Gender
AND **jobs**
Sex segregation of
occupations in the world

Gender

AND jobs

Sex segregation of occupations in the world

Richard Anker

INTERNATIONAL LABOUR OFFICE   GENEVA

331.4133
A61g

Anker, Richard
Gender and jobs: Sex segregation of occupations in the world
Geneva, International Labour Office, 1998

/Comparison/, /Labour market segmentation/, /Sexual division of labour/, /Sex discrimination/, /Woman worker/, /Men/, /Trend/, /Developed country/, /Developing country/. 13.01.2
ISBN 92-2-109524-X

ILO Cataloguing in Publication Data

Printed in the United Kingdom   ALD

CONTENTS

ACKNOWLEDGEMENTS

This book has been a long time in the making—from ideas and publications one decade ago with Catherine Hein, to collection of the required data, to processing and tabulation of these data, and of course to the analysis and write up. This means that there are many people to be thanked.

Jim Windell provided most of the statistical support in the earlier stages of the work and made valuable contributions, especially to Chapters 6, 7 and 8. Esperanza Magpantay did most of the statistical data processing and tabulations. It is fair to say that without her assistance this book would not have been completed; anyone who has worked with such complicated, and not always comparable data for so many countries will understand what this involved. Laszlo Zsoldos was responsible for the graphs and figures which improve the presentation so much. Emiko Soyama and Helina Melkas also provided statistical assistance. Tracy Murphy, Sally Outterside and Rowena Ferranco did the typing; Rowena also made sure that the text, bibliography and figures were consistent and in the correct format.

In the ILO's Bureau of Statistics, which was responsible for collecting most of the occupational data, its chief Farhad Mehran had the openness of mind to see the usefulness of collecting a supplemental, detailed occupational data set. Eivind Hoffmann was not only partly responsible for making sure that these data were collected, but also provided useful comments and suggestions. Adriana Mata-Greenwood had the main responsibility for compiling the data received from member States; Adriana also provided indispensable inputs into matching the national classifications across data years described in Chapter 4.

My various chiefs are to be thanked for their forbearance in giving me time and support beyond the call of duty—Bud Clatanoff, Juhani Lönnroth, Gek-Boo Ng, Werner Sengenberger and Guy Standing. Guy, in particular, deserves thanks because his support was also substantive as he is himself a recognized scholar on gender issues. I would also like to thank Eugenia Date-Bah who was responsible for the original concept of this work under the ILO interdepartmental project which she directed.

There were also a number of persons who took care to read the manuscript and to make constructive suggestions. These included Eugenia

Date-Bah, Deborah DeGraff, Catherine Hein, Gavin Jones, M.E. Khan, and Alexander Samorodov. Thanks are also due to Lilian Neil and John Myers, who helped edit this book.

Finally, I want to reserve my greatest thanks for my wife Martha. Her help and support went far beyond that often provided by a spouse. We discussed the work as it progressed and in several places she made important contributions to the approach and presentation which were taken.

Richard Anker

PART I

INTRODUCTION AND BACKGROUND

INTRODUCTION

1

1.1 Background

This book explores the extent to which labour markets are divided on the basis of sex. Using detailed occupational data for 41 countries or areas, it investigates how occupational segregation by sex differs across countries in the world, how this has been changing over the past two decades and the factors contributing to it.

Occupational segregation by sex is extensive and pervasive and is one of the most important and enduring aspects of labour markets around the world. This is despite the fact that there have been large increases in the labour force participation of women worldwide. As will be shown in this book, occupational segregation by sex is *extensive in all countries*: in industrialized capitalist countries; former communist countries; and developing countries. Occupational segregation by sex has *probably always been very high*, as evidence from the United States and Canada indicate that there was little or no change in overall levels of sex segregation in these countries from the beginning of this century until approximately the 1960s (Reskin and Hartmann, 1986; Fox and Fox, 1987).

1.2 Special aspects of this book

In several ways, **this book differs from previous studies of occupational segregation by sex.** First, it is mainly *based on unusually detailed data*. For most of the empirical analysis in this book, the minimum number of non-agricultural occupations classified for a country is roughly 50, and on average there are approximately 175 non-agricultural occupations classified per study country. This level of detail in the occupational data is unusual for an empirical study involving a large number of countries, and in particular, studies which include developing countries. In contrast, most previous cross-national analyses have relied on crude occupational data consisting of only about six non-agricultural occupations per country (see Chapter 3). Yet, as will be demonstrated in this book (Chapter 6), crude one-digit occupational data are often misleading for investigations of cross-national differences and national trends over time. Indeed, the need for more detailed data than the widely available one-digit data was the reason why the ILO collected these new data in the first place—in part in response to the widespread knowledge that one-digit occupational data hide a great deal of occupational segregation by sex, and partly on the basis of analysis in an earlier book on sex segregation in Third World labour markets which contained detailed occupational data (Anker and Hein, 1986).

Second, the data used in this book *cover a large number of countries or areas as well as a broad range* (see Chapter 4): 17 from Europe, 5 from the Americas, 6 from the Middle East and North Africa, 6 from Asia, 3 from Oceania and 4 from Africa. This broad coverage is important for a cross-national investigation of sex segregation, since it makes it possible to observe whether levels and trends in occupational segregation by sex differ by region, socio-economic level or labour market conditions. It also makes it possible to observe whether or not there are distinctly different levels and patterns for different groups of countries.

Third, another feature of this book is that *time series data* for 32 countries and areas are analysed in Part IV. In this way, it is possible to observe whether or not sex segregation of occupations is increasing or decreasing in the world as a whole, as well as whether or not increases or decreases are found in some countries, subregions and regions only.

Fourth and fifth, *new methodologies are developed* in order to help increase the comparability of national occupational data. Two new inequality statistics are developed in Chapter 5; this includes a relative measure of gender-integrated and gender-dominated occupations, and an inequality statistic which combines into one index the effects of both whether or not women participate in the labour force, and the level of occupation segregation by sex for those in the labour force. In Chapter 6, a way of increasing the comparability of national estimates of occupational segregation by sex is developed; observed levels of occupational segregation are adjusted by taking into consideration the mathematical relationship we estimated in Chapter 6 between the number of occupations classified and the observed level of occupational segregation by sex. These adjustments are extremely important because, as found in Chapter 6, the observed level of occupational segregation by sex is quite sensitive to the number of occupations classified; yet, the number of occupations classified in the national data provided by study countries and areas in this book range from around 50 to 500 occupations.

Sixth, *a number of different statistics are used* to measure and understand the multi-dimensional nature of occupational segregation by sex. These include, for example, representation ratios; inequality indices; percentage of workers in male-dominated and female-dominated occupations; percentage female and male for 17 important "male" and "female" occupations; and lists of the most important "male" and "female" occupations. This use of multiple statistics and measures of sex segregation is somewhat unusual for cross-national analyses, which typically rely on only one inequality statistic (even though a number of researchers have recommended the use of multiple statistics).

The extent to which labour markets are segmented based on workers' sex is startling. As shown in Chapter 10, a typical country has approximately 55 per cent of its non-agricultural labour force (based on study data for around 75 non-agricultural occupations) in what most people would consider "male" or "female" occupations, defined as occupations where male or female workers comprise more than 80 per cent of all workers. This percentage increases to about 60 per cent when based on data for around 250 non-agricultural occupations; approximately 60 per cent of male non-agricultural workers are in a "male" occupation and approximately 25 per cent of female non-agricultural workers are in a "female" occupation.

Given the extensive nature of occupational segregation by sex and its undesirable effects on the economy, women and society (see section 1.4 below on these negative effects), **reducing sex segregation of occupations should receive urgent and priority attention by policy-makers, laypersons and researchers.** While national laws and initiatives (such as women's bureaux, anti-discrimination and equal opportunity laws, and affirmative action pro-grammes) as well as recent international conferences and ILO Conventions (see below) indicate that actions are being taken, this topic is not being taken as seriously as it should be in my opinion. It is hoped that this book will help increase the interest of policy-makers in the degree of sex segregation of occupations and the important role it plays in determining women's status in society and in achieving the main goals of labour market policies: efficient labour markets, equitable labour markets, economic growth and social justice (ILO, 1993a).

1.3   Indications of international concern

The following quotes from recent international conferences and ILO Conventions and Recommendations indicate that there is some recognition at the international level of the need to reduce occupational segregation by sex (and especially to increase the representation of women in higher-level positions). At the same time, these quotes are only small snippets from large documents and in any case are not particularly strong statements, raising some doubt about the seriousness with which this topic is being considered.

The recent platform of action adopted by the 1995 Beijing Conference on Women (*Fourth World Conference on Women—4 to 15 September*) which marked the end of the second women's decade, recommends the following:

"elimination of occupational segregation and all forms of employment discrimination" (strategic objective F5);

"ensure women's equal access to and full participation in power structures and decision-making" (strategic objective G1);

"guarantee the rights of women and men to equal pay for work of equal value" (paragraph 165 of platform).

The recent 1995 Copenhagen World Summit on Social Development commits countries to:

"ensure gender balance and equity in decision-making processes at all levels" (commitment 5b).

ILO Conventions and Recommendations—such as the Equal Remuneration Convention, 1951 (No. 100) and Recommendation No. 90, the Human Resources Development Recommendation, 1975 (No. 150), the Workers with Family Responsibilities Convention, 1981 (No. 156) and Recommendation No. 165, and the Discrimination (Employment and Occupation) Convention, 1958 (No. 111), include the following statements:

"promote equality of opportunity and treatment for men and women workers" (Recommendation No. 165);

"the term 'equal remuneration for men and women workers for work of equal value' refers to rates of remuneration established without discrimination based on sex" (Convention No. 100);

"ensure the application to all workers of the principle of equal remuneration for men and women workers for work of equal value" (Convention No. 100);

"discrimination includes (a) any distinction, exclusion or preference made on the basis of race, colour, sex, religion, political opinion, national extraction or social origin, which has the effect of nullifying or impairing equality of opportunity or treatment in employment or occupation". (Convention No. 111).

1.4   Why occupational segregation of men and women is an important topic

The reasons why occupational segregation by sex should be of critical concern to researchers and policy-makers extend well beyond the very important equity concerns and a desire to improve the situation for women. First, occupational segregation by sex (where, as at present, women tend to have lower paying and lower status jobs, and where work in female-dominated occupations is similar to activities women perform at home) *has an important negative effect on how men see women as well as how women see themselves by reinforcing and perpetuating gender stereotypes.* This, in turn, negatively affects women's status and empowerment and consequently many social variables such as mortality and morbidity, poverty and income inequality.

Second, occupational segregation based on the sex of workers has a negative effect on labour *market efficiency and labour market functioning*. When most women are effectively excluded from most occupations, human resources are wasted and consequently income levels are reduced, as many of the best suited and most skilled people are excluded from working in the occupation where they would be the most productive.

Third, sex segregation is *a major labour market rigidity,* greatly reducing a labour market's ability to respond to change. In this regard, it is important to note that labour market rigidity caused by sex segregation of occupations includes not only the exclusion of women from "male" occupations but also the exclusion of men from "female" occupations (or perhaps an unwillingness of men to work in these occupations). When these labour market inefficiencies and rigidities are seen in the context of the recent large increases in female labour force participation rates throughout the world and the need for labour markets to adjust to rapid economic changes, it is clear that countries can ill afford to ignore occupational segregation by sex and still remain competitive in today's global market-place.   *indirect effects*

Fourth, the segregation of men and women into different *occupations negatively affects the education and training of future generations.* Decisions by parents, youngsters and schools regarding how much education to provide girls and boys, as well as which fields of study they should pursue, are based to a significant extent on labour market opportunities. This means that women's restricted labour market opportunities and lower pay for "female" occupations help perpetuate women's inferior position in society and the labour market into the next generation, thereby also perpetuating this important source of labour market inefficiency and inequality.

Fifth, occupational segregation probably keeps many women out of wage employment altogether (especially in developing countries where the formal sector is small). This has an undesirable effect of raising fertility rates *ceteris paribus*, since female wage employment, especially in the formal sector, *helps reduce fertility rates in developing countries* (United Nations, 1985b). This undesirable effect is of particular importance in countries where reducing high population growth is a major policy objective.

Sixth, sex segregation is a major *determinant of male–female wage differentials, a point which is stressed in the research literature.* Indeed, most of the research literature on occupational segregation by sex is embedded within an analysis of male–female pay differentials and the fact that "female" occupations have lower pay as compared to "male" occupations. Some authors even go so far as to say that occupational segregation is mainly of interest as a subject because of its effect on the female–male pay gap (e.g. Jacobs and Lim, 1992). While the proportion of the male–female pay differential attributable to sex segregation of occupations is hotly debated in the research literature, there is general agreement that it is one of its most important determinants (see Chapter 2 for discussion on this).

Seventh, the low pay and incomes for women workers that accompany occupational segregation are becoming an increasingly important *contributor to poverty and inequality in society* as a whole (Anker, 1995). It is important to keep in mind that a high percentage of households in the world are headed by a woman and that this percentage is increasing. According to some estimates, this percentage varies from approximately the mid-teens in South and South-East Asia to almost one-half in parts of Africa and the Caribbean (Buvinic, 1995). It is also important to keep in mind that women generally spend a higher proportion of their income on children and family necessities as compared to men (Mason Oppenheim, 1995).

1.5 Should occupational segregation by sex be completely eliminated?

The above discussion has been about why it is important to *reduce* (not eliminate) the sex segregation of occupations. There are, for example, innate physiological differences between men and women (e.g. strength on average) and these affect labour force options for individual men and women, but this effect should be small overall, since there is a broad overlap in the abilities of individual men and women—see section 1.7). **The total elimination of occupational segregation by sex** is not only impossible, but is, in my opinion, **an inappropriate policy objective.** Men and women should be free to choose their occupation, and employers should have considerable freedom in hiring. This means that there will never be the same (or even approximately the same) percentage female in each and every occupation. Nor should there be.

However, in light of the facts presented in this book indicating that female and male workers are very unequally distributed across occupations all around the world and that "female" occupations are very sex-stereotyped worldwide in terms of characteristics and skills, it is clear that effective freedom of choice is missing for many men and women in the world. This means that **equality of opportunity in the labour market is missing, and changing this should be the policy objective.**

1.6 Occupational segregation is not always bad for women and good for men

Both the research and the popular literature are mainly concerned about the sex segregation of occupations because this is felt to be an important aspect and determinant of women's disadvantaged position in the labour market and society. Thus, occupational segregation by sex is almost always seen as a "female" subject by researchers, policy-makers and laypersons alike, with higher segregation seen as indicating a worse situation for women (and by implication a better situation for men).

While it is true that a higher level of occupational segregation by sex is generally associated with a poorer labour market for many working women, since it is generally associated with a reduced range of "female" occupations (which generally have lower pay, status, independence and career opportunities), **sex segregation of occupations is not always bad for women; nor is it always good for men.** One positive aspect of occupational segregation for women is that it helps protect some women from competition from another large group of workers (men). In recent years, this has been a valuable advantage, since job growth has been fastest in areas of the labour market where women's occupations are concentrated (such as clerical and services occupations). In contrast, many countries (especially industrialized countries) have experienced job losses in production occupations where men dominate.

Even though many "female" occupations are relatively low paid, have relatively little employment security and have relatively little authority or career opportunities, they are jobs. It is a dilemma faced by women—whether it is better to have a poor quality job than no job at all. Now, many men, especially in industrialized countries, including those who have lost jobs in production occupations because of the globalization of trade, are now facing this same dilemma: whether a poor quality job is better than no job at all. It will be very interesting to see how many men in the future will seek work in what are currently "female" occupations, and in the process reduce occupational segregation and break down sex stereotyping in labour markets and society.

1.7 Difference between sex and gender

The research literature as well as policy documents distinguish between the words "sex" and "gender". Sex is a biological characteristic determined at conception. It is fixed for a person's life. And, the same biological differences between men and women exist in all countries of the world and do not change over time.

The word "gender", on the other hand, refers to differences between men and women that are learned. It is not fixed but determined by social and cultural values. This means that gender differences between men and women vary across countries and regions as well as over time within countries—and consequently (and unlike sex) can be changed by education, government policy, media images and opinion leaders.

Some differences between men and women are biologically determined (for example, men tend to have greater physical strength); yet, aside from differences in the reproductive process, these differences are small on average. And there is a large overlap in the abilities of men and women based on biologically determined differences. For example, while men have greater physical strength than women on average, many women are stronger than many men. This implies the importance of considering men and women as individuals and not according to small biologically determined average differences between the sexes. Thus, the virtual exclusion of women from occupations requiring physical strength is not defensible. Unfortunately, average differences between men and women often do lead to the sex segregation of occupations; this is sometimes explained by economists using statistical discrimination theory (see discussion on this theory in Chapter 2).

An important implication that the concept of "gender" has for policies aimed at reducing occupational segregation by sex is its recognition that non-labour market factors play a critical role in determining occupational segregation by sex. Indeed, the empirical analysis in this book demonstrates the important role played by non-labour market factors such as stereotyping in determining occupational segregation by sex. In particular, as long as women remain almost exclusively responsible for child care and household work as at present, it will be impossible to achieve gender equality in the labour market. Another important implication of the concept of gender is that it is possible to eliminate most gender differences in the labour market, since these differences are based on learned behaviour and societal values which are not fixed for all time and for all countries.

1.8 Usefulness of cross-national analysis

Measuring, understanding and explaining occupational segregation by sex should be enhanced by cross-national studies such as in this book. They help to identify the extent to which various aspects of occupational segregation by sex are universal in nature as opposed to being specific to a particular culture, country or region. Cross-national studies also encourage analysts and others to explain unusual national or regional situations, again something which national studies do not have the perspective for; in any case, national studies are prone to take for granted long-standing relationships as normal and so not question them. These advantages of cross-national studies are important, since they help identify fruitful areas for policy action.

Cross-national studies also enable one country to learn from the experiences and policies of other countries. They also provide a basis for evaluating the national situation and recent progress (or lack of progress) in reducing occupational segregation by sex. These advantages can be very important for policy formulation, evaluation and advocacy.

There are also, of course, important disadvantages of cross-national studies. There are problems with data comparability in particular. This is a serious problem on which this book spends a considerable amount of time and effort. Despite these efforts, comparability of data across countries remains a major problem. This is easy to visualize by considering how a large occupation such as salesperson differs in an industrialized country where one would often work in a modern store, as compared to a less developed country where one would generally work in an informal sector establishment located on the street. Data quality and comparability is a larger problem in cross-national studies with broad coverage as compared to national studies. Further, detailed knowledge of all the countries included in a cross-national study (especially in a study with 41 countries and areas such as in this book) is impossible. On the other hand, the use of a wide range of countries, in order to better understand national differences and regional and global similarities, is one of the most important advantages of cross-national analysis.

1.9   Description of contents of this book

This book is divided into five parts. *Part I provides introductory and background information about occupational segregation by sex.* This includes the above introductory discussion on the concept of occupational segregation by sex, advantages of this book and why occupational segregation by sex is an important subject for men and women, policy-makers and researchers (Chapter 1). It also includes a description of economic and non-economic theories explaining the reasons for occupational segregation by sex (Chapter 2), and a review of previous cross-national empirical studies (Chapter 3). The following questions are among those addressed in this part of the book:

(i)   why is occupational segregation by sex an important topic for men and women, policy-makers, and researchers?
(ii)   how do economists, sociologists, feminists and others explain the existence and persistence of occupational segregation by sex?
(iii)   what do we already know from previous cross-national studies about the extent and patterns in the world of occupational segregation by sex?

Part II describes the study data used for most of the analysis in this book. This includes a description of socio-economic and labour market conditions in study countries and areas and study regions (Chapter 7); comparability of study data in terms of coverage, coding procedures, etc. (Chapter 4);

definitions and meaning of the different statistics used in the analysis (Chapter 5); mathematical relationship between the level of occupational segregation by sex observed and the number of occupations classified, along with a procedure (developed in Chapter 6) to adjust national inequality statistics to increase cross-country comparability. Since analysis and discussion in Chapters 4 to 7 are fairly detailed and technical in nature, readers only interested in the empirical evidence for levels and trends in occupational segregation by sex might wish to skip (or skim over) much of Part II. The following questions are among those addressed in this part of the book.

(i)   why is it important to use a number of different statistics to measure and understand occupational segregation by sex?

(ii)   what are the best inequality statistics to use in a cross-national analysis of occupational segregation by sex where there is such great variation in national data, labour markets and female labour force participation?

(iii)   how can the comparability of national data be increased by taking into account differing levels of detail in national occupational classifications?

Part III describes and analyses current levels and patterns around the world in occupational segregation by sex. This includes an analysis of the situation based on crude one-digit data (with six non-agricultural occupations) for 56 countries and areas (Chapter 8). This analysis uses representation ratios and provides a broad picture of the general types of non-agricultural occupations in which men and women work. Chapters 9 to 13 use various inequality measures and statistics to describe and analyse occupational segregation by sex, based on the detailed ILO data set for 41 countries and areas, which has approximately 175 non-agricultural occupations per country. Chapter 9 uses the index of dissimilarity (ID), the most commonly used index in the research literature, to measure the overall level of segregation. Chapter 10 analyses the extent to which the female, male and total non-agricultural labour forces are divided into "female" occupations. Chapter 11 investigates the extent to which 17 specific occupations (e.g. teacher, secretary, construction worker) are feminized around the world, and identifies the largest female occupations in each study country in terms of female employment. Chapter 12 investigates the extent to which the various measures of women's position in the labour market used in earlier chapters are related to each other, whether there are distinct patterns between these measures; and how these patterns differ across regions and groups of countries. The following questions are among those addressed in this part of the book:

(i)   In which major occupational groups are women most likely to be concentrated based on national data for six major non-agricultural occupations? How does this differ across regions and subregions in the world?

(ii) How do current levels of occupational segregation by sex vary across countries, subregions and regions based on detailed occupational data with an average of 175 occupations per country?

(iii) Is the level of occupational segregation by sex in a country related to the level of socio-economic development and/or women's labour force participation?

(iv) Which specific non-agricultural occupations do women tend to dominate? Which specific non-agricultural occupations are the most important in terms of employment for women? How much variation is there across countries, regions and subregions?

(v) How common is the sex-stereotyping of occupations? To what extent does the sex-stereotyping of occupations correspond to typical pre-conceived beliefs about appropriate roles and behaviours for men and women?

(vi) How are various measures of occupational segregation by sex and women's position in the labour market related to each other? Are there distinct patterns in these relationships that differ by regions and/or subregions of the world?

Part IV contains a similar analysis to that in Part III—the difference being that *Part IV is concerned with recent changes in occupational segregation by sex over the past two decades*, whereas Part III is concerned with the current situation. Thus, Chapter 13 uses inequality indices to measure changes in occupational segregation by sex; Chapter 14 looks at the extent to which there have been changes in the number and size of "female", "male" and gender-integrated occupations; Chapter 15 investigates changes in the feminization and masculinization of 17 important non-agricultural occupations. The following questions are among those addressed in this part of the book:

(i) How has occupational segregation by sex been changing in the past two decades?

(ii) How have recent changes in occupational segregation by sex differed across countries, groups of countries, areas and regions?

(iii) Are recent changes in occupational segregation by sex related to labour market or socio-economic changes?

Part V contains a discussion of the main findings and conclusions (Chapter 16).

THEORIES AND EXPLANATIONS FOR OCCUPATIONAL SEGREGATION BY SEX

2

Researchers usually distinguish between labour supply and labour demand factors when explaining occupational segregation by sex. Factors related to labour supply generally focus on why women "prefer" certain types of occupations—for example, women may "prefer" occupations with flexible hours in order to allow time for child care, and may also prefer occupations which are relatively easy to interrupt for a period of time for maternity or child care. Explanations related to labour demand focus on why employers generally "prefer" to hire women or men for particular occupations and why women and men have different opportunities for promotion and career development within firms.

The word "prefer" has been put in quotes in the previous paragraph, because even when an individual chooses to accept work in a particular occupation or an employer chooses mainly workers of one sex, these decisions are constrained by learned cultural and social values that often discriminate against women (and sometimes discriminate against men) and stereotype occupations into "male" and "female" occupations. In other words, this "preference" is usually caused by learned, gender-related factors.

Theories explaining the existence of occupational segregation by sex can be classified into three broad categories: (i) neoclassical and human capital theories; (ii) institutional and labour market segmentation theories; and (iii) non-economic and feminist (gender) theories. Although these three sets of theories overlap, this classification none the less provides a useful basis for discussion in this chapter.

Before proceeding, it is important to point out that most of the research literature dealing with occupational segregation by sex is *not* concerned with occupational segregation *per se*, but with the effect occupational segregation by sex has on female–male pay differentials. For this reason, many theories and explanations treat the determinants of occupational segregation by sex and male–female pay inequality as if they are synonymous. This is unfortunate, since female–male pay differentials have many sources and occupational segregation is only one of them (see the end of this chapter). Also, as noted in Chapter 1, there are a number of reasons why the sex segregation of occupations is an important topic in its own right.

2.1 Neoclassical, human capital model

Neoclassical economics assumes that workers and employers are rational and that labour markets function efficiently. Workers seek out the best paying-jobs after taking into consideration their own personal endowments (e.g. education and experience), constraints (e.g. young child to take care of) and preferences (e.g. for a pleasant work environment). Employers try to maximize profits by maximizing productivity and minimizing costs as much as possible. But because of competition and efficient labour markets, employers pay workers their marginal product.

Labour supply

On the labour supply side, neoclassical/human capital theories stress women's lower levels of human capital—both (i) what women bring to the labour market (such as less education and less relevant fields of study), as well as (ii) what women acquire after joining the labour market (such as less experience due to intermittent or truncated labour market participation because of marriage and/or household/child-care responsibilities).[1] In short, women are viewed as rightfully receiving lower pay than men because of lower productivity.

These productivity-related variables of education and labour market experience are believed to also affect women's choice of occupation. The effect of education on choice of occupation would hardly seem to need comment. However, two observations are worth making here. First, in low income countries with small formal/modern labour markets, there are often many more educated, qualified persons (men and women) than (sought after) formal sector jobs. This implies, everything else being equal, that women should be reasonably well represented in a wide range of occupations in the formal sector (and at least in proportion to female–male educational levels). When this is not the case, it probably implies discrimination. Second, the relationship of women's education and experience with occupation is bi-directional in nature. While women may not choose or be offered work in particular occupations because they do not have the education or experience to qualify for these occupations, it is also true that many parents decide to give their daughters less education (and in less relevant subjects for the labour market) than their sons, and women decide to accumulate less labour market experience than men partly because women do not have the same labour market opportunities as men. These are very important factors helping to determine occupational segregation in the labour market. This reinforcing phenomenon is not generally considered by neoclassical theory, which typically represents a static rather than a dynamic, longitudinal perspective.

Neoclassical theories also stress the fact that women are almost exclusively responsible for housework and child care around the world (e.g.

UNDP, 1995; UN, 1991).[2] These family responsibilities cause many women to have less work experience due either to early and permanent withdrawal from the labour force (for example because of marriage), and/or temporary withdrawal from the labour force in order to care for young children. According to neoclassical economic theory, this implies that women would rationally choose occupations with relatively high starting pay, relatively low returns to experience, and relatively low penalties for temporary withdrawal from the labour force—including occupations which are flexible in terms of entry and working hours.

There are several problems with using the neoclassical/human capital theory as the only explanation for occupational segregation by sex. First, women's labour force commitment has increased greatly in recent decades, as indicated by the disappearance in many countries of the double-humped (also sometimes referred to as m-shaped) age-specific labour force participation curve. Second, the amount of household and family-based work which needs to be done (almost always by women) has fallen in many countries in recent years due to increasing age at marriage and falling fertility almost everywhere, as well as the use of machines for housework such as washers, cookers, vacuum cleaners, etc. in higher income countries. Third, the increasing importance of female-headed households all over the world (Buvinic, 1995) implies that more and more women need to work continuously in order to earn money. These various changes imply that women are having increasing labour market experiences—and according to neoclassical theory, this should imply major changes in the types of occupations women prefer and are offered. Despite this, occupational segregation by sex has remained very high worldwide (although it is true that occupational segregation by sex has fallen in many countries in the past two decades, see Part IV).

Fourth, when one looks at the most important occupations for men and women (see Chapter 11), one finds that many important male-dominated occupations (such as transport driver and auto mechanic) do not require more experience or continuity of employment than many important female-dominated occupations (such as secretary and other clerical worker). If anything, the opposite is true. For example, comparable worth job evaluations (see section 2.4 below) indicate that secretary (one of the most important "female" occupations in the world, see Chapter 11) requires considerably more knowledge, skills and mental demands than delivery truck driver (one of the most important "male" occupations in the world, again see Chapter 11); yet secretaries receive lower pay.

Labour demand

According to neoclassical/human capital theory, many of the same factors which influence women's and men's preferences for particular occupations also influence employers' preferences for male or female workers. Thus, occupations requiring a relatively high level of education are more likely to be offered to men (although it should be noted that the relevance of this argument is especially questionable in the many countries where education levels of men and women are now similar) as are occupations where experience and on-the-job training is relatively important (although again it should be noted that the relevance of this argument is decreasing in importance in many countries along with women's increasing labour force commitment).

Second, women are often considered to be higher cost workers as compared to male workers (even when men and women receive the same monetary wage rate) due to a number of supposedly higher indirect labour costs for women workers. According to neoclassical/human capital theory, this should affect the types of occupations employers offer women, depending on the relative importance of each of these factors for each occupation. For example, women are often said to have higher absenteeism rates than men (partly due to family responsibilities which cause women to miss work in order to care for family members). Women are often said to be tardy more often than men (again because of family responsibilities). Women are often said to have higher labour turnover rates (i.e. leave their job more often) than men; this can be an important indirect cost for employers, since new workers have to be found and trained. This higher turnover rate is said to occur because many women leave jobs in order to take care of young children (and in some countries because of marriage). Women workers may require facilities at the workplace for toileting[3] and/or for their children, since women do not want to leave their children at home unattended.[4] Women are sometimes said to be less flexible than men in not being able to stay late or work on official leave days.

It is important to question the veracity of statements (such as those in the previous paragraph) which assume that there are higher direct and indirect labour costs for female workers as compared to males. This is especially important in light of the fact that there is relatively little empirical evidence to support or reject such statements.

In this regard, a series of empirical studies in Third World countries for which I was responsible (Anker and Hein, 1986) are very informative. A total of 423 employers, 2517 women workers and 803 male workers were interviewed with structured survey questionnaires in five developing countries (Cyprus, Ghana, India, Mauritius and Sri Lanka). Results from these studies call into question a number of the above assumptions. For example, while women were found to have higher absenteeism rates (mainly due to family responsibilities) and many employers stressed the importance of this factor, the difference between male and female absenteeism rates was small on average. Also, study results indicated similar labour turnover rates for women and men. This unexpected result was due to men being much more likely to leave one job for another, while women were much more likely to leave their job for family reasons.

Labour laws and regulations sometimes directly affect the demand for women workers. Protective legislation sometimes prohibits women from working in certain occupations and/or working under certain conditions. For example, women may be prohibited from night work—see the Night Work (Women) Convention, 1919 (No. 4); or working underground in mines—see the Underground Work (Women) Convention, 1935 (No. 45); or carrying heavy loads—see the Maximum Weight Convention, 1967 (No. 127). Although protective laws and conventions were set up with the best intentions to protect women, many observers now believe that these laws are no longer relevant and should be changed (see for example, Lim, 1996). Indeed, many ILO Conventions dealing with protective legislation are currently under review.

Labour laws and regulations can also increase the cost of female workers as compared to males. For example, paid maternity leave increases the cost of women workers relative to men and therefore can become an indirect form of sex discrimination when employers bear this cost.[5] Partly for this reason, and partly because reproduction of the next generation is a societal need, ILO Conventions on maternity leave recommend that maternity leave costs be borne by the state and not by employers. Another example sometimes mentioned is laws which require separate toilet facilities for men and women; this could be important in Third World countries where single sex workplaces are common at present.

Faced by the fact that the sex segregation of occupations and female–male pay differences continue to persist and cannot be fully explained by differences in male and female characteristics, neoclassical economists have developed other, complementary theories to explain the persistence of occupational segregation by sex, without abandoning the basic assumptions of rationality and efficient labour markets. Two of these theories (employers' taste for discrimination, and compensating differentials) are briefly described in the present section. For the most part, these complementary theories focus on the demand side and employers' motivation and behaviour. Other complementary economic theories related to labour market segmentation are described in the next section (such as dual labour markets, statistical discrimination, occupational overcrowding, and efficiency wages).

According to a model of employer behaviour developed by Becker (1971), employers (like many others) are prejudiced against certain groups of workers. Usually, but not always, this prejudice is against persons who are visibly different, based on characteristics, such as on race, disability, age and sex (Anker, 1995). Because of this prejudice, employers are said to sustain disutility (i.e. a cost) when they hire someone from the discriminated group. Therefore according to this theory, employers are rational in hiring fewer people from this group, as this enables them to avoid this "cost".

There are two main problems with the Becker model. First, it is unclear (as pointed out by a number of researchers) how this system can be sustained in a competitive economy. One would expect less prejudiced employers to hire more people from the discriminated group in order to decrease costs and increase profits; this implies that over time the behaviour of unprejudiced employers would prevail due to competitive forces in the capitalist system. A second problem with this theory is that even if one assumes that some employers have a "taste" for discrimination, the great overlap in the skills, preferences, etc. of individual men and women should make it likely that every occupation would include substantial percentages of each sex—which is not the case. On the other hand, these criticisms could be explained by the existence of very strong social values and stereotypes (see discussion below on feminist/gender theories) and statistical discrimination theory (see discussion below on institutional and labour market segmentation theories).

One other neoclassically based economic theory sometimes mentioned as helping to explain why women prefer certain occupations as well as why pay is lower in typical female occupations is the compensating differentials model. According to this model, women are said to prefer occupations with good working conditions, wishing to avoid unpleasant and dangerous working conditions and/or to have jobs with good fringe benefits such as health insurance and crèches; the former aspect could be especially important when men are the main breadwinners and most working women are secondary earners. Under these circumstances, lower monetary rewards (i.e. pay) in typical "female" occupations are said to be partly explained by some "pay" being taken in non-wage forms. While there may be some truth in this argument in countries where cultural values restrict the types of jobs women should do, it is much more difficult to accept the former argument in countries where a substantial percentage of women work and/or for women who are the principal earner in the family. In any case, typical "female" occupations (for example, maids, salespersons, and sewers are three of the most common female occupations in the world according to study data presented in Chapter 11) hardly seem to be occupations where low pay is partly explained by pleasant working conditions.

In summary, neoclassical economics and human capital theory make valuable contributions to our understanding of occupational segregation by sex and the lower pay which women workers tend to receive. This theory highlights the important role played by systematic differences in the human capital accumulated by men and women. For example, as compared to men, women tend to have lower levels of education; women's fields of study tend to be less relevant for the labour market; women tend to have shorter working lives as some women permanently withdraw from the labour force upon marriage and other women temporarily withdraw from the labour force and/or do part-time work in order to care for their children.

All of these factors negatively affect women's productivity (and pay) and the types of occupations for which women are qualified. **For these reasons, neoclassical/human capital theories stress the need for policies to**

address non-labour market factors in order to reduce occupational segregation by sex. This implies for example that policy-makers should be concerned with non-labour market variables such as education, family policy, family planning, male responsibility and the more equal sharing of child care/household work. Regarding labour market policies, these theories imply that policy-makers should be concerned with increasing women's human capital, especially education and training in non-traditional occupations; improving women's ability to combine work and child care/housework, possibly through provision of crèches, or reorganization of work-time, or parental leave provisions that indirectly discriminate against female workers; and elimination of provisions in labour laws that prohibit the employment of women in certain occupations.

2.2   Institutional and labour market segmentation theories

Institutional and labour market segmentation theories also rely on well-established economic thought and neoclassical logic. They begin with the assumption that institutions (such as unions and large enterprises) play an important role in determining who is hired, fired and promoted and how much they are paid. Institutional theories also begin with the assumption that labour markets are segmented in certain ways. And while each labour market segment may function according to neoclassical theory, it is difficult for workers to pass between these segments.

The best known labour market segmentation theory is dual labour market theory (Doeringer and Piore, 1971). It distinguishes between a "primary" sector and a "secondary" sector. Other labour market segmentation theories divide the labour market into "static" and "progressive" jobs (Standing, 1978) and "formal" and "informal" sectors (ILO, 1972). Jobs in the primary sector are relatively good jobs in terms of pay, security, opportunities for advancement and working conditions. Secondary sector jobs tend to be relatively poor quality jobs, with low pay, poor chances for promotion, poor working conditions and little protection or job security. These two labour markets are seen as functioning independently of each other to a substantial degree, largely because firms in the primary sector have some market power which insulates them somewhat from competition, whereas firms in the secondary sector face fierce competition. Although this distinction between primary and secondary sectors has become less marked in recent years in both industrialized and developing countries (because of increased subcontracting and globalization of trade), it still retains a significant degree of relevance.

It is a relatively short step to adapt the concept of dual labour markets to occupational segregation by sex, with one labour market segment comprised of "female" occupations and another segment comprised of "male" occupations. This segmentation implies relatively low wage rates in "female" occupations, because many women workers are *"overcrowded"* into a small number of "female" occupations (Bergmann, 1974; Edgeworth, 1922). "Male" occupations, on the other hand, benefit from reduced competition within this wider set of occupations and consequently these "male" occupations tend to have relatively high wage rates.

The nature of primary sector jobs implies that women should be underrepresented in this sector. Since jobs in the primary sector are more secure, firm-specific experience and low labour turnover should be relatively highly valued by firms in this sector. Consequently, male workers should tend to be favoured by primary sector employers, because they tend to have more continuous labour market experience than women. Also, since primary sector firms are able to pay higher wages, they are in a position to cream off the best qualified workers; this again implies that men, who tend to be better educated and more experienced than women, should tend to be preferred by primary sector firms.

An additional economic theory related to labour market segmentation is *statistical discrimination* theory. It is based on there being (i) differences, on average, in the productivity, skills, experiences, etc. of different groups of workers (such as men and women) and (ii) high search and information costs to identify and decide on whom to hire or promote. In such circumstances (which are said to be common), it is argued that it is rational for employers to discriminate against groups of workers (such as women) when differences, on average, between the abilities of persons from different groups (e.g. women and men) are less than decision-making costs. Thus, statistical discrimination theory provides an explanation for how entire occupations can be comprised of mostly males even though many individual women have more ability, education, etc. than many individual men.[6]

One aspect ignored by statistical discrimination is the role occupational segregation by sex plays in perpetuating labour market discrimination into the next generation. Because women are discriminated against, they are likely to obtain less education than men and to pursue work careers that reinforce this current situation. A second possible problem with statistical discrimination is that it may be less relevant for explaining discrimination in promotions as compared to recruitment, since information costs for the former may be less than for the latter in many enterprises.

In summary, labour market segmentation theories are very useful for understanding occupational segregation by sex, since they stress the existence of segregated labour markets and occupations. At the same time, they do not explain why occupations are segmented by sex; after all, the same occupations are found in both the primary and the secondary labour markets. Rather, labour market segmentation theory is better at explaining vertical occupational segregation by sex; that is, why men are more likely than women to have better quality jobs in the same occupation (which is a major source of female–male wage differentials).

Despite the valuable contributions of neoclassical/human capital theory and institutional and labour market segmentation theories to the understanding of sex inequality in the labour market (e.g. explaining that: women receive less pay because they have less human capital and so are less productive; labour markets are segmented in different ways), *they make only a partial contribution to our understanding of occupational segregation by sex.* In particular, they do not address very well a number of critical non-economic and non-labour market variables and behaviour, mainly because these are felt to be outside the competence (and often interest) of economists, such as: why women come to the labour market with less education and less relevant education than men; why housework and child care are almost always the sole responsibility of women; why labour market segregation based on sex remains important despite a large overlap in the abilities of individual men and women; why the stereotyping of "female" occupations is so consistent with the sex stereotyping of women in society at large; why occupational segregation by sex has persisted to such an extent despite major increases in recent years in the education and labour force commitment of women. In my opinion, these types of non-economic issues are critical to understanding occupational segregation by sex. Non-economic/feminist (gender) theories, which are discussed in the next section, address many of these issues.

2.3   Feminist (gender) theories and other explanations

Feminist (gender) theories[7] are mainly concerned with non-labour market variables which economists take as given. A basic premise of gender theories is that women's disadvantaged position in the labour market is caused by, and is a reflection of, patriarchy and women's subordinate position in society and the family.[8] In all societies, household work and child care are seen as the main responsibility of women, while men are seen as mainly responsible for being the breadwinner. That these societal norms and perceptions differ from reality for many women, men and families does not detract from their influence on behaviour and their effect in causing discrimination against women.

This division of responsibilities and patriarchal ordering of society helps determine why women tend to accumulate less human capital as compared to men before entering into the labour market—that is, why female children receive less education than male children, and girls are less likely to pursue fields of study which are relevant for the labour markets such as sciences and crafts. Women are seen as having less need for labour market skills.

This patriarchal ordering of society and women's responsibility for household work/child care[9] helps determine why women acquire less labour market experience, on average, as compared to men—why many women withdraw from the labour force early and why many other women withdraw from the labour force temporarily.

Gender theory makes a valuable contribution to explaining occupational segregation by sex by pointing out how closely the characteristics of "female" occupations correspond to typical stereotypes of women and their supposed abilities. To illustrate this, table 2.1 presents a list of 13 typical female stereotypes which might affect occupational segregation by sex. These are divided into three groups of stereotypes (positive, negative and other stereotypes). Table 2.1 extends the author's earlier work on why employers' prefer men (Anker and Hein, 1985 and 1986), by expanding the list of stereotyped female characteristics, hypothesizing the occupations each stereotype might affect, indicating why these occupations might be affected, and commenting on the factual nature of this reasoning. This list of stereotypes is much more complete than the common observation that "female" occupations are an extension of household activities.

Five "positive" stereotypes (caring nature; skill and experience at household-related work; greater manual dexterity; greater honesty; and physical appearance) are noted in table 2.1. It would seem logical to hypothesize that these characteristics, if true, would help "qualify" women for the following types of ISCO occupations: nurse, doctor, social worker, teacher, maid, housekeeper, cleaner, cook, waiter, launderer, hairdresser, spinner, weaver, knitter, tailor/dressmaker, midwife, sewer, typist, cashier/book-keeper, salesperson, accountant, receptionist and shop assistant.

Five "negative" stereotypes (disinclination to supervise others; less physical strength; less ability to do science and maths; less willingness to travel; and less willingness to face physical danger and use physical force) are noted in table 2.1. These characteristics negatively affect women's accept-ability for various occupations—which help ensure that these become typical "male" occupations as a consequence. These stereotypes, if true, would help "disqualify" women for the following types of ISCO occupation: manager, supervisor, government executive officer/administrator, legislative official, construction worker, miner/quarrier, well driller, physical scientist, architect, engineer, mathematician, statistician, aircraft officer and worker, ship officer and worker, transport equipment driver/operator, fire-fighter, police officer and security guard.

Three other stereotypes (greater willingness to take orders, greater docility and less likelihood to complain about work or working conditions, less likelihood to join labour unions, greater willingness to do monotonous/repetitive work; greater willingness to accept lower wages and less need for income; and greater interest in working at home) are noted in table 2.1. These characteristics have a greater influence on the general characteristics

Table 2.1. Common stereotyped characteristics of women and their expected effect on occupational segregation by sex

Common stereotyped characteristics of women[a]	Effect on occupational segregation	Examples of typical occupations affected[b]	Comments
Positive			
1. Caring nature	Helps qualify women for occupations where others are cared for, such as children, the ill, older people.	Nurse Doctor Ayah Social worker Teacher Midwife	Often felt to be biological (i.e. sex difference), because women are mainly responsible for child care in all societies. This is, however, a learned, gender-based difference. Note that occupations which require care but which also require greater authority, such as medical doctor, are often male-dominated.
2. Skill (and experience) at household-related work	Helps qualify women for occupations that are frequently done in the home (almost always by women), often as unpaid household work.	Maid Housekeeper Cleaner Cook Waiter Launderer Hairdresser Spinner Sewer Weaver Knitter Tailor/dressmaker	Skills easy to learn (therefore, women's greater experience before entering the labour market should not be very important).
3. Greater manual dexterity (especially smaller, nimble fingers)	Helps qualify women for occupations where finger dexterity is important.	Sewer Knitter Spinner Weaver Tailor/dressmaker Typist	Belief is partly based on: − biological (sex) difference; and − experience (gender) differences in house before joining the labour market (also see stereotype 2). Skill is easy to learn. Occupations often similar to those noted under household-related work activities (see stereotype 2).
4. Greater honesty	Helps qualify women for occupations where money is handled and/ or trust is important.	Cashier/ bookkeeper Salesperson Accountant	Higher paying and higher status occupations (such as accountant which is a professional occupation) are often male-dominated.

Table 2.1.   (contd.)

Common stereotyped characteristics of women[a]	Effect on occupational segregation	Examples of typical occupations affected[b]	Comments
5. Physical appearance	Helps qualify women for occupations where physical appearance would help attract and/ or please customers.	Receptionist Salesperson Shop assistant	This advantage is often thought to be combined with a more pleasant and accommodating personality of women (e.g. for receptionist or salesperson).
			Other times, sex appeal is used to attract male customers (e.g. barmaid or prostitute).
			In certain cultures and countries where public interaction between men and women is frowned upon, this characteristic disqualifies/ excludes women from certain occupations (e.g. salespersons in the Middle East).
Other 6. Greater willingness to take orders Greater docility and less likelihood of complaining about work or working conditions Less likelihood of joining trade unions Greater willingness to do monotonous/ repetitive work	General characteristics which help qualify women for occupations and sectors of the economy where working conditions are poor, labour laws are not applied (e.g. informal sector) and work is routinized.	Note: These general characteristics (6, 7, 8) "qualify" women for many jobs which are low paid, unskilled, unprotected and repetitious in nature.	These stereotypes have been combined because they are similar in that all imply a subservient nature. These are archetypal learned (gender-type) characteristics.
7. Greater willingness to accept lower wages Less need for income	General characteristics which help qualify women for low-paid occupations and sectors of the economy.		Often related to (and often justified by) belief that women are secondary earners (i.e. not main "breadwinner"). This is despite: – increase in incidence of female-headed households; and – need of many families for multiple incomes.

Table 2.1. (contd.)

Common stereotyped characteristics of women[a]	Effect on occupational segregation	Examples of typical occupations affected[b]	Comments
			Often implies occupations which are in highly competitive industries, where cost considerations are very important. This often includes export products such as textiles.
			Low-paid occupations may be partly low paid because they are highly feminized.
8. Greater interest in working at home	Helps qualify women for occupations and sectors of the economy where work is organized in a home-based "putting out" type of production system.		Home-based work is usually poorly remunerated and often based on piece-work.
			Home-based work is easy to combine with household/child care.
			"Putting out" production system is often set up specifically to make use of the available cheap female labour.
			Home-based work is increasing in importance.[c]
Negative			
9. Disinclination to supervise others	Helps disqualify women for all types of supervisory and managerial occupations.	Manager (general; production; trade, catering and lodging) Supervisor (clerical; sales; production) Government executive officer and administrator Legislative official	This is in many ways the opposite of willingness to take orders (see no. 6).
			This often affects vertical occupational segregation (with lower level jobs for women).
10. Less physical (muscular) strength	Helps disqualify women for occupations requiring heavy lifting and/or physical effort.	Construction worker Miner/quarrier Well driller	There is considerable overlap in the physical strength of individual women and men which means that many women are physically capable of doing this work.
			Becoming less and less important in today's economy.

Table 2.1. (contd.)

Common stereotyped characteristics of women[a]	Effect on occupational segregation	Examples of typical occupations affected[b]	Comments
11. Less able to do science and maths	Helps disqualify women for occupations where high levels of science and maths are required.	Physical scientist (chemist/physicist) Architect Engineer Mathematician Statistician	Gender discrimination here begins in school where girls are discouraged from majoring in maths or science.
			Some believe that this is a biological (i.e. sex) difference. If so, it is a small average difference with a large overlap in the abilities of individual men and women.
12. Less willing to travel	Helps disqualify women for occupations where considerable travel is required.	Aircraft officer and worker Ship officer and worker Transport equipment driver/ operator	Many women are willing to travel, as evidenced by, for example, airline stewardesses (who were originally sought for their physical appearance— see stereotype 5).
			Many drivers do not travel overnight.
13. Less willing to face physical danger and use physical force	Helps disqualify women for occupations where physical danger is relatively great.	Fire-fighter Police officer Security guard Miner/Quarrier	This is a learned gender difference.
			Many women are willing to do these occupations.

Notes: [a] Many of these stereotypes overlap in their effects. While some stereotypes help reinforce sex segregation of particular occupations (e.g. greater manual dexterity and skill at household-type work for sewer), the effects of other stereotypes counterbalance each other (e.g. physical appearance and disinclination to supervise others for sales supervisors). [b] Almost all examples of occupations are taken from two- and three-digit ISCO-68 occupational classifications. [c] Bidi maker (local Indian cigarette), which is the largest non-agricultural occupation for women in India according to 1981 census data, is almost exclusively a home-based industry.
Source: Author's impressions and Anker and Hein (1985; 1986).

typifying "female" occupations (such as low pay, high flexibility, low status, less decision-making authority) than on qualifying or disqualifying women for particular occupations.

That sex stereotyping, such as discussed just above, plays an important role in affecting occupational segregation by sex is brought out very clearly by a series of establishment surveys sponsored by the ILO in transition economies (Bulgaria, the Czech Republic, Hungary and Slovakia) and developing countries (India, Cyprus, Sri Lanka and Ghana). In these enterprise surveys, employers were directly asked whether they preferred men or women for certain occupations and types of work. Given that these questions were so blunt and so direct, it seems reasonable to assume that responses admitting sex bias represent only the tip of the iceberg. Despite the direct nature of these questions, many employers indicated that a person's sex is an important characteristic affecting hiring and promotion decisions. In the Czech Republic, Hungary and Slovakia surveys (in 1992/1993), roughly 90 per cent of the employers interviewed indicated that they preferred men for repair occupations as well as maintenance occupations, whereas virtually none preferred women; roughly 35 to 55 per cent of employers questioned preferred men for professional occupations, general production occupations and skilled operative occupations as compared to only about 10 per cent who preferred women for each of these occupations (Paukert, 1994). In other enterprise surveys in Hungary and Bulgaria (in 1991/1992), roughly 55 to 65 per cent of the employers questioned preferred men for production occupations compared to roughly 15 to 25 per cent who preferred women (Sziraczki and Windell, 1992). In Cyprus (1981), when employers were asked a general question about whether certain types of job are considered more suitable for women or men, 85 per cent indicated that men are preferred for certain jobs and 89 per cent indicated that women are preferable for certain (other) jobs (House, 1986). In Lucknow, India (1982), roughly 60 per cent of the employers interviewed reported that women were unsuitable or less suitable than men for sales, production, service and executive/supervisory occupations (Papola, 1986). In Accra, Ghana (1982), 21 per cent of the employers interviewed indicated that they sometimes refused to hire women because of fear that they would become pregnant.

In addition to female stereotypes, there are also masculine stereotypes which play a role in determining what are typical "male" occupations (such as engineer, truck driver, police officer, construction worker). Therefore, in order to break down the sex segregation of occupations, **it is important to change male stereotypes as well as female stereotypes and to integrate men into "female" occupations as well as women into "male" occupations.** Integrating men into typical "female" occupations is controversial, since most labour market discrimination is against women, not men; in addition, this would help eliminate one of the few labour market advantages women have. In my opinion, however, breaking down occupational segregation by sex is critical for improving women's labour market situation, and to accomplish this goal, it is necessary to break down the sex stereotyping of men, women and occupations.

Cross-national analyses (such as those in Parts III and IV of this book) are excellent for investigating whether or not typical "male" and "female" occupations are consistent with (and by implication possibly determined by) the typical stereotyped characteristics of women listed in table 2.1. The conclusion of these analyses is that they are.

Why are "female" occupations flexible?

It seems clear that women's responsibility for housework and child care affects the type of jobs many women prefer, since flexible jobs in terms of hours (or part-time jobs) and relatively easy entry/exit/re-entry enable women to combine work and family responsibilities more easily. In this, feminist (gender) theories and neoclassical theories agree.

However, there are two possible reasons why "female" occupations tend to be flexible in terms of hours and labour turnover. It could be that women gravitate towards occupations with these characteristics (either because of women's preferences and characteristics and/or because employers prefer women for occupations with these characteristics), as explained by economic theory (see discussion in previous sections). Or, it could be that occupations become "female", because of the type of sex stereotyping described just above—with flexible working conditions a *consequence* of the fact that these are "female" occupations.[10]

While according to neoclassical economic/human capital theory, preferences of women and employers are responsible for the concentration of women in flexible occupations, there can not be an unequivocal conclusion according to feminist (gender) theory, since both of the possibilities noted above are supportable. While family responsibilities should increase women's preferences for flexible occupations, sex stereotyping of appropriate work for women should affect the types of occupations available to them.

The empirical analysis in Part III provides some evidence on the above issue. Without going into the details of these results, suffice it to say that they indicate a high degree of consistency between an occupation being a "female" or "male" occupation and the feminine stereotypes listed in table 2.1. They support the conclusion that the flexibility and low pay associated with many typical "female" occupations is due, to a large extent, to the fact that these are "female" occupations. There is no reason why many typical "male" occupations (for example, driver) could not be much more flexible, and why many typical "female" occupations (for example, maid) could not be much less flexible.[11]

Cultural restrictions on women's physical movement and public interaction with men

Gender theories also point out how cultural restrictions help define what is acceptable work for women and in some countries effectively bar women from certain occupations. This is an extreme form of sex stereotyping. For example, in many Muslim countries, *purdah* effectively forbids women from interacting with men in public. As a result, many Muslim women are strongly discouraged from taking sales jobs except in shops where customers are all women; women are excluded from factory jobs except when the entire factory is comprised of women.[12] Many other examples could be described. Cultural restrictions on women's physical movement are enforced through strong social sanctions. This often includes sexual harassment or rude behaviour by men.

2.4 Female-male pay differentials and occupational segregation by sex

Women receive lower pay than men throughout the world. As indicated by ILO data presented in table 2.2, this is true in all regions of the world; whether one is comparing pay computed on a daily, weekly or monthly basis; or whether one is comparing non-agricultural workers as a whole or only manufacturing workers. Average female–male pay ratios in the world are roughly 60–70 per cent based on a monthly reference period, 70–75 per cent based on daily and weekly reference periods and 75–80 per cent based on an hourly reference period, with reasonably similar averages for OECD and developing countries. Ratios appear to be especially low in East and South-East Asian countries as well as in some European countries (with Japan, the Republic of Korea, Malaysia, Singapore, Luxembourg and Cyprus the only countries from table 2.2 having a ratio below 0.60). Ratios appear to be relatively high in Scandinavia, as well as in some other OECD and Third World countries (with Denmark, Iceland, Norway, Sweden, Australia, Sri Lanka, Turkey and Swaziland the only countries from table 2.2 with a ratio clearly above 0.80).

Gunderson (1994) identifies *five sources of male–female pay differentials:* (i) differences in human capital endowments such as education and experience (caused mainly by non-labour market factors), (ii) differences in pay within the same occupation (caused by pure discrimination and dual labour markets), (iii) differences in pay for work of "equal value" (caused by the relationship between pay level in an occupation and the degree to which it is feminized), (iv) differences in jobs desired, and (v) differences in jobs available. *Occupational segregation by sex plays an important direct role in determining the last three sources of female–male pay differentials.*

Comparable worth exercises provide good illustrations of how wage rates tend to be lower in "female" occupations as compared to "male" occupations. In these exercises, jobs are objectively evaluated and point scores established for factors such as responsibility, skill, education, physical effort, working conditions. The summation of these factor scores indicates in some sort of objective sense the "value" of a job, and therefore its comparable worth. The greater the number of total points, the greater a job's "worth" or "value". Figure 2.1 and table 2.3 provide examples for the Washington State government and the Toronto municipal government. Notice that for

Table 2.2. Female-male wage ratios in the world, around 1990[a]

Region/country/area	Reference period[b,c]	Female-male wage ratio	
		All non-agricultural	Manufacturing
OECD[d]			
Australia	Hourly	88.2	82.5
Belgium	Hourly	75.1	74.5
Denmark	Hourly	82.6	84.6
Finland	Hourly		77.3
France	Hourly	80.8	78.9
Germany (West)	Hourly	73.2	72.7
Greece	Hourly		78.4
Iceland	Hourly	87.0	
Ireland	Hourly		69.2
Luxembourg	Hourly	67.8	62.2
Netherlands	Hourly	77.5	75.0
New Zealand	Hourly	80.6	74.9
Norway	Hourly		86.4
Portugal	Hourly	69.1	69.0
Sweden	Hourly		88.9
Switzerland	Hourly	67.6	68.0
United Kingdom	Hourly	70.5	68.4
Average (unweighted)		**76.7**	**75.7**
Cyprus	Daily/weekly	59.0	58.0
Turkey	Daily/weekly	84.5	81.0
Average (unweighted)		**71.8**	**69.5**
Developing countries or areas[d]			
Sri Lanka	Hourly	91.2	
Average (unweighted)			
Egypt	Daily/weekly	80.7	68.0
Hong Kong	Daily/weekly	69.5	69.0
Sri Lanka	Daily/weekly	89.8	88.0
Average (unweighted)		**80.0**	**75.0**
Costa Rica	Monthly	66.0	74.0
Japan	Monthly	49.6	41.0
Kenya	Monthly	78.3	73.0
Korea (Rep. of)	Monthly	53.5	50.0
Malaysia	Monthly		50.1
Paraguay	Monthly	76.0	66.0
Singapore	Monthly	71.1	55.0
Swaziland	Monthly	106.6	88.0
Average (unweighted)		**71.6**	**62.1**
World averages (unweighted)	Hourly	**77.8**	**75.7**
	Daily/weekly	**76.7**	**71.2**
	Monthly	**71.6**	**62.1**

Notes: [a] Data year is 1990. [b] Countries are grouped according to reference period over which wages are estimated, because the female-male wage ratio increases as the reference period increases (since women work fewer hours than men on average). For purposes of exposition, estimates for daily and weekly reference periods are combined. [c] Preference is given to estimate for shorter reference period if data are available for two or more reference periods. [d] Japan is included with other Asian countries (which are developing countries). Sri Lanka appears twice because of different reference periods.
Sources: Various issues of ILO *Yearbook of Labour Statistics*.

**Figure 2.1.   Relationship between monthly salary and job worth points for men and women
in the Washington State public service, 1974**

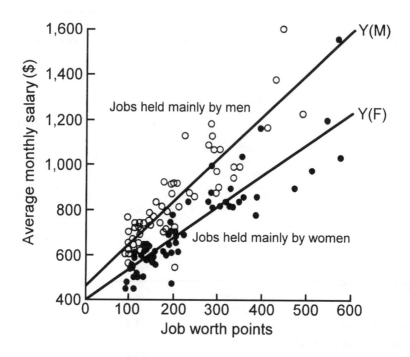

Source: Donald J. Treiman and Heidi I. Hartmann, eds., *Women, work and wages* (Washington, DC: National Academy
Press, 1981), p. 61.

jobs with similar worth (i.e. point scores), occupations held mainly by men
have substantially higher pay rates as compared to occupations mainly held
by women.[13] Based on these evaluations, pay rates are increased in the
female jobs in order to help equalize pay in male and female jobs with similar
point scores (or worth).

Empirical studies analysing the determinants of male–female pay
differences typically rely on regression analysis to separate out the proportion
attributable to (i) differences in productivity-related variables (including
human capital)[14] and other factors which affect wage rates[15] and (ii) differences in the returns men and women receive for their endowments. The first
set of factors is felt to measure justifiable differences in wage rates, whereas
the second set of variables deals mainly with the functioning of the labour
market and is seen as measuring discrimination (Oaxaca, 1973).

There have been scores of empirical studies of the female–male pay
differential. A review of American studies concludes that *around one-third of
the female–male differential is due to occupational segregation by sex* (Treiman

GENDER AND JOBS

Table 2.3. Pay equity job evaluations for selected male and female job classes, Toronto

Total points	Pay rate	Selected female job class	Total points	Pay rate	Selected male job classes
1 559	17.22	Early childhood educator grade 1	1 563	20.94	Automotive mechanic foreman
1 399	15.44	Early childhood educator grade 2	1 179	16.36	Junior microcomputer technician
1 155	12.49	Nursing attendant	1 179	16.36	Junior microcomputer technician
1 034	13.02	Day-care housekeeper	1 034	14.28	Cook grade 1
839	11.68	Housekeeping attendant	879	15.22	Security guard
652	11.42	Cleaner, light duties	694	14.21	Cleaner, heavy duties

Notes: Pay rates are hourly pay rates in Canadian dollars as of 1 January, 1990. Total points are obtained from a comparable worth review on 4 September, 1992. The phrases "pay equity" and "comparable worth" are equivalent. The former phrase is used in Canada and the latter phrase is used in the United States. Total points for job evaluation are based on the summation of points for the following factors using the following weights shown in brackets: skill (45%); responsibility (33%); effort (14%); and working conditions (8%). Job classes selected for this table are based in part on the job classes chosen as the main male comparators in the pay equity evaluations and in part on what are typical female jobs around the world.
Source: Canadian Union of Public Employees, mimeo, 1992.

and Hartmann, 1981; World Bank, 1994), as do reviews of different national studies (Terrell, 1992; Gonzalez, 1991).[16]

Studies relating occupational segregation by sex to female–male pay differentials are also greatly affected by the level of disaggregation of the occupational data being analysed. When very aggregated data are utilized, such as the usual seven major ISCO occupations, occupational segregation's effect is underestimated, mainly because most occupational segregation by sex is hidden/unobserved. As occupational data become more disaggregated, the observed level of sex segregation increases, and the portion of the female–male pay differential explained by occupational segregation tends to increase. A study from the United States (Treiman and Hartmann, 1981) illustrates this. The percentage of the female–male earnings gap explained by occupational segregation by sex in this study rose from about 10 per cent when 12 occupational categories were used, to 10 to 20 per cent when 222 occupations were used and to at least 30 per cent when 479 occupations were used. Similarly, a study by Kidd and Shannon (1996) found that the percentage of the female–male wage gap explained rose from 12 to 18 and 27 per cent as the number of occupations classified increased from 9, to 17 and 36 using the same Oaxaca (1973) approach used by Treiman and Hartmann (1981) (although no change was observed in this percentage when the Brown (1980) approach was used, which estimates a separate equation for each occupation). OECD (1988) reports that average female earnings would have been 93.2 per cent of average male earnings in 1986, if men and women had been paid the same median earnings for each occupation based on 18 broad occupational groups; in contrast, this would have been 84.1 per cent based on a much more disaggregated classification with 238 occupations.

After a fairly high level of detail in the occupational classification is reached, however, further disaggregation of the occupational data probably reduces the proportion of the female–male pay differential observed to be attributable to occupational segregation by sex. At the extreme of detailed job descriptions within establishments, there is usually very little difference in pay for men and women, since anti-discrimination laws in almost all countries make it illegal to pay different wages for the identical job within an enterprise.

The research literature on wage differentials provides a useful context in which to understand occupational segregation by sex, since it indicates that female–male pay differentials are due to many factors other than occupational segregation and differences in the human capital of men and women. It is only when these other factors are also taken into consideration that a coherent explanation can be found for both the level of female–male pay differentials and occupational segregation by sex in countries around the world. Indeed, several previous cross-national studies based on aggregated occupational data have noted that the simple correlation between the female–male pay ratio and occupational segregation by sex is not statistically significant and that sometimes this relationship is even positive (Rosenfeld and Kalleberg, 1990; Jacobs and Lim, 1992; Barbezat, 1993).

For example, the review of literature in Chapter 3 (as well as analysis in Part III) finds that occupational segregation by sex is lower in Asia than in Europe, and within Europe highest in Scandinavia. These results are unexpected and counter-intuitive if one is thinking only about female–male pay ratios, since as shown in table 2.2 and elsewhere (see for example, Anker and Hein, 1986; Standing, 1989; Terrell, 1992), European countries tend to have higher female–male pay ratios as compared to Asian countries. And within European countries, female–male pay ratios are highest in Scandinavia.

First, a major determinant of female–male pay differences across countries is the general level of pay differentials in a country (Blau and Khan, 1992; Gunderson, 1989). Second, in a related point, female–male pay differentials tend to be lower in countries with centralized wage setting (Gunderson, 1994; Rosenfeld and Kalleberg, 1991). Both of these factors undoubtedly help explain the relatively high female–male pay ratios in Scandinavia.

A third major source of pay differentials within countries is enterprise size. Large enterprises pay higher wage rates than small enterprises for seemingly similar occupations (Gunderson, 1989; 1994). Various explanations have been offered for this. One theory (compensating differentials theory) postulates that large enterprises pay a higher, so-called efficiency wage in order to attract the best talent. This has important implications for the average female–male wage ratio in a country, because men are more likely to be employed in large enterprises as compared to women. This factor could be especially important in a country like Japan where about one-third of the labour force works in large enterprises, in which seniority is an especially important determinant of pay. That women have been largely excluded from these large firms undoubtedly helps to explain the low female–male wage ratio in Japan (despite having a relatively low level of occupational segregation by sex).

Fourth, the research literature distinguishes between two different forms of occupational segregation by sex. Horizontal segregation refers to the distribution of men and women across occupations—for example, women may work as maids and secretaries and men as truck drivers and doctors. Vertical segregation refers to the distribution of men and women in the same occupation but with one sex more likely to be at a higher grade or level—for example, men are more likely to be production supervisors and women production workers, men more likely to be senior managers and women junior managers. Some authors stress the point that vertical segregation is more important (Hakim, 1992) or at least as important (Barbezat, 1993) a determinant of the female–male pay ratio as horizontal segregation. Of course, depending on the detail of the occupation classification, the same phenomenon could be observed as horizontal or vertical segregation. For example, if men work as doctors and women as nurses, this would be horizontal segregation in a three-digit ISCO classification where these two occupations are classified separately; but this same phenomenon would be vertical segregation in a two-digit ISCO classification where medical, dental and veterinary workers are combined into one occupational group. Irrespective of this measurement problem, it is clear that vertical segregation is a very important phenomenon determining female–male pay differentials, because even a relatively detailed occupational classification of 250 or so occupations is rather crude for a modern economy. Again referring to the situation in Japan, it seems likely that vertical segregation is an especially important determinant of Japan's low female–male pay ratio. For example, Japanese women are more or less excluded from the managerial career path in large corporations, so that even when they get a job in a large company, they rarely get into a career track position (Lam, 1993).[17]

Notes

[1] A number of researchers have commented on the fact that female–male wage differentials are very small for single persons and that married persons account for almost all of the observed female–male wage differential (see for example, Blau and Khan, 1992 and World Bank, 1994 for general conclusions; Hakim, 1992 for the United Kingdom; Ogawa and Clark, 1995 for Japan).

[2] Even in Scandinavia, women continue to be mainly responsible for housework and child care according to time use data (UNDP, 1995; UN, 1991).

[3] Papola (1986) reports that this was one of the most common reasons for not hiring women by employers in his enterprise survey in Lucknow, India.

[4] The need for women to bring their children to the workplace is even found for older female children in Bangladesh, where garment manufacturers say that women workers are

unwilling to leave their 11–13 year old daughters at home alone, because this would negatively affect their daughter's reputation and consequently marriage prospects (Myers, personal communication).

[5] It is possible, of course, to design maternity and child-care leave programmes as parental leave programmes. However, experience from countries which give new parents the choice of maternal leave or paternal leave indicates that relatively few fathers use the paternity leave provision. An interesting policy to get men to take paternity leave is found in Norway where at least four weeks of a possible total of 52 weeks of parental leave must be taken as paternal leave; if the *father* does not use this four weeks of paternal leave, it is lost (Melkas and Anker, forthcoming).

[6] Two interesting institutional aspects of Scandinavian labour markets (see for example, Melkas and Anker, forthcoming) are strong public commitments to: (i) gender equity and (ii) full employment for all citizens. These public commitments directly affect the sex segregation of occupations. They help create many public sector jobs in order to help women combine their dual responsibilities of family and work. For example, it is estimated in Melkas and Anker (forthcoming) that in 1990 approximately 10 per cent of non-agricultural women workers in Finland and Norway and 19 per cent of non-agricultural women workers in Sweden were in one of the following generally public sector occupations of this nature: child day-care centre staff, social worker, municipal home help and assistant nurse/attendant. Since these occupations are highly feminized (96, 75, 96, 92 per cent female respectively in Sweden, for example), this substantially increases occupational segregation by sex in Scandinavia and in part helps cause it to be higher than in other European countries.

[7] This division of theories into three separate categories is done for heuristic purposes, as there is substantial overlap between them. For example, while the perpetuation of sex segregation in an occupation through sexual harassment by male workers is usually described as part of feminist theory, it could easily be incorporated into a neoclassical model of the labour market as an added expense for employers (since introduction of female workers in such a situation might disrupt the workplace and affect labour productivity).

[8] The following story, told in the form of a riddle, illustrates quite well how strong gender stereotypes can be.

A boy was riding in a car driven by his father. They got into a car accident and both were hurt. The boy was seriously hurt. An ambulance took the boy and his father to the hospital. The boy went directly to the emergency room for an operation, accompanied by his father. In walked a doctor who took one look at the boy and said to the surprised father who was himself a doctor, "I'm sorry, but I cannot operate on this boy as he is my son".

RIDDLE FOR THE READER: Why won't the doctor operate? (Answer: the doctor who refuses to operate is the boy's mother).

[9] This point is illustrated by an experience of mine during field work several years ago in Egypt. In response to a typical question on labour force participation ("What was your main activity in the past week?"), a female school teacher reported that she was a housewife. I stopped the interview to find out why she gave this answer when she, in fact, was a teacher. She responded by saying that teaching involved 20–30 hours of work per week, but that housework involved many more hours—and that the question had enquired about her "main activity" in terms of time.

[10] The idea that women's occupations are flexible because they are "female" is, in essence, the concept of an article on the increasing feminization of the labour force in the world, where it is argued that labour markets worldwide are becoming more "flexible" (Standing, 1989).

[11] A similar conclusion was reached in a recent European Union report regarding how teaching is organized (Rubery and Fagan, 1993). "Characteristics of this profession (emphasis on caring role, convenient working hours, relatively low pay) may be a reflection of, and not a cause of the dominance of women".

[12] A solution to this problem used by some garment factories in Bangladesh is to have single sex shop-floors. In this way, factories have both male and female workers, but there is no interaction between men and women at the worksite.

[13] See Chapter 5 for discussion of how "male jobs" and "female jobs" are defined in comparable worth exercises.

[14] Variables which are typically used to measure a worker's human capital and productivity include the following: education, field of study, training, experience in the enterprise, experience in the labour market, age, size of firm, hours of work and health.

[15] Typical factors used to measure macro, meso and establishment level aspects that might affect a worker's wage rate, include the following: size of establishment, sector of establishment, whether public or private, region, city size, whether unionized. Also sometimes included is the percentage female in the occupation, although this variable is sometimes interpreted as measuring sex discrimination.

[16] Scott (1986) discusses the interesting case of Peru where female education levels increased over several decades to a point where they exceeded male levels—yet the average female–male pay ratio showed little change.

[17] Even in Nikko Securities, a large Japanese corporation which is considered a leader in promoting women's employment, very few women enter the career promotion track. According to a recent report (Manpower, 1994), Nikko Securities recruited a relatively high percentage of women for its managerial positions (148 men and 75 women), but not into the career, *sogoshoku* rank, track (148 men and only 3 women).

REVIEW OF CROSS-NATIONAL STUDIES OF OCCUPATIONAL SEGREGATION BY SEX

3

In the previous chapter on theories of occupational segregation by sex, it was indicated that male and female workers are often segregated into different occupations, with women's occupations typically having lower status and pay as compared to men's occupations. It was also indicated that certain types of occupations tend to be dominated by men (e.g. managerial and production occupations) while other occupations tend to be dominated by women (e.g. services and some types of clerical and care-giving professional occupations such as nursing and teaching). The reasons why certain occupations tend to be dominated by men and other occupations by women is debated, with competing theories providing explanations as discussed in Chapter 2.

But what of the available empirical evidence on occupational segregation by sex? What does it reveal? The present chapter investigates this based on results from previous cross-national studies. This review is important both to set a context for the detailed empirical analysis of occupational segregation by sex which follows, as well as to help indicate aspects of the present book that are new and unusual.

There have been a reasonably large number of empirical studies on the sex segregation of occupations. However, most have been national studies, with those for the United States the most common. We were able to locate roughly 20 studies with data on occupational segregation by sex which are cross-national in nature, each covering at least five countries and in several cases more than 50 countries. It is important to note that a number of these studies are not mainly interested in occupational segregation by sex, but with female inequality in general and/or the effect occupational segregation has on male-female pay. This means that several of these studies contain data on, but little or no analysis *per se* of, occupational segregation by sex.

Table 3.1 summarizes findings for these earlier empirical cross-national studies. Indicated for each study is: author, data source, data years, countries covered, detail of occupational classification, inequality measures, and selected findings. Based on this review of previous empirical cross-national studies, the following issues are addressed and general conclusions drawn in the remainder of this chapter:

Table 3.1. Earlier cross-national studies of occupational segregation by sex

Author and study	Data source	Data year(s)	Regions and countries covered	Detail in occupational data	Inequality measures used	Selected findings
Anker and Hein (1985, 1986)	ILO *Yearbook* National surveys and censuses	1960s, 1970s, 1980s	52 developing countries with 1 digit data (5 Africa, 13 North Africa and Middle East, 21 Latin America, 13 Asia) 5 developing countries with 2 or 3 digit data (Cyprus, Ghana, India, Mauritius, Peru)	1 digit (6 occupations) for 52 developing countries 2 or 3 digits for 5 developing countries	ID Representation ratio Percentage of labour force in gender-dominated occupations	Women overrepresented in professional/technical and services. Women are underrepresented in administrative/ managerial and production. Based on detailed occupational data, many male-dominated occupations but few female-dominated occupations. Largest female-dominated occupations are highly gender-stereotyped.
Bakker (1988)	OECD 1980 (taken from ILO *Yearbook* and National enquiries)	1968 to 1978	5 industrialized countries (Canada, France, W. Germany, Sweden, United States)	Not indicated. (Note: must be 1 digit as OECD 1980 used this.)	ID Representation ratio	Occupational segregation lower across industries than across occupations. ID and female LFPR are positively related.
Blau and Ferber (1992)	ILO *Yearbook*	1988 to 1990 (mostly)	World, 94 countries	1 digit (7 occupations)	ID	ID highest in Latin America, Caribbean and Middle East. ID lowest in sub-Saharan Africa and East Asia.

Table 3.1. (contd.)

Author and study	Data source	Data year(s)	Regions and countries covered	Detail in occupational data	Inequality measures used	Selected findings
Blau and Ferber (1992) cont.						Variations across countries in percentage female for particular occupations, such as clerical, implies that social, cultural and religious norms important.
Boserup (1970)	ILO Yearbook UN Demographic Yearbook National data	1953–1966 (mostly 1960s)	34 developing countries (4 Africa, 6 North Africa/ Middle East, 13 Latin America, 11 Asia)	1 digit (no. of occupations varies by country; mostly 8)	Percentage female by employment status	
Boulding (1976)	ILO Yearbook UN Demographic Yearbook	1950–1971 (1965 on average)	World, 86 countries (13 Africa, 9 North Africa and Middle East, 24 Latin America, 23 Europe/ North America, Asia)	1 digit (7 occupations)	ID Representation ratio	ID highest in Latin America (approx .49) and lowest in Africa and Asia (approx .30). ID similar in Europe and North Africa/Middle East (approx .38).
Charles (1992)	ILO Yearbook	1985 or closest year	25 industrialized countries	1 digit (6 occupations)	Ratio index[a]	Structural characteristics of modern economies (large service sector and high proportion of employees) positively associated with occupational segregation. Female LFPR not associated with occupational segregation.

Study	Source	Period	Level of disaggregation	Measure	Comments
Charles (1992) cont.					Lowest occupational segregation in Italy and highest in Luxembourg.
Horton (1993)	National censuses and surveys (sometimes from ILO *Yearbook*)	1950 to 1990	7 Asian countries (India, Indonesia, Republic of Korea, Japan, Malaysia, Philippines, Thailand)	1 digit (7 occupations)	ID	ID is low at .09 to .19, except for Philippines at .37, for latest year. ID appears to have recently risen in most of these countries. Suggested that a major reason for low ID in Asia may be large size of agricultural sector.
Jacobs and Lim (1992)	ILO *Yearbook*	1960 to 1980	World, 39 countries (13 Americas, 12 Asia, 14 Europe)	7 occupations (also 9 industries)	ID Size-standardized ID[b]	ID declined in Americas. ID changes for Europe and Asia are mixed. Size-standardized ID is consistently decreasing around the world.
Nordic Council of Ministers (1995)	National data	1990 to 1992	5 Nordic countries (Denmark, Finland, Iceland, Norway, Sweden)	Not indicated (must be 2 digit)	Percentage of male LF and female LF working in occupations with 10, 40, 60 and 90 per cent female	65 to 75 per cent of women work in occupations with over 60 per cent women. Slightly more of male LF compared to female LF work in occupations with over 60 per cent men or women.
OECD (1985)	ILO *Yearbook*	1970 to 1983	8 OECD countries (Australia, Canada, W. Germany, Japan, New Zealand, Norway, Sweden, United States)	1 digit (7 occupations)	ID WE index[c]	ID lowest in Japan (.23) in latest available year and highest in Australia and Norway (approx. 48).
OECD (1988)	ILO *Yearbook*	1960 and 1970 (or nearest year)	23 OECD countries	1 digit (7 occupations)	ID	Italy, Japan, Greece and Portugal lowest ID in 1980s.

Table 3.1. (contd.)

Author and study	Data source	Data year(s)	Regions and countries covered	Detail in occupational data	Inequality measures used	Selected findings
OECD (1988) cont.		1980–1986				Slight overall decrease in ID with considerable variation across countries. ID not related to average female LFPR.
Psacharopoulos and Tzannatos (1992)	ILO *Yearbook*	1950s/1960s to 1970s/ 1980s	15 Latin American countries (also United States, Canada, Japan, Norway, Sweden for comparison)	1 digit (7 occupations)	ID Representation ratio	ID generally higher among employees than among self-employed or unpaid family workers. ID high at .49 on average. ID decreased in 7 countries and increased in 6 countries. ID decrease due more to changes in occupational structure than to changes in sex composition of occupations.
Reubens and Harrison (1983)	National censuses	1970 to 1975	4 industrialized countries (United Kingdom, Japan, Sweden, United States)	3 digits (223 to 426 occupations; also 3 age groups: 15–19, 20–24, 25+)	ID Most common occupations	Japan had lowest and Sweden highest occupational segregation. Occupational segregation by sex greater than occupational segregation by age.

Study	Source	Period	Countries	Occupations	Indices/Measures	Findings
Roos (1985)	National surveys	1970s	12 "countries" (Same 9 countries in Treimann and Roos plus Great Britain, Japan and Northern Ireland)	14 occupations (high and low prestige occupations. For 7 ISCO one digit occupations.)	ID Representation ratio	Women overrepresented in high prestige clerical, low prestige sales and low prestige services occupations. Women underrepresented in administrative and managerial and high prestige production occupations. Extensive uniformity across countries in patterns of occupational segregation by sex. ID lowest in Japan (.28) and highest in Sweden (.60).
Rosenfeld and Kalleberg (1990)	National surveys ILO *Yearbook*	1980 to 1987	9 industrialized countries (United States, Canada, Norway, Sweden, Japan, W. Germany, Denmark, United Kingdom, Australia)	1 digit (6 occupations)	ID	ID lowest in Japan (.28) and highest in Norway (.51). ID and female–male pay ratio positively related. Mainly interested in ID to relate it to male–female pay ratio. Centralization of wage setting is important determinant of male–female pay ratio.
Rubery and Fagan (1993)	Eurostat National labour force surveys	1983, 1987, 1990	12 European Union countries (Belgium, Denmark, France, W. Germany, Greece, Ireland, Italy, Luxembourg, Netherlands, Portugal, Spain, United Kingdom)	2 digit (80 occupations)	Indices (ID, Index of segregation[d], "0" index[e]) Percentage of LF in gender-concentrated occupations	High level of occupational segregation in all European Union countries. No evidence that occupational segregation related to economic development or female share of LF.

Table 3.1. (contd.)

Author and study	Data source	Data year(s)	Regions and countries covered	Detail in occupational data	Inequality measures used	Selected findings
					15 most female dominated occupations and 15 most male dominated occupations 6 specific occupations (teacher, computer professional, clerical in public administration, clerical in finance, driver, caterer)	Considerable similarity in EU countries in most important occupations for men as well as for women. Occupational segregation did not change much over 1983–90 time period.
Treiman and Roos (1983)	National surveys	1970s	9 industrialized countries (Austria, Denmark, Finland, W. Germany, Israel, Netherlands, Norway, Sweden, United States)	14 occupations (high and low prestige occupations for the 7 one-digit ISCO occupations)	ID Representation ratio	Substantial sex segregation in all nine countries. ID highest in Sweden (.60) and lowest at around .40 in four countries
UN ECE (United Nations, 1985a)	ILO *Yearbook* National statistics	1970s 1980s	26 countries (2 North America, 6 Eastern Europe and USSR, 18 other Europe) Note: ID available only for 13 countries	1 digit (6 occupations)	ID Representation ratio WE	Little change in ID from 1970–80 except in North America. WE often declined in Europe.

| World Bank (1994) | 1950s/1960s compared to 1970s/1980s | World, 45 countries (4 Africa, 11 Asia, 5 North Africa and Middle East, 11 Americas, 14 Europe) | 1 digit (7 or 8 occupations) | ID | No consistent change from 1950s/1960s to 1970s/1980s. ID highest in North Africa (approx .55) and lowest in West Africa (approx .20). |

Notes: ID is abbreviation for index of dissimilarity (see Chapter 5 and Appendix 5.1 to Chapter 5 for definition). LF is abbreviation for labour force; and LFPR is abbreviation for labour force participation rate. Generally six occupations implies agriculture is excluded. Representation ratio is the percentage female in an occupation divided by the average percentage female for the LF as a whole.

[a] Ratio index indicates the sum of occupation-specific deviations from proportionate representation of the sexes. [b] Size-standardized ID assumes that all occupations are exactly the same size. [c] WE index is equal to ID times twice the ratio of male to female workers. [d] Index of segregation is the same as marginal matching index (see Chapter 5). [e] Starting point for "0" is a truly desegregated labour market characterized by women comprising 50 per cent of LF as well as 50 per cent of each occupation. See also Barbezat, 1993, for an excellent paper which reviews many national and cross-national studies on occupational segregation by sex.

- what data sources tend to be relied upon?
- what is the usual level of aggregation/disaggregation in the occupational data which are used?
- what countries tend to be included; do they tend to come from particular regions or development levels?
- what inequality measures tend to be used?
- what conclusions are reached on how occupational segregation varies across countries and over time?

Previous cross-national studies have relied heavily on data reported in the ILO Yearbook of Labour Statistics. This is the case for 14 of the 19 studies covered in table 3.1—although it is worth noting that six of these 14 studies also use data from national sources. All five studies which rely exclusively on national data cover only OECD countries, with a total of only 20 different OECD countries included: these are the 12 original European Communities countries, four additional Nordic countries and Austria (several of which were soon to join the EU), in addition to the United States, Israel and Japan. The fact that the ILO *Yearbook of Labour Statistics* is used so often means that there are not as many independent studies as table 3.1 would seem to indicate—especially for developing countries—as a number of studies, in essence, analyse the same data over and over again.

Previous cross-national studies relied on one-digit occupational data for 14 of the 19 studies—all covering OECD countries—included in table 3.1. Indeed, there is a close match between use of the ILO *Yearbook of Labour Statistics* and one-digit occupational data as well as the use of national sources and two-digit occupational data. This means that analysis of occupational segregation is often—too often—based on only seven occupations (and only six non-agricultural occupations). Yet as discussed in Chapter 2 and as will be demonstrated in Chapter 6, one-digit occupational data not only hide a great deal of occupational segregation by sex but can also be misleading as regards cross-national differences and trends over time.

By far the most commonly used measure of occupational segregation by sex is the index of dissimilarity (generally referred to as ID). This inequality statistic is used in virtually every cross-national empirical study. There are only three exceptions in table 3.1 (Charles, 1992 which uses a newly derived inequality index; Boserup, 1970 which uses only percentage female; and Nordic Council of Ministers, 1995 which uses percentage of the male and female labour forces working in gender-dominated occupations).

The widespread use of ID as *the* measure of occupational segregation is due to its common usage, the ease with which it can be calculated, and its seemingly simple interpretation which allows analysts to compare levels and trends in occupational segregation between and across countries. In actual fact, there is a good deal of unease among many analysts with the use and interpretation of ID, in particular to measure changes over time. It is for this reason that there is a raging debate in the research literature about the appropriateness of ID, and a number of analysts have recently proposed alternative inequality statistics (readers are referred to Chapter 5 for a detailed discussion of this research literature). It is also for this reason that *most of the studies included in table 3.1 use one, and sometimes several, additional measures of occupational segregation besides ID.* The most commonly used additional statistic is the representation ratio (defined as the percentage female in an occupation divided by the average percentage female for the labour force as a whole). This statistic is a good complement to ID, since it provides an easy-to-understand measure of the extent to which women are over-represented or underrepresented in *specific* occupational groups, whereas ID provides a composite measure of inequality for the labour force as a whole.

A number of analysts make it clear in their papers that one or even two inequality measures are not sufficient to understand the phenomenon of occupational segregation by sex in the world. Partly for this reason, the present study uses a number of different inequality statistics (see Chapter 5) to describe, measure and analyse the sex segregation of occupations in the world in Parts III and IV.

In summary, there have been two different basic types of empirical cross-national studies of occupational segregation by sex. One type relies on rather crude one-digit occupational data taken from the ILO *Yearbook of Labour Statistics* and uses ID and representation ratios to measure the extent of sex inequality in and across occupations. Virtually all previous studies which have included large numbers of developing countries are of this type. Indeed, one of the few exceptions to this generalization appears to be my own earlier work with Catherine Hein (Anker and Hein, 1986). The second type of study uses national data sources, more detailed two-digit or three-digit occupational data and several inequality statistics. Almost all of the studies which fall into this category cover industrialized countries only. In this regard, the Rubery and Fagan (1993) study for the European Union is worth a special mention, as it is rather unique, covering twelve (European Union) countries, using many different inequality measures, and using two-digit data with 80 occupations per country for three points in time.

Despite the obvious weaknesses and limitations of previous cross-national empirical studies, it is possible, and useful, to **point out noteworthy findings and draw some general conclusions.** This is done in the remainder of this chapter.

First, most, if not all, authors stress that *occupational segregation by sex is very extensive in every country.* This is important, since it documents the universality of occupational segregation by sex—and how it cuts across national boundaries, religions, cultures and development levels.

Second, a large percentage of the labour force works in occupations that are dominated by one sex to such an extent that *many occupations are in essence "female" or "male" occupations*—as shown for developing countries

(Anker and Hein, 1986), Nordic countries (Nordic Council, 1995), and a number of industrialized countries (Roos, 1985 and Rubery and Fagan, 1993). At the same time, "male" occupations are found to be much more important than "female" occupations in terms of their number and overall size. Once again, male workers have an advantage over female, this time in the extent to which they are protected from competition from the other sex.

Third, in terms of regional differences based on crude one-digit data, it appears that *inequality is greatest in Latin America and the Caribbean region*. This was found by Boulding (1976) based on data for the 1950s and 1960s, Psacharopoulos and Tzannatos (1992) based on data for the 1970s and 1980s and Blau and Ferber (1992) based on data for the late 1980s and 1990. At the other end of the spectrum, previous studies indicate that *inequality is lowest in Asia and sub-Saharan Africa* based on crude one-digit data (although it is worth pointing out that the relatively low ID observed in sub-Saharan Africa is greatly influenced by the fact that one occupation, agriculture, is extremely large in this region). Interestingly, industrialized countries in Europe, North America and Oceania tend to have average levels of inequality. Some of the above observations are confirmed, while others are contradicted by the analysis in Part III of this book.

Fourth, in terms of differences among industrialized countries, several studies comment on how *Scandinavian countries, and in particular Sweden, have among the greatest inequalities* (e.g. Reubens and Harrison, 1983; Treiman and Roos, 1983; Rosenfeld and Kalleberg, 1991). Within Europe, ID seems to be lowest in southern European countries such as in Greece, Portugal, Italy and Spain (OECD, 1988; Charles, 1992 and Rubery and Fagan, 1993). Many analysts have also commented on how *Japan has relatively low inequality* (e.g. Roos, 1985; OECD, 1985; OECD, 1988). This result for Japan is so surprising that some analysts have tried to explain it by suggesting that the Japanese occupational classification may not be comparable to those used in Europe (Hakim, 1992). Analysis in Part III based on detailed occupational data, while broadly confirming these results for Europe and Japan (in a much weakened form partly because more recent data are utilized), also provides a much more complete explanation for these results (both because more detailed occupational data and a number of inequality measures are used).

Fifth, *occupational segregation by sex and female labour force participation are not found to be significantly related among industrialized countries—* that is, industrialized countries with higher (lower) female participation rates do not tend to have lower (higher) levels of occupational segregation (as one would expect if the entry of women into the labour market implies that they would find work in "male" as well as "female" occupations). An insignificant relationship was found by Charles (1992) and OECD (1988), while Bakker (1988) found a slightly positive relationship.

Sixth, there appears to be *considerable consistency across regions in the extent to which women workers are concentrated in certain major occupational groups*, while at the same time there appears to be considerable variability across regions for other major occupational groups (see Boulding, 1976 for earlier evidence worldwide; Anker and Hein, 1986 for earlier evidence on developing countries; OECD, 1988 and Rubery and Fagan, 1993 for earlier evidence on OECD countries). Thus, women are strongly underrepresented in the production and administrative/managerial major occupational groups as well as strongly overrepresented in service occupations in both developing and OECD countries. Sales and clerical occupations show considerable variability across regions of the world in terms of female representation; for example, women are strongly overrepresented in clerical occupations in Middle Eastern and North African countries. In terms of professional/technical occupations, women workers seem to be slightly overrepresented relative to their share of the non-agricultural labour force as a whole in most of the world, but most women professional/technical workers are in just two specific occupations (teachers and nurses).

Seventh, there is a high degree of uniformity around the world in *the feminization of specific occupations*, and this *closely matches gender stereotypes in society* regarding the types of work that are appropriate for men and women (Anker and Hein, 1986 for developing countries; Rubery and Fagan, 1993 for European Union countries; Roos, 1985 for industrialized countries). At the same time, there are some noteworthy differences across countries in the feminization of certain occupations; for example, Blau and Ferber (1992) point out how India and Pakistan have a low percentage female in clerical occupations, and Anker and Hein (1986) show how Middle Eastern and North African countries have a very low percentage female for sales occupations—implying that social and cultural factors affect the form of occupational segregation by sex.

Eighth, *sex inequality tends to be higher when measured across occupations* as compared to when measured across industries or age groups (e.g. Bakker, 1988, for industries; Reubens and Harrison, 1983, for age groups). These results imply that the sex segregation of occupations is one of the main aspects on which labour markets segment.

Ninth, a number of cross-national studies investigated how the sex segregation of occupations has changed over time. Analysts have generally been sanguine about the *lack of change for broad groupings of countries in recent years and decades*. Regarding industrialized countries, the UNECE (United Nations, 1985a) found little change in the 1970s outside of North America. The OECD (1988) found a slight overall decrease in OECD countries between the 1960s/1970s and the 1980s, but with considerable variation in national trends. Rubery and Fagan (1993) found little overall change between 1983 and 1990 in European Union countries. Regarding developing countries, once again the available evidence indicates that there has been no consistent change in the sex segregation of occupations in recent decades. Horton (1993) found a slight rise in recent years for seven Asian countries. The World Bank (1994) found no consistent change for the 1950s/1960s as compared to the 1970s/1980s. Psacharopoulos and Tzannatos (1992) found mixed results for Latin America and the Caribbean, as occupational segregation by sex was found to have decreased in seven countries and increased in six others; in contrast, Jacobs and Lim (1992) found that ID fell in 7 of 10 Latin American and Caribbean countries between 1960 and 1980. In short, while previous cross-national studies indicate that occupational segregation by sex has decreased in some countries in recent decades, they do not find that there has been a general improvement in industrialized or developing countries. In contrast, Part IV, which analyses recent changes in sex segregation of occupations, draws a different conclusion. We conclude that the glass is half full rather than half empty; we find that while there has been a general decrease in the world in occupational segregation by sex in recent decades, there has been no change in some countries, regions and subregions.

PART II

DESCRIPTION OF STUDY DATA AND OCCUPATIONAL SEGREGATION STATISTICS

This section of the book provides a description of the national data on which this book is based. Chapter 5 describes the comparability of national data across countries and areas as well as within countries or areas over time. This includes discussions of data coverage, definitions of employment, occupational classifications and adjustments made to improve data comparability.

Chapters 6 and 7 deal with issues related to the measurement of occupational segregation. Chapter 6 is concerned with the various concepts and statistics which have been used for measuring occupational segregation—and argues that several different types of inequality statistics are needed in order to obtain a reasonably complete picture and perspective of occupational segregation. Chapter 6 also describes and defines the different types of inequality statistics used in this book. Chapter 7 is concerned with one of the most important problems in cross-national comparison of occupational segregation—the fact that the measured/observed level of occupational segregation by sex in a country or area is significantly affected by the level of disaggregation in its national occupational classification. The more disaggregated the classification, the higher occupational segregation by sex is observed to be. In order to increase the cross-national comparability of our study data, the relationship between the observed level of occupational segregation by sex and the level of disaggregation in an occupational classification is analysed in Chapter 7. And, most importantly, Chapter 7 describes the procedures developed to derive national inequality statistics which take into account the level of disaggregation in the national occupation classification.

COMPARABILITY OF DATA BETWEEN COUNTRIES AND WITHIN COUNTRIES OVER TIME[1]

4

A variety of factors influence the extent to which occupational data can be said to be comparable, both across countries at one point in time and within countries over time. Six such factors are discussed in this chapter.

First, *differing data sources* can pose a problem in that data collected through labour force surveys and censuses involve different enumeration and coding techniques, and therefore sometimes produce somewhat different results; censuses, being large undertakings, tend to have relatively poor data quality but no sampling errors as compared to labour force surveys which generally have better data quality and sampling errors. Second, *country coverage is more complete for some regions* than for others. This means that there is greater representativeness of experiences and situations in some regions (especially OECD) than in others (especially developing countries and transition economies). Third, *the working population covered by study data varies across countries.* Some country data cover the employed population, while others cover the total labour force (i.e. include the unemployed); some include the armed forces, others do not. Fourth, *countries sometimes define and measure employment in different ways.* This is especially a problem for measuring women workers who are often incompletely enumerated (and therefore often invisible) in the official statistics. This is more important for certain occupations (e.g. agricultural) and certain types of jobs (e.g. informal sector occupations). Fifth, *occupational classification systems differ* from country to country; in addition, this system sometimes changes over time within a country. Sixth, there are *often major differences across countries in the rules and procedures used for coding* up the responses recorded on questionnaire forms. This often manifests itself in unrealistically large "other" and "not elsewhere classified" occupations.

Sections 4.1–4.8 examine how each of the above six factors limit the comparability across countries of occupational segregation data and describe the adjustments made to our study data in order to improve comparability. Table 4.1 provides information on the characteristics of study data as regards year, source, coverage and coding scheme. In addition to these six factors, comparability of national data on occupational segregation is also greatly affected by the degree of disaggregation in these data. **The more disaggregated**

Table 4.1. Characteristics of study data in terms of year, source, coverage and occupational classification scheme

Country or area	1970	1980	1990
Australia	70 LFS E NOC	80 LFS E NOC	90 LFS E NOC
Austria	71 C L A NOC	80 LFS L A NOC	90 LFS L A NOC
Canada			90 LFS E NOC
Cyprus		81 ES P ISCO68	89 ES P ISCO88
Finland	70 C E A NOC	80 C E A NOC	90 LFS E A NOC
France		82 C E NOC	90 C E NOC
Germany (West)	76 LFS E NOC	80 LFS E NOC	89 LFS E NOC
Italy	71 C E NOC	81 C E NOC	
Luxembourg	70 C L A ISCO68	81 C E A ISCO68	91 LFS E A ISCO68
Netherlands	73 LFS E A ISCO68	79 LFS E A ISCO68	90 LFS E A ISCO68
New Zealand		81 C L ISCO68	86 C E ISCO68
Norway	70 C E A NOC	80 C E A NOC	90 C E A NOC
Spain	75 LFS L A NOC	80 LFS E A NOC	90 LFS E A NOC
Sweden[a]		80 LFS L A NOC	91 LFS L A NOC
Switzerland	70 C E A NOC	80 C E A NOC	
United Kingdom		81 LFS E NOC	90 LFS E NOC
United States	70 C E NOC	80 C E NOC	91 LFS E NOC
Bulgaria		75 C L NOC	85 C L NOC
Hungary		80 C E NOC	90 C E NOC
Poland		78 C L NOC	88 C L NOC
Former Yugoslavia	71 C L NOC	81 C E NOC	
Bahrain	71 C L A ISCO58	81 C E ISCO68	91 C L NOC
Egypt		76 C E ISCO68	86 C E ISCO68
Iran, Islamic Rep.			86 C E NOC
Jordan	61 C L ISCO58	79 C E ISCO68	
Kuwait		75 C E ISCO68	85 C E ISCO68
Tunisia		75 C L ISCO68	89 C L NOC
China[b]		82 C E NOC	
Fiji		76 C E ISCO68	86 C E ISCO68
Hong Kong	71 C E NOC	81 C E A NOC	91 C E A NOC
India		81 C E NOC	
Japan	70 C E A NOC	80 C E A NOC	90 C E A NOC
Rep. of Korea		83 LFS E ISCO68	
Malaysia		80 C L ISCO68	
Angola			92 LFS E ISCO68
Costa Rica	73 C E NOC	87 LFS E NOC	91 LFS E NOC
Ghana		84 C E ISCO68	
Haiti			86 IES E ISCO68
Mauritius	72 C E ISCO68	83 C E ISCO68	90 C E ISCO88
Netherlands Antilles		81 C L ISCO68	
Senegal		76 C L ISCO68	88 C L NOC

Notes:
For source: C indicates population census; LFS indicates labour force or general household survey; IES indicates income and expenditure survey; ES indicates establishment survey.
For coverage: E indicates the employed population only; L indicates the labour force; P indicates paid employment only. A indicates that armed forces are included in the original data. (These data are deleted for the analysis in this book.)
For occupational classification: ISCO58, ISCO68, ISCO88 indicate the international standard classification of occupations for 1958, 1968 and 1988. NOC indicates a national occupational classification (except for non-metropolitan territories).
For year: Countries and areas are placed under 1970, 1980 or 1990 column depending on whether the data year is closest to 1970, 1980 or 1990. The only exceptions are: Germany (West) 1976, which is placed under 1970 column because there are data for 1980; Bulgaria, Kuwait and Tunisia for 1975 are assigned to the 1980 column and Bulgaria and Tunisia for 1985 are assigned to the 1990 column as these are midpoints for each decade and the most up-to-date years for these countries.
[a] Subsequent to compilation of the full data set, this table and the analysis of the current situation (Part III), much more disaggregated data became available for Sweden for 1970, 1980 and 1990. These data deleted for the analysis in this book.) These more disaggregated data are used for the time series analysis in Part IV. Occupational segregation by sex is qualitatively similar for both data sets. [b] Subsequent to compilation of the full data set, this table and the analysis of the current situation, data became available for 1990 for China. These 1982 and 1990 data are used for the analysis of time trends in Part IV. Occupational segregation by sex in 1990 is qualitatively similar to that in 1982 for China.

is the occupational classification, the greater the level of occupational segregation which is observed. How we adjusted study data to take this into account is described in Chapter 7.

4.1 Country coverage

Detailed occupational data from 41 countries and areas are used in this book. These data were obtained from National Statistical Offices who were requested by the ILO's Bureau of Statistics to provide detailed occupational data for men and women for 1970, 1980 and 1990, or if unavailable for those years, for the closest year(s) available. This request from the ILO specified that occupational data needed to be at least at the two-digit level of disaggregation. Approximately one-half of the 41 economies covered in this book provided three-digit data and the other half two-digit data (see section 4.7 and table 4.2). Figure 4.1 illustrates graphically the 41 study countries and areas covered.

It is apparent from figure 4.1 that there is an excellent coverage among OECD countries in Europe, North America and Asia/Oceania. It is also apparent from figure 4.1 that coverage is weak among some developing country regions, especially outside Asia—despite the fact that this coverage is much better than in any previous cross-national study of the sex segregation. While the reason for the limited coverage of developing countries is mainly the non-availability of detailed occupational data, some available country data are not included in this book. The data supplied by the Mexican (1980, 1990) national statistical office to the ILO were insufficiently detailed with fewer than 20 non-agricultural occupations; the Republic of Korea (1989) did not include data for professional/technical, administrative/managerial or clerical occupations; the data for Haiti (1986) were felt to be of insufficient quality. It is clear that some countries with detailed occupational

Figure 4.1.   Study countries and areas

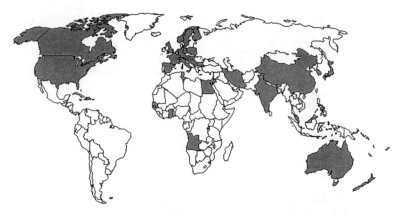

Note: Study countries and areas are marked in grey. Those countries or areas which are too small to mark are Bahrain, Costa Rica, Cyprus, Fiji, Haiti, Hong Kong, Kuwait, Luxembourg, Mauritius and Netherlands Antilles.
Source: Table 4.1.

data did not respond to the ILO request for data. In light of this, the ILO plans to update the data set used in this book and at the same time to expand the country coverage. In particular, a special effort will be made to include other countries where there is reason to believe that data are available. Because of the limited coverage for some developing country regions, readers always need to keep in mind that regional averages for developing country regions reported in Parts III and IV are based on select sets of countries.

4.2   Data sources

Study data were obtained from four different types of sources: population censuses, labour force surveys, establishment surveys and income and expenditure surveys. **Censuses and labour force surveys are the main data sources.** Censuses account for 78, 73 and 52 per cent of the data sources for around 1970, 1980 and 1990 respectively. The much lower percentage for censuses for 1990 is explained by the fact that countries were requested to send data for their most recent year and this often implied a labour force survey and not a census; also, data were often not yet available for the latest round of censuses for a number of developing countries especially. Most of the countries having a labour force survey as its source were OECD countries (100, 78 and 85 per cent of such countries for 1970, 1980 and 1990 respectively).

Each data source uses different data collection and processing techniques, and this affects comparability. In population censuses, which are massive undertakings, the quality of the information collected and the coding procedures used are not as good as in labour force surveys. On the other hand, statistics for small occupational groups have greater precision for population censuses as compared to labour force surveys. While no adjustments were made to study data on this issue, readers should be aware that changes in the sex composition of occupations, especially for small occupations, may be substantially affected by changes in the type of data source. On the other hand, sampling variations should not pose a major problem for most segregation statistics, since small occupations have low weightings in these statistics. It is not possible to know the effect of better quality coding and data collection associated with labour force surveys as compared to censuses, but as noted above, when a labour force survey was the source, it was usually an OECD country (approximately 85 per cent) where sample size tends to be reasonably large. It is worth noting here, however, that the data for Cyprus (which are based on enterprise surveys) and Haiti (which are based on an income and expenditure survey) are not quite comparable with the data from other study countries, especially the Cypriot data which cover only wage and salary workers.

4.3 Worker coverage

Most study data refer to the number of persons in employment (roughly 65, 75 and 77 per cent of countries and areas for 1970, 1980 and 1990 respectively). The remaining data cover only the labour force (i.e. unemployed and employed workers). There are only three study countries where coverage differs across data years. We did not carry out any adjustments to increase data comparability in this regard, as we did not have the information required to make this adjustment.

Our implicit assumption is that including or excluding unemployed persons has a relatively small effect on measures of occupational segregation by sex. This is, we feel, a reasonable assumption because unemployment rates were low in virtually all study categories where data included unemployed persons—either because of favourable labour market conditions as in OECD countries in the 1970s and 1980s (five countries),[2] or because of state policy to avoid unemployment as in former communist countries (three countries), or because measured unemployment rates are low as in developing countries (six countries).

Eleven of the 41 study economies included the armed forces as a separate occupational category in the original data provided to the ILO. As this occupation is highly sex segregated for reasons other than those related to labour market functioning, inclusion of armed forces for only some countries would have had an adverse effect on cross-national comparability. For this reason, data on workers in the armed forces are deleted from the data set used in this book and thus excluded from the analysis.

4.4 Definition and measurement of employment

Countries frequently differ in the extent to which they measure certain types of workers, especially the self-employed, unpaid family workers, persons who work relatively few hours and home-based workers. This tends to be especially important in measuring the labour force participation of women, youth and older workers. Methodological surveys of approximately 2000 households, which the author conducted in rural India and rural Egypt, illustrate these points quite well (see Anker, Khan and Gupta, 1987; Anker and Anker, 1995). In the Indian methodological survey, for example, measured female labour force activity rates varied from approximately 16 to 88 per cent depending on how the labour force questions were asked and the labour force was defined. In the Egyptian methodological survey, the reporting of any female labour force activity rates varied from about 20 to 90 per cent depending on how the labour force questions were asked; reported rates went from about 16 to 55 per cent when a minimum work-time of at least 20 hours a week was imposed.

Measurement and definitional differences in what constitutes labour force activity across countries are also likely to affect occupational segregation measures, since particular types of occupations (such as agriculture, informal sector activities and business-related activities done for family or self) are especially sensitive to these differences in definition and data collection techniques.[3] In the ILO Indian (and Egyptian) methodological surveys in rural areas, for example, use of an improved questionnaire caused the reporting of wage employment to increase from about 3(7) to 11(15) per cent, whereas the increase was very much larger, when broader, more typical labour force definitions were used (which include in particular unpaid agricultural activities on the family farm and/or with family-owned animals), from about 16(20) to 88(85) per cent.

To increase the comparability of the study data across countries we *excluded* **employment in agriculture from our analysis.** This decision to exclude agricultural employment has major implications for the empirical analyses in Parts III and IV, because so many men and women work in these occupations, especially in less industrialized countries. There were several reasons for this decision.

First, the size and gender composition among agricultural occupations reported in the ILO database were often inconsistent over time, probably reflecting reporting and coding errors. In Senegal for example, the occupation "general farmer" accounted for 32.0 per cent of total employment in 1976 and

68.3 per cent in 1988. Furthermore, while only 3.1 per cent of all women enumerated in Senegal in 1976 were reported to be in this one occupation, this reportedly "rose" to 77.2 per cent in 1988.[4] Finland provides a similar example—this time from an industrialized country. The 1990 Finnish labour force survey data indicate that 73 per cent of female farm workers are "farmers" and 27 per cent are "farm workers". This is in stark contrast with the 22 and 78 per cent respectively according to 1980 census data. (Note that percentages for men for 1980 and 1990 are within three percentage points of each other for each of these same two agricultural occupations.) Because of problems in distinguishing between these two categories of agricultural workers (which together comprised around 17 per cent of the Finnish labour force in 1970 and eight per cent in 1990), Finland collapsed these two occupations into one occupation when coding 1990 census data. Second, the very large size of the agricultural sector in a number of study countries in the developing world meant that the level of occupational segregation in these countries would be virtually determined by the percentage female in agriculture. Third, coding schemes are very crude amongst agricultural occupations with very little disaggregation (see Chapter 7). Fourth, and most importantly from an analytical point of view, **the reasons for gender segregation in non-agricultural and agricultural occupations are quite different, since a large proportion of agricultural employment is family labour which does not enter the labour market.**

4.5   Rules and procedures for coding occupations

The procedures used to code information on the occupation of workers represent another important source of variation in the comparability of occupational data. Indeed, even when countries follow the same occupational classification scheme, data may not be completely comparable as coding rules and procedures may differ. For example, different coding procedures may classify persons working on a family farm as "farm managers" or as "farmers" (see ISCO-68 classification in Appendix 6.1). Detecting this source of variation in a systematic way is virtually impossible, and we did not attempt to do this. The Finnish example noted in the previous section illustrates a typical problem with the coding of agricultural occupations, since the practice in many countries in the past was to code women working on a family farm as "farmer" and men as "farm manager".

Coding rules also have an important effect on the size of "ignored" or "unclassifiable" occupational groups. The size of these groups depends on the quality of the data collected, the training and supervision of the coders and the coding strategies used. The number of workers included in "unclassified" groups will tend to be relatively small when sufficient information is available for the classifier, when computer-assisted coding is used, and when the coding strategy hinders the use of unclassified groups, but relatively high when these groups are used as "dump" categories (i.e. when all "difficult" or "unclear" occupations are systematically coded into these occupational groups). "Ignored" and "unclassified" occupational groups were excluded from our analysis.

It is important to note that "ignored" and "unclassifiable" occupations are different from occupations "not elsewhere classified" and "other" occupations; the latter two occupations are included in our analysis. In principle, "not elsewhere classified" and "other" groups cover well-defined occupations which are too small to deserve a separate occupational group in the classification. For this reason, included in our analysis are "not elsewhere classified" and "other" occupations that belong to a clearly defined occupational group. Examples include "engineering technicians not elsewhere classified", "managers not elsewhere classified", "clerks not elsewhere classified", "sales workers not elsewhere classified", etc. It is important to note, however, that these occupations can sometimes be used as "dump" or "catch all" categories with unreasonably large numbers of workers. This obviously affects the usefulness and comparability of national data. For example, 22 per cent of female non-agricultural workers are "other clerical workers" in Australia, 21 per cent are "general clerical workers" in Japan, and 24 per cent are "clerical and related workers" in Egypt.

4.6 National classifications of occupations

A very important source of variation in the comparability of occupational data (between countries at one point in time and across time within countries) relates to differences in national occupational classification schemes. Although many study countries used the International Standard Classification of Occupations (ISCO) adopted in 1958, 1968 and 1988, the majority of study countries (about 60 per cent) used their own national occupational coding scheme (although it should be noted that many national classifications are similar to ISCO, because countries often adapt ISCO to national realities and objectives). This is potentially a serious problem for the empirical analysis in this book, since study data include 29 different occupational classification schemes.

A flavour of the difficulty involved in comparing specific occupations in countries with different national occupational classifications can be illustrated by information provided in Chapter 11 for two ISCO-68 occupations which we feel are sometimes subject to a noticeable degree of non-comparability across countries. Take for example cooks, waiters, bartenders and related workers which is a two-digit ISCO-68 occupation. Several study countries (such as Finland, the Netherlands, Norway and Austria) specifically mention and include kitchen helpers within this occupational group; it is not generally clear whether or not almost all other study countries do or do not include kitchen helpers. Bahrain includes waiters and bartenders in this occupational group for 1971 and 1981 (and does not include cooks for 1971 or 1981); yet, all three sub-occupations (waiters, bartenders and cooks) are included for 1991. Austria includes cooks and kitchen assistants but not waiters or bartenders for 1970 and 1980; yet, all three of these occupations are included for 1990. Hong Kong included maids as well in this occupational group for 1991. Similarly, the two-digit ISCO-68 occupation of bookkeepers, cashiers and related workers presents various difficulties in comparability. Several countries (West Germany, Switzerland, Austria) specify accountants (*comptable* in French), not bookkeepers, and include this occupation together with cashiers in the area of their occupational classification where clerical occupations are located. Norway includes accountants and bookkeepers in one occupational group. In Japan, this occupation is entitled "accounting clerks". Canada specifies bookkeepers only and does not mention cashiers. China and Bahrain do the opposite, specifically mentioning only cashiers. Of the 17 specific occupations analysed in Parts III and IV, the above two occupational groups were probably the most difficult to compare across countries.

4.7 Comparability over time of national occupational classifications and of adjusted data

A number of countries update and revise their national occupational classifications to take into account the emergence of new occupations and the demise of obsolete occupations. Revisions of national classifications typically involve either: (a) splitting an occupational group into several more detailed occupational groups; (b) merging occupational groups into a more aggregated group; (c) creating new occupational groups which cut across previous groups; or (d) creating (or deleting) new (or obsolete) occupational groups. In order to establish a national time trend of occupational segregation, it is best to have comparable coding classifications for each time point (i.e. to have identical occupational groups).[5] For this reason, whenever possible, a data set was created for each study country with time series data that had comparable occupational classifications for each data year. The procedures followed to develop this so-called mapped data set are described below.

Because the process of adjusting for comparability over time involved merging occupational categories, the number of categories in the adjusted or mapped national data sets is always smaller than in the unadjusted or original data set. The number of occupational categories lost in the process is shown in column four of table 4.2.

Table 4.2. **Comparison of the number of non-agricultural occupations in data provided by national statistical organizations and the mapped (i.e. comparable) data**

Country or area	Number of non-agricultural occupations in original/unmapped data	Number of non-agricultural occupations in adjusted/mapped data	Difference: Mapped vs. unmapped
One time period only			
Angola	67[**]	n/a	n/a
Canada	44[**]	n/a	n/a
China[a]	277[**]	270[a]	n/a[a]
Ghana	75[**]	n/a	n/a
Haiti	75[**]	n/a	n/a
India	423[**]	n/a	n/a
Iran, Islamic Rep. of	21[**]	n/a	n/a
Malaysia	76[**]	n/a	n/a
Netherlands Antilles	76[**]	n/a	n/a
Rep. of Korea	56[**]	n/a	n/a
Not mapped (as especially difficult to map/make comparable over time)			
Australia	279[**]	n/a	n/a
Cyprus	376[**]	n/a	n/a
Kuwait	268[**]	n/a	n/a
Poland	361[**]	n/a	n/a
Bahrain	86[**]	n/a[b]	n/a
Difference in number of occupations in mapped and original data sets is relatively small[c]			
Austria	72	64[**]	8
Bulgaria	45	43[**]	2
Costa Rica	56	55[**]	1
Egypt	79	74[**]	5
Fiji	77	75[**]	2
France	433	433[**]	0
Hungary	118	118[**]	0
Italy	234	231[**]	3
Japan	279	259[**]	20
Luxembourg	74	71[**]	3
Netherlands	170	150[**]	20
Sweden[d]	49[**]	261x[d]	0[d]
Switzerland	517	452[**]	65
Tunisia	55[**]	49x[e]	6
United Kingdom	510	509[**]	1
United States	473	461[**]	12
Former Yugoslavia	208	206[**]	2
Difference in number of occupations is relatively large[e] and number of occupations in mapped data is within 20 per cent of median number for countries in the region[f]			
Finland	451	264[**]	187
Jordan	75	61[**]	14
Mauritius	381	70[**]	311
Norway	464	291[**]	173

Table 4.2.   (contd.)

Country or area	Number of non-agricultural occupations in original/unmapped data	Number of non-agricultural occupations in adjusted/mapped data	Difference: Mapped vs. unmapped
Difference in number of occupations is relatively large[c] and number in mapped data set differs by more than 20 per cent from median number for countries or areas in the region[f]			
Germany (West)	268**	150x	118
Hong Kong	73**	45x	28
New Zealand	281**	75x	206
Senegal	80**	46x	34
Spain	77**	52x	25

Notes: **Indicates classification used in the analysis for the latest year in Part III, i.e. current situation. x Indicates classification used in the analysis for time trends in Part IV if it differs from data used in Part III. [a] Subsequent to compilation of the full data set and this table, data became available for 1990 for China. When these data are mapped, there are 270 non-agricultural occupations for the time-series analysis in Part IV. The 1982 data (with 277 non-agricultural occupations) are used for the cross-section analysis of the current situation in Part III as the 1990 data were not available at the time Part III was written. [b] It is possible to have mapped/comparable data for Bahrain for 58 non-agricultural occupations but only for 1970 and 1980. These mapped data are used in trend analysis in Part IV. [c] Relatively small is defined as a difference of 10 or fewer occupations per 75 occupations classified, or roughly a difference of about 15 per cent. Relatively large is defined as a difference of 11 or more occupations per 75 occupations classified. [d] Subsequent to compilation of the full data set and this table, much more disaggregated data became available for Sweden. This means that there are 261 non-agricultural occupations for the time-series analysis for Part IV. However, for analysis of the current situation in Part III, 49 non-agricultural occupations are used, as the more disaggregated data were not available at the time Part III was written. [e] Substantial degree of objective judgment was used to map Tunisian data and for this reason original data are used for analysis in Part III. [f] Mean number of occupational categories is based on an unweighted average of original unmapped data for countries in the region.

Described below are the reasons why it was decided to use the mapped or the original data sets for each study country in the analysis of the current situation (Part III) and/or the analysis of changes over time (Part IV).

For the cross-national analysis in Part III, it was not obvious whether the mapped data or the unmapped data should be used. Use of the mapped data had three advantages. First, it increased the comparability of the cross-national data for the most recent year with the data for changes over time, since both analyses would be based on the same data. Second, use of the mapped data avoided any possible confusion in having different occupational segregation values for the same year appearing in different analyses and parts of this book. Third, the amount of work required for both analyses would be considerably reduced as only one data set would be involved. On the other hand, there was one potentially important disadvantage of using the mapped data set for the cross-national analyses of the most recent year—it reduced the level of disaggregation in the occupational data. With the above in mind, it was decided to use the mapped data set whenever (i) the disadvantage noted above was felt to be relatively small, which we felt occurred when there was relatively little difference in a study country's mapped and unmapped data sets in terms of the number of occupations for the latest available year; or (ii) the number of occupations for other study countries in the region tended to be similar to those in country x's mapped data set, as this would increase the comparability of data for study countries within the region.

Occupational classifications for 27 study countries or areas were mapped, i.e. adjusted to increase comparability over time (see table 4.2). This was generally a straightforward procedure as most national statistical offices (24 out of 27) provided us with the necessary information. The procedure involved merging occupational categories or reassignment of codes. For three countries—Finland, Senegal and Tunisia—adjustments required considerable judgment on our part as the occupational classifications used in various data years differed conceptually; for this exercise we looked at each occupational title and decided on what we felt were necessary backwards and forwards merging of occupational groups. As this procedure sometimes resulted in large and heterogeneous occupational groups for Senegal and Tunisia, the comparability over time for Senegal and Tunisia is definitely less secure than it is for other countries (although it should be noted that for this reason, we used the original, more complete national data for these two countries for analysing the current situation in Part III and the mapped data in Part IV).[6]

Nine countries had data available for one year only and so no adjustments were required other than deletion of armed forces, "ignored" and "unclassified" occupations.[7,8]

For five study countries, we did not feel that we could create comparable occupational classifications for all available time periods (Australia, Cyprus, Kuwait, Poland and Bahrain), because the occupational classification systems differed conceptually and/or we did not have the necessary information to make the national classifications comparable. For these five countries, the original data were used for analysis in Part III and rough adjustments were made for the analysis in Part IV to take account of differences in the number of occupations classified in each data year (see notes to tables in Parts III and IV).

For 17 countries, differences in the number of occupations between the "mapped" data (which have been adjusted through "mapping" across years so that occupational classifications for two or three points in time are comparable) and the unadjusted/"original" data are relatively small (with "relatively small" defined in an ad hoc manner as less than 10 occupations per 75 occupations classified in the original data). For these 17 countries, it was felt that this difference is sufficiently small so as to favour the use of the mapped data set for both the analysis of occupational segregation by sex for the current situation undertaken in Part III, as well as the analysis of time trends (as use of these mapped data increase the comparability of the cross-section and time-series analyses undertaken in Part IV).[9]

For nine countries, a relatively large number of occupations were lost in the mapping process (with relatively large defined in an ad hoc manner as

---

GENDER AND JOBS

more than 10 occupations per 75 occupations in the original classification). The decision was also taken to use the mapped data for both the cross-national analysis of the current situation (Part III) and the time-series analysis comparisons (Part IV) for four of the nine study countries, when the number of occupations in the mapped data set for a study country was similar to that in other countries in its region (i.e. when the number of occupations in a country's mapped data is within 20 per cent of the mean number of occupations for other countries in its region)—as this increased intra-regional comparisons. This means that for five study countries the mapped data are used for the time trend analysis (Part IV) whereas the original unmapped data are used for the cross-national analysis of the current situation (Part III).

4.8 Consistency and possible errors in national data

Data quality obviously varies across countries as well as within countries over time. In order to detect (and correct) obvious errors in the data, we looked at the consistency of the national data with regard to: (i) the share (%) of each occupation in the total non-agricultural labour force, (ii) percentage female in each occupation, and (iii) changes in (i) and (ii) over time for countries with data for two or more years. As we did not want to inadvertently make changes in what are real (but unusual) phenomenon, we used very rough criteria to "flag" possible errors in the data: (a) change in percentage female in an occupation greater than two absolute percentage points per year plus the average percentage point change in the female share of total non-agricultural employment during the period in question; (b) change in the percentage share of an occupation in the non-agricultural total labour force greater than one absolute percentage point per year in a ten-year reporting period; (c) percentage of non-agricultural employment greater than 10 per cent for one occupation in any one data year.

When any one of these criteria was met, we used judgment about whether or not to change the original data by, for example, merging occupational categories or dropping the country data altogether from our analysis.[10] In the end, we were *very cautious* in making changes in the original data, since we did not have detailed knowledge of many country situations and were concerned about inappropriately eliminating real changes and differences. In some instances, we even left unchanged some obvious data errors (such as an observed change in percentage female for an occupation which went from 0 to 100 per cent or from 100 to 0 per cent in a ten-year period)[11] when small occupations were involved, as these changes could be due to sampling variations and, in any case, small occupations have only a minor effect on aggregate segregation statistics.

In the end, we made very few adjustments to the original data provided by national statistical offices.[12] What few changes we did make were done in response to the consistency checks described above.[13] When a change was made, employment in that occupation was generally combined with employment in the "other" category corresponding to that occupation's own minor or unit occupational group.

Notes

[1] A debt is owed to Adriana Mata-Greenwood for important inputs to this chapter.

[2] Also, two OECD study countries (Austria and Sweden) included unemployed persons in their official statistics for the data year closest to 1990. At this time, unemployment rates were relatively low at 3.2 per cent in Austria and 2.7 per cent in Sweden.

[3] For Senegal, it was found that women workers in the maids and other related house-keeping service workers occupation were very clearly under-enumerated in the 1988 census. Whereas 42.4 per cent of women in non-agricultural occupations were reported to be in this occupation in 1976, the figure was only 0.3 per cent in 1988. This is a typical example of women's work becoming invisible (see Anker, Khan and Gupta, 1987, for a general discussion on this type of under-enumeration and invisibility of the economic work done by women). For this reason, we adjusted the 1988 Senegalese data by assuming that the number of "maids and related household workers" (as observed in 1976) grew by the same overall percentage increase between 1976 and 1988 as observed for all workers (which was approximately 158 per cent).

[4] These results for Senegal in 1988 appear to be due to two factors: (1) different procedures for classifying agricultural workers in 1976 and 1988 and (2) a more complete enumeration of women agricultural workers in 1988. The large increase in this occupation's share of employment between 1976 and 1988 is offset only somewhat by a decline for "agricultural and animal husbandry workers"; female agricultural workers according to these data numbered approximately 12,000 in 1976 and 387,000 in 1988.

[5] Having mapped (i.e. comparable) occupational classifications over time for a country does not necessarily mean that the number of occupations is identical at each time point. It is possible for a small number of new occupations to appear and old occupations to disappear.

[6] Subsequent to compilation of this table and analyses in Parts III and IV, comparable census data for Finland for 1970, 1980 and 1990 became available. These new Finnish data are analysed together with comparable data for Norway and Sweden and reported in a separate publication (Melkas and Anker, forthcoming).

[7] For three of these nine study countries (Canada, the Republic of Korea and Haiti), data were available for two or more years in the original ILO data set, but data for only one year was retained. The 1970 and 1980 data for Canada were not retained as they included too few occupational groups (only 11 and 19 respectively). The Republic of Korea data from 1989 were dropped as the 41 occupational groups represented did not include any disaggregation for ISCO-68 Major Groups 1, 2 and 3 (i.e. professional/technical, managerial/administrative and clerical). For Haiti, we retained only the 1986 data (and excluded the 1971 data), because when data from these two years were examined, numerous and unreasonably large changes in occupational shares and female employment shares within occupations were common; perhaps the fact that the 1986 data for Haiti are based on an Income and Expenditure Survey while the 1971 data are drawn from a national census has something to do with this.

[8] Subsequent to compilation of table 4.2 and analysis of the current situation in Part III, data became available for 1990 for China (with 270 occupations) which enabled us to include China in the analysis of recent changes in occupational segregation by sex in Part IV.

[9] There were two exceptions to this decision. Because of the substantial subjectivity used in the mapping process for Tunisia (see discussion in the text on this), it was decided to use the original data set for Part III and the mapped data for Part IV. For Sweden, subsequent to compilation of table 4.2 and analysis of the current situation in Part III, much more disaggregated, yet comparable, data with 261 non-agricultural occupations became available, and so these data were used for the time-series analysis in Part IV.

[10] The only country data point dropped for this reason was Haiti (1971).

[11] In the United Kingdom for example, in what are admittedly unusual cases, four of 502 occupations changed from 0 to 100 per cent female or 100 to 0 per cent female between 1981 and 1990.

[12] It should be noted that many more changes would have been required if we had also included agricultural occupations in this consistency analysis, as these are large occupations in almost all countries and it was fairly common to observe unreasonably large changes over time for agricultural occupations in both their share of total employment and in percentage female. See discussion on this in section 4.5.

[13] Data for Senegal, Austria, Bulgaria, Japan and former Yugoslavia were adjusted. The occupations combined with the appropriate "other" category were as follows: Austria, chimney sweeps (with reported change of +89.9% in percentage female in the occupation, 1981–90); Bulgaria, workers in water transport (with reported change of +100%, 1975–85); Japan, nutritionists (with reported change of −86.6%, 1970–90); former Yugoslavia, building cleaners (with reported change of −37.5%, 1971–81). See footnote 3 in this chapter for details on change introduced for Senegal.

MEASURING OCCUPATIONAL SEGREGATION

5

The literature on occupational segregation by sex is replete with different types of statistics.[1] Each provides a different perspective. For this reason, **the present book uses several statistics to measure occupational segregation by sex in order to piece together a more complete picture than is possible to obtain from only one statistic such as an inequality index.** In this way, we avoid the (unfortunately) common practice in the research literature of relying on only one inequality index.

This report describes occupational segregation by sex in four different ways. First, we use *descriptive statistics,* such as the extent to which an occupation is female (percentage female in an occupation); extent to which women are concentrated in an occupation (percentage of all women workers in an occupation); and extent to which women are over- or under-represented in an occupation (ratio of the percentage female in an occupation to the average percentage female for the non-agricultural labour force as a whole). Second, we use two types of *indices of inequality* (index of dissimilarity and marginal matching index). Third, the labour force is divided into *gender-dominated and gender-integrated occupations using relative and absolute concepts of domination:* "male", "female" and "gender-integrated" occupations. Fourth, we look at *specific occupations* and the extent to which they are feminized. In order to assist readers, table 5.1 presents in an easy-to-follow format a listing of the various inequality statistics used in this book along with their abbreviation, their mathematical definition, a description of their conceptual use and the main chapters in which they are used.

The discussion in this chapter begins with a detailed description of two of these four measures of occupational segregation. In the first instance (indices of inequality, section 5.1), there is a debate in the research literature regarding what is the most appropriate index for measuring occupational segregation. In the second instance (gender-dominated occupations, section 5.2), there is considerable variation in the definition of gender-dominance, within both the research and policy fields; in addition, previous analysis is almost exclusively restricted to industrialized countries where women now comprise a large proportion of the labour force, and this has important implications for defining gender-domination. Chapter 6 investigates a major difficulty faced by cross-national analyses of occupational segregation—the sensitivity of statistics on occupational segregation by sex to the level of aggregation in the occupational data on which these statistics are based.

5.1 Inequality indices for measuring occupational segregation by sex

First and foremost, previous studies of occupational segregation by sex have relied on indices of inequality. Such indices have the advantage of simplicity, as they condense into one number all variation in the distribution of jobs between men and women. At the same time, they have the disadvantage of all indices, their simplicity: they often hide changes in inequality over time; they are often difficult to understand and explain in common sense terms; there are methodological problems attached to all indices; and many practical and policy-related aspects cannot be addressed by such an aggregated statistic.

Index of dissimilarity

By far the most commonly used inequality index is the index of dissimilarity, or ID (see Chapter 3), an index described by Duncan and Duncan (1955). ID has not only been used extensively in the analysis of occupational segregation by sex but also in various other types of inequality analyses, such as poverty, schooling and housing.

In recent years, the index of dissimilarity has, however, come under criticism as inappropriate for measuring occupational segregation by sex, especially over time (e.g. Siltanen et al., 1995; Watts, 1992, 1993; Hakim, 1993). For this reason, several other inequality indices have been proposed in recent years for measuring occupational segregation by sex. There is the WE index proposed by the OECD for a report on women and employment (OECD, 1980). There is the sex ratio index (SR) developed for the United Kingdom's Department of Employment, sometimes called the Hakim index after its originator (Hakim, 1981). There is the Gini coefficient (which is not used very widely in the occupational segregation literature but is used widely in other types of inequality studies such as for investigating income distribution). There is an index proposed by Karmel and MacLachlan (1988), dubbed KM index, which has been developed further by Watts and Rich in a series of recent articles (Watts and Rich, 1991; 1992; 1993). There is the marginal matching index (MM) developed by Blackburn, Siltanen and Jarman in a series of recent publications (Blackburn, Jarman and Siltanen, 1993; Siltanen, 1990; Siltanen, Jarman and Blackburn, 1995)—the 1995 publication includes a lengthy description of, and argument for MM;

Table 5.1. Statistics used to measure occupational segregation

Statistic	Abbreviation used in book	Mathematical definition	Concept and description	Chapters mainly used in book
Descriptive statistics				
Percentage female in occupation	% fem	$\dfrac{\text{females in occupation } i}{\text{all workers in occupation } i} \times 100$	Extent to which an occupation is feminized	8, 11, 15
Percentage male in occupation	% male	$\dfrac{\text{males in occupation } i}{\text{all workers in occupation } i} \times 100$	Extent to which an occupation is masculinized	11, 15
Female share of non-agricultural employment	PFEM	$\dfrac{\text{female non-ag LF}}{\text{total non-ag LF}} \times 100$	Women's percentage share of non-agricultural employment	4, 8, 9, 12
Occupation's share of non-agricultural employment	OCCSH	$\dfrac{\text{workers in occupation } i}{\text{total non-ag LF}} \times 100$	Relative size of an occupation	4, 8
Share of female non-agricultural employment	FEMSH	$\dfrac{\text{females in occupation } i}{\text{all female workers in non-ag LF}} \times 100$	Extent to which women workers are concentrated in an occupation	8
Representation ratio for women in an occupation	—	$\dfrac{\text{\% fem in occupation } i}{\text{PFEM}}$	Extent to which women are overrepresented (values > 1.0) or underrepresented (values < 1.0) in an occupation relative to women's share of non-agricultural employment in general.	4, 11, 15
Largest female non-agricultural occupations	—	—	Largest non-agricultural occupations for women workers are those with largest number of women workers.	11
			Largest female-dominated non-agricultural occupations for women workers are those with largest number of women workers among non-agricultural occupations where women comprise at least 80 per cent of the workers.	11

Inequality indices

		Formula	Description	Refs
Index of dissimilarity	ID	$\dfrac{1}{2}\sum \left\lvert \dfrac{\text{f in non-ag occ i}}{\text{f non-ag LF}} - \dfrac{\text{m in occ i}}{\text{m non-ag LF}} \right\rvert$ with | | indicating positive value of difference enclosed.	Measure of statistical association which ranges from 0 (no segregation) to 1 (total segregation). It equals minimum proportion of women plus minimum proportion of men who would need to change occupation so that proportion female is the same in all occupations.	9, 13
Adjusted index of dissimilarity	ID75	ID + b[ln (75) − ln (number of occupations in national classification)] with b generally determined by country's ID value based on one-digit level data as given in equations 4-6, table 6.6 (see Chapter 6 and table 9.7 in Appendix 9.1 for details).	ID adjusted in an approximate way so as to be for an occupational classification with 75 non-agricultural occupations. For this reason, the abbreviation for the adjusted ID is represented by ID75.	9, 12, 13
ID index which takes account of female labour force participation rate	IDHALF	ID recalculated (see above formula for ID) after assuming that women comprise one-half of non-agricultural labour force and that all non-working women are in a created occupation entitled "unpaid housepersons and care-givers".	Index combines two separate aspects of labour market inequality: (i) women being left out of the non-agricultural labour force; and (ii) occupational segregation for women in the non-agricultural labour force. Since this ID index is calculated using the assumption that women comprise one-half of all non-agricultural workers, the abbreviation used for this index is represented by IDHALF.	9, 13
Size standardized ID	—	ID recalculated after assuming: (i) that all occupations have an equal number of workers and (ii) percentage female in each occupation is as actually observed (see Chapter 6 for mathematical formula).	Size standardized ID (see Appendix 13.1) is used to measure changes over time caused by changes in the feminization of occupations, since index can only be affected by changes in per cent female in occupations.	13

Table 5.1. (contd.)

Statistic	Abbreviation used in book	Mathematical definition	Concept and description	Chapters mainly used in book
Inequality indices				
Decomposed changes in ID	SEX, OCC, RES	ID changes over time decomposed into changes due to changes in sex composition of occupations (SEX), size distribution of occupations (OCC) and a residual (RES) (See Chapter 6 for mathematical formula).	Typical decomposition method where calculations are redone for end of time period after alternatively keeping sex composition of occupations and size distributions of occupations the same as at the beginning of the time period.	13
Marginal matching index	MM	See Chapter 6 for mathematical definition.	Measure of statistical association which ranges from 0 (no segregation) to 1 (total segregation).	9, 13
Gender domination				
Absolute concept			Domination of men or women in non-agricultural occupations in the same absolute sense for both sexes and all countries (defined as any occupation where at least 80% of workers are women or men).	10, 11, 12, 14, 15
Female-dominated occupations	FDOM	[Summation of females in non-ag occupations where >80% of workers are women]/[total female non-ag LF] × 100	Percentage of female non-agricultural workers in a female-dominated occupation.	10, 11, 12, 14, 15
Adjusted FDOM	FDOM75	FDOM + b [ln(75) - ln (number of occupations classified)] with b determined by observed national or regional logarithmic change in FDOM along with disaggregation of occupational classification (see Chapter 6 and table 10.8 in Appendix 10.1 for details).	FDOM adjusted in an approximate way so as to be for a classification with 75 non-agricultural occupations.	10, 11, 14, 15

Concept	Abbreviation	Formula	Description	
Male-dominated occupations	MDOM	[Summation of males in non-ag occupations where >80% of workers are men]/[total male non-ag LF] × 100	Percentage of male non-agricultural workers in a male-dominated occupation (defined as an occupation where at least 80 per cent of workers are men).	10, 11, 12, 14, 15
Gender-dominated occupations	TDOM	[Summation of workers in non-ag occupations where >80% of workers are either male or female]/[total non-ag LF] × 100	Percentage of all non-agricultural workers in a gender-dominated occupation (defined as an occupation where at least 80 per cent of workers are either male or female).	10, 12
Adjusted TDOM	TDOM75	TDOM + b [ln (75)−ln (number of occupations classified)] with b determined by observed national or regional logarithmic change in TDOM along with disaggregation of occupational classification (see Chapter 6 and table 10.10 in Appendix 10.1 for details).	TDOM adjusted in an approximate way so as to be for a classification with 75 non-agricultural occupations.	10, 12
Gender-integration *Relative concept*			Relative representation of women in non-agricultural occupations in a relative sense (relative to women's average share of all non-agricultural employment).	
Gender-integrated occupations	–	[summation of females in non-ag occupations where per cent female is between 0.5 and 1.5 times PFEM]/[total female non-ag LF]×100	Percentage of female non-agricultural employment in occupations where there is a *relative* integration of male and female workers.	10, 11, 14, 15
Female-concentrated occupations	–	[summation of females in non-ag occupations where per cent female is >1.5 times PFEM]/[total female non-ag LF]×100	Percentage of female non-agricultural employment in occupations where there is an overrepresentation of women workers *relative* to women's average share of total non-agricultural employment.	10, 11, 14, 15

Table 5.1. (contd.)

Statistic	Abbreviation used in book	Mathematical definition	Concept and description	Chapters mainly used in book
Gender-integration				
Relative concept				
Female-underrepresented occupations	–	[summation of females in non-ag occupations where per cent female is <0.5 times PFEM]/[total female non-ag LF]×100	Percentage of female non-agricultural employment in occupations where there is an underrepresentation of women workers *relative* to women's average share of the total non-agricultural employment.	10, 11, 14, 15

also, a recent EC publication (Rubery and Fagan, 1993) on occupation segregation by sex in the European Communities uses three indices in its analysis, including MM and ID.

The present book uses ID to measure and analyse recent cross-national differences as well as ID and MM to analyse national time trends. These analyses are presented in Parts III and IV of this book.

The ID (Duncan and Duncan, 1955) is defined as one-half of the summation over all occupations of the absolute differences between the proportion of all females (F_i/F) and the proportion of all males (M_i/M) in each occupation. It has a minimum value of 0 (no segregation; same percentage female in each occupation) and a maximum value of 1.0 (complete segregation; each occupation is completely female or completely male).

$$ID = \frac{1}{2} \sum_i |F_i/f - M_i/M|$$

ID may be interpreted as the sum of the minimum proportion of women plus the minimum proportion of men who would have to change their occupation in order for the proportion female to be identical in all occupations. This interpretation differs from the more common, but erroneous, interpretation that ID equals the minimum proportion of men *or* women who need to change occupation. Readers are referred to Appendix 5.1 for a detailed discussion on, and proof of, our interpretation.

Siltanen, Blackburn and Jarman (1995) have shown that ID can be expressed in terms of a basic segregation table which they developed (table 5.2). Thus, ID equals the proportion of women in "female" occupations

Table 5.2. Basic segregation table for calculating ID

	Men	Women	Total
"Male" occupations	M_m	F_m	N_m
"Female" occupations	M_f	F_f	N_f
Total	M	F	N

with:
M_m Number of men in "male" occupations
M_f Number of men in "female" occupations
M   Number of male workers in total
F_m Number of women in "male" occupations
F_f Number of women in "female" occupations
F   Number of female workers in total
N   Total number of workers in labour force
N_m Total number of workers in "male" occupations
N_f Total number of workers in "female" occupations

Note: "Male" ("female") occupations are defined as those where the percentage male (female) is higher than the average percentage male (female) in the total labour force.
Source: Siltanen et al., 1995.

(F_f/F) minus the proportion of men in "female" occupations (M_f/M), with "female" occupations defined as those where the proportion female is higher than for the labour force as a whole.[2] Thus, using the basic segregation table 5.2:

$$ID = F_f/F - M_f/M$$

Using the above formula, it becomes relatively easy to explain why some analysts are not completely happy with ID as a measure of occupational segregation.[3]

There is extensive discussion in the research literature of the fact that ID values change over time from both changes in: (i) the occupational structure of the labour force and (ii) the extent to which occupations are feminized.[4] Many analysts do not like this property as they are more interested in (ii) than (i). To illustrate this issue, suppose that the percentage share of each and every occupation remained unchanged between time periods t and t + 1, but that the number of workers increases only in highly sex segregated occupations (say services) and production occupations during this time period. In one sense there would have been no change in segregation as the percentage female remained unchanged in each and every occupation. Yet, in another sense there would have been an increase in average inequality for the labour force as a whole. Thus, ID would have increased in this example due to an increase in the relative importance of highly sex segregated occupations—even though per cent female remained the same in all occupations.

For this reason, analysts sometimes decompose ID changes over time into: (i) changes in the sex composition of occupations, and (ii) changes in the relative size or distribution of occupations (as well as (iii) a residual or interaction effect of both the sex composition and occupational distribution effects). Similarly, analysts sometimes calculate a size-standardized version of ID (where all occupations are assumed to be of equal size) in order to control for changes over time in the relative size of occupations. Both of these standardization procedures are described below by drawing on derivations provided in Blau and Hendricks (1979) for the decomposition methodology and Jacobs (1989) for the size standardization methodology.

The decomposition methodology begins by recalculating ID for the latest year in two different ways—once using the same occupational distribution as in the earlier year and once using the same percentage female for each occupation as in the earlier year. The differences between the actual ID in the latest year and these newly calculated IDs are, then, taken to indicate how much occupational segregation changed due exclusively to changes in the sex composition of occupations (since occupational structure was standardized, i.e. forced to stay the same in both years) in the former case, and how much occupational segregation changed due exclusively to changes in the occupational structure of the labour force (since sex composition of all occupations was standardized) in the latter case.

$$\text{SEX} = \frac{1}{2}\left[\sum_i \left| \frac{q_{i2}T_{i1}}{\sum_i q_{i2}T_{i1}} - \frac{p_{i2}T_{i1}}{\sum_i p_{i2}T_{i1}} \right| - \sum_i \left| \frac{q_{i1}T_{i1}}{\sum_i q_{i1}T_{i1}} - \frac{p_{i1}T_{i1}}{\sum_i p_{i1}T_{i1}} \right| \right]$$

$$\text{OCC} = \frac{1}{2}\left[\sum_i \left| \frac{q_{i1}T_{i2}}{\sum_i q_{i1}T_{i2}} - \frac{p_{i1}T_{i2}}{\sum_i p_{i1}T_{i2}} \right| - \sum_i \left| \frac{q_{i1}T_{i1}}{\sum_i q_{i1}T_{i1}} - \frac{p_{i1}T_{i1}}{\sum_i p_{i1}T_{i1}} \right| \right]$$

with:

q_{it} per cent female in occupation i in time t
p_{it} per cent male in occupation i in time t
T_{it} total number of workers in occupation i in time t (i.e. $M_{it} + F_{it}$)

One problem with this standardization methodology is that the weights (i.e. distributions) chosen for this standardization (i.e. the initial year's distribution) do not provide unique results in the sense that there would be different results if other weights (e.g. the final year's distribution, or initial year's average for the region or the world) were used. Another problem is that the changes calculated as due to changes in the sex composition of occupations (SEX) and due to changes in the occupational structure of the labour force (OCC) do not sum up to the actual observed change (as always occurs when this type of standardization methodology is used). For this reason, a residual value (RES) is always calculated (which is equal to actual change in ID minus SEX and minus OCC); it "may be interpreted as due to the interaction between changes in sex composition and employment mix over the period" (according to Blau and Hendricks, 1979). On the other hand, this residual is basically meaningless, being as the term implies, a residual.

The size-standardized methodology calculates ID after assuming that all occupations are equal in size. In this way, occupational structure is held constant, and so ID can only change over time due to changes in the sex composition of occupations.

$$\text{Size-standardized ID} = \frac{1}{2}\sum_i \left| \left(\frac{q_i}{\sum q_i} \right) - \left(\frac{p_i}{\sum p_i} \right) \right|$$

This simple standardization methodology has one very important drawback: it gives the same weight to changes in percentage female in all occupations, small and large occupations. This means that change in the size standardized ID is strongly influenced by changes in the feminization of small occupations. Yet such changes are often (1) erratic because of the small numbers of workers and (2) strongly influenced by what happens in small "male" occupations because of the fact that occupational classifications tend to be much more disaggregated where male workers are concentrated as compared to where female workers are concentrated.

Fully realizing the shortcomings and advantages of ID (especially its widespread use), we use ID in this book and complement it with several other statistics in order to describe and analyse occupational segregation for the current situation in Part III. We also decompose changes over time in ID for the time trends in Part IV.

Marginal matching index

An alternative inequality index "recommended" in a recent ILO publication is the marginal matching index, or MM. This index is advertised as correcting for the main difficulty associated with ID,[5] the fact that the value of ID is affected by shifts in occupational structure over time—although it is necessary to note that Watts (see for example Watts, 1995) argues strongly against MM and criticizes its properties. MM was developed to *measure changes over time* in occupational segregation by sex *resulting exclusively from changes in the sex composition of occupations*. MM does this by using a different definition for "male" and "female" occupations as compared to ID. MM defines "female" occupations as those which contain the same number of workers (male plus female) as there are women workers in the labour force as a whole. This calculation is done after ordering occupations according to their degree of feminization and then cumulating workers starting with the occupation having the lowest (or highest) per cent female. This can be represented in a modified basic segregation table (table 5.3) where rows and columns are forced to be equal or "matched". The table is also symmetrical so that M_f equals F_m, with MM defined as a measure of association as follows:

$$MM = (F_f * M_m - F_m * M_f)/F * M$$

An obvious and important methodological issue is the relationship between MM and ID, whether they differ in any systematic way. It can be demonstrated algebraically that ID and MM are basically equal when the labour force is 50 per cent female.[6] But what about when the labour force is

Table 5.3.   **Modified segregation table for calculating marginal matching index (MM)**

	Men	Women	Total
"Male" occupations	M_m	F_m	N_m
"Female" occupations	M_f	F_f	N_f
Total	M	F	N

Note: By assumption, the total number of workers (male and female) in "female" occupations (N_f), equals the total number of women workers in the labour force as a whole (F). After sorting occupations and starting with occupations having lowest to highest per cent female, the analyst stops defining occupations as "female" occupations when the sum of all workers in these occupations (N_f) equals F.
Source: Siltanen et al., 1995.

GENDER AND JOBS

Figure 5.1. Difference between ID and MM national values as a function of the female share of non-agricultural labour force (PFEM)

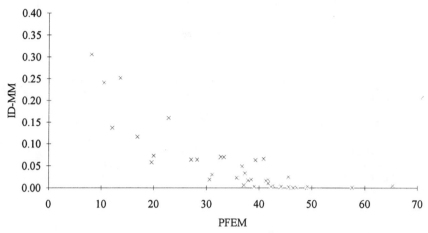

Source: Study data.

not close to 50 per cent female, how are ID and MM related? And, is there a consistent pattern to this relationship? To investigate these questions, we used data for our 41 study countries and areas. We plotted the difference between ID and MM values as a function of the percentage female in the non-agricultural labour force (figure 5.1) and investigated this relationship using multiple regression analysis (table 5.4).

Figure 5.1 indicates that *the difference between ID and MM is very strongly related to the percentage of the non-agricultural labour force which is female*. Regression results reported in table 5.4 indicate that this relationship is highly significant.[7] Furthermore, this relationship is strongly nonlinear. For our full sample of 41 economies, over 80 per cent of the variation in ID-MM is explained by percentage female (equation 2). According to equation 2, ID and MM are approximately equal when PFEM is 50 per cent, which is consistent with the above discussion (see bottom of table 5.4). Successive increases in PFEM beginning from zero per cent female are associated with smaller and smaller reductions in the differences in ID-MM, until approximately 50 per cent, after which the relationship is symmetrical to that for levels below 50 per cent. Thus, the difference between ID and MM based on equation 2 is estimated to be 0.216, 0.122, 0.055, 0.014 and −0.002 respectively when PFEM is 10, 20, 30, 40 and 50 per cent.

Indeed in our opinion, countries with very low labour force participation rates of women have unrealistically low levels of inequality according to MM.[8] For example, when we rank order 26 study countries or areas for which there is two-digit occupational data (so that there is some rough control for level of disaggregation in the occupational data), we find that the rank order of countries with relatively low female participation rates (where

Table 5.4. Regression analysis (OLS) of the difference between ID and MM national values as a function of percentage female for the non-agricultural labour force (t values in brackets)

Explanatory variables	All countries and areas ($N = 41$)	
	Equation 1	Equation 2
Constant	0.213 (10.96)	0.336 (13.22)
PFEM	−0.0046 (8.87)	−0.0133 (8.64)
PFEM^2	x	1.31×10^{-4} (5.84)
R^2	0.67	0.83
Adjusted R^2	0.66	0.82
F value	78.7	89.9
Significance F	0.01	0.01
Degrees of freedom	39	38
Implied turning point		50.8

Notes: PFEM is percentage female for the non-agricultural labour force as a whole.
All coefficients are significant at the 0.01 level.
Estimated value of ID-MM at various levels of PFEM (based on equation 2)
PFEM	Estimated ID-MM
10	0.216
20	0.122
30	0.055
40	0.014
50	−0.002

Source: Study data.

women comprise less than 25 per cent of the labour force) is always lower when based on MM as compared to when based on ID. Furthermore, there are several striking differences for countries with very low female participation rates. For example, Egypt is ranked 3rd based on MM and 15th based on ID; Jordan is ranked 7th based on MM and 26th based on ID. In our opinion, these results imply that MM is not an especially good index for analysing point-in-time, cross-national differences where there is a very wide range in average percentage female, especially when this includes countries with low female labour force participation rates.

As the above results do not indicate whether ID or MM is preferable for investigating trends in inequality over time for countries with middle to high female labour force participation rates, both indices are used in Part IV where trends in occupational segregation by sex are analysed.

5.2 Dividing the labour force into gender-dominated and gender-integrated occupations

It is reasonably common for analysts to divide occupations according to whether or not they are highly segregated on the basis of sex, that is into so-called

"male-dominated" and "female-dominated" occupations. This provides easy to understand, policy-relevant information. One might observe, for example, that architects are overwhelmingly male whereas nurses are overwhelmingly female, thereby implying a need to determine why this is so in order to design appropriate action to help increase equality of opportunity for men and women.

The main difficulty with this approach is knowing how to define "male" and "female" occupations. Should the dividing line be, for example 50 per cent (i.e. equal numbers of men and women); or 60 or 70 per cent (as is common in industrialized country research studies and comparable worth regulations); or extreme values such as 80 or 90 per cent (in order to identify occupations where there is consistently reduced opportunity for one sex as in a previous publication by the author—Anker and Hein, 1986); or the average percentage female in the labour force as a whole (which has intuitive meaning and is used to calculate the ID index). It is even possible that one number/dividing line may be inappropriate for all needs and in all national circumstances.[9]

Table 5.5 provides information on how "female-dominated", "male-dominated" and "gender-integrated" occupations have been defined in previous research studies and comparable worth regulations.[10] Table 5.6 provides a summary of the findings for "gender-integrated" occupations. Included are 22 research studies covering nine countries, along with six examples of comparable worth regulations from Canada and the United States. In the research literature, the most common (modal) definition for gender-dominated occupations is 40 per cent female ±20 per cent female (implying a range of 20 to 60 per cent female for gender-integrated occupations), with the average (mean) range for gender-integrated occupations slightly smaller (from about 27 to 58 per cent female). In comparable worth regulations, the average range is slightly smaller, at about 25 per cent, from about 35 to 60 per cent; although it is common for authors to refer to the so-called typical "70 per cent rule" for defining gender-dominance (see, for example, Gunderson, 1994 and Barbezat, 1993) which has an implied range of 40 per cent, that is from 30 to 70 per cent female or male.

Two observations are worth making regarding the various definitions which have been used. First, *the centre-point for "gender-integrated" occupations has generally been somewhere near the mean percentage female for the labour force as a whole.* In some instances this is explicit (see, for example, Jusenius, 1975; Izraeli, 1979); in other instances this is mentioned in the text (see, for example, Hakim, 1993). For industrialized countries—and almost all of the examples in table 5.5 are from industrialized countries—the mean percentage female is generally between 35 and 45 per cent. Second, *research studies generally use a higher cut-off point for defining "male-dominated" as compared to "female-dominated" occupations.* This comes about because "gender-integrated" occupations are seen from the women's point of view

Table 5.5. Definitions of "male-dominated", "female-dominated" and "gender-integrated" occupations from previous research studies and comparable worth regulations

Male-dominated (in % male)	Female-dominated (in % female)	Gender-integrated range implied (in % female)	Rule followed to set gender-integrated range (in % female)	Country, year and source
Research studies				
>80%	>60%	20%–60%	40% ± 20%	USA 1970 and 1980 Fields & Wolff (1991)
>74%	>46%	26%–46%	36% ± 10%	USA 1970 Jusenius (1977)
>66.9%	>43%	33%–43%	38% ± 5%	USA 1970 Jusenius (1977)
>80%	>60%	20%–60%	40% ± 20%	USA 1975 Rytina (1981)
>80%	>60%	20%–60%	40% ± 20%	USA 1980 Bianchi & Rytina (1986) (note: female share was about 37% in 1970 and 42% in 1980)
>60%	>60%	40%–60%	as set	USA 1990 Reskin & Roos (1992)
>male share+5%	x	x	x	USA 1960, 1970, 1971, 1977 Beller (1982 & 1984)
>70%	>70%	30%–70%	50% ± 20%	USA 1986 Jacobs (1989)
x	>75%	x	x	UK 1971 Joseph (1983)
>75%	>55%	25%–55%	40% ± 15%	UK 1971, 1981, 1991 (note: female share was roughly 40%: 37%, 39% and 44% in 1971, 1981 and 1991) Hakim (1993)
>70%	>70%	30%–70%	50% ± 20%	UK 1971, 1981 Hakim (1993)
>75%	>46%	25%–46%	Approx. female share of 32% ± ≈10%	Israel 1979 Cohen et al. (1987)
>69%	>51%	31%–51%	Approx. female share of 39.1% ± 10%	Israel 1983 Cohen et al. (1987)
>75%	>44%	25%–44%	Approx. female share of 33% ± 10%	Israel 1972 Izraeli (1979)

Table 5.5. (contd.)

Male-dominated (in % male)	Female-dominated (in % female)	Gender-integrated range implied (in % female)	Rule followed to set gender-integrated range (in % female)	Country, year and source
Research studies				
x	>70% >60% >50%	x	x	New Zealand, 1971 Moir (1977)
x	twice female share	x	x	New Zealand 1981 Gwarney–Gibbs (1988)
>80%	>60%	20%–60%	40% ± 20%	New Zealand 1971 Van Mourik et al. (1989)
>male share + 5%	>female share + 5%	x	x	Australia 1989 Watts & Rich (1991)
x	>female share	x	x	Cyprus 1984 House (1984)
>80%	>63%	20%–63%	a	UK 1980 Martin & Roberts (1984)
>80%	>80%	20%–80%	a	India, Cyprus, Ghana, Mauritius, Peru & USA 1970–1980 Anker & Hein (1986)
>90%	>90%	10%–90%		
Comparable worth regulations (all cited in Gunderson, 1994 except the first entry)				
>70%	>70%	30%–70%	a	Based on Washington State, for USA GAO (1992)
>70%	>60%	30%–60%	a	Ontario Province, Canada
>70%	>60%	30%–60%	a	New Brunswick Province, Canada
>70%	for enterprise with < 100 workers	30%–70%	a	Canada Federal Jurisdiction (% varies by size of enterprise to ensure equivalent statistical certainty of gender–dominance and so not due to random chance)
>60%	for enterprise with 100–500 workers	40%–60%		

Table 5.5. (contd.)

Male-dominated (in % male)	Female-dominated (in % female)	Gender-integrated range implied (in % female)	Rule followed to set gender-integrated range (in % female)	Country, year and source
Research studies				
>55%	for enterprise with >500 workers	45%–55%		
>60%	>60%	40%–60%	a	Nova Scotia Province, Canada
>60%	>60%	40%–60%	a	Prince Edward Island Province, Canada

Notes: x indicates not applicable or not applied.
a indicates no rule used. We calculated a range based on definitions for male–dominated and female–dominated occupations.
Sources: Note that several of these references are found in Barbezat (1993), Hakim (1993) and Gunderson (1994).

and generally centred on mean percentage female, which is below 50 per cent. The same is generally not the case for comparable worth regulations which are concerned with equal treatment and so generally use the same definition for men and women, with the range for "gender-integrated" occupations a gratuitous outcome.

Absolute concept and definition for gender-dominated occupations

In light of the above discussion—and in order to account for different policy perspectives as well as wide variations in female labour force participation

Table 5.6. Summary for "gender-integrated" occupations

	Range (in % female)	Size of range (in % female)
Average (mean)		
Research studies	26–58	32
Comparable worth regulations (note average female share of LF slightly less than 40%)	36–61	25
Average (mode)		
Research studies	20–60	40
Comparable worth regulations	30–60	20 and 30

Notes: In calculating mean and mode for comparable worth regulations, value for Canada taken as that for large establishments only.

GENDER AND JOBS

Table 5.7. Relationship between percentage female in an occupation and ratio of female to male workers in that occupation

Percentage female	Ratio of females to males	Ratio of males to females
10	0.11	9.00
20	0.25	4.00
30	0.43	2.30
40	0.67	1.50
50	1.00	1.00
60	1.50	0.67
70	2.30	0.43
80	4.00	0.25
90	9.00	0.11

rates around the world—two conceptually different approaches for dividing the labour force into gender-dominated occupations can be identified. One approach employs **an absolute concept where the** *same* **dividing line is used for all countries and both sexes**; this concept is similar to the definition used in a previous study by the author (Anker and Hein, 1986) and most comparable worth regulations. Thus, the male- and female-based versions of "gender-dominated" occupations are the same. In this concept, it makes no difference if many occupations are almost exclusively male due to a relatively low average female labour force participation rate or an unequal distribution of men and women across occupations; in either situation, it is assumed that women would be in a disadvantaged position in obtaining and/or holding a post in such occupations.

To help in defining an absolute concept of "male-dominated" and "female-dominated" occupations for the present study, we constructed table 5.7 and figure 5.2 which show the relationship between percentage female and the ratio of male to female workers. This table demonstrates how *very sensitive this ratio is to small changes in percentage female (or male) when a high percentage of workers are from one sex.* Thus, while this ratio is 1.5 when 60 per cent are men or women, it increases to 2.3 at 70 per cent, 4.0 at 80 per cent and 9.0 at 90 per cent. Even a seemingly small change in this percentage when it is high has a big effect on the ratio; thus, going from 75 per cent to 80 per cent causes the ratio to go from 3.0 to 4.0.

In defining the cut-off point for the absolute concept, the chosen percentage should identify occupations where one sex predominates to such an extent that the other sex does not have anywhere near an equal opportunity of obtaining a job in this occupation, nor would persons with this sex

Figure 5.2. Relationship between percentage female in an occupation, ratio of female to male and male to female workers in that occupation and absolute type definition of male-dominated and female-dominated occupations used in this book

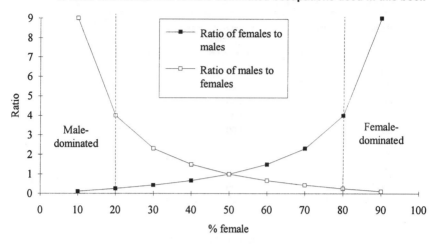

Note: The definition of gender-dominated occupation used in this book is when one sex comprises at least 80 per cent of workers in occupation.
Source: Table 5.7.

generally feel comfortable working in such an occupation even if they were able to get a job there. Such an occupation would be "sex-stereotyped". This implies the need for a definition which uses a rather extreme percentage so as to represent an extreme situation where sex-stereotyping is clear.

For this book, we decided to use at least 80 per cent of one sex as our definition of gender-dominated occupations—that is, occupations where the ratio of male (female) to female (male) workers is at least 4 to 1. We felt that 85 and 90 per cent (ratios of 5.7 and 9.0) are too stringent while 75 or 70 per cent (ratios of 3.0 and 2.3) are not strong enough. While the decision to use 80 per cent is partly ad hoc in nature (as 75 per cent and a ratio of 3.0, or 85 per cent and a ratio of 5.7 could have been acceptable), occupations with a ratio greater than 4.0 in the number of male and female workers, we feel, represents reasonably well the situation where sex-stereotyping is clear.

Relative concept and definition of gender-integrated occupations

A second approach employs a relative concept where the dividing line between gender-dominated and **gender-integrated occupations is defined in relation to the average percentage female for the labour force as a whole.** This is similar to the definition used in most previous research studies where "gender-inte-grated" occupations represent occupations where women have a reasonable degree of opportunity, thereby allowing for randomness as well as individual variations in preferences and circumstances.

86 GENDER AND JOBS

Table 5.8. Relationship between per cent female in non-agricultural labour force and definitions of "female-concentrated", "female-underrepresented" and "gender-integrated" occupations used in this book

Female share of non-agricultural labour force (%)	Female-underrepresented occupations (% male)	Female-concentrated occupations (% female)	"Gender-integrated" occupations (% in female)	
			Range	Size of range
10	>95%	>15%	5%–15%	10%
20	>90%	>30%	10%–30%	20%
30	>85%	>45%	15%–45%	30%
40	>80%	>60%	20%–60%	40%
50	>75%	>75%	25%–75%	50%
60[a]	>70%	>80%[a]	30%–80%	50%
70[a]	>65%	>80%[a]	35%–80%	45%

Note: [a] Maximum percentage female set at 80 per cent. Only two of our 41 study economies (Ghana and Haiti) could be affected by this, as their female share of the non-agricultural labour force exceeds 53.3 per cent (which when multiplied by 1.5 becomes 80 per cent).

We felt that for a cross-national analysis such as in the present monograph (where there is a wide range of female labour force participation rates) that the definition used for this relative concept of "gender-integrated" occupations should be a function of the average percentage female for the non-agricultural labour force as a whole.[11] With this in mind, we made an ad hoc decision to define "gender-integrated" occupations in a country as those where the percentage female is between 0.5 and 1.5 times the average female share of employment in the non-agricultural labour force for the country. In this way, "gender-integrated" occupations are centred around the mean percentage female for the non-agricultural labour force as a whole. **"Female-concentrated" occupations are thus defined as those having more than 1.5 times the mean percentage female, while "female-underrepresented" occupations are those having less than 0.5 times the mean percentage female.**

Table 5.8 and figure 5.3 illustrate what this relative definition implies in terms of "female-concentrated", "gender-integrated" and "female-underrepresented" occupations at different levels of average percentage female for the non-agricultural labour force as a whole. The first thing to notice is that *the size of the range for "gender-integrated" occupations is the same as the average percentage female.* Second, *at a percentage female of 40 per cent (approximately the average for OECD countries), the range for "gender-integrated" occupations is the same as the most commonly used definition in the research literature* (which is based almost exclusively on industrialized country examples). Third, and a corollary of the first point, the *size of the range for "gender-integrated" occupations increases as percentage female*

Figure 5.3. **Relationship between the percentage female share of non-agricultural labour force (PFEM) and relative type definition of "female-concentrated", "female-underrepresented" and "gender-integrated" occupations used in book**

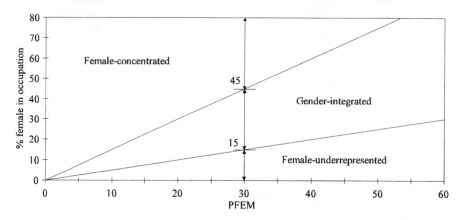

Note: Gender-integrated occupations are defined as occupations where percentage female is between 0.5 and 1.5 times the average percentage female for total non-agricultural labour force. For example, an occupation in a country with PFEM equals 30% would be considered as female-concentrated if percentage female for that occupation is above 45%, gender-integrated if percentage female is between 15% and 45%, and female-underrepresented if percentage female is below 15%. Source: Table 5.8.

increases. While this might seem to cause a comparability problem since countries with higher female shares of employment would have larger ranges for "gender-integrated" occupations, these occupations remain conceptually comparable across countries, since they are defined relative to the mean female share of the labour force for each country.

Appendix 5.1. Intuitive meaning of the index of dissimilarity (ID)

The index of dissimilarity (ID) is the most widely used statistic for analysing occupational segregation by sex. One of the supposed advantages of ID is that it is easy to understand, because it has an intuitively meaningful interpretation. This supposed advantage of ID is one of the reasons why we chose to use ID in this monograph.

Unfortunately, **there is a great deal of confusion (and inaccuracy) in the research literature regarding the intuitive interpretation of ID.** This appendix investigates this issue and demonstrates what ID can be interpreted to mean. As it turns out, this meaning differs from that contained in the research literature, which is not correct (and this even includes the 1955 Duncan and Duncan article to which analysts always refer).[12]

A few quotes provide a good flavour regarding the confusion, and as it turns out inaccuracy, in the research literature.

> It [ID] may be interpreted as the proportion of non-whites who would have to change their tracts of residence to make $q_i = q$ [where q_i is per cent non-white in tract i and q is per cent non-white for all tracts] for all i (hence the term, displacement). (Duncan and Duncan, 1955, pp. 211).

> The actual value of the [ID] index may be interpreted as the percentage of women (or men) who would need to change occupations for the employment distribution of the two groups to be identical (Blau and Hendricks, 1979).

> The index is interpretable as the minimum percentage of women (or alternatively men) who would have to change their occupations so as to equalize the occupational distributions of men and women (Fox and Fox, 1987).

> The index of dissimilarity has a convenient interpretation: it represents the proportion of women who would have to change occupations in order to be distributed in the same manner as men. The measure, D, is symmetrical; that is, the same proportion of men and women would have to change occupations to be distributed in the same manner as women (Jacobs, 1989).

As the above quotes indicate, ID is frequently interpreted as equal to the minimum proportion of men *or* women who would need to change occupations in order to bring about an equal proportion by sex across all occupations. Yet, this could not possibly be true except when the labour force has equal numbers of male and female workers, an observation made by Tzannatos (1990).

To begin with, in calculating ID, it is necessary to obtain the same percentage of workers who are women in every occupation (and therefore by definition the same percentage of workers who are men in every occupation, as the percentage male plus the percentage female in an occupation must equal 100). Since in calculating ID one leaves unchanged the distribution of employment across occupations and the percentage of all workers who are female ($\overline{PFEM}$), this implies that the percentage female in any occupation i ($PFEM_i$) must have the same percentage female as for the total labour force. Thus, the number of women (men) who need to shift occupation can then be expressed as follows:

Total number of females who must shift:

$$\frac{1}{2}\sum_i |(\text{PFEM}_i - \overline{\text{PFEM}})| * (M_i + F_i)$$

Total number of males who must shift:

$$\frac{1}{2}\sum_i |(1 - \text{PFEM}_i) - (1 - \overline{\text{PFEM}})| * (M_i + F_i)$$

Notice that the total number of males who must shift equals the number of females who must shift, which equals:

$$\frac{1}{2}\sum_i |(\overline{\text{PFEM}} - \text{PFEM}_i)| * (M_i + F_i)$$

Now it can be demonstrated that when total number of men *or* women who would need to shift their occupation (indicated above) is expressed as a proportion of the total number of male workers and a proportion of the total number of female workers in the labour force, the summation of these two proportions equals ID. This is, then, *the intuitive meaning of ID: the proportion of male workers* plus *the proportion of female workers who would need to change occupations in order to have the same proportion of women in every occupation* (and the same proportion of men in every occupation but with a different value).

ID = minimum number of females or males who would need to shift occupation to get the same proportion female in every occupation (which would equal the average proportion female for the total labour force) expressed as a proportion of the female labour force.
+ the same minimum number of females or males expressed as a proportion of the male labour force.

The following algebraic exercise demonstrates that ID is equivalent to the above "intuitively meaningful" formula for the ID.[13]
Algebraically the definition of ID equals:

$$\frac{1}{2}\sum_i |(F_i/F - M_i/M)|$$

And our intuitive definition of ID based on the necessary shifting of male and female workers noted above in the first two equations equals:

$$\text{ID} = \frac{1}{2}\sum_i \left[\left[|(\text{PFEM}_i - \overline{\text{PFEM}})| * \frac{(M_i + F_i)}{F} \right] \right.$$
$$\left. + \left[|(\text{PFEM}_i + \overline{\text{PFEM}})| * \frac{M_i + F_i}{M} \right] \right]$$

If our intuitive definition is correct, the above two equations must be equal. After equating these two equations, eliminating the 1/2 and summation sign and on both sides of the equation, putting everything into common denominators, we get:

$$|F_i M - M_i F| = \left(\left| \left(\frac{F_i}{F_i + M_i} - \frac{F}{F + M} \right) \right| * (M_i - F_i) * M \right)$$

$$+ \left(\left| \left(\frac{F_i}{F_i + M_i} - \frac{F}{F + M} \right) \right| * (M_i - F_i) * F \right)$$

Then eliminating this common denominator yields:

$$|F_i M - M_i F| = \left| \frac{F_i}{(M_i + F_i)} - \frac{F}{M + F} \right| * (M + F) * (M_i + F_i)$$

Putting the right hand side (RHS) of the equation into a common denominator yields:

$$\left| \frac{F_i(M + F) - F(M_i + F_i)}{(M_i + F_i)(M + F)} \right| * (M + F)(M_i + F_i)$$

Simplifying this, we get the same formula as on the LHS:

$$|F_i M + FF_i - FM_i - F_i F| = |F_i M - FM_i|$$

Based on the above formula, it is possible to calculate the percentage of the female and male labour forces which would have to change occupation for different ID values. These proportions, which are presented in table 5.9 and figure 5.4 are themselves dependent on the level of PFEM. Notice that: (i) the implied percentage shifts for men and women are equal only when the labour force is one-half female and one-half male; (ii) when PFEM is less than 50 per cent, the implied percentage shift for women is greater than it is for men; (iii) for low PFEM values, there is a very small implied percentage shift for males and a large implied shift for females; (iv) for a given PFEM value, the implied percentage shift increases along with

Table 5.9.   Implied percentage shift in the female (F) and male (M) labour forces implied by the index of dissimilarity (ID) as a function of ID and average percentage female in the labour force (PFEM)

PFEM		ID					
		0.30	0.40	0.50	0.60	0.70	0.80
10	F	27	36	45	54	63	72
	M	3	4	5	6	7	8
20	F	24	32	40	48	56	64
	M	6	8	10	12	14	16
30	F	21	28	35	42	49	56
	M	9	12	15	18	21	24
40	F	18	24	30	36	42	48
	M	12	16	20	24	28	32
50	F	15	20	25	30	35	40
	M	15	20	25	30	35	40

Figure 5.4. **Percentage shift in the female and male labour forces implied by the index of dissimilarity (ID) as a function of ID and percentage female in the labour force (PFEM)**

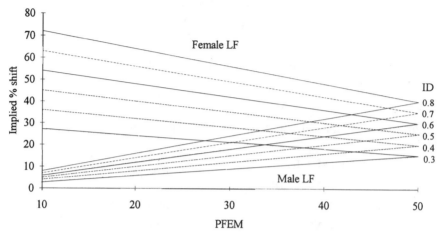

Source: Table 5.9.

increases in ID; (v) for a given ID value, the implied percentage shift for women (men) decreases (increases) along with increases in PFEM.

In conclusion, there is an intuitively understandable interpretation for ID. This interpretation is, however, different from that stated (incorrectly) in the research literature. The usefulness of our (correct) interpretation is questionable, however, as it is not so intuitively meaningful.

Notes

[1] A distinction is sometimes made between segregation and concentration (see e.g. Siltanen et al., 1995; Rubery and Fagan, 1993). "Whereas segregation refers to the separation of the two sexes across occupations, concentration refers to the representation of one sex within occupations" (Siltanen et al., 1995). We do not feel that stressing this distinction is especially helpful and for this reason do not use it in this book. For us, occupational segregation by sex is about men and women having unequal opportunities in the labour market, specifically in finding and keeping jobs in a broad range of occupations.

[2] Alternatively, ID could be defined in terms of "male" occupations using the basic segregation table 5.2:

$$ID = M_m/M - F_m/F$$

[3] Using the basic segregation table, it is also possible to show how several of the newly proposed alternative indices of inequality are similar to, or different from, ID in ways that do not recommend them. For example, Siltanen, Jarman and Blackburn (1995), demonstrate that the WE index proposed by OECD is a direct function of ID and is weighted by the proportion of the labour force which is male. Furthermore, they demonstrate how WE and the SR index proposed by Hakim do not have a constant upper limit, nor are they symmetrical with respect to their male and female versions. For these reasons, we do not feel that the WE and SR indices are useful additions to ID.

[4] Two other possible problems with ID much less extensively discussed in the research literature are: (i) the single cut-off point used for calculating ID (see the basic segregation

table) can conceivably cause large and basically random variations in ID over time, since each occupation has to be either a "male" or "female" occupation; and (ii) changes over time in percentage female among highly feminized and masculinized occupations may have no effect on ID values. The latter observation is apparent from the basic segregation table and how ID is calculated. This means that changes over time in the feminization of relatively highly sex-segregated occupations will not generally affect the ID value. The former observation is more or less neglected by analysts, but it can be very important when occupations are very large in size (which is much more likely to occur when there are relatively few occupations classified, such as for one-digit data where there are only six non-agricultural occupations as in ISCO-68). To illustrate this latter point, suppose that percentage female for the labour force as a whole is 30.0 per cent and percentage female is 29.9 for one very large occupation. Then in time $t + 1$, suppose that this occupation becomes 30.9 per cent female while per cent female for the labour force as a whole remains unchanged. ID values for time periods t and $t + 1$ in this example would be different (possibly considerably different) due solely to the basically fluke "movement" of this one occupation from being a "male" occupation to being a "female" occupation.

[5] Also, MM does not have the problem that all occupations have to be *exclusively* "male" or "female" occupations and so the possibility that they could shift from one category to the other over time due to a very small change in per cent female (see hypothetical example in previous footnote on this for ID). MM does this by apportioning men and women in the borderline occupation to "male" and "female" occupations. MM, however, has the same problem as ID with regard to its being insensitive to most changes in the feminization of highly sex-segregated occupations (again see previous footnote on this for ID).

[6] The definition of MM is as follows:

$$MM = (F_f * M_m - F_m * M_f)/F * M$$

$$= (F_f/F) * (M_m/M) - (F_m/F) * (M_f/M)$$

Since the modified segregation table is symmetrical, and M equals F when the labour force is one-half female, this implies that F_f/F equals M_m/M; F_m/F equals M_f/M; and F_m/F equals $1 - (F_m/F)$ as well as $1 - (M_f/M)$ when F equals M. Therefore, if F_f/F is set equal to x, then:

$$MM = x * x - (1 - x) * (1 - x)$$

$$= 2x - 1$$

It can be demonstrated that this is equal to ID when 50 per cent of the labour force is female (and the distribution of occupations by their degree of feminization is not very skewed and the occupation on the borderline dividing "male" and "female" occupations is not large). Thus, referring to the basic segregation table, which is symmetrical at 50 per cent female, and again setting F_f/F equal to x, then:

$$ID = F_f/F - M_f/M$$

$$= x - (1 - x)$$

$$= 2x - 1$$

This is the same value as for MM above. Indeed, readers are referred to figure 5.1, table 5.3 and discussion in the text where it is shown that ID and MM have very similar values when women comprise over 40 per cent of the labour force.

[7] It is interesting to note that specifying in table 5.4 the number of occupations classified in the national data (unreported regressions) does not significantly improve the fit. The variable representing the number of occupations (NOCCUP) is always insignificant at the 0.10 level.

[8] MM appears to have a lower value as compared to ID when women comprise a small percentage of the labour force because of how "male" and "female" occupations are defined for MM as compared to ID. Using the example of Egypt where women are reported to be 13.6 per cent of the non-agricultural labour force, we find that while 19 occupations are "female"

occupations according to ID, there are only 8 "female" occupations according to MM. This difference is due to inclusion in MM of two large "relatively female" occupations (teachers; bookkeepers and cashiers), and therefore inclusion of large numbers of male workers in these occupations when calculating the MM statistic.

[9] In an international comparative study such as the present one, for certain purposes it is important to take into consideration varying levels of female participation in the labour force. A dividing line which might be appropriate in a country such as India where women comprise only about 12 per cent of the non-agricultural labour force might not be appropriate in a country such as Sweden where women comprise approximately 49 per cent of the non-agricultural labour force. See figure 5.3 and table 5.8 and the text for a discussion of a relative concept of gender dominance based on average percentage female in the non-agricultural labour force.

[10] Comparable worth regulations are concerned with bringing about equal pay for work of equal value. They try to accomplish this by correcting for the underpayment of female workers which would exist even if occupational segregation by sex ceased to exist. They stipulate that occupations which are similar in terms of the "value" of the work done should have the same pay. Comparable worth settlements then attempt to equalize the pay in equivalent (in terms of the value of the work done) "male" and "female" occupations. To do this, they need to define "male" and "female" occupations—the aspect which interests us here.

[11] Notice that if a fixed range were used, such as the mean percentage female ±10 percentage points or ±20 percentage points as is done in some research studies, this range would be relatively enormous for countries with low female shares of employment.

[12] Although almost all articles on occupational segregation refer to Duncan and Duncan (1955) as their source for the ID index, with some even calling it the Duncan index, it is interesting to note that the original 1955 article refers back to two earlier articles as the source for this index (Jahn, Schmid and Schrag, 1947; and Williams, 1948). It is also interesting to note that Duncan and Duncan describe several different segregation indices and that they **do not recommend any one index.** Indeed, they conclude that it is wrong to think that any one particular index will always be preferable. They say that it is best to use several different indices or statistics (an approach which is followed in the present book). **"As we have suggested, no single index will be sufficient, because of the complexity of the notion of segregation,** involving as it does considerations of spatial pattern, unevenness of distribution, relative size of the segregated group, and homogeneity of sub-areas, among others" (Duncan and Duncan, 1955).

[13] A recent publication by Psacharopoulos and Tzannatos (1992) comes up with a similar result without quite realizing it. They find that the necessary shift of male or female workers implied by ID (defined below as R_k) equals the following:

$$R_k = ID * LF_m * \frac{LF_f}{LFtotal}$$

It is easy to show algebraically that this equation can be transformed to show that

$$ID = \frac{R_k}{LF_m} + \frac{R_k}{LF_f}$$

This is our above intuitive definition of ID.

SENSITIVITY OF SEGREGATION STATISTICS TO DEGREE OF DISAGGREGATION IN OCCUPATIONAL CLASSIFICATION

6

It is well known that the level of occupational segregation by sex as measured by segregation indices, such as the index of dissimilarity (ID) and the marginal matching index (MM), is a function of the degree of disaggregation in the occupational data itself. The same is almost always true for the percentage of the labour force in gender-dominated or mixed occupations.

The greater the level of detail in the occupational data, the greater the level of measured occupational segregation by sex *ceteris paribus*. Indeed, there is a mathematical certainty in this for ID, which can be demonstrated quite easily. To illustrate this using a typical example, suppose that a classification scheme becomes more detailed in that teachers are subdivided into the following occupations (as in ISCO-68): university and higher education teachers; secondary school teachers; primary education teachers; pre-primary education teachers; special education teachers; teachers not elsewhere classified. The value of an inequality index such as ID would increase unless percentage female is identical in each teacher occupation, something which does not occur in the real world. A similar conclusion would almost always apply for statistics measuring the extensiveness of gender-dominated occupations.

The main issue addressed in the present chapter is the sensitivity of inequality statistics to the level of disaggregation in the occupational data[1], and whether one-digit, two-digit and three-digit occupational data yield similar conclusions regarding relative rank orders of countries and time trends. Also investigated is the consistency of the relationship between ID and the number of occupations on which it is based as well as between the degree of detail in the occupational classification and the extent of gender-dominated occupations in the labour force.

These are important questions for analysts, policy-makers and laypersons. First, in order to avoid misleading interpretations, it is important to establish whether or not the relative levels of occupational segregation by sex across countries as well as the trends over time in occupational segregation by sex within countries differ, depending on whether or not occupational data are classified at the one-digit level, or at a more detailed two- or three-digit level. In particular, it is important to know if inequality statistics based on much more widely available one-digit occupational data provide a misleading or accurate reflection of occupational segregation by sex across countries in the world.

Second, it is important to know if relationships between occupational detail and inequality statistics are sufficiently consistent to allow an analyst the possibility of calculating adjusted national values with roughly comparable values by taking into account the detail of the national occupational data.

The international standard classification of occupations (ISCO) is the most widely used classification scheme in the world and our data set; in addition, many national coding schemes are similar to ISCO. ISCO-68 (the most widely used classification in our data set and the world) has six major non-agricultural occupational groups, and divides these up into 75 occupations at the two-digit level and 265 occupations at the three-digit level.[2] This increasing detail along with examples of specific occupations in each major occupational group are shown in table 6.1 and figure 6.1. Appendix 6.1 to this chapter reproduces full details on the occupations included in ISCO-68.

Some **aspects of this ISCO classification scheme, which have important implications for inequality statistics, are worth noting.** First, *the degree of detail in ISCO-68 is much greater in the two largest major occupational groups: (i) professional and technical, and (ii) production and related workers* - as compared to the other four major non-agricultural groups. Second, this greater *disaggregation for these two major occupational groups is even more marked at the three-digit level as compared to the two-digit level.* Thus, these two major groups include: 2 (33.3 per cent) of the 6 one-digit non-agricultural occupations, 46 (61.3 per cent) of the 75 two-digit non-agricultural occupations and 212 (80.0 per cent) of the 265 three-digit non-agricultural occupations. This aspect of ISCO-68 is illustrated quite well by figure 6.1 which shows how most three-digit ISCO-68 occupations are production or professional/technical occupations.

Third, an examination of one-, two- and three-digit occupational groups in ISCO-68 (see Appendix 6.1) indicates that *considerable occupational segregation by sex is hidden within the one-digit classification as compared to the two- and three-digit classifications.* Consequently, it is possible (and indeed common) for the professional and technical occupational major group to be relatively feminized (see Chapter 8) even though almost all professional and technical occupations are highly masculinized (e.g. most physical scientists, architects, engineers, ship officers, aircraft officers, life scientists, etc. are men). What happens is that most women working in professional and technical occupations work in just two occupations (teachers and medical workers). This means that when one disaggregates from a one- to a two-digit classification considerably more occupational segregation is observed.

Two-digit data also hide a considerable degree of occupational segregation by sex. For example, when one disaggregates from a two-digit to a three-digit classification, one finds among teachers that pre-primary and primary

Table 6.1. ISCO-68: Number of occupations at 1-, 2- and 3-digit classification levels, with examples of some important occupations

ISCO-68 Major Group	Number of occupations at 2-digit level	Examples at 2-digit level	Number of occupations at 3-digit level	Examples at 3-digit level
Professional & Technical	16	Physical scientists	81	Chemists Physicists
		Medical, dental and veterinary workers		Medical doctors Professional nurses
Administrative & Managerial	2	Managers	5	General managers Production managers
Clerical & related workers	10	Clerical and related workers not elsewhere classified	20	Stock clerks Receptionists and travel agency clerks Library and filing clerks Correspondence and reporting clerks
Sales	7	Salespersons, shop assistants and related workers	12	Salespersons, shop assistants and demonstrators Street vendors, canvassers and news vendors
Services	10	Protective services workers	16	Fire-fighters Police officers and detectives
Agricultural, animal husbandry, forestry and fishermen and hunters	5	Agricultural and animal husbandry workers	16	General farm workers Dairy farm workers Poultry farm workers
Production and related workers, transport equipment operators and labourers	30	Spinners, weavers, knitters, dyers and related workers	131	Knitters Bleachers and dyers Spinners and winders
		Blacksmiths, toolmakers and machine-tool operators		Toolmakers, machine-tool operators Metal grinders, polishers and sharpeners
		Transport equipment operators		Railway engine drivers and firepersons Motor vehicle drivers
Total	80		281	
Total non-agricultural	75		265	

Source: ILO, *International Standard Classification of Occupations*, Geneva, 1968.

Figure 6.1.   Percentage of all non-agricultural occupations included in each of six major non-agricultural categories based on 1-, 2- and 3-digit ISCO-68 classifications

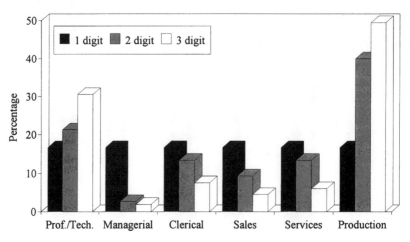

Source: Table 6.1.

school teachers are much more likely to be women as compared to secondary and university teachers; in the medical professions, women are much more likely to be nurses than doctors or dentists. In Italy in 1991, for example, while women comprised 72 per cent of all teachers, they were 100, 90, 69 and 27 per cent respectively of nursery, primary, secondary and university teachers (Rubery and Fagan, 1993).

On the other hand, disaggregation of occupational data from a two- to three-digit classification often does not reveal much more occupational segregation, since many times all three-digit sub-occupations have similar percentages of women. Again, using an example from professional occupations, in most countries each of the four physicist sub-occupations, the 18 engineer or architect sub-occupations, and the three aircraft and ship officer sub-occupations tend to be similarly dominated by men.

Two important implications of the above discussion for measuring occupational segregation are:

(i)   A one-digit occupational classification, such as in ISCO-68, conceals a great deal of occupational segregation by sex. This implies that going from a one-digit to a two-digit classification scheme should cause a large increase in measured levels of occupational segregation. This also implies that one-digit occupational data are likely to provide a misleading basis for measuring the extensiveness of occupational segregation.

(ii)   Since the difference in the amount of occupational segregation by sex which is hidden by a two-digit classification as compared to a three-digit classification appears to be considerably less than between one-digit and two-digit classifications, it just might be acceptable to measure relative differences and national time trends in occupational segregation by gender using two-digit occupational data. Whereas one-digit data are likely to be too aggregated, three-digit data may be unnecessarily detailed (as well as being available for fewer countries).

Analysis in the remaining parts of Chapter 6 investigate the above hypotheses.

6.1 Study evidence on sensitivity of inequality statistics to degree of disaggregation in occupational classification

In the above discussion, it was shown that the level of an inequality index must, by definition, increase as the number of occupations on which it is based is increased. Then, based on a discussion of ISCO-68 coding, it was hypothesized that the change in inequality statistics, such as ID and MM, would display a large change as the occupational classification is disaggregated. We further hypothesized that this change would be greater as one went from a one- to a two-digit classification as compared to going from a two- to a three-digit classification.

These hypotheses are supported by data (table 6.2) provided in a literature review by Barbezat (1994). The average ID value for the four economies reviewed is approximately .41 based on a one-digit classification (about 7 occupations) as compared to .58 and .61 respectively when based on two- and three-digit classifications (about 65 and 300 occupations respectively). The average changes in ID, of about .17 and .03 as the coding classification becomes more detailed, are consistent with the above hypothesis of greater sensitivity in inequality indices between one- and two-digit classifications as compared to between two- and three-digit classifications. In this example from Barbezat (1993), the rank order of the four countries is the same whether based on one-, two- or three-digit data.[3] As we will later observe based on a more extensive analysis of our own study data, this similarity of rank orders is often not the case.

In the remainder of this section, this hypothesis is further investigated using study data for the most recent year (generally around 1990) for 26 of our 41 study countries and areas. These data are presented in tabular form (table 6.3) and then related using multiple regression analysis in the following subsection.

Subsequent subsections investigate how the rank order of countries based on ID at one point in time as well as for trends over time differ depending on whether ID is calculated using one-, two- or three-digit occupational data. The 26 study economies used in this analysis provide an excellent cross-section of the world and our own data set. Included are 6 (of our 7)

Table 6.2. Relationship between index of dissimilarity (ID) and the number of occupations classified, based on data in a literature review

Country or area	1 digit		2 digits		3 digits		Change in ID	
	ID	No. occup.	ID	No. occup.	ID	No. occup.	1 to 2 digits	2 to 3 digits
New Zealand	.4190	7	.5760	80	x	x	.16	x
Australia	.4299	6	.5887	71	.6230	292	.16	.03
Israel	.4230	7	.5898	86	.6162	303	.17	.03
Puerto Rico	.3579	11	x	x	.5728	296	x	x
Unweighted average	.4075	7.75	.5848	79	.6040	297	.16	.02
Unweighted average (excluding Puerto Rico)[a]	.4240	6.67	.5848	79	.6196	298	.16	.03
Unweighted average (excluding Puerto Rico & New Zealand)[a]	.4265	6.50	.5893	61	.6196	298	.16	.03

Notes: x indicates not available.
[a] These additional averages calculated to increase compatibility, because of missing information for Puerto Rico (2-digit data) and New Zealand (3-digit data).
Sources: Drawn from Barbezat (1993): Australia, Lewis (1985); Puerto Rico, Presser and Kishor (1991); New Zealand, Gwarney-Gibbs (1988); Israel, Neuman (1991).

Table 6.3. Relationship between index of dissimilarity (ID) and the level of aggregation (1-, 2- and 3-digit levels) in the occupational classification, based on national and regional study data

Region/country or area	1 digit		2 digits		3 digits		Change in ID	
	ID	No. occup.	ID	No. occup.	ID	No. occup.	1 to 2 digits	2 to 3 digits
OECD (minus Japan)								
Cyprus	.25	6	.60	104[H]	.63	376[H]	.35[+]	.03[−]
Finland	.46	6	.61	64	.67	264	.15	.06
France	.39	5	.58	119[H]	.61	433[H]	.19[+]	.03[−]
Luxembourg	.45	6	.59	71	x	x	.14	x
Netherlands	.38	6	.56	63	.59	151[L]	.18	.03[−]
New Zealand	.43	6	.58	77	.62	281	.15	.04
Norway	.43	6	.56	65	.65	291	.13	.09
Switzerland	.29	8	.57	66	.65	452[H]	.28	.08[+]
Average	.39	6	.58	79	x	x	.20	x
Average (countries with 3-digit data)	.38	6	.58	80	.63	321	.20	.05
Middle East and North Africa								
Bahrain	.47	6	.63	86	x	x	.16	x
Egypt	.53	6	.59	74	x	x	.06	x
Jordan	.68	6	.77	61	x	x	.09	x
Kuwait	.50	6	.73	75	.74	268	.23	.01
Tunisia	.15	6	.66	55	x	x	.51	x
Average	.47	6	.68	70	x	x	.21	x
Average (countries with 3-digit data)	.50	6	.73	75	.74	268	.23	.01
Asia/Pacific								
China	.09	6	.29	38[L]	.44	277	.20[−]	.15[+]
Fiji	.40	6	.60	75	x	x	.20	x
India	.17	6	.46	83	.49	423[H]	.29	.03[+]
Japan	.26	6	.46	49[L]	.53	259	.20[−]	.07[+]
Korea (Rep. of)	.23	6	.40	56	x	x	.17	x

Table 6.3. (contd.)

Region/country or area	1 digit		2 digits		3 digits		Change in ID	
	ID	No. occup.	ID	No. occup.	ID	No. occup.	1 to 2 digits	2 to 3 digits
Malaysia	.19	6	.49	76	x	x	.30	x
Average	.22	6	.45	63	x	x	.23	x
Average (countries with 3-digit data)	.17	6	.40	57	.49	320	.23	.08
Other Developing								
Angola	.53	6	.65	67	x	x	.12	x
Costa Rica	.22	6	.57	55	x	x	.35	x
Ghana	.45	6	.71	75	x	x	.26	x
Haiti	.61	6	.67	75	x	x	.06	x
Netherlands Antilles	.49	6	.64	76	x	x	.15	x
Mauritius	.12	6	.59	70	x	x	.47	x
Senegal	.39	6	.52	80	x	x	.13	x
Average	.40	6	.62	71	x	x	.22	x
Totals								
Average	.37	6	.58	71	x	x	.21	x
Average (countries with 3-digit data)	.33	6	.55	73	.60	316	.21	.06
Average non-OECD countries (incl. Japan)	.36	6	.58	68	x	x	.22	x
Average non-OECD countries (incl. Japan) with 3-digit data	.26	6	.49	61	.55	307	.23	.07
Average OECD countries	.39	6	.58	79	x	x	.20	x
Average OECD countries with 3-digit data	.38	6	.58	80	.63	321	.20	.05

Notes: Averages based on unweighted average of country values. H implies a higher than usual number of occupations for this digit level. L implies a lower than usual number of occupations for this digit level. + implies an upward bias in change in ID between occupational classification levels (1 to 2, or 2 to 3) due to an usual number of non-agricultural occupations at one or both digit level. − implies a downward bias in change in ID between occupational classification levels (1 to 2, or 2 to 3) due to an usual number of non-agricultural occupations at one or both digit level. See footnotes 4 and 5 for explanations indicating which study countries and areas are included in this table.
Source: Study data.

Asian/Pacific countries and areas, 5 (of our 6) Middle Eastern and North African countries, 7 (of our 7) Other Developing countries and areas and 8 (of our 17) OECD countries.[4,5] It should be noted that for expositional purposes, we took some liberty in defining the number of occupations considered as representing two-digit data.[6]

Table 6.3, which uses study data, again indicates a much greater absolute change in ID[7] when going from a one-digit to a two-digit classification as compared to going from a two- to a three-digit classification—although these changes are larger (approximately .21 and .06 respectively) as compared to results (approximately .17 and .03 respectively) based on a literature review of only four industrialized countries from table 6.2. As will be shown below, the larger change in our study data results partly from the fact that ID is more sensitive to disaggregation from a one- to a two-digit classification in developing countries as compared to industrialized countries.[8]

6.1.1 Estimating the relationship between index of dissimilarity (ID) and number of occupations classified

As indicated above, ID values must increase as the number of occupations increase. This, together with the fact that there is considerable variation across study countries in the numbers of occupations classified reduces the comparability of calculated ID values for study countries. In this subsection, we investigate this problem further and devise an adjustment procedure which helps increase the comparability of study ID values.

We began by using regression analysis to estimate the relationship between ID and the number of occupations on which it is based. To control for country, country binary variables are included in the estimated equations.[9] Thus:

$$\text{ID} = \text{f(number of occupations classified, country binaries)}$$

Linear and various nonlinear functional forms (ln, quadratic and cubic) are estimated. Equation 1 uses a linear function, equation 2 a natural log function, equation 3 a quadratic, and equation 4 a cubic. Countries included in the analysis are: (i) the 26 study countries for which we have data for at least two levels of aggregation (i.e. at least at the one- and two-digit levels and also possibly at the three-digit level), and (ii) similar data provided in a literature review by Barbezat (1993) for four countries or areas (Australia, Israel, New Zealand, Puerto Rico). Table 6.4 provides results based on the data reported in Barbezat (1993). Table 6.5 provides results based on our own study data.

For illustrative purposes, study data are also presented in graphical form in figures 6.2 to 6.4. Figure 6.2 shows ID values based on one- and two-digit levels data for countries with relatively low, medium and high ID values based on one-digit data. Figure 6.3 graphs average ID values based on one-, two-, and three-digit level data for the seven OECD study countries

Figure 6.2. Index of dissimilarity (ID) as a function of number of non-agricultural occupations classified based on 1- and 2-digit classifications, for countries with relatively low, medium and high ID values based on 1-digit classification

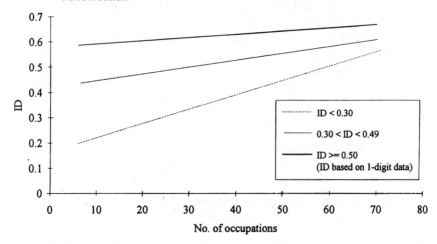

Note: For expositional purposes, points connected by straight lines. There are two points for each set of countries, with values based on average of one- and two-digit occupational classifications for each set of countries.
Source: Study data.

Figure 6.3. Index of dissimilarity (ID) as a function of number of non-agricultural occupations classified based on 1-, 2- and 3-digit classifications, for study countries with 3-digit data

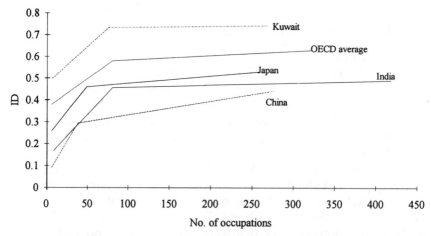

Note: For expositional purposes, points connected by straight lines. There are three points for each set of countries, with values based on average of 1-, 2- and 3-digit occupational classifications for each set of countries.
Source: Table 6.3.

Figure 6.4.   Average index of dissimilarity (ID) as a function of number of non-agricultural occupations classified based on 1- and 2-digit classifications, by region

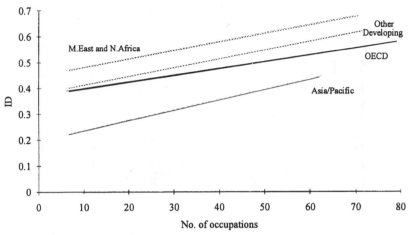

Note: For expositional purposes, points connected by straight lines.
Source: Study data.

with three-digit data, along with China, India and Kuwait which also have three-digit data. Figure 6.4 shows average ID values based on one- and two-digit data for four study regions. Data points are connected by straight lines for expositional purposes. **It seems apparent from these graphs that: (i) there is a strong relationship between ID and number of occupations classified; (ii) the relationship is nonlinear; (iii) the relationship for the range between one- and two-digit occupational data is steeper among non-OECD countries as compared to OECD countries; and (iv) the relationship is progressively less steep the higher the ID is based on one-digit level.**

Regression results shown in tables 6.4 and 6.5 are similar and corroborate the observations made above based on figures 6.2–6.4. As expected, the relationship between ID and NOCCUP is *strongly non-linear*. Whereas the linear relationship estimated (equation 1) has an adjusted R^2 of approximately 0.40 and an F statistic of approximately 3, all of the non-linear equations in table 6.5 have F values generally around 10 and adjusted R^2s of approximately 0.80. Among the non-linear relationships, the log function (equation 2) and the cubic function (equation 4) have the best fits.

Earlier discussion and figures 6.2–6.4 indicated that the relationship between ID and the number of occupations classified differs between OECD and non-OECD countries as well as between countries with differing levels of ID at the one-digit level. For this reason, equation 2 (log function) from tables 6.4 and 6.5 was re-estimated in table 6.6 for: (i) different regions/types of countries (equations 1–3) and (ii) countries with differing ID levels based on one-digit level data (equations 4–6).[10]

Table 6.4. Estimated relationship (using OLS) between index of dissimilarity (ID) and number of occupations classified (NOCCUP), based on literature review data (t values in brackets)

Explanatory variables	Equation number			
	(1)	(2)	(3)	(4)
Constant	.469 (10.19)	.3248 (14.20)	.4099 (40.75)	.4068 (37.04)
NOCCUP	6.367×10^{-4} (3.40)[b]	x	.0029 (14.74)[a]	.0035 (4.51)[b]
ln (NOCCUP)	x	.0569 (11.96)[a]	x	x
$(\text{NOCCUP})^2$	x	x	-7.129×10^{-06} (11.66)[a]	-1.632×10^{-05} (1.53)
$(\text{NOCCUP})^3$	x	x	x	2.375×10^{-08} (0.86)
R^2	.73	.97	.99	.99
Adjusted R^2	.52	.95	.98	.98
F value	3.5	40.8	104.5	81.6
Significance F	.10	.01	.01	.01
Degrees of freedom (residual)	5	5	4	3

Notes: All equations also include country binary variables (to control for country).
Countries and areas included in data are taken from Barbezat, 1993. They are Australia, Israel, Puerto Rico and New Zealand (see table 6.2).
NOCCUP means number of non-agricultural occupations classified.
[a] Significant at .01 level. [b] Significant at .05 level. [c] Significant at .10 level.
x Not specified.
Source: Study data.

Table 6.5. Estimated relationship (using OLS) between index of dissimilarity (ID) and number of occupations classified (NOCCUP), based on data for 26 study countries and areas (t values in brackets)

Explanatory variables	Equation number			
	(1)	(2)	(3)	(4)
Constant	.370 (4.86)	.194 (3.84)	.389 (6.74)	.299 (5.86)
NOCCUP	7.800×10^{-4} (5.16)[a]	x	.0026 (7.13)[a]	.0046 (8.59)[a]
ln (NOCCUP)	x	.076 (11.70)[a]	x	x
$(NOCCUP)^2$	x	x	-4.95×10^{-6} (5.28)[a]	-2.005×10^{-5} (5.69)[a]
$(NOCCUP)^3$	x	x	x	2.600×10^{-08} (4.39)[a]
R^2	.67	.88	.82	.88
Adjusted R^2	.44	.80	.68	.79
F value	2.8	10.3	5.8	9.2
Significance F	.01	.01	.01	.01
Degrees of freedom (residual)	36	36	35	34

Notes: All equations also include country binary variables (to control for country).
NOCCUP means number of non-agricultural occupations classified.
Based on study data for 26 countries and areas having at least one- and two-digit level data and possibly three-digit level data (see table 6.3).
[a] Significance at .01 level. [b] Significance at .05 level. [c] Significance at .10 level.
x Not specified.
Source: Study data.

Table 6.6. Estimated relationship (using OLS) between ID and number of occupations classified (NOCCUP) for different regions and ID values based on one-digit level data, based on study data (t values in bracket)

Independent variable	Region			ID based on 1-digit data		
	OECD	Asia/Pacific	Non-Asian Non-OECD	<.30	.30–.49	.50+
	(1)	(2)	(3)	(4)	(5)	(6)
Constant	0.254	−0.037	0.142	0.081	0.311 (13.09)	0.488
	(6.69)	(1.04)	(1.47)	(1.25)		(19.07)
In (NOCCUP)	0.066[a]	0.085[a]	0.087[a]	0.103[a]	0.061[a]	0.034[b]
	(10.54)	(11.90)	(4.65)	(9.55)	(15.51)	(5.11)
R^2	0.89	0.96	0.80	0.89	0.95	0.97
Adjusted R^2	0.83	0.93	0.58	0.81	0.91	0.92
F value	14.7	30.9	3.6	11.2	26.1	21.9
Significance F	0.01	0.01	0.02	0.01	0.01	0.02
Degrees of freedom (residual)	14	8	11	14	17	3

Notes: All equations also include country binary variables (to control for country).
NOCCUP means number of non-agricultural occupations classified.
Based on study data for 26 countries and areas having at least one- and two-digit level data, and possibly three-digit data (see table 6.3).
[a] Significant at .01 level. [b] Significant at .05 level. [c] Significant at .10 level.
Source: Study data.

The estimated relationships between ID have better fits in table 6.6 as compared to table 6.5. With the exception of equation 3 (for non-Asian and non-OECD countries), adjusted R^2s in table 6.6 range from .81 to .93 and F statistics from 11 to 31. These are excellent fits indeed. In contrast, the same functional form in table 6.5 has an adjusted R square of .80 and F statistic of around 10.

Using the estimated relationships from table 6.6, it is possible to calculate typical changes in ID as the level of disaggregation in the occupational data increases. These are presented in table 6.7. For OECD countries and countries with medium ID values based on one-digit data (note that almost all of OECD countries are in this category), ID values typically increase by around .17 as the occupational data are disaggregated from 6 non-agricultural occupations (one-digit) to 75 non-agricultural occupations (two-digit), and by approximately a further .08 when the data are disaggregated from 75 (two-digit) to 265 occupations (three-digit). The estimated changes in ID are considerably larger in Asian countries and non-Asian non-OECD countries (about .22 and .11 respectively).

6.1.2 Consistency in rank ordering of economies based on index of dissimilarity (ID) as a function of the number of the occupations classified

As observed above, there is a distinct pattern whereby ID is a positive, non-linear function of the number of occupations classified, with ID increasing much more as the data is disaggregated from a one- to a two-digit occupational classification as compared to disaggregation from a two- to a three-digit

Table 6.7. Predicted changes in ID for 1-digit data as compared to 2-digit data, and 2-digit data as compared to 3-digit data, based on regression results reported in table 6.6

ID based on 1-digit level data	Change in ID predicted by regression equations	
	from 1-digit (6 occup.) to 2-digit (75 occup.) data	from 2-digit (75 occup.) to 3-digit (265 occup.) data
<.30	.26	.13
.30–.49	.15	.08
>.50	.09	.04
Region		
OECD	.17	.08
Asia	.22	.11
Non-Asian Non-OECD	.22	.11

Note: Number of non-agricultural occupations used here are those found in 1-, 2- and 3-digit ISCO-68 classifications.
Source: Table 6.6.

classification. The issue addressed in this subsection is the consistency of the rank ordering of countries when based on one-, two- and three-digit occupational data. Data from the same 26 economies as in previous sections are used here. *A priori* expectations are that the rank order of a country will differ more frequently when comparing rank orders based on one- and two-digit data than for a comparison of rank orders based on two- and three-digit data. Such expectations are consistent with results reported in previous sections.

In table 6.8, countries/areas are put in rank order based on national ID values. For expositional purposes, rank orders are shaded when there are large differences between those based on one- and two-digit data or based on two- and three-digit data.

It is possible to make a number of general observations. First, rank orders based on one-, two- and three-digit data are similar, as indicated by the significant relationship (at the .01 level) between the rank orders of countries or areas based on one- and two-digit level data, as well as between rank orders based on two- and three-digit level data.

Second, the consistency of rank orders based on occupational data at different levels of aggregation is much greater for comparisons of two- and three-digit level data than it is for comparisons of one- and two-digit level data. This is indicated by (i) the lower rank order correlation coefficient for one- and two-digit data comparisons (0.68) as compared to that for two- and three-digit data comparisons (0.85)[11] and (ii) the larger number of instances where rank orders are demonstratively different when comparing one- and two-digit data (shaded rows in table 6.8). This result is consistent with the above discussion which indicated that the ID value changes much more when the occupational data are disaggregated from one to two digits as compared to disaggregation from two to three digits.

One basic lesson from this analysis is that **one-digit data often provide misleading information for a comparison of occupational segregation by sex across countries**—although they do provide significantly similar results to those based on two-digit data. A second lesson is that **two-digit data, although not perfect, tend to provide reasonably good information on relative levels of inequality across countries in the sense that country rankings tend to be very similar to those based on three-digit data.**[12]

6.1.3 Comparisons of trends in inequality indices based on one-, two- and three-digit occupational classifications

This section investigates whether trends in occupational segregation by sex, as measured by the most commonly used inequality statistic (ID) and another inequality statistic developed in order to measure trends (MM), are similar when based on one-, two- or three-digit occupational data. This is an important issue for policy-makers interested in monitoring the effectiveness of policies intended to reduce sex inequality in the labour market.

Table 6.8. Rank order according to ID values based on 1-, 2- and 3-digit occupational classifications, for 26 study countries or areas

Country/area	ID			ID rank order for countries/areas with 1- and 2-digit data		ID rank order for countries/areas with 2- and 3-digit data	
	1 digit	2 digit	3 digit	1 digit	2 digit	2 digit	3 digit
China	.091	.293^L	.443	1	1	1	1
Mauritius	.123	.586		2	14		
Tunisia	.150	.663		3	22		
India	.168	.457	.492^H	4	3	2	2
Malaysia	.185	.490		5	5		
Costa Rica	.219	.566		6	9		
Korea (Rep. of)	.231	.402		7	2		
Cyprus	.254	.604^H	.634^H	8	17	9	7
Japan	.256	.458^L	.529	9	4	3	3
Switzerland	.293	.573	.654^H	10	10	6	9
Netherlands	.381	.556	.588^L	11	7	4	4
Senegal	.388	.523		12	6		
France	.393	.585^H	.607^H	13	12	8	5
Fiji	.395	.600		14	16		
New Zealand	.431	.583	.620	15	11	7	6
Norway	.434	.564	.646	16	8	5	8
Ghana	.452	.710		17	24		
Luxembourg	.454	.586		18	13		
Finland	.461	.606	.673	19	18	10	10
Bahrain	.467	.635		20	19		
Netherlands Antilles	.486	.645		21	20		
Kuwait	.499	.733	.743	22	25	11	11
Egypt	.527	.586		23	15		
Angola	.528	.652		24	21		
Haiti	.607	.669		25	23		
Jordan	.682	.769		26	26		

Notes: H implies an unusually high number of non-agricultural occupations for this level.
L implies an unusually low number of non-agricultural occupations in this level.
Rank orders are shaded when they are considered to be substantially different – which is defined here as a difference of 8 or more in rank orders based on 1- and 2-digit data, and a difference of 4 or more in rank orders based on 2- and 3-digit data.
Source: Study data.

Table 6.9 presents ID and MM values for the seven study countries with data at the one-, two- and three-digit levels for two or three points in time. Figures 6.5 and 6.6 present these data graphically.

Results indicate that trends over time in occupational segregation by sex are quite similar when based on two- or three-digit information, as the same trend (using the crude ad hoc assumption that a change of more than 2

Table 6.9. **ID and MM values over time based on 1-, 2- and 3-digit occupational classifications for seven study countries**

Country[a]/year	ID			MM		
	1 digit	2 digit	3 digit	1 digit	2 digit	3 digit
Netherlands						
1973	.462	.639	.671	.317	.553	.614
1979	.448	.622	.654	.339	.555	.622
1990	.381	.556	.588	.336	.508	.586
Norway						
1970	.513	.680	.744	.447	.605	.701
1980	.502	.650	.719	.443	.623	.710
1990	.434	.564	.646	.385	.540	.644
Finland						
1970	.460	.672	.735	.446	.655	.729
1980	.459	.656	.714	.441	.644	.714
1990	.461	.606	.673	.428	.602	.673
Japan						
1970	.257	.448	.526	.242	.364	.469
1980	.284	.450	.529	.267	.367	.460
1990	.256	.458	.529	.255	.382	.467
France						
1982	.379	.613	.636	.378	.591	.615
1990	.393	.586	.607	.389	.578	.602
Switzerland						
1970	.304	.584	.667	.209	.502	.614
1980	.293	.573	.654	.181	.495	.605
Kuwait						
1975	.508	.732	.743	.248	.573	.621
1985	.499	.733	.743	.226	.624	.670

Note: [a] The seven countries included in this table met the following conditions: (i) data were available for two or three years; (ii) data were available at the three-digit level and were relatively easy to aggregate to the one- and two-digit levels. Source: Study data.

percentage points during approximately a ten-year period indicates a clear trend) is observed for all 11 country-time periods for MM and for 10 out of 11 country-time periods for ID. In contrast, ID or MM trends based on one-digit information are often different; six of our eleven country-time periods are observed to have a different trend for ID and MM when based on one-digit data as compared to when based on two-digit data.

GENDER AND JOBS

Figure 6.5. ID values over time based on 1-, 2- and 3-digit occupational classifications for seven study countries

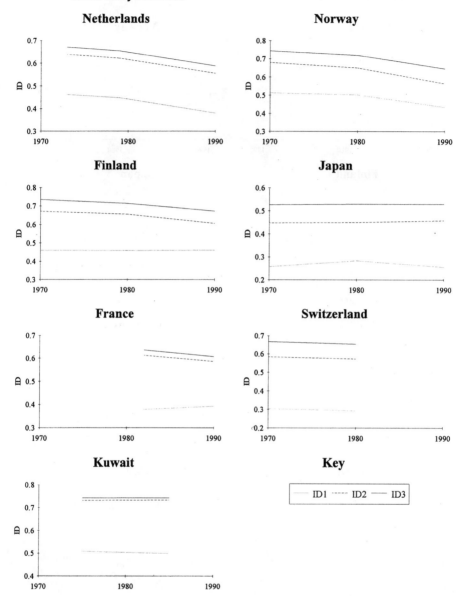

Notes: ID1, ID2 and ID3 refer to the index of dissimilarity based on 1-, 2- and 3-digit data respectively. For expositional purposes, points connected by straight lines.
Source: Study data, table 6.9. All study countries included which have data for two or more time periods and all three levels of occupational classification.

Figure 6.6.   MM values over time based on 1-, 2- and 3-digit occupational classifications for seven study countries

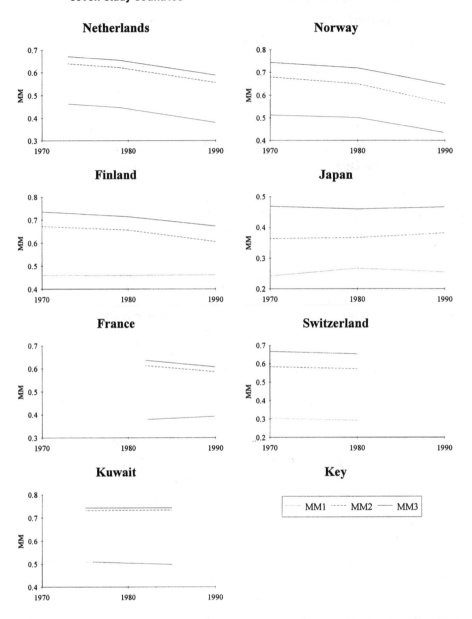

Notes: MM1, MM2 and MM3 refer to the Marginal Matching index based on 1-, 2- and 3-digit data respectively. For expositional purposes, points connected by straight lines.
Source: Study data, table 6.9. All study countries included which have data for two or more time periods and three levels of occupational classification.

GENDER AND JOBS

The conclusion is that **one-digit occupational data are often inappropriate for analysing time trends in occupational segregation by sex within countries.** Also once again, **two- and three-digit data provide similar conclusions.** One needs to keep in mind that the analysis in this section has been based largely on data from industrialized countries with reasonably high female labour force participation rates, and it is possible that patterns might differ for countries with low female labour force participation rates.

6.2 Estimating adjusted national ID values with increased comparability by taking into account the number of occupations in national classification

Given the high R^2 and F values in the regression equations in section 6.1, **it seems reasonable to use the above estimated relationships between ID and the number of occupations on which ID is based to adjust national ID values in a way so as to increase comparability among countries by taking into account differing numbers of occupations classified.** Obviously, any such adjusted national ID values would not be strictly comparable in that they would not take into consideration differences in national occupational classification schemes, coding practices and labour market conditions (see Chapter 5).

In developing a set of adjusted national ID values for study countries, we used 75 occupations as the benchmark to which we adjusted national ID values. There were several reasons for choosing 75 occupations as the benchmark. First, this is the number of non-agricultural occupations at the two-digit level in ISCO-68, the most commonly used classification scheme. Second, a majority of study countries have data at the two-digit level. Third, as demonstrated above, the sensitivity of ID to disaggregation in the occupational data is increasingly less important the further the occupational classification is disaggregated.

National adjusted ID values for the most recent year (which we call ID75) and the size of the adjustment factor applied are presented in Appendix 9.1 to Chapter 9. To calculate the adjustment factor for each country, we began with the 34 study countries which have two-digit data in either our basic data set (see Chapter 5) or in the data set used in the present chapter to analyse the sensitivity of inequality statistics to the level of disaggregation in the occupational data on which it is based (considering that up to 119 occupations is two-digit data).[13,14] For these 34 countries, we took a study country's observed ID value based on their two-digit data and added (or subtracted) an adjustment factor which was estimated using the relevant coefficient from equations 4-6 in table 6.6. In this way, adjusted values were estimated for 75 occupations (i.e. ID75) for these 34 study countries.

To illustrate this adjustment procedure, suppose countries x and z both have an ID of .550, but based on 60 occupations for country x and 90 occupations for country z. We would adjust country x's ID upwards and country z's ID downwards, with the size of the adjustment partly dependent on the country's ID based on one-digit level data (in keeping with results from equations 4–6 in table 6.6).[15] For country x, this would imply an adjustment factor (and adjusted ID) of either .023 (.573), .014 (.564) or .008 (.558), depending on whether country x's ID based on one-digit data had a relatively low (below .30), middle (between .30 and .49) or high (above .50) value. For country z, this would imply an adjustment of either −.019, −.011 or −.006, and therefore an adjusted ID of either .531, .539 or .544 depending on country z's ID based on one-digit data. These two examples illustrate three important properties of this adjustment procedure. First, adjustments are greater, *ceteris paribus*, the lower the number of occupations before adjustment (as illustrated in the above example by the greater adjustment from 60 to 75 occupations as compared to the adjustment from 90 to 75 occupations). Second, the adjustment is smaller, *ceteris paribus*, the higher is a country's ID when based on highly aggregated one-digit data. Third, the adjustment is positive for countries with occupational classifications having fewer than 75 occupations and negative for countries having more than 75 occupations.

Adjustments for the 34 countries with available two-digit data are relatively small. They are less than .013 for 22 of these 34 countries. For twelve countries, adjustment factors range from about .03 (for France, Sweden, Canada, Cyprus, Hungary, Bulgaria, Tunisia, Australia and the Republic of Korea), to about .04 (for the Islamic Republic of Iran and Japan), and to about .07 for China. The adjusted ID values (i.e. ID75) for these twelve countries are somewhat less precise than for other study countries and so are qualified by an asterisk in tables in Chapter 9 in order to indicate that they include a relatively large adjustment factor.

Seven study countries remained where the only study data available were three-digit data (i.e. more than 119 occupations: Australia, West Germany, Italy, Poland, the United Kingdom, the United States and former Yugoslavia). For these seven study countries, we looked through the published research literature for ID estimates based on two-digit data. We were able to find usable values for Australia and United Kingdom, and we used these published ID estimates for the United Kingdom and Australia after making some necessary adjustments.[16] (We were also able to find a value for the combined East and West Germany; however, we did not feel it appropriate to use these data.) For the remaining five study countries with only three-digit data, we used equation 5 in table 6.6 to estimate adjusted ID75 values in basically the same way as described above for countries with two-digit data.[17] Since this involved relatively large adjustments ranging from about 0.06 to about .11, the adjusted ID75 values for these five countries are qualified by two asterisks in tables in Chapter 9.[18,19]

Table 6.10. Comparison of ID from study data and from Rubery and Fagan (1993) for six EC countries

Country	ID (according to Rubery and Fagan 1993)	Ratio of ID without agriculture and ID with agriculture based on study data	Adjusted ID (Rubery and Fagan)[a]	Adjusted ID, i.e. ID75 (study data)
France	0.54	1.0369	0.556	0.556
Germany (West)	0.54	0.9756	0.523	0.523
Luxembourg	0.59	1.0135	0.594	0.589
Netherlands	0.57	0.9671	0.548	0.567
Spain	0.53	1.0779	0.567	0.569
United Kingdom[b]	0.57	1.0016	0.567	0.567

Notes: [a] The values of ID reported by Rubery and Fagan (1993) are adjusted in two ways: (1) reduced by 0.0039 to take into account the difference between 80 and 75 occupations as indicated by the relationship reported in table 6.6; and (2) multiplied by the ratio of ID without agricultural occupations and ID with agricultural occupations, based on our study data (column 3). [b] Values for the United Kingdom are the same, because we used values reported in Rubery and Fagan (1993) for calculating our ID75 (see footnote 16).

6.3 Study evidence on the relationship between the percentage of workers in female-dominated and male-dominated occupations to the degree of detail in the occupational classification

Previous sections in this chapter investigated the sensitivity of the index of dissimilarity (ID) to the level of detail in the occupational data being analysed. The present section provides a similar—but truncated—analysis for the percentage of the male, female and total labour forces working in "gender-dominated" occupations, which are defined as occupations where men or women comprise at least 80 per cent of the workers (see Chapter 5 for a discussion on how this definition was derived).

A priori, expectations are that the percentage of employment in a gender-dominated occupation will be much higher when based on two-digit data as compared to when based on one-digit data, since broad one-digit non-agricultural occupations are unlikely to reveal much, if any, of the extensive sex-stereotyping of occupations that is known to exist. There are no *a priori* expectations regarding whether the extensiveness of gender-dominated occupations will be very sensitive to further disaggregation from two-digit to three-digit data. While, on the one hand, three-digit data are expected to reveal greater numbers of gender-dominated occupations (e.g. nursery, primary, secondary and university teachers are separate occupations in the three-digit ISCO-68 data whereas there is only one composite teacher occupation in the two-digit ISCO-68 data; nurses and physicians are separate occupations in three-digit data whereas there is one composite occupation of medical, dental, veterinary and related workers in the two-digit data), it is uncertain how much of the sex segregation of the labour market is already revealed by two-digit data.

Table 6.11 presents results based on one-, two-, and three-digit level data on the percentage of the female, male and total employment in a gender-dominated occupation for the same 26 study countries. Table 6.12 summarizes these data by aggregating them into regional averages.

For women, results are generally consistent with *a priori* expectations. One-digit data reveal virtually no female-dominated occupations. There are no female-dominated occupations in 22 of the 26 study countries or areas represented in table 6.11 according to one-digit data. Only Finland, Haiti, Angola and Ghana have any female-dominated occupations based on one-digit non-agricultural data.[20] In the three developing countries, women are observed to dominate the major occupational group of sales, where they are mainly petty traders in the informal sector.

In contrast to the one-digit data, two- and three-digit data reveal many female-dominated occupations. On average, approximately one quarter of female workers are in a female-dominated occupation according to both two- and three-digit data (25 and 29 per cent on average respectively). A closer look at these data, however, indicate that three-digit data are in fact very important for identifying female-dominated occupations.[21] Thus, when we look at results for the 10 study countries with both two- *and* three-digit data, we find that the percentage of the female labour force in a female-dominated occupation increases from about 20 to 31 per cent on average; from about 30 to 43 per cent in the seven OECD study countries represented in table 6.11, and from about 3 to 11 per cent, in the four other study countries with such data (India, China, Japan and Kuwait).

The general conclusions based on information for female employment contained in tables 6.11 and 6.12 are: (i) one-digit data are not at all useful for investigating the extent to which there are female-dominated occupations in the labour force; (ii) two-digit data are much better for this purpose, as they reveal many female-dominated occupations; (iii) three-digit data are better still as they reveal many additional female-dominated occupations; and (iv) there is considerable variability across countries in the sensitivity of results to disaggregation of the occupational data (notice, for example, that there is an increase of only 2 per cent for Cyprus and 3 per cent for India as compared to 18 per cent for Switzerland and 19 per cent for France when going from two-digit data to three-digit data). Our data do not allow us to observe how many more female-dominated occupations would be observed by even more detailed occupational data, but we expect that more detailed data would reveal additional female dominated occupations.

Results for male-dominated occupations (shown in tables 6.11 and 6.12) are qualitatively quite different compared to those for the female-dominated occupations discussed above. For men, one-digit data reveal

Table 6.11. Percentage of male, female and total non-agricultural employment in gender-dominated occupations (using absolute concept of gender-dominance)[a] based on one-, two- and three-digit data for 26 study countries or areas with relevant data (number of occupations classified indicated in brackets in columns 1-3)

Region/country or area	Female employment[b]			Male employment[b]			Total employment[b]		
	1 digit	2 digits	3 digits	1 digit	2 digits	3 digits	1 digit	2 digits	3 digits
OECD (minus Japan)									
Cyprus	0 (6)	29 (104)	31 (376)	5	61	63	3	53	54
Finland	22 (6)	55 (64)	61 (264)	53	56	59	46	62	64
France	0 (5)	26 (119)	45 (433)	43	52	55	31	44	54
Luxembourg	0 (6)	37 (71)	n/a	52	63	n/a	36	57	n/a
Netherlands	0 (6)	30 (63)	37 (151)	45	59	61	30	51	54
Norway	0 (6)	34 (65)	48 (291)	49	51	60	31	47	59
New Zealand	0 (6)	20 (77)	46 (281)	60	58	57	41	46	58
Switzerland	0 (8)	16 (66)	34 (452)	36	62	68	25	49	58
Average (unweighted)	3 (6)	31 (79)	43 (321)	43	58	60	30	51	57
Middle East and North Africa									
Bahrain	0 (6)	0 (86)	n/a	56	81	n/a	49	70	n/a
Egypt	0 (6)	0 (74)	n/a	70	80	n/a	63	72	n/a
Jordan	0 (6)	6 (61)	n/a	85	89	n/a	80	83	n/a
Kuwait	0 (6)	0 (75)	7 (268)	51	84	87	41	70	73
Tunisia	0 (6)	44 (55)	n/a	81	84	c	78	81	c
Average (unweighted)	0 (6)	10 (70)	c	69	84	c	62	75	c
Asia/Pacific									
China	0 (6)	8 (38)	15 (277)	8	41	43	6	31	36
Fiji	0 (6)	26 (75)	n/a	55	70	n/a	44	61	n/a
India	0 (6)	0 (83)	3 (423)	91	87	86	90	83	81
Japan	0 (6)	5 (49)	17 (259)	7	52	54	5	37	42
Korea (Rep. of)	0 (6)	0 (56)	n/a	2	40	n/a	1	28	n/a
Malaysia	0 (6)	10 (76)	n/a	2	56	n/a	2	46	n/a
Average (unweighted)	0 (6)	8 (63)	12 (320)	28	58	61	25	48	53

Table 6.11. (contd.)

Region/country or area	Female employment[b]			Male employment[b]			Total employment[b]		
	1 digit	2 digits	3 digits	1 digit	2 digits	3 digits	1 digit	2 digits	3 digits
Other developing									
Angola	52 (6)	52 (67)	n/a	53	60	n/a	59	59	n/a
Costa Rica	0 (6)	46(55)	n/a	0	53	n/a	0	55	n/a
Ghana	54 (6)	77 (75)	n/a	2	60	n/a	36	76	n/a
Haiti	69 (6)	76 (75)	n/a	2	59	n/a	50	75	n/a
Mauritius	0 (6)	14 (70)	n/a	3	66	n/a	2	53	n/a
Netherlands Antilles	0 (6)	33 (76)	n/a	52	67	n/a	33	56	n/a
Senegal	0 (6)	2 (80)	n/a	57	77	n/a	50	69	n/a
Average (unweighted)	25 (6)	43 (71)	n/a	24	63	n/a	33	63	n/a

Notes: Averages are unweighted averages of country values.
[a] Gender-dominated occupations are defined as occupations where at least 80 per cent of the workers are male or female. [b] For female and male employment, it is percentage in a female-dominated or male-dominated occupation respectively. For total employment, it is the percentage in either a male-dominated or female-dominated occupation; note that, on average, about 2 per cent of male workers are in a female-dominated occupation and about 8 per cent of women workers are in a male-dominated occupation. [c] Not reported because only one country in this region (Kuwait) has three-digit data.
n/a indicates not available.
Source: Study data.

Table 6.12. Regional summaries on percentage of female, male and total non-agricultural employment in gender-dominated occupations (using absolute concept of gender-dominance)[a], based on 1-, 2- and 3-digit data for 26 study countries and areas with relevant data

Region	Female employment[b]			Male employment[b]			Total employment[b]		
	1 digit	2 digits	3 digits	1 digit	2 digits	3 digits	1 digit	2 digits	3 digits
OECD (excluding Japan)									
Average (unweighted)	3	31	43	43	58	60	30	51	57
Change in average[c] (overall)		28	12		15	2		21	6
Change in average[c] (for countries with 2 and 3 digits)		27	13		15	2		20	7
Middle East and North Africa									
Average (unweighted)	0	10	d	69	83	d	62	75	d
Change in average[c] (overall)		10	d		14	d		13	d
Asia/Pacific									
Average (unweighted)	0	8	12	27	58	61	25	48	53
Change in average[c] (overall)		8	4		31	3		23	5
Change in average[c] (for countries with 2 and 3 digits)		4	8		25	1		16	3
Other developing									
Average (unweighted)	25	43	n/a	24	63	n/a	33	63	n/a
Change in average[c] (overall)		18	n/a		39	n/a		30	n/a
Change in average[c] (for countries with 2 and 3 digits)		n/a	n/a		n/a	n/a		n/a	n/a
All 26 countries and areas									
Average (unweighted)	8	25	31	39	64	63	36	58	58
Change in average (overall)		17	6		25	–1		22	0
Change in average (comparable countries with 2 and 3 digits)		19	12		18	3		19	6

Notes: Averages are unweighted averages of country values.
[a] Gender-dominated occupations are defined as occupations where at least 80 per cent of the workers are male or female. [b] For female and male employment, it is percentage in a female-dominated or male-dominated occupation respectively. For total employment, it is the percentage in either a male-dominated or female-dominated occupation; note that, on average, about two per cent of male workers are in a female-dominated occupation and about eight per cent of women workers are in a male-dominated occupation. [c] Change in average is difference between average for 1- and 2-digit data (reported under 2-digit column) or 2- and 3-digit data (reported under 3-digit column). [d] Not reported because only one country in this region (Kuwait) has three-digit data.
n/a indicates not available.
Source: Table 6.11.

many male-dominated occupations. Approximately 40 per cent of male workers are observed to be in a male-dominated occupation based on one-digit data in our 26 study countries and areas, with regional averages ranging from 25 to 70 per cent. These large national and regional differences for males are partly due to the fact that males make up a large percentage of the labour force in some countries (an especially important factor in the Middle East and North Africa) and partly due to male dominance of some major one-digit occupational groups such as in the quantitatively important production occupation (an especially important factor in OECD countries).

Two-digit data reveal many more male-dominated occupations as compared to one-digit data. On average, the percentage of male employment in a male-dominated occupation rises from about 40 to 65 per cent when the occupational data are disaggregated from a one- to a two-digit classification.

Three-digit data reveal very little additional in terms of male employment in male-dominated occupations as compared to two-digit data. For the 10 study countries in table 6.11 with two- and three-digit data, this increase is only about 3 per cent on average.[22]

Results for total employment are a weighted average of those for female and male employment. Consequently, a considerable degree of gender-dominance in total employment (around 36 per cent of total employment on average) is observed based on one-digit data due to the identification of important male-dominated major occupations. Two-digit data reveal considerable additional employment in gender-dominated occupations due to the identification of both additional male-dominated *and* female-dominated occupations. Three-digit data, on the other hand, reveal relatively little additional gender-dominated employment as compared to two-digit data (an additional 6 per cent on average for the 10 study countries with relevant data); this result is due to the relative insensitivity here for male employment (which waters down the important effect observed for female employment).

It is also possible to use the rank ordering of countries and areas to observe how consistent national data are based on one-, two- and three-digit data. Country rank orders based on two- and three-digit data (based on data in table 6.13) are generally—but not always—similar. Country rank orders are, however, frequently quite different when based on one- and two-digit data. Once again, at least two-digit data seem to be required to analyse the relative importance of gender-dominated occupations across countries (just as they are for analysing inequality indices as indicated in previous sections).

In conclusion, and as expected, **one-digit data are not sufficiently detailed for studying gender-dominance of occupations, especially for women workers. Two-digit data appear to be sufficiently detailed for analysing the extent to which men are in a male-dominated occupation, but insufficiently detailed for observing the extent to which women are in a female-dominated occupation.**

Table 6.13. Rank order of countries and areas based on the percentage of female, male and total non-agricultural employment in gender-dominated occupations (using absolute concept of gender-dominance)[a], based on 1-, 2- and 3-digit data for 26 study countries and areas with relevant data[b]

Country/area	Total employment				Female employment				Male employment			
	1 digit	2 digit	Comparable 2 digit	Comparable 3 digit	1 digit[c]	2 digit	Comparable 2 digit	Comparable 3 digit	1 digit	2 digit	Comparable 2 digit	Comparable 3 digit
Costa Rica	1	12							1	6		
Korea (Rep. of)	2	1							3	1		
Malaysia	3	5							4	8		
Mauritius	4	11							6	17		
Cyprus	5	10	8	3			8	5	7	14	8	8
Japan	6	3	2	2			3	4	8	4	3	2
China	7	2	1	1			4	3	9	2	1	1
Switzerland	8	8	6	7			5	6	10	15	9	9
Netherlands	9	9	7	5			9	7	12	11	7	7
Norway	10	7	5	8			10	10	13	3	2	6
France	11	4	3	4			7	8	11	5	4	3
Netherlands Antilles	12	13							15	18		
Ghana	13	23			25	26			2	12		
Luxembourg	14	14							16	16		
New Zealand	15	6	4	6			6	9	22	9	6	4
Kuwait	16	19	10	10			2	2	14	24	10	11
Fiji	17	16							19	19		
Finland	18	17	9	9	23	24	11	11	17	7	5	5
Bahrain	19	20							20	22		
Haiti	20	22			26	25			5	10		
Senegal	21	18							21	20		
Angola	22	15			24	23			18	13		

Table 6.13. (contd.)

Country	Total employment		Comparable		Female employment		Comparable		Male employment		Comparable	
	1 digit	2 digit	2 digit	3 digit	1 digit[c]	2 digit	2 digit	3 digit	1 digit	2 digit	2 digit	3 digit
Egypt	23	21							23	21		
Tunisia	24	24							24	23		
Jordan	25	26							25	26		
India	26	25	11	11			2	1	26	25	11	10

Notes: [a] Gender-dominated occupations are defined as occupations where at least 80 per cent of workers are either male or female. Percentages for female and male employment refer only to persons from that sex (i.e. men in male-dominated occupations and women in female-dominated occupations). [b] Values are shaded when rank order differs by six or more when comparing one- and two-digit based rank orders and by four or more when comparing two- and three-digit based rank orders. These represent, in our opinion, reasonably clear differences resulting from aggregation of the occupational data. [c] All but four countries have zero per cent of female employment in female-dominated occupations based on one-digit data.
Source: Table 6.11.

6.3.1 Estimating adjusted national values with increased comparability by taking into account the number of occupations in national classification

Since the extent to which employment (especially female employment) is observed to be segregated into gender-dominated occupations is affected by the level of disaggregation in the available occupational data on which it is based, the subsequent cross-national analysis of gender-dominated occupations in Part III would be subject to a substantial degree of non-comparability across countries unless observed national values are adjusted to take into account differences in the numbers of occupations classified (ranging from 21 in the Islamic Republic of Iran to 509 in the United Kingdom).

The adjustment procedure used here is simpler than the one described in the previous section for ID, in that the procedure here is based on interpolation rather than regression results. Similar, however, to the procedure used for calculating our adjusted ID values is that: (i) national values are adjusted to 75 occupations and consequently, the adjustment factor is positive when the number of occupations classified in a country's data is fewer than 75 and negative when the number of occupations classified is greater than 75; (ii) the adjustment factor is greater the further away from 75 occupations is the number of occupations in the national data. Also as for ID, the adjustment procedure here is far from exact and particular national estimates must be treated cautiously, especially those with a large adjustment factor; for this reason, adjusted national values with relatively large adjustments are identified with an asterisk in tables in Chapter 10. Different from the adjustment procedure used for ID, the size of the adjustment here is dependent on the observed rate of change in the percentage of female (male or total) employment between two levels of aggregation based on national occupational data when they exist, and based on the observed regional rate of change (as shown in table 6.12) when they do not exist.

The procedure used to make these adjustments is described below. (Readers are referred to tables in Appendix 10.1 to Chapter 10 which provide the adjustments factors, along with unadjusted and adjusted national values). First, for each study country, available national values based on different levels of aggregation in the national data were listed (based on our original data, the "mapped" data for increased comparability over time, see table 7.2, and the sensitivity data used in the present section). Second, a rate of change between values for these different aggregation levels was estimated for each country. For example, if national values were available based on 6, 38 and 277 occupations (as for China), we used the national values for 38 and 277 occupations as these bracketed 75; if two values were available which did not bracket 75 occupations, as for Luxembourg, Egypt, Tunisia, Angola, Costa Rica and Mauritius, the observed national rate of change for the available range was used; if only one national value was available, as for Italy, the average rate of change observed for the region was used; if data for different aggregation levels are not available (as for the United Kingdom and the United States), the average rate of change for other countries in the region was used. The rate of change was calculated assuming that the pattern is logarithmic in nature (as this is the pattern observed for ID, and it fits the present data reasonably well and much better than a linear relationship). This means that the assumed rate of change decreases along with increases in the number of occupations classified. Third, the size of the national adjustment factor was calculated by multiplying the relevant rate of change described in step 2 above by the difference in the number of occupations classified (expressed in log units). For example, for China, the ln rate of change in the total labour force in a gender-dominated occupation for each ln unit change in the number of occupations was calculated as 2.67; and since the number of ln units between 38 and 75 occupations is 0.68 ln units, this implied an adjustment factor of 1.82 percentage points for China for the total labour force in a gender-dominated occupation. Lastly, adjusted national values were then calculated by adding the estimated adjustment factor to the observed national value from the national classification closest to 75 occupations.

Most adjustment factors are small, especially for the male-dominated non-agricultural labour force. The adjustment factor is greater than 5 percentage points for only 2, 11 and 12 of our 41 study countries and areas for the male, female and total labour forces respectively (and greater than 10 percentage points for only 0, 6 and 0 countries respectively). In order to assist readers, adjusted national values where the adjustment factor is relatively large (arbitrarily defined as greater than 5 percentage points) are qualified by an asterisk in the relevant tables in Chapter 10.

Notes

[1] For reasons of parsimony, discussion and analysis in this section concerning inequality indices are presented only for ID. Similar conclusions are found for MM as well.

[2] In ISCO-68, inclusion of agricultural occupations increases the number of occupations from 6 to 7, 75 to 80 and 265 to 281 for one-, two- and three-digit level classification respectively.

[3] A similar conclusion was reached regarding time trends in ID in a recent cross-national analysis of occupational segregation by sex for eight countries using occupational data at two levels of aggregation (Jacobs and Lim, 1992). Unfortunately, there was little difference in this study in the number of occupations classified in these one- and two-digit level data (generally only 7 and 19 occupations respectively, although they also present ID estimates based on 7 and 80 occupations for New Zealand and 7 and 483 occupations for the United States).

[4] All four transition economy study countries were excluded in this analysis, because they used a different conceptual approach in their occupational classification.

[5] This data set includes all study countries or areas with roughly comparable occupational classification schemes, and so data which could be reasonably easily aggregated to one- or two-digit levels of aggregation; thus, we included countries which used either ISCO-68 (because these data were easy to aggregate), or an occupational classification system that was roughly similar to ISCO-68 and/or was not overly difficult to aggregate from the three-digit to the two-digit level, or from two-digit to one-digit level. We also made a special effort

to include three large Asian countries (China, India and Japan) because of their importance, despite their quite different classification schemes.

[6] While 22 of the 26 study countries and areas included in this analysis have between 55 and 86 occupations for their two-digit data, we also considered China and Japan (with 38 and 49 occupations respectively) as well as Cyprus and France (with 104 and 119 occupations respectively) as having two-digit data, since these were the number of occupations in the second level of aggregation for these countries. Inclusion of these four data points has the added advantage of providing intermediate values between the usual number of occupations at the two-digit level (i.e. 75); this is useful in estimating relationships between inequality statistics and the number of occupations in the coding classification.

[7] Results for ID discussed in the text are similar to those when MM is used. Results for MM are not presented here for reasons of parsimony.

[8] It is not possible to draw strong conclusions on differences between developing and OECD countries regarding disaggregation from the two- to the three-digit level based data provided in table 6.3, as three-digit data are available only for three greatly differing non-Western and non-OECD countries: China, India and Kuwait (as well as Japan which we have included in our Asian region).

[9] Inclusion in the regression equations of country binaries means, in essence, that the estimated equations reported in tables 6.4 to 6.6 are an average of many separate country curves.

[10] Equations 2 and 4 have similar F statistics and adjusted R squares. However, the estimated relationship in equation 4 in table 6.5 has a conceptual problem. It indicates incorrectly that ID falls at first as the number of occupations increases up to about 11 occupations—a theoretical impossibility. For this reason, equation 2 is felt to provide the best fit.

[11] Correlation coefficients are also significant at the .01 level for comparisons of actual ID values (rather than for rank orders as in the text) based on data at different levels of aggregation. Again, correlation coefficients are much higher for comparisons of two and three-digit data (0.95) as compared to comparisons of one- and two-digit data (0.69).

[12] It is interesting to note that unreported correlation analysis also indicates that one-digit data tend to provide a much better representation of the *relative* pattern of occupational segregation by sex in OECD countries as compared to non-OECD countries, especially non-Asian developing countries.

[13] Thus, Cyprus, Hungary and France are included as countries having two-digit data even through technically speaking they do not, as they have 103, 118 and 119 occupations respectively. We felt that these were close enough to 99 occupations to be considered as two-digit data. In this regard, note that the absolute differences between natural log values of 75 and natural log values of 103, 118 and 119 are the same as that between 75 as compared to 55, 48 and 47 respectively.

[14] Note that while for seven countries the number of occupations is closer to 75 in the mapped data set (see table 5.2) than in either the basic data set or the sensitivity analysis data set, differences in number of occupations between these two data sets are almost always small (Austria 72 versus 64; Bulgaria 45 versus 43; Costa Rica 56 versus 55; Luxembourg 74 versus 71; Jordan 75 versus 61; New Zealand 75 versus 77). For this reason, we ignored the mapped data in order to simplify calculations and the discussions. The only exception in this regard was West Germany; yet its estimated ID75 is remarkably similar whether derived from its data based on 150 or 268 occupations.

[15] It is not too difficult to calculate ID values based on one-digit data for study countries. One-digit data are available for 26 countries and areas included in the data set used in the sensitivity analysis in the present chapter. Another 9 have one-digit data reported in table 8.2 in Chapter 8. For the remaining 6 study countries or areas, it is possible to estimate the likely range of their ID value based on 6 occupations using coefficients from equations 4, 5 and 6 in table 6.6; in all cases, these estimates fall for each of these six study countries or areas within either the low (<.30), medium (.30 −.49) or high (>.50) ID category. For two OECD countries (Italy and Switzerland), whose ID based on one-digit data are just below .30 (.28 and .29 respectively), however, the medium (.30 −.49) equation coefficient is used, as this

seemed more in keeping for countries in the OECD region; this decision has a substantial effect on Italy's adjusted ID value which none the less remains relatively low for the OECD region.

[16] For the United Kingdom, Rubery and Fagan (1993) report an ID of .57 for 1990 based on 80 occupations, including agricultural occupations. We adjusted this figure downwards by .0039 to take into account the likely difference in ID between 80 and 75 occupations (based on equation 5 in table 6.6). This adjusted figure (.5661) was then multiplied by 1.0016 (which, based on our study data, is the ratio between the ID when agricultural occupations are and are not included in calculating ID) to arrive at our adjusted ID value for United Kingdom. This adjusted ID for United Kingdom (.5670), as it turns out, is similar to the value (.5534) which would have been calculated for the country using the procedure described in the text, based on our estimated relationship between ID and number of occupations classified.

For Australia, Lewis (1985) reports ID values for 1981 of .5887 based on 71 occupations and .6320 based on 292 occupations. We use this ratio of .5887 to .6230 to adjust our ID value for 1990 (which is based on 279 non-agricultural occupations) on the assumption that this ratio is the same whether or not agricultural occupations are included. In this regard, note that according to our study data Australia's ID is hardly affected by inclusion of agricultural occupations as it is 0.6110 with, and 0.6148 without, agricultural occupations in 1990. (Also note that the difference between natural log values for 71 and 279 occupations is virtually the same as the difference between ln values for 75 and 292: 1.368 and 1.359 respectively.)

[17] The only difference here is that the possible effect on ID of increases in the number of occupations above 300 was ignored. This assumption is made for the following reasons. First, very few data points with more than 300 occupations were used to estimate the regression results reported in table 6.6. Second, evidence from Australia (Lewis, 1985) indicates a very low sensitivity of ID to increases in the number of occupations above 300 (ID of .6230, .6201 and .6240 for 292, 355 and 382 occupations respectively). For these reasons, we felt that the predicted effects on ID from our estimated regression equations due to increases in the number of occupations above 300 are likely to be unrealistically large (e.g. predicting an increase in ID for an OECD country of .034 for an increase in number of occupations from 300 to 500). This assumption only affects estimates for Poland and the United States (which, as a result, are higher by about .011 and .026 respectively because of this assumption than if this assumption had not been made). After completing the draft of this book, ID values for the United States based on 7 and 483 occupations (i.e. including agricultural occupations) in a paper by Jacobs and Lim (1992) were noted: .414 and .676 for 1970 and .349 and .598 for 1980. These values imply that ID increased by .062 in 1970 and .059 in 1980 along with each natural log unit increase in the number of occupations classified. Note that this relationship is very similar to the .061 used to estimate ID75 for the United States. These data, thus, add some degree of confidence to the ID75 estimate for the United States used in this book (although as we assumed no effect of disaggregation in the occupational classification above 300 occupations, our ID75 for the United States is probably a bit overestimated, by approximately .02 and .03).

[18] It is possible to compare some of our adjusted ID (i.e. ID75) values to those reported in Rubery and Fagan (1993) for European Communities countries for 1990 (which are based on comparable data that use the same occupational classification for 80 occupations). In this way, it is possible to observe how well our adjustment procedure has done for these countries, since we would expect our ID75 to be similar to the ID reported in Rubery and Fagan (1993). Before making this comparison, we adjusted the Rubery and Fagan ID estimates to take into account that they (i) are for 80 occupations whereas our adjusted ID estimates are for 75 occupations and (ii) include agricultural occupations whereas our estimates exclude agricultural occupations. We took the first point into account by using the relationship between ID and number of occupations from equation 5 in table 6.6. The second point was taken into account by applying the ratio between ID values based on data which exclude or include agricultural occupations. Table 6.10 (see above) provides these comparisons. For all six EC countries, our adjusted ID values (i.e. ID75) are quite similar to those reported in Rubery and Fagan (1993).

[19] It should be noted that our adjusted ID value for West Germany (.523) is quite similar to the value of .528 which would have been estimated if we had utilized our mapped data set for 150 occupations as the basis for our adjustment rather than 268 occupations as we have done.

[20] In Finland, women dominate the one-digit clerical occupational group. It is also worth noting that several OECD countries very nearly have a female-dominated occupation based on one-digit non-agricultural data. For example, between 70.0 and 79.9 per cent of clerical workers are female in six of our 17 OECD study countries (Australia, Canada, Finland, New Zealand, Norway and the United States). Furthermore, women comprise between 70.0 to 79.9 per cent of service workers in five of our OECD study countries (Austria, Finland, Luxembourg, Netherlands and Norway).

[21] The similarity in the overall average for two- and three- digit data is due in large part to the different composition of study countries having three-digit data as compared to the full set of study countries and areas.

[22] These results do not necessarily imply that very few additional male-dominated occupations are revealed by three-digit data as compared to two-digit data, since it is possible for there to be counterbalancing effects, because gender-dominated occupations can disappear as well as appear along with increasing disaggregation of occupational data. To illustrate this possibility, suppose that production workers are 85 per cent male. This would make all production occupations male-dominated based on one-digit data. Therefore, *all* male workers in this major occupational group would be counted as being in a male-dominated occupation. When this major group is disaggregated into two-digit data, one or more production occupations may be found to have less than 80 per cent male; this would cause the total number of male workers in male-dominated production occupations to decrease. Indeed, there are three country examples in table 6.11 where this percentage is lower based on three-digit data as compared to two-digit data (and two examples based on two-digit data as compared to one-digit data). Some of these counterbalancing effects undoubtedly help explain part of the insensitivity for the percentage of the male labour force in male-dominated occupations based on two-digit data as compared to three-digit data.

Appendix 6.1. International standard classification of occupations (ISCO-68)

MAJOR, MINOR AND UNIT GROUPS

Major Group 1   **Professional, Technical and Related Workers**

0-1   *Physical Scientists and Related Workers*

0-11	Chemists
0-12	Physicists
0-13	Physical scientists not elsewhere classified
0-14	Physical science technicians

0-2/0-3   *Architects, Engineers and Related Technicians*

0-21	Architects and town planners
0-22	Civil engineers
0-23	Electrical and electronics engineers
0-24	Mechanical engineers
0-25	Chemical engineers
0-26	Metallurgists
0-27	Mining engineers
0-28	Industrial engineers
0-29	Engineers not elsewhere classified
0-31	Surveyors
0-32	Draughtsmen
0-33	Civil engineering technicians
0-34	Electrical and electronics engineers
0-35	Mechanical engineering technicians
0-36	Chemical engineering technicians
0-37	Metallurgical technicians
0-38	Mining technicians
0-39	Engineering technicians not elsewhere classified

0-4   *Aircraft and Ships' Officers*

0-41	Aircraft pilots, navigators and flight engineers
0-42	Ships' desk officers and pilots
0-43	Ships' engineers

0-5   *Life Scientists and Related Technicians*

0-51	Biologists, zoologists and related scientists
0-52	Bacteriologists, pharmacologists and related scientists
0-53	Agronomists and related scientists
0-54	Life sciences technicians

0-6/0-7   *Medical, Dental, Veterinary and Related Workers*

0-61	Medical doctors
0-62	Medical assistants
0-63	Dentists
0-64	Dental Assistants
0-65	Veterinarians
0-66	Veterinary assistants
0-67	Pharmacists
0-68	Pharmaceutical assistants
0-69	Dietitians and public health nutritionists
0-71	Professional nurses
0-72	Nursing professionals not elsewhere classified
0-73	Professional midwives
0-74	Midwifery personnel not elsewhere classified
0-75	Optometrists and opticians

Major Group 1   **Professional, Technical and Related Workers (contd.)**

0-6/0-7   *Medical, Dental, Veterinary and Related Workers (contd.)*

0-76   Physiotherapists and occupational therapists
0-77   Medical X-ray technicians
0-79   Medical, dental, veterinary and related workers not elsewhere classified

0-8   *Statisticians, Mathematicians, Systems Analysts and Related Technicians*

0-81   Statisticians
0-82   Mathematicians and actuaries
0-83   Systems analysts
0-84   Statistical and mathematical technicians

0-9   *Economists*

1-1   *Accountants*

1-2   *Jurists*

1-21   Lawyers
1-22   Judges
1-33   Jurists not elsewhere classified

1-3   *Teachers*

1-31   University and higher education teachers
1-32   Secondary education teachers
1-33   Primary education teachers
1-34   Pre-primary education teachers
1-35   Special education teachers
1-39   Teachers not elsewhere classified

1-4   *Workers in Religion*

1-41   Ministers of religion and related members of religious orders
1-49   Workers in religion not elsewhere classified

1-5   *Authors, Journalists and Related Writers*

1-51   Authors and critics
1-59   Authors, journalists and related writers not elsewhere classified

1-6   *Sculptors, Painters, Photographers and Related Creative Artists*

1-61   Sculptors, painters and related artists
1-62   Commercial artists and designers
1-63   Photographers and cameramen

1-7   *Composers and Performing Artists*

1-71   Composers, musicians and singers
1-72   Choreographers and dancers
1-73   Actors and stage directors
1-74   Producers, performing arts
1-75   Circus performers
1-79   Performing artists not elsewhere classified

1-8   *Athletes, Sportsmen and Related Workers*

1-9   *Professional, Technical and Related Workers Not Elsewhere Classified*

1-91   Librarians, archivists and curators
1-92   Sociologists, anthropologists and related scientists
1-93   Social workers
1-94   Personnel and occupational specialists
1-95   Philologists, translators and interpreters
1-99   Other professional, technical and related workers

Major Group 2 **Administrative and Managerial Workers**

2-0 *Legislative Officials and Government Administrators*

2-01 Legislative officials
2-02 Government administrators

2-1 *Managers*

2-11 General managers
2-12 Production managers (except farm)
2-19 Managers not elsewhere classified

Major Group 3 **Clerical and Related Workers**

3-0 *Clerical Supervisors*

3-1 *Government Executive Officials*

3-2 *Stenographers, Typists and Card- and Tape-Punching Machine Operators*

3-21 Stenographers, typists and teletypists
3-22 Card- and tape-punching machine operators

3-3 *Bookkeepers, Cashiers and Related Workers*

3-31 Bookkeepers and cashiers
3-39 Bookkeepers, cashiers and related workers not elsewhere classified

3-4 *Computing Machine Operators*

3-41 Bookkeeping and calculating machine operators
3-42 Automatic data-processing machine operators

3-5 *Transport and Communication Supervisors*

3-51 Railway station masters
3-52 Postmasters
3-59 Transport and communication supervisors not elsewhere classified

3-6 *Transport Conductors*

3-7 *Mail Distribution Clerks*

3-8 *Telephone and Telegraph Operators*

3-9 *Clerical and Related Workers Not Elsewhere Classified*

3-91 Stock clerks
3-92 Material and production planning clerks
3-93 Correspondence and reporting clerks
3-94 Receptionists and travel agency clerks
3-95 Library and filing clerks
3-99 Clerks not elsewhere classified

Major Group 4 **Sales Workers**

4-0 *Managers (Wholesale and Retail Trade)*

4-1 *Working Proprietors*

4-2 *Sales Supervisors and Buyers*

4-21 Sales supervisors
4-22 Buyers

4-3 *Technical Salesmen, Commercial Travellers and Manufacturers' Agents*

4-31 Technical salesmen and service advisors
4-32 Commercial travellers and manufacturers' agents

4-4 *Insurance, Real Estate, Securities and Business Services Salesmen and Auctioneers*

4-41 Insurance, real estate and securities salesmen
4-42 Business services salesmen
4-43 Auctioneers

Major Group 4		Sales Workers (contd.)
4-5		*Salesmen, Shop Assistants and Related Workers*
	4-51	Salesmen, shop assistants and demonstrators
	4-52	Street vendors, canvassers and news vendors
4-9		*Sales Workers Not Elsewhere Classified*

Major Group 5		**Service Workers**
5-0		*Managers (Catering and Lodging Services)*
5-1		*Working Proprietors (Catering and Lodging Services)*
5-2		*Housekeeping and Related Service Supervisors*
5-3		*Cooks, Waiters, Bartenders and Related Workers*
	5-31	Cooks
	5-32	Waiters, bartenders and related workers
5-4		*Maids and Related Housekeeping Service Workers Not Elsewhere Classified*
5-5		*Building Caretakers, Charworkers, Cleaners and Related Workers*
	5-51	Building caretakers
	5-52	Charworkers, cleaners and related workers
5-6		*Launderers, Dry-cleaners and Pressers*
5-7		*Hairdressers, Barbers, Beauticians and Related Workers*
5-8		*Protective Service Workers*
	5-81	Fire-fighters
	5-82	Policemen and detectives
	5-83	Protective service workers not elsewhere classified
5-9		*Service Workers Not Elsewhere Classified*
	5-91	Guides
	5-92	Undertakers and embalmers
	5-93	Other service workers

Major Group 6		**Agricultural, Animal Husbandry and Forestry Workers, Fishermen and Hunters**
6-0		*Farm Managers and Supervisors*
6-1		*Farmers*
	6-11	General farmers
	6-12	Specialized farmers
6-2		*Agricultural and Animal Husbandry Workers*
	6-21	General farm workers
	6-22	Field crop and vegetable farm workers
	6-23	Orchard, vineyard and related tree and shrub crop workers
	6-24	Livestock workers
	6-25	Dairy farm workers
	6-26	Poultry farm workers
	6-27	Nursery workers and gardeners
	6-28	Agricultural and animal husbandry workers not elsewhere classified
6-3		*Forestry Workers*
	6-31	Loggers
	6-32	Forestry workers (except logging)
6-4		*Fishermen, Hunters and Related Workers*
	6-41	Fishermen
	6-42	Fishermen, hunters and related workers not elsewhere classified

Major Group 7/8/9   **Production and Related Workers, Transport Equipment Operators and Labourers**

7-0   *Production Supervisors and General Foremen*

7-1   *Miners, Quarrymen, Well Drillers and Related Workers*

        7-11   Miners and quarrymen
        7-12   Mineral and stone treaters
        7-13   Well drillers, borers and related workers

7-2   *Metal Processors*

        7-21   Metal smelting, converting and refining furnacemen
        7-22   Metal rolling-mill workers
        7-23   Metal melters and reheaters
        7-24   Metal casters
        7-25   Metal moulders and coremakers
        7-26   Metal annealers, temperers and case-hardeners
        7-27   Metal drawers and extruders
        7-28   Metal platers and coaters
        7-29   Metal processors not elsewhere classified

7-3   *Wood Preparation Workers and Paper Makers*

        7-31   Wood treaters
        7-32   Sawyers, plywood makers and related wood-processing workers
        7-33   Paper pulp makers
        7-34   Paper makers

7-4   *Chemical Processors and Related Workers*

        7-41   Crushers, grinders and mixers
        7-42   Cookers, roasters and related heat-treaters
        7-43   Filter and separator operators
        7-44   Still and reactor operators
        7-45   Petroleum-refining workers
        7-49   Chemical processors and related workers not elsewhere classified

7-5   *Spinners, Weavers, Knitters, Dyers and Related Workers*

        7-51   Fibre preparers
        7-52   Spinners and winders
        7-53   Weaving- and knitting-machine setters and pattern-card preparers
        7-54   Weavers and related workers
        7-55   Knitters
        7-56   Bleachers, dyers and textile product finishers
        7-59   Spinners, weavers, knitters, dyers and related workers not elsewhere classified

7-6   *Tanners, Fellmongers and Pelt Dressers*

        7-61   Tanners and fellmongers
        7-62   Pelt dressers

7-7   *Food and Beverage Processors*

        7-71   Grain millers and related workers
        7-72   Sugar processors and refiners
        7-73   Butchers and meat preparers
        7-74   Food preservers
        7-75   Dairy product processors
        7-76   Bakers, pastry cooks and confectionery makers
        7-77   Tea, coffee and cocoa preparers
        7-78   Brewers, wine and beverage makers
        7-79   Food and beverage processors not elsewhere classified

Major Group 7/8/9   Production and Related Workers, Transport Equipment Operators and Labourers (contd.)

7-8   *Tobacco Preparers and Tobacco Product Makers*

      7-81   Tobacco preparers
      7-82   Cigar makers
      7-83   Cigarette makers
      7-89   Tobacco preparers and tobacco product makers not elsewhere classified

7-9   *Tailors, Dressmakers, Sewers, Upholsterers and Related Workers*

      7-91   Tailors and dressmakers
      7-92   Fur tailors and related workers
      7-93   Milliners and hatmakers
      7-94   Pattern makers and cutters
      7-95   Sewers and embroiderers
      7-96   Upholsterers and related workers
      7-99   Tailors, dressmakers, sewers, upholsterers and related workers not elsewhere classified

8-0   *Shoemakers and Leather Goods Makers*

      8-01   Shoemakers and shoe repairers
      8-02   Shoe cutters, lasters, sewers and related workers
      8-03   Leather goods makers

8-1   *Cabinetmakers and Related Woodworkers*

      8-11   Cabinetmakers
      8-12   Woodworking-machine operators
      8-13   Cabinetmakers and related woodworkers not elsewhere classified

8-2   *Stone Cutters and Carvers*

8-3   *Blacksmiths, Toolmakers and Machine-Tool Operators*

      8-31   Blacksmiths, hammersmiths and forging-press operators
      8-32   Toolmakers, metal patternmakers and metal markers
      8-33   Machine-tool setter-operators
      8-34   Machine-tool operators
      8-35   Metal grinders, polishers and tool sharpeners
      8-39   Blacksmiths, toolmakers and machine-tool operators not elsewhere classified

8-4   *Machinery Fitters, Machine Assemblers and Precision Instrument Makers (except Electrical)*

      8-41   Machinery fitters and machine assemblers
      8-42   Watch, clock and precision instrument makers
      8-43   Motor vehicle mechanics
      8-44   Aircraft engine mechanics
      8-49   Machinery fitters, machine assemblers and precision instrument makers (except electrical) not elsewhere classified

8-5   *Electrical Fitters and Related Electrical and Electronics Workers*

      8-51   Electrical fitters
      8-52   Electronics fitters
      8-53   Electrical and electronic equipment assemblers
      8-54   Radio and television repairmen
      8-55   Electrical wiremen
      8-56   Telephone and telegraph installers
      8-57   Electric linemen and cable jointers
      8-58   Electrical fitters and related electrical and electronics workers not elsewhere classified

8-6   *Broadcasting Station and Sound Equipment Operators and Cinema Projectionists*

      8-61   Broadcasting station operators
      8-62   Sound equipment operators and cinema projectionists

Major Group 7/8/9 Production and Related Workers, Transport Equipment Operators and Labourers (contd.)

8-7   *Plumbers, Welders, Sheet Metal and Structural Metal Preparers and Erectors*

     8-71   Plumbers and pipe-fitters
     8-72   Welders and flame-cutters
     8-73   Sheet-metal workers
     8-74   Structural metal preparers and erectors

8-8   *Jewellery and Precious Metal Workers*

8-9   *Glass Formers, Potters and Related Workers*

     8-91   Glass formers, cutters, grinders and finishers
     8-92   Potters and related clay and abrasive formers
     8-93   Glass and ceramic kilnmen
     8-94   Glass engravers and etchers
     8-95   Glass and ceramic painters and decorators
     8-99   Glass formers, potters and related workers not elsewhere classified

9-0   *Rubber and Plastic Product Makers*

     9-01   Rubber and plastic product makers (except tyre makers and tyre vulcanizers)
     9-02   Tyre makers and vulcanizers

9-1   *Paper and Paperboard Products Makers*

9-2   *Printers and Related Workers*

     9-21   Compositors and typesetters
     9-22   Printing pressmen
     9-23   Stereotypers and electrotypers
     9-24   Printing engravers (except photo-engravers)
     9-25   Photo-engravers

9-3   *Painters*

     9-31   Painters, construction
     9-39   Painters not elsewhere classified

9-4   *Production and Related Workers Not Elsewhere Classified*

     9-41   Musical instrument makers and tuners
     9-42   Basketry weavers and brush makers
     9-43   Non-metallic mineral product makers
     9-44   Other production and related workers

9-5   *Bricklayers, Carpenters and other Construction Workers*
     9-51   Bricklayers, stonemasons and tile setters
     9-52   Reinforced-concreters, cement finishers and terrazzo workers
     9-53   Roofers
     9-54   Carpenters, joiners and parquetry workers
     9-55   Plasterers
     9-56   Insulators
     9-57   Glaziers
     9-59   Construction workers not elsewhere classified

9-6   *Stationary Engine and Related Equipment Operators*

     9-61   Power generating machinery operators
     9-69   Stationary engine and related equipment operators not elsewhere classified

9-7   *Material-Handling and Related Equipment Operators, Dockers and Freight Handlers*

     9-71   Dockers and freight handlers
     9-72   Riggers and cable splicers
     9-73   Crane and hoist operators
     9-74   Earth-moving and related machinery operators
     9-79   Material-handling equipment operators not elsewhere classified

Major Group 7/8/9   **Production and Related Workers, Transport Equipment Operators and Labourers (contd.)**

9-8   *Transport Equipment Operators*

     9-81   Ships' deck ratings, barge crews and boatmen
     9-82   Ships' engine-room ratings
     9-83   Railway engine drivers and firemen
     9-84   Railway brakemen, signalmen and shunters
     9-85   Motor vehicle drivers
     9-86   Animal and animal-drawn vehicle drivers
     9-89   Transport equipment operators not elsewhere classified

9-9   *Labourers Not Elsewhere Classified*

Major Group 10   **Workers Not Classifiable by Occupation**

X-1   *New Workers Seeking Employment*

X-2   *Workers Reporting Occupations Unidentifiable or Inadequately Described*

X-3   *Workers Not Reporting Any Occupation*

Armed Forces: Members of the Armed Forces

Source: ILO, *International Standard Classification of Occupations*, ISCO-68, Geneva, 1968.

DESCRIPTION OF STUDY REGIONS

7

For most of the empirical analysis in this book, the 41 study countries and areas are divided into geographic/economic groupings (see figure 5.1 and table 5.1 for a listing and graphical indication of study countries). Our *a priori* feeling was that socio-economic, cultural, historical and policy/legal factors which vary by region are important determinants of occupational segregation by sex (see Chapter 2). This turned out to be a good decision, since analyses below in Parts III and IV indicate that occupational segregation by sex tends to be similar for countries within each region, yet differ greatly across regions.

As indicated below, study countries and areas are divided into the following five, basically regional, groupings for the empirical analysis in Parts III and IV:

1. OECD countries
2. Transition Economies in Central and Eastern Europe
3. North Africa and the Middle East
4. Asia (and Pacific)
5. Other Developing Countries and Areas

The largest number of study countries is in the OECD region (17), while the smallest is in the Transition Economy region (4), with 6 or 7 study countries or areas in each of the other three groupings. Readers need to keep in mind when interpreting the empirical results reported in Parts III and IV that non-OECD regional averages are less representative of their region than averages for the OECD region. For example, study economies from the Asian (and Pacific) region include only one country from South-East Asia as well as the Indian subcontinent; the Transition Economy region does not include countries from the former USSR; the Other Developing region includes only three sub-Saharan countries and no South American countries. At the same time, it is worth pointing out that the number and percentage of study countries or areas with at least two-digit occupational data from non-OECD countries (approximately 60 per cent of study countries) is uniquely high for a cross-national study of occupational segregation by sex (see Chapter 3).

The present chapter provides a brief description of each of the above five study regions. Tables 7.1–7.5 provide key indicators of social and economic development for study countries or areas and regions: per capita gross domestic product (GDP) for 1990,[1] mean number of years of schooling in 1990 for men and women aged 25 and older, percentage of the national work-force employed in agriculture, and female share of both total employment and non-agricultural employment.[2]

7.1 OECD countries

The OECD grouping (table 7.1) covers the two industrialized North American member countries (the United States and Canada), the two Oceanic industrialized countries (Australia and New Zealand), and a good cross-section of OECD European countries (12 countries). Although not an OECD member, Cyprus was included in this grouping, because it is relatively developed and somewhat comparable with European countries. Japan, although an OECD member, was included in the Asian region rather than the OECD grouping. We felt that these adjustments to actual OECD membership improved the homogeneity of our OECD grouping, because of our *a priori* feeling that cultural and historical factors are more important in determining occupational segregation than development levels.[3] In general, our OECD grouping is fairly representative of the organization's membership, although some of the least developed OECD countries such as Greece, Portugal and Turkey are missing from the data set.

As expected, our OECD countries have relatively high income levels and small agricultural sectors. Average GDP per capita was approximately US$16,500 in 1990. It was highest in the United States (approximately $21,500) and lowest in Cyprus (approximately $10,000). Less than 10 per cent of the labour force was in the agricultural sector on average (5.7 per cent), with only three countries (Italy, Spain and New Zealand) barely surpassing the 10 per cent level.[4]

Women are now an integral part of the labour force in OECD countries and an earlier pattern, whereby many women withdraw from the labour force in large numbers to marry and raise children, has disappeared in many OECD countries. This increased labour force commitment of women is reflected in their historic entry into the labour force in recent decades. For example, women's share of non-agricultural employment in Norway rose from 34.8 per cent in 1970 to 47.1 per cent in 1990; in the Netherlands it rose from 24.0 per cent to 39.1 per cent during the same time period. For the nine OECD countries for which we have data for 1970, 1980 and 1990,[5] on average, women's share of the non-agricultural

Table 7.1. **Key development and employment indicators, OECD study countries (including Cyprus but excluding Japan)**

Country	Real GDP per capita 1990 (PPP$)	Mean years of schooling 1990 (age 25+)			Most recent data year for study data	% of employment in agriculture (in data year)	% female share in total employment (in data year)	% female share in non-agricultural employment (in data year)
		Men	Women	M/F ratio				
Australia	16 051	11.6	11.4	1.02	1990	3.3	41.4	41.7
Austria	16 504	11.7	10.5	1.11	1990	7.8	41.2	40.8
Canada	19 232	12.3	11.9	1.03	1990	4.2	44.7	45.9
Cyprus	9 953	7.6	6.5	1.12	1989	0.3	37.2	37.3
Finland	16 446	10.7	10.5	1.02	1990	8.5	47.8	49.1
France	17 405	11.5	11.7	0.98	1990	4.4	42.4	42.6
Germany (West)	18 213	11.7	10.6	1.10	1989	3.8	38.8	41.7
Italy	15 890	7.4	7.3	1.01	1981	10.7	33.0	32.6
Luxembourg	19 244	10.3	9.8	1.05	1991	4.3	35.4	35.9
Netherlands	15 695	10.4	10.8	0.96	1990	5.2	38.4	39.1
New Zealand	14 481	10.2	10.6	0.96	1986	10.9	40.7	42.3
Norway	16 028	11.7	11.5	1.02	1990	6.2	45.8	47.1
Spain	11 723	7.0	6.5	1.08	1990	11.8	32.0	32.7
Sweden	17 014	11.1	11.1	1.00	1991	3.3	48.3	49.1
Switzerland	20 874	11.5	10.7	1.07	1980	6.6	36.0	36.7
United Kingdom	15 804	11.4	11.6	0.98	1990	2.4	43.4	44.0
United States	21 449	12.2	12.4	0.98	1991	2.9	45.6	46.5
Average (unweighted)	**16 562**	**10.6**	**10.3**	**1.03**		**5.7**	**40.7**	**41.5**

Figure 7.1.   Women's share of non-agricultural employment, OECD study countries, 1970–90

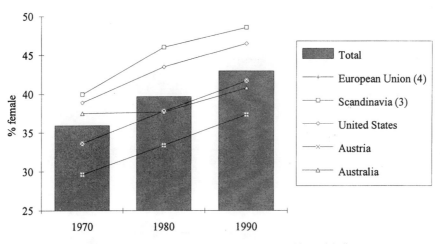

Note: For expositional purposes, values for 1970, 1980 and 1990 are connected by straight lines.
Source: Includes all ten OECD study countries with data for 1970, 1980 and 1990.

labour force rose from 33.8 per cent in 1970 to 37.9 per cent in 1980 and 41.2 per cent in 1990.

Women now constitute approximately 42 per cent of the non-agricultural labour force, on average, in our 17 OECD countries. In 1990, women's share of non-agricultural employment was highest in Finland and Sweden at about 49 per cent and lowest in Italy and Spain at about 33 per cent. Figure 7.1 displays trends since 1970 for the ten OECD study countries with detailed occupational data for 1970, 1980 and 1990. Notice that there is an upward trend in all of these examples. Figure 7.2 shows age-specific female labour force participation rate profiles for 1950, 1970 and 1990 for developed countries based on recent ILO labour force estimates that use common definitions of labour force participation. Again the upward time trend in female labour force participation is quite apparent.[6]

The number of years of schooling completed by adult men and women in OECD countries is roughly equal, being 10.6 years for men and 10.3 years for women on average. Although there are inequalities between men and women in terms of educational opportunity, it is not in terms of years of schooling completed. **Gender differences in education in OECD countries occur more in the types of subjects and fields of study** (e.g. women are concentrated more in humanities and men in sciences) and in types of vocational training received (e.g. in the craft professions such as carpentry and masonry, where men predominate); this has important implications for

Figure 7.2. Female age-specific labour force participation rates for developed regions, 1950, 1970, 1990

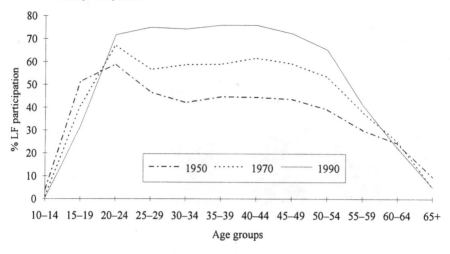

Source: ILO, forthcoming, *Labour force estimates and projections, 1950–2010* (Geneva, ILO). Based on estimates for countries from developed regions out of 176 countries in the world.

the establishment and perpetuation of occupational segregation by sex in OECD countries.

7.2 Transition Economies

Our Central and Eastern European Transition Economy group (table 7.2) includes three former COMECON states of the region: Bulgaria, Hungary and Poland. Former Yugoslavia, which was not part of COMECON, is also included here because of its geographical proximity, its somewhat similar political system and a level of development more comparable to this region than to the European Communities. Missing are countries from the former USSR.

The social, historical, legal and economic characteristics of this region are in sharp contrast to those of the OECD. Throughout the second half of the twentieth century, these countries pursued an ideological path which emphasized the labour market integration of women. And a cornerstone of communist ideology was equality of the sexes. Government policy encouraged women to remain in the labour force, and families were offered extensive social support such as maternity leave, extended child-care leave and subsidized creches. The general perception was that women had greater occupational choice and advancement than elsewhere in the world, although

Table 7.2. Key development and employment indicators, Transition Economy study countries

Country	Real GDP per capita 1990 (PPP$)	Mean years of schooling 1990 (age 25+)			Most recent data year for study data	% of employment in agriculture (in data year)	% female share in total employment (in data year)	% female share in non-agricultural employment (in data year)
		Men	Women	M/F ratio				
Bulgaria	4,700	7.6	6.4	1.19	1985	12.4	46.5	45.6
Hungary	6,116	9.5	9.7	0.97	1990	6.0	44.5	45.6
Poland	4,237	8.3	7.7	1.08	1988	24.9	45.4	44.1
Former Yugoslavia	–	–	–	–	1981	2.8	33.0	33.3
Average (unweighted)	**5,018**	**8.5**	**7.9**	**1.08**		**11.5**	**42.4**	**42.2**

there was considerable evidence that these labour markets were still far from equal for men and women (Bodrova and Anker, 1985).

It should be noted that our study data cover the time period before the tumultuous political and economic changes of the late 1980s and 1990s; what impact these changes have had on gender inequalities in the labour market is therefore beyond the scope of this book. However, these data are of considerable "historical" interest. These data are important for monitoring and understanding how women have been doing in the transition to a market economy, which is only possible when pre-transition data are compared to post-transition data.

Although these Transition Economies were generally considered to be industrialized, their **level of development was considerably below that of the OECD grouping.** Average GDP per capita in 1990, for example, was only US$5,018 in the three former COMECON states, roughly one-third of the level found in OECD grouping, and much more in line with middle-income developing countries.

Educational levels are also lower in the former socialist countries than in OECD countries, with the average number of years of schooling in 1990 only about eight years. Similar to the OECD, however, is the small difference between men and women in terms of the length of schooling. Also similar to OECD countries is that men and women tend to study different subject areas in school and women tend to receive less vocational training (Bodrova and Anker, 1985).

The share of employment in agriculture is relatively low (but generally higher than in the OECD), at about 12 per cent on average. This average, however, hides considerable variation across Transition Economy study countries as almost 25 per cent of the labour force in Poland is in the agricultural sector, compared to 6 per cent and 3 per cent respectively in Hungary and former Yugoslavia.

Whereas high female labour force participation in the OECD countries is a relatively recent phenomenon, **women** in Transition Economies in Central and Eastern Europe **began entering the labour market in large numbers soon after the Second World War.** In fact, while elsewhere in the world female participation rates have been increasing in recent years, especially in OECD countries, in the Transition Economies they reached relatively high levels earlier. In Poland, for example, women accounted for 44.7 per cent of total employment in 1950; this only increased to 45.4 per cent in 1988 (ILO *Yearbook of Labour Statistics*). In Hungary, the female share of employment rose from 35.5 per cent in 1960 to 44.5 per cent in 1985 (ILO *Yearbook of Labour Statistics*); indeed, the increasing female participation accounted for most of the growth in the labour force between 1950 and 1980 in most Transition Economies (Bodrova and Anker, 1985). This relatively long history of high female labour force participation, coupled with an active government policy of promoting equality in employment, is expected to have produced relatively low levels of sex segregation of occupations in Transition Economy countries.

7.3 Middle East and North Africa

The Middle Eastern and North African region (table 7.3) includes one Maghreb country (Tunisia), the most populous country in the region (Egypt), two Gulf oil states (Bahrain and Kuwait), as well as the Islamic Republic of Iran and Jordan. The countries included in this grouping are fairly representative of the region. The unweighted average per capita GDP for the countries in this grouping, excluding Bahrain and Kuwait, is approximately $2,800, a reasonably representative figure for non-oil rich North African and the Middle Eastern countries.

The share of employment in agriculture displays great variation across the study countries in this region. It is fairly high in Egypt, the Islamic Republic of Iran and Tunisia (38.8 per cent, 34.0 per cent and 26.9 per cent respectively), and more in line with industrialized countries in Jordan, Bahrain and Kuwait.

In all study countries in this region, **the female share of non-agricultural employment is small,** ranging from a high of about 20 per cent in Tunisia and Kuwait to a low of about 8 per cent in Jordan. Women in this region have not entered the labour market in the vast numbers seen in the OECD and Transition Economy countries, although their share of employment has increased over the past few decades. In Bahrain, for example, women accounted for 9.9 per cent of the non-agricultural labour force in 1971 and 16.9 per cent in 1991. Women's share of non-agricultural employment is reported to have risen slightly in Egypt, from 9.7 per cent in 1976 to 13.6 per cent in 1986.[7]

The number of **years of schooling is low for both men and women in this region,** with the average only 4.7 years for men and 3.0 years for women. This large gender differential is found in all six countries in the region.

A key feature of this region is the predominance of Islam, an influence that undoubtedly plays a major role in affecting occupational segregation by sex, as well as female labour force participation. At the same time, it is important to keep in mind that the status of women varies greatly across Islamic countries. In some, women are somewhat integrated into professional and educational life, while in others the traditional functions of housewife and mother are virtually the only socially acceptable roles for women. The influence of Islam and tradition undoubtedly helps explain why women have considerably lower educational levels and labour force participation rates than men in this region—as well as restricted occupational choices as will be shown in Part III.

Table 7.3. Key development and employment indicators, Middle Eastern and North African study countries

Country	Real GDP per capita 1990 (PPP$)	Mean years of schooling 1990 (age 25+)			Most recent data year for study data	% of employment in agriculture (in data year)	% female share in total employment (in data year)	% female share in non-agricultural employment (in data year)
		Men	Women	M/F ratio				
Bahrain	10,706	4.7	3.2	1.47	1991	2.6	16.4	16.9
Egypt	1,988	3.9	1.6	2.43	1986	38.8	8.9	13.6
Iran, Islamic Rep.	3,253	4.6	3.1	1.48	1986	34.0	9.7	10.5
Jordan	2,345	6.0	4.0	1.50	1979	11.4	7.3	8.1
Kuwait	15,178	6.0	4.7	1.28	1985	2.0	19.6	20.0
Tunisia	3,579	3.0	1.2	2.50	1989	26.9	19.5	19.6
Average (unweighted)	**6,175**	**4.7**	**3.0**	**1.78**		**19.3**	**13.6**	**14.8**

7.4   Asia/Pacific

The Asian (and Pacific) countries and areas covered in this book (table 7.4) provide a fairly representative sample of this region. Included are the two most populous countries in the world (India and China), two Asian economies with relatively high per capita income (Japan and Hong Kong), and two newly industrializing states (the Republic of Korea and Malaysia). The Pacific island state of Fiji is also included in this group. Representation is weak for South-East Asia as well as South Asia. The seven Asian study economies illustrate the immense diversity of the region, and the occupational segregation by sex is expected to vary accordingly. Data from India and China are from the early 1980s, a time when these nations were considered among the least developed countries of the world.[8]

In 1990, real per capita GDP was only about $1,400 and $2,000 in India and China respectively. Japan and Hong Kong had high average incomes, with 1990 per capita GDPs above $15,000, while the Republic of Korea and Malaysia are examples of the East Asian "tiger" economies, with average per capita GDPs between $6,000 and $7,000 in 1990.

Educational levels also vary greatly, with men generally receiving more education than women. In terms of the mean number of years of schooling, educational levels are lowest in India, where the average is 3.5 years for men and 1.2 years for women, and highest in Japan where the average for both men and women is about 10.5 years. In Japan and Malaysia, there is very little difference between men and women in the length of schooling, while in all the other study countries and areas, the male to female ratio in years of schooling exceeds 1.5, with India's nearly 3.0.

Agricultural employment in China accounted for 72.0 per cent of total employment in 1982. India reportedly had a roughly comparable level, with 66.4 per cent of all employment in agriculture in 1981. Agricultural employment was lowest in Hong Kong and Japan (1 and 7 per cent respectively of total employment), and relatively high in Malaysia, the Republic of Korea and Fiji (approximately 39, 33 and 48 per cent respectively).

The female share of non-agricultural employment also varied widely. It was low in India (12 per cent), and roughly between 30 and 40 per cent in the remaining countries or areas. Female labour force participation rates in China, Hong Kong, Japan and the Republic of Korea are approaching those found in certain parts of Europe and North America. In Japan, they have remained fairly stable during the past two decades as the female share of non-agricultural employment rose only slightly, from about 36 per cent in 1970 to about 39 per cent in 1990. In the Republic of Korea and China on the other hand, women's share of total non-agricultural employment has increased recently. In the Republic of Korea, their share rose from about 35 per cent in 1960 to about 40 per cent in 1990 (and was approximately 47 per cent in 1992 when agriculture was also included, ILO, 1994b). In China,

Table 7.4. Key development and employment indicators, Asian/Pacific study countries/areas

| Country/area | Real GDP per capita 1990 (PPP$) | Mean years of schooling 1990 (age 25+) | | | Most recent data year for study data | % of employment in agriculture (in data year) | % female share in total employment (in data year) | % female share in non-agricultural employment (in data year) |
		Men	Women	M/F ratio				
China	1,990	6.0	3.6	1.67	1982	72.0	43.7	35.7
Fiji	4,427	5.6	4.6	1.22	1986	48.1	19.5	27.1
Hong Kong	15,595	8.6	5.4	1.59	1991	0.9	37.9	37.9
India	1,400	3.5	1.2	2.92	1981	66.4	26.9	12.1
Japan	17,616	10.8	10.6	1.02	1990	7.1	39.7	39.3
Republic of Korea	6,733	11.0	6.7	1.64	1983	33.1	34.0	30.6
Malaysia	6,140	5.6	5.0	1.06	1980	39.2	32.0	28.2
Average (unweighted)	**7,700**	**7.3**	**5.3**	**1.59**		**38.1**	**33.4**	**30.1**

GENDER AND JOBS

the female share of non-agricultural employment rose from about 36 per cent in 1982 to about 38 per cent in 1990.

7.5 Other Developing Countries and Areas

The final **regional grouping is quite heterogeneous** as its six developing countries and one area come from sub-Saharan Africa, the Indian Ocean, the Caribbean and Central America (table 7.5). There was insufficient data available to subdivide this grouping into more homogeneous regional groupings. Although the study data set includes only seven economies, this multi-regional grouping is still useful for comparative purposes.

It is difficult to make generalizations for such a heterogeneous set of countries or areas. Angola and Haiti are among the poorest countries in the world. Mauritius, Costa Rica and the Netherlands Antilles are examples of small, middle-income developing economies, while Senegal and Ghana are poor, but somewhat better off African countries. The size of the agricultural sector also shows great variation, ranging from 0.9 per cent in the Netherlands Antilles to 70.4 per cent in Senegal. The data for Angola refer to the capital city only.

Female shares of total employment are generally similar to those in Asia, being much higher than in North Africa and the Middle East, but generally lower than in the OECD and Transition Economies. At the same time,

Figure 7.3. Women's share of non-agricultural employment, Asian, Middle Eastern and Other Developing study countries and areas, 1970–90

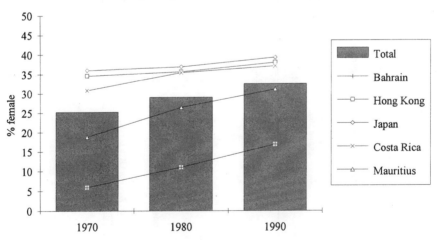

Notes: For expositional purposes, values for 1970, 1980 and 1990 are connected by straight lines. Includes all five study Asian, Middle Eastern and Other Developing Countries and Areas with data for 1970, 1980 and 1990.
Source: Study data.

Table 7.5. Key development and employment indicators, Other Developing study countries and areas

Country/area	Real GDP per capita 1990 (PPP$)	Mean years of schooling 1990 (age 25+)			Most recent data year for study data	% of employment in agriculture (in data year)	% female share in total employment (in data year)	% female share in non-agricultural employment (in data year)
		Men	Women	M/F ratio				
Angola	840	2.0	1.0	2.00	1992	3.2[a]	41.2	41.3
Costa Rica	4,542	5.8	5.6	1.04	1991	24.5	29.4	37.1
Ghana	1,016	4.8	2.2	2.18	1984	60.7	51.4	57.6
Haiti	933	2.0	1.3	1.54	1986	38.4	45.8	65.2
Mauritius	5,750	4.8	3.3	1.45	1990	16.2	30.4	31.1
Netherlands Antilles	2,392	–	–	–	1981	0.9	38.2	38.5
Senegal	1,248	1.3	0.4	3.25	1988	70.4	23.7	22.8
Average (unweighted)	**2,389**	**3.5**	**2.3**	**1.91**		**30.6**	**37.2**	**41.9**

Notes: [a] Data for Angola refer to only capital city.
Sources for tables 7.1–7.5: GDP per capita and education levels: UNDP, *Human Development Report*, 1993. Employment levels and data year are from study data except for India which is drawn from other national statistics.

Figure 7.4.   Female age-specific labour force participation rates for less developed regions, 1950, 1970, 1990

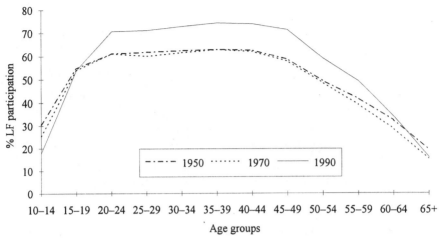

Source: ILO, forthcoming, *Labour force estimates and projections, 1950–2010* (Geneva, ILO). Based on estimates for countries from developed regions out of 176 countries in the world.

Haiti and Ghana represent an interesting situation, since female non-agricultural workers outnumber male non-agricultural workers. Educational levels in this grouping are low, being only about three years on average, with men having more education than women.

Figures 7.3 and 7.4 indicate in graphical form how female non-agricultural labour force activity has been changing in study Asian, Middle Eastern, North African and other developing countries and areas. There has been a consistent increase in female activity rates in recent decades. Further, women in these countries or areas are generally committed to labour force activity, as their age-specific activity patterns tend to be similar to that for men.

Notes

[1] GDP per capita figures are adjusted for purchasing power parity (PPP). These estimates provide greater cross-national comparability than GDP per capita figures based on exchange rates, as the former more fully take into account differences in living costs.

[2] Note that the female share of employment is similar for total employment and non-agricultural employment—except in countries with large agricultural sectors. Indeed, for 32 of our 41 study countries and areas, female shares in these two labour forces are within three percentage points of each other. For the nine countries where this difference exceeds 3 per cent, the share of agricultural employment is 16.5 per cent on average. It seems clear for OECD and Transition Economy countries that excluding agricultural occupations from the analysis in Parts III and IV (see Chapter 5) is unlikely to have much of an effect on the empirical results. After all, among OECD and Transition Economy countries, the percentage of total employment in agriculture is always below 12 per cent (except Poland), and the female shares of employment for the total labour force and non-agricultural labour force are always within three percentage points of each other.

For most non-OECD and non-Transition Economy countries on the other hand, agriculture is a very important sector for workers, and so excluding it from the analysis in Parts III and IV is likely to have had a major effect on the empirical results. But excluding agricultural employment from the analysis is, I feel, necessary, in large part for conceptual reasons (see Chapter 5 for a detailed discussion on this).

[3] In any case, basing our typology on per capita income levels alone would have resulted in entirely different groupings, as not all OECD study countries have relatively high income per capita levels whereas some non-OECD countries do.

[4] According to study data, women's share of employment in OECD countries tends to be lower for the agricultural labour force as compared to the total labour force. It is our feeling that this is due in part to measurement problems, with women working on family farms often undercounted in censuses and labour force surveys. (Readers are referred to previous publications by the author which document how female labour force activity in unpaid family work such as in agriculture often goes unreported in response to typical questions used in labour force surveys and censuses, such as Anker, 1994; Anker and Anker, 1995; and Anker, Khan and Gupta, 1987.)

[5] Among OECD study countries, data are available for 1970, 1980 and 1990 for Australia, Austria, Finland, West Germany, Luxembourg, the Netherlands, Norway, Spain, Sweden and the United States.

[6] There is also a downward trend over time in male labour force participation rates around the world. This has important implications for women in the labour market, since the female share of employment has increased due to both rising female participation and falling male participation.

[7] It is possible that this increased share in Egypt is due in part to a conscious effort by the Egyptian central statistical office to increase the enumeration of women workers (Fergamy, 1995).

[8] Subsequent to completion of all the analysis in Part III, data became available for 1990 for China. These more recent Chinese data are used for the trend analysis in Part IV.

PART III

OCCUPATIONAL SEGREGATION AROUND THE WORLD—
THE PRESENT SITUATION

This part of the book examines recent information on occupational segregation by sex using several different perspectives. It begins by describing the occupational structure of the economy and occupational segregation by sex based on data for six broad non-agricultural occupational categories in Chapter 8.

Chapters 9 to 11 carry this analysis forward by using the detailed ILO data set described in Chapter 5, which includes, on average, approximately 175 non-agricultural occupations for 41 countries or areas. Inequality indices described in Chapter 6 are used in Chapter 9 to examine the overall level of occupational segregation by sex in national labour markets, as well as to investigate similarities and differences across countries or areas, regions and subregions. This is followed in Chapter 10 by an analysis of the percentages of the female or male total non-agricultural labour force working in "gender-dominated" or "gender-integrated" occupations. Chapter 11 examines 17 typical "male" and "female" occupations; and whether or not they are consistently gender-dominated or gender-integrated within and between study regions and subregions. Finally, Chapter 12 investigates how various inequality statistics analysed in Chapters 9, 10 and 11 are interrelated and whether there are distinct patterns in these relationships.

Subsequently, Part IV of this book investigates recent trends in occupational segregation by sex in order to determine whether or not this has increased or decreased in recent years.

Before beginning the following analyses of the current situation around the world, readers need to be reminded that cross-national comparisons of occupational segregation by sex are difficult to make and not only because of differences in the level of disaggregation in national occupational classifications—an issue which is discussed at length in Chapter 7. There are also problems discussed in Chapter 5 with comparing the same occupation in different countries even when the same classification system, definition, sampling technique, enumeration procedure and coding scheme are used. The same occupational title (for example, cashier or sales-person) may involve different work across countries, depending on the types of machines and equipment used and the knowledge and education required of the workers. Also, the occupational structure of the non-agricultural labour force differs across countries, and this affects observed levels of occupational segregation. Despite the usual limitations of cross-national data, the following analysis of the "current" situation of occupational segregation by sex in the world, permits, I feel, reasonable—and interesting—comparisons, especially for groups of countries.[1]

Note

[1] Readers need to keep in mind that the occupational data for three study countries have an unusual data source (see Chapter 4). This means that they are definitely less comparable to data for other study countries or areas. The data for Cyprus and Haiti are based on income and expenditure surveys whereas the data for all other countries or areas are based on censuses or labour force surveys. Also, the Cypriot data cover only non-agricultural wage earners whereas all other national data cover all non-agricultural employment or the entire non-agricultural labour force. The data for Angola cover only its capital city.

OCCUPATIONAL SEGREGATION BY SEX BASED ON DATA FOR SIX NON-AGRICULTURAL OCCUPATIONS

8

A unique aspect of this book is the high level of detail in the occupational data used throughout most of the text. As described in earlier chapters, detailed occupational data are essential to understanding occupational segregation; yet, as noted in Chapter 3, with very few exceptions, which are almost always for industrialized countries, previous empirical cross-national studies have relied on aggregated one-digit occupational data.

Notwithstanding the importance of disaggregated occupational data, the use of *only* highly disaggregated occupational data runs the risk of missing the broad picture of the general types of jobs held by men and women—that is, by concentrating on the proverbial "trees", the proverbial "forest" can be missed. It is for this reason that **Part II begins with an analysis of one-digit ISCO-68 occupational data for six non-agricultural occupations.** The remainder of the book uses more detailed two- and three-digit occupational data. In ISCO-68, there are six major non-agricultural occupations. There are three generally non-manual white-collar major occupational groups (professional/technical, administrative/managerial and sales); two heterogeneous major occupational groups, which are generally white-collar but less well paid (clerical and services) and one primarily manual major occupational group (production).

Data for our 41 study countries or areas are supplemented by comparable data for six non-agricultural occupations for non-study countries when these were readily available (mainly in the ILO *Yearbook of Labour Statistics*) in order to provide a more complete picture of the world. In all, data are presented for 56 countries and areas in this chapter. The Transition Economies of Central and Eastern Europe are omitted from this chapter because their occupational classification systems, except for Yugoslavia's, previously were conceptually different from ISCO.[1]

Analysis of the aggregate one-digit data reveal wide variation around the world in employment structures (section 8.1) and to a lesser extent in occupational segregation by sex in each of the six ISCO major non-agricultural occupational groups (section 8.2). At the same time, **there are distinct regional patterns,** reflecting the different social, cultural, historical, economic and labour market contexts in which occupational segregation by sex occurs.

8.1 Occupational structure based on six major non-agricultural occupations

Figure 8.1 illustrates the occupational structure of non-agricultural employment for study regions based on one-digit level data (see Appendix 8.1, table 8.3). In all but two study countries, the largest major occupational group in terms of non-agricultural employment is production occupations, while the smallest is administrative and managerial occupations.[2] Each of the remaining major groups—professional and technical; clerical; sales; and services—generally represent between 10 and 20 per cent of all non-agricultural employment, although national and regional differences are quite marked.

One striking difference between OECD countries and most developing countries is the relative size of professional and technical occupations. While in Asia and in our other developing country/area group, the percentage of non-agricultural employment in professional and technical occupations is less than 13 per cent on average, it is 19 per cent on average in OECD countries; northern European OECD countries (Finland, Sweden, Norway and the Netherlands) have a particularly high share at approximately 25 per cent. Interestingly, Middle Eastern and North African countries also have a

Figure 8.1. Occupational structure of the non-agricultural labour force based on the six ISCO major non-agricultural occupational groups, latest available year, by study region

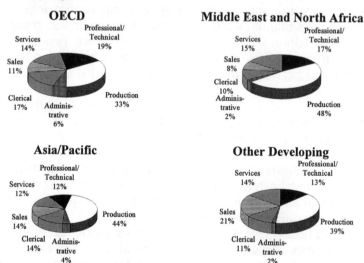

Notes: Percentage of non-agricultural labour force in a major occupational group is defined as the number of workers in the occupational group divided by the total number of workers in the non-agricultural labour force times 100.
Due to the rounding off of values there may be slight differences between the percentages shown in figure 8.1 and those in table 8.3.
Source: Based on data for study countries and areas only. Appendix 8.1, table 8.3.

comparatively high share of non-agricultural employment in this group (16 per cent on average).

There is also wide regional variation in the proportion of non-agricultural employment in *production occupations*. These generally *account for a lower share of employment in OECD countries* as compared to non-OECD countries. Whereas approximately 33 per cent of employment on average is in production occupations in OECD countries, this is 43 per cent on average in non-OECD countries. Asian study economies have a particularly high regional average (44 per cent); the more developed economies in the region, Japan, the Republic of Korea and Hong Kong, have a relatively low share in production occupations (36 per cent, 42 per cent and 37 per cent respectively); while the least developed, China and India, have the highest shares (57 per cent and 50 per cent respectively). Such contrasting occupational structures reflect differences in development levels and the organization of national economies (as well as possible differences in occupational classification schemes).

Other major differences worth noting are the following. *OECD countries generally have a relatively high proportion of non-agricultural employment in the clerical occupations,* a reflection of the importance of administrative support activities in their economies. The administrative and managerial category is, on average, larger in OECD countries than in other regions. *In the Other Developing Countries/Areas group, sales is a relatively large major occupational group*, comprising over one-fifth of employment on average; Ghana and Haiti have particularly high employment shares in sales at 35 and 49 per cent respectively. Throughout much of the developing world, small-scale female entrepreneurs in the informal sector—street hawkers and petty traders—constitute a major source of non-agricultural employment.

8.2 Occupational segregation by sex for six major non-agricultural occupations

There is great variation both within and between regions in the extent to which women are concentrated in the six major ISCO non-agricultural occupational groups. Table 8.2, which presents national data on the extent to which women are over- or underrepresented in each of these six Major Occupational Groups, is based on data for 56 countries and areas (34 of our 41 study countries and areas, supplemented by data from other sources for 22 other countries).[3] (Interested readers are referred to table 8.3 in Appendix 8.1 for national values for study countries.) Table 8.1 summarizes these data by indicating the average representation ratios and the number of countries within each region where women are under- or overrepresented in each major occupational group. Figure 8.2 indicates graphically the extent of

Table 8.1. Representation ratios for women workers in six major non-agricultural occupational groups, by region (study and other countries/areas)

Major Occupational Group	Representation ratio	Region OECD	Middle East and North Africa	Asia/Pacific	Latin America	Africa	Overall
Professional & technical	≥1.00	19	6	9	10	5	49
	<1.00	0	0	1	3	3	7
	Average	1.25	2.43	1.35	1.21	1.13	1.47
Admin. & managerial	≥1.00	0	0	0	1	0	1
	<1.00	19	6	10	12	8	55
	Average	0.47	0.46	0.34	0.58	0.36	0.44
Clerical	≥1.00	19	6	7	12	6	50
	<1.00	0	0	3	1	2	6
	Average	1.62	1.85	0.95	1.37	1.26	1.41
Sales	≥1.00	16	0	5	10	8	39
	<1.00	3	6	5	3	0	17
	Average	1.15	0.28	1.02	1.25	1.55	1.05
Services	≥1.00	18	4	10	13	6	51
	<1.00	1	2	0	0	2	5
	Average	1.45	1.25	1.42	1.53	1.11	1.35
Production	≥1.00	0	0	2	0	0	2
	<1.00	19	6	8	13	8	54
	Average	0.42	0.33	0.74	0.43	0.46	0.48

Notes: Regional averages are based on an unweighted average of country values.
Representation ratio indicates the extent to which women are overrepresented or underrepresented in a relative sense, in a Major Occupational Group, with a ratio of 1.00 being the dividing line. Representation ratio is defined as the percentage female in the Major Group divided by the average percentage female in the non-agricultural labour force as a whole. A value greater than 1.0 indicates that women are overrepresented in a relative sense. A value less than 1.0 indicates that women are underrepresented in a relative sense.
Source: Based on data in table 8.2.

Table 8.2. Representation ratios for women for six major non-agricultural occupational groups, latest available year, by country/area and region (study and non-study countries/areas)

Region/country/area	Major Occupational Group					
	Professional and technical	Admin. and managerial	Clerical	Sales	Services	Production
OECD (study countries)						
Australia 1990	1.04	0.52	1.83	1.39	1.36	0.29
Austria 1990	1.19	0.41	1.65	1.48	1.76	0.36
Canada 1990	1.12	0.89	1.78	1.01	1.26	0.31
Cyprus 1989	1.15	0.23	1.63	1.32	1.13	0.59
Finland 1990	1.17	0.55	1.75	1.21	1.56	0.40
Germany, West 1989	1.09	0.46	1.59	1.46	1.41	0.39
Italy 1981	1.43	0.43	1.34	1.24	1.37	0.60
Luxembourg 1991	1.02	0.32	1.36	1.49	2.02	0.19
Netherlands 1990	1.08	0.34	1.47	1.08	1.80	0.22
New Zealand 1986	1.15	0.42	1.76	1.11	1.49	0.39
Norway 1990	1.21	0.66	1.59	1.14	1.55	0.32
Spain 1990	1.42	0.28	1.46	1.34	1.75	0.38
Sweden 1991	1.25	0.69	1.63	0.99	1.32	0.37
United States 1991	1.11	0.88	1.73	1.07	1.29	0.39
OECD average (unweighted average of above study countries)	**1.17**	**0.51**	**1.61**	**1.24**	**1.51**	**0.37**
OECD (non-study countries)						
Denmark 1990	1.30	0.30	1.36	1.00	1.51	0.44
Greece 1990	1.31	0.31	1.52	1.13	1.31	0.52
Ireland 1988	1.24	0.39	1.67	0.93	1.36	0.41
Portugal 1990	1.31	0.46	1.24	1.02	1.58	0.64
Turkey 1991	2.16	0.39	2.49	0.42	0.73	0.78
Average—non-study OECD	1.46	0.37	1.66	0.90	1.30	0.56
Average—non-study OECD (excluding Turkey)	1.29	0.36	1.45	1.02	1.44	0.50
Average—all OECD	**1.25**	**0.47**	**1.62**	**1.15**	**1.45**	**0.42**

Table 8.2. (contd.)

Region/country/area	Major Occupational Group					
	Professional and technical	Admin. and managerial	Clerical	Sales	Services	Production
Middle East and North Africa (study countries)						
Bahrain 1991	1.91	0.46	1.53	0.45	1.74	0.13
Egypt 1986	2.07	0.84	2.49	0.44	0.45	0.18
Iran, Islamic Rep. 1986	3.09	0.22	1.19	0.15	0.67	0.60
Jordan 1979	4.25	0.55	3.20	0.15	1.65	0.12
Kuwait 1985	1.67	0.18	1.19	0.13	1.90	0.01
Tunisia 1989	1.56	0.48	1.51	0.34	1.09	0.93
Average Middle East and North Africa (study countries)	**2.43**	**0.46**	**1.85**	**0.28**	**1.25**	**0.33**
Asia/Pacific (study countries/areas)						
China 1982	1.07	0.29	0.69	1.28	1.34	0.99
Fiji 1986	1.47	0.34	1.74	1.07	1.78	0.35
Hong Kong 1991	1.20	0.71	1.68	0.97	1.13	0.62
India 1981	1.69	0.19	0.53	0.55	1.48	1.06
Japan 1990	1.01	0.22	1.53	0.94	1.43	0.70
Republic of Korea 1983	0.89	0.08	1.04	1.30	1.70	0.66
Malaysia 1980	1.35	0.29	1.53	0.88	1.13	0.76
Average Asia/Pacific (study countries/areas)	**1.24**	**0.30**	**1.25**	**0.99**	**1.43**	**0.73**
Pakistan 1991	2.28	0.39	0.34	0.36	1.73	1.06
Philippines 1990	1.40	0.61	1.20	1.44	1.28	0.44
Thailand 1980	1.16	0.26	1.00	1.38	1.22	0.80
Average (other non-study Asian countries)	**1.61**	**0.42**	**0.84**	**1.06**	**1.41**	**0.77**
Average Asia/Pacific	**1.35**	**0.34**	**0.95**	**1.02**	**1.42**	**0.74**

Latin America and Caribbean

Barbados 1991	1.15	0.75	1.50	1.25	1.25	0.42
Chile 1991	1.43	0.54	1.27	1.25	1.99	0.33
Colombia 1991	1.03	0.68	1.36	1.01	1.65	0.50
Costa Rica 1991	1.25	0.70	1.33	0.88	1.60	0.62
El Salvador 1991	0.98	0.51	1.05	1.33	1.45	0.64
Haiti 1986	0.71	0.15	0.72	1.41	1.11	0.39
Honduras 1991	1.22	0.73	1.43	1.35	1.31	0.40
Netherlands Antilles 1981	1.27	0.24	1.35	1.51	1.66	0.08
Panama 1991	1.22	0.69	1.75	0.96	1.30	0.29
Paraguay 1982	1.53	0.70	1.81	1.21	1.76	0.54
Peru 1981	1.31	0.28	1.16	1.21	1.79	0.41
Trinidad and Tobago 1991	0.97	1.12	1.40	1.99	1.37	0.63
Venezuela 1990	1.60	0.49	1.70	0.91	1.64	0.30
Average Latin America and Caribbean	**1.21**	**0.58**	**1.37**	**1.25**	**1.53**	**0.43**

Africa

Angola 1992	0.78	0.26	1.27	2.09	1.04	0.21
Cape Verde 1990	1.38	0.66	1.52	1.99	1.64	0.37
Ghana 1984	0.62	0.15	0.52	1.54	0.60	0.78
Malawi 1987	1.55	0.44	1.23	1.07	1.15	0.61
Mauritius 1990	1.25	0.57	1.18	0.76	1.29	0.90
Nigeria 1986	0.66	0.14	0.47	1.61	0.28	0.38
Rwanda 1989	1.42	0.36	1.46	1.43	1.15	0.60
Senegal 1988	1.34	0.41	2.46	1.56	1.24	0.35
South Africa 1988	1.33	0.50	1.69	1.14	1.79	0.39
Average Africa	**1.15**	**0.39**	**1.31**	**1.47**	**1.13**	**0.51**

Notes: Average is unweighted average of national values.
Representation ratio indicates the extent to which women are relatively overrepresented or underrepresented in a major group, with a ratio of 1.0 being the dividing line.
Representation ratio is defined as the percentage female in the Major Group divided by the average percentage female in the non-agricultural labour force. A value greater than 1.0 indicates that women are overrepresented in a relative sense. A value less than 1.0 indicates that women are underrepresented in a relative sense.
Sources: Study data for study countries and areas from table 8.3 in Appendix 8.1 except for Austria, Germany (West) and the United States which are from ILO *Yearbook of Labour Statistics*. Various issues of the ILO *Yearbook of Labour Statistics* for non-study countries.

Figure 8.2. Female representation ratio in the six ISCO major non-agricultural occupational groups, latest available year, by region

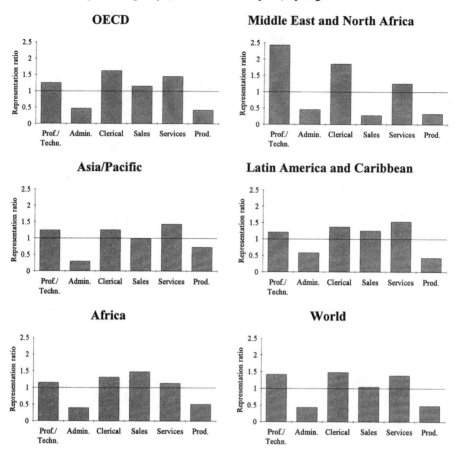

Notes: Representation ratio is defined as the percentage female in an occupational group divided by the average percentage female for the non-agricultural labour force as a whole. A value greater than 1.0 implies women are overrepresented relative to their overall share of the non-agricultural labour force. A value of less than 1.0 implies underrepresentation in a relative sense.

Source: Based on data for 56 (study and non-study) countries and areas. Table 8.2.

over- and underrepresentation at the regional level, while figure 8.3 indicates the percentage female by study region.

Representation ratio is defined, in a relative sense, as the percentage female in the major occupational group divided by the average percentage female for the non-agricultural labour force as a whole. A ratio of 1.00 indicates an employment share equal to women's share of non-agricultural employment as a whole. Women can, therefore, be said to be overrepresented (compared to their share of the total non-agricultural labour force) when the representation ratio is above 1.00, and underrepresented when it is below 1.00.

Figure 8.3. Percentage female in the six ISCO major non-agricultural occupational groups, latest available year, by study region

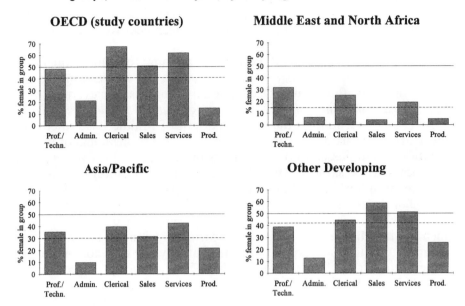

Note: Each dashed line shows the average female share for the region.
Source: Based on data for study countries and areas only. Table 8.3.

Two provisos are in order before beginning the following discussion. First, it is important to stress that **overrepresentation or underrepresentation within a major occupational group is a relative concept which is a function of women's average share of the non-agricultural labour force.** (For this reason, it is possible for women in a country with low female participation rates to be overrepresented in a Major Group while comprising only a small percentage of its workers.) Second, no attempt is made to provide detailed explanations for many national differences as we are primarily interested in general observations and patterns in the present section—in order to highlight major differences and similarities around the world. Subsequent chapters go into more detail using more disaggregated occupational data.

8.2.1 Professional and technical occupations

Throughout the world, women tend to be overrepresented (i.e. relatively concentrated) in the Professional and Technical Major Group. Women are overrepresented in this occupational group in all six of the regions examined, and in *49 of the 56 countries or areas* reviewed. For three of the seven exceptions (Angola, Ghana and Haiti), the comparatively low representation ratios can be attributed to exceptionally high female shares of non-agricultural employment and a concentration of women in informal sector sales

---

SEGREGATION BY SEX FOR SIX NON-AGRICULTURAL OCCUPATIONS 163

occupations.[4] It is also interesting to note that Japan and the Republic of Korea have relatively low ratios (1.01 and 0.89) as compared to other countries; this undoubtedly has important implications for average female pay levels (see table 2.2) as professional and technical workers tend to be relatively highly paid.

Particularly striking—and perhaps surprising to some readers—are results for the *Middle East and North African region,* where women's share of employment in this Major Occupational Group is, on average, *almost two and a half times their share in the non-agricultural labour force.* Turkey, an OECD member, follows the typical pattern of Middle Eastern countries where a large proportion of working women are in a professional or technical occupation. As discussed in other sections in this book, this overrepresentation appears to be largely attributable to social and cultural factors that help create both low female labour force participation rates as well as restrict the range of occupations which are considered to be suitable occupations for women. In short, social and cultural factors seem to ensure that most adult women in the Middle East and North African region do not work in the non-agricultural labour force, but for the relatively few who do, an unusually high percentage (by world standards) have a professional or technical job (often teacher or nurse).

The overrepresentation of women in professional and technical occupations should be quite positive for women, since these occupations have relatively good pay and high status. This positive picture, however, needs to be greatly tempered, since there is considerable segregation within this Major Group. For example, in the United States in 1991 almost one-half of women in the professional and technical category worked in only two occupations: nurses and teachers (15.9 per cent and 32.5 per cent of all women professional and technical workers respectively). In Japan, 46.6 per cent of women professional and technical workers were in these same two occupations in 1990 (25.3 per cent as nurses and 21.3 per cent as teachers), while for India and Hong Kong over 80 per cent of women professional and technical workers were either nurses or teachers. Although the popular press often discusses new and greater opportunities for women in professional and technical occupations such as aircraft pilots, engineers, and computer programmers, the fact is that *women remain largely confined in the professional and technical sphere to traditional women's occupations such as teacher and nurse,* a topic discussed in more detail in Chapter 11.

8.2.2 Administrative and managerial occupations[5]

Women are very much underrepresented in the administrative and managerial Major Group in all regions of the world, as indicated by the fact that the average representation ratio is below 0.60 for all six regions, and the global average is only 0.42. This underrepresentation is least pronounced in the

Latin American and Caribbean region (with an average ratio of 0.58) and most pronounced in the Asian/Pacific region (0.34).

Among our study countries/areas, three stand out as having relatively high representation ratios, although still below 1.0: Canada (0.89) the United States (0.88) and Egypt (0.84). For Canada and the United States, this result appears to be partly related to a more encompassing classification of managerial workers than in ISCO-68. In Canada, clerical, sales, services and production supervisors are included in this occupational group but not in ISCO.[6] In the United States, a range of "management-related" occupations are included in this occupational group but not in ISCO.[7] In Egypt, the "high" representation ratio appears to be real, since women are equally well represented in both of the sub-occupations in this Major Group (government officials; and administrators/general managers) at around 11 per cent female. Although indicating an unusual situation in that women are not strongly underrepresented in this Major Group, the comparatively high representation ratio for Egypt must be viewed in light of women's very low share of non-agricultural employment (approximately 14 per cent).[8]

Although always small in size, administrators and managers are an important occupational group. Both in the government and the private sector they are decision-makers, and they tend to earn a relatively high income. The degree to which women participate in these activities can be seen as a proxy for women's position in society and the labour market. Obviously, women have a long way to go towards equality in this area.

8.2.3 Clerical occupations

Women are highly overrepresented in most countries of the world in this Major Occupational Group, reflecting the work done by women office workers who ensure that phones are answered, letters are typed, and data are entered. Indeed, women are overrepresented in this Major Group in 50 of the 56 countries or areas examined.

On the other hand, the six exceptions where women are underrepresented in clerical occupations (China, India, Pakistan, Haiti, Nigeria and Ghana) are very important exceptions indeed as some are among the most populous countries in the World. So it seems that while the sex-stereotyping of clericals, such as secretaries, is true for the vast majority of countries in the world, **this is only true for about one-half of the world's population.**

Women's representation ratio in clerical occupations is highest on average in North Africa and the Middle East (1.88) and the OECD (1.62). This ratio is lowest in Asia (0.95) where women are slightly underrepresented in clerical occupations. The low relative share of women clerical workers in Asia and the high relative share in North Africa and the Middle East may be attributable largely to historical and cultural factors, an issue discussed in detail in Chapter 11.

8.2.4 Sales occupations

In terms of gender concentration, sales occupations display considerable variation across regions. Women are overrepresented in this Major Occupational Group in 16 of 19 OECD countries and 18 of 21 Latin American and African countries.[9] In contrast, women are very much underrepresented in sales occupations in North Africa and the Middle East, with an average representation ratio of only 0.28. Asia presents a mixed picture, with women overrepresented in five of ten countries/areas, and very underrepresented in two: India and Pakistan, where purdah and restrictions on women's interaction with men are common. The reasons behind these differences are discussed in more detail in subsequent chapters, such as Chapter 11 which investigates the feminization and masculinization of 17 specific occupations typically held by men and women. It appears that sales occupations, which require public contact between men and women, are not considered acceptable for women in a number of countries, such as in the Middle East/North Africa, India and Pakistan.[10]

8.2.5 Service occupations

Women are overrepresented in service occupations in all regions. Furthermore, the representation ratio exceeds 1.0 in *51 of the 56 countries/areas* for which we have data. Three of these five *exceptions are countries where Islam predominates;* a fourth is Nigeria where Islam is important.[11] Service occupations are a major source of employment for women as they include traditional women's occupations such as maids, ayahs, launderers, hairdressers and housekeepers. The five country exceptions reflect the fact that there are sizeable numbers of male barbers, launderers and houseboys in some countries.

8.2.6 Production occupations

Production occupations represent the largest Major Occupational Group as about 40 per cent of all non-agricultural employment is found here, ranging from about 33 per cent in the OECD to about 48 per cent in North Africa and the Middle East. As with the administrative and managerial Major Group, **women are greatly underrepresented in production occupations in all regions** and in *54 of the 56 countries/areas* reviewed. The only national exceptions to this generalization are in Asia (India and Pakistan; as well, China's representation ratio is 0.99).

There are, however, sharp contrasts within and between regions. At the regional level, *women have greater representation in production occupations in Asia* (although still underrepresented), with an average representation ratio of 0.74. In China, India and Pakistan, the female share of employment in production occupations is roughly equivalent to their overall share in non-agricultural employment. And, although women are underrepresented in the production occupations in other Asian countries such as Japan, Malaysia and the Republic of Korea, this ratio (0.70, 0.76 and 0.66 respectively) is relatively high when compared to the average for OECD countries, which is just 0.37.

The major role played by women in export-led industrialization is a much discussed topic, and our data confirm that women play an important role in production activities in these fast-growing Asian countries.[12] In particular, two garment-related occupations (spinners/weavers and tailors/ dressmakers) account for many of the women production workers in these countries. In the Republic of Korea, for example, 44 per cent of women in the production occupations in 1986 were employed in these two occupational groups. The same two occupational groups in the early 1980s accounted for about 27 per cent of all female production workers in Malaysia, India and China (although Indian women are mainly working in the traditional cottage industry sector doing spinning and weaving activities mainly for national consumption).

It is noteworthy that although the average representation ratio for North Africa and the Middle East is very low (0. 33), it approaches 1.0 in Tunisia (0.93). As with some Asian NICs, women work as spinners and weavers (50.4 per cent of all women in non-agricultural employment and 82.2 per cent of those in production occupations). It is also noteworthy that Mauritius has a representation ratio approaching those in Asia (0.90); Mauritius has pursued an economic growth strategy based on exports, and study data reflect the important role played by women in making this strategy successful.

The above discussion has identified some of the major similarities and differences between and within regions based on data for six non-agricultural Major Groups of occupations. The following chapters investigate occupational segregation of men and women based on much more detailed occupational data.

Notes

[1] Due to the difficulties in aggregating national classification systems to ISCO-comparable one-digit occupational groups, France, Switzerland and the United Kingdom are also omitted from analysis in the present chapter.

[2] The unusually high share of non-agricultural employment (approximately 13 per cent) in the administrative and managerial group in Canada and the United States is at least partly attributable to use of a wider classification for managerial workers than that generally provided by ISCO, encompassing some workers who, under ISCO guidelines, would usually be classified as self-employed managers in other major groups.

[3] As the coverage of Latin American and sub-Saharan African countries among study countries with detailed occupational data is relatively poor (see Chapters 4 and 7), we included information from the ILO *Yearbook of Labour Statistics* on the degree to which women are overrepresented or underrepresented for an additional seven Latin American and Caribbean countries and an additional five sub-Saharan African countries (table 8.2).

[4] In Haiti, for example, women comprised 65.2 per cent of non-agricultural workers in 1986 according to study data, while their share of professional and technical positions was 46.1 per cent. Employment was heavily concentrated in the sales sector (48.7 per cent of all non-agricultural employment) where 91.9 per cent of all such jobs were held by women.

[5] In ISCO-68, this Major Group is comprised of: (i) legislative officials and government administrators, and (ii) general managers. It does not, however, include all administrative and managerial workers; within each of the other Major Groups, certain occupations are defined as supervisory in nature (e.g. clerical supervisors are classified in the clerical major group).

[6] In Canada, women are underrepresented in two of the three managerial sub-categories—government officials and administrators (34 per cent female) and other managers and administrators (36 per cent female)—while they are overrepresented in the management and administrative-related category (50 per cent female).

[7] In the United States in 1991, 41 per cent of administrative and managerial workers were women. In the United States, this major group also includes administrators in education (55 per cent female), a group that is classified within the professional and technical category in ISCO-68.

[8] This result for Egypt may be partly due to an earlier government policy which guaranteed university graduates a government job, a policy that may have worked to the advantage of university-educated women.

[9] The concentration of women in sales occupations appears to be greater in Africa than in Latin America. The representation ratio is above 1.5 in five of eight African countries, while in only two Caribbean economies (Netherlands Antilles and Trinidad and Tobago). One obvious explanation for this difference is the greater importance of informal sector activities in African countries.

[10] It is noteworthy that in our other developing country/area group, sales occupations account for over 20 per cent of non-agricultural employment. Furthermore, women are very much overrepresented in sales occupations in three of the seven countries in this grouping, with their share of employment here approximately twice their average share of all non-agricultural employment. As indicated in subsequent chapters, informal sector activities, such as petty trading, shop-keeping and street hawking, account for the female domination in sales occupations in these countries.

[11] Women's underrepresentation in service occupations in Egypt appears to be due to male dominance of what in many other countries is a female-concentrated occupation: building caretakers and cleaners. In Egypt, fewer than 7 per cent of those workers were women.

[12] For an overview of this issue in Asia and the Pacific, see UNIDO, 1994.

Appendix 8.1

Table 8.3. Occupational structure and percentage female for six major non-agricultural occupational groups (one-digit data), latest available year (for study countries/areas)

Region/country/area	Major Occupational Group						
	Professional & technical	Admin. and managerial	Clerical	Sales	Services	Production	Total non-agricultural
OECD							
Australia 1990							
group as % of non-agr. LF	18.9	8.1	17.9	12.0	13.4	29.6	100.0
% female in group	45.0	16.5	77.3	58.6	57.2	11.8	42.2
Austria 1990							
group as % of non-agr. LF	16.2	6.1	17.4	9.9	12.0	38.5	100.0
% female in group	47.9	16.4	66.4	59.7	70.8	14.3	40.3
Canada 1990							
group as % of non-agr. LF	20.8	13.1	17.0	9.8	13.4	25.9	100.0
% female in group	50.4	40.7	80.0	45.6	56.9	14.0	45.0
Cyprus 1989							
group as % of non-agr. LF	22.5	3.2	8.9	14.6	18.4	32.7	100.0
% female in group	42.7	8.6	60.7	49.2	42.3	21.9	37.3
Germany (West) 1989							
group as % of non-agr. LF	17.4	4.0	21.7	9.8	12.0	35.1	100.0
% female in group	42.1	17.9	61.3	56.2	54.5	15.0	38.6
Finland 1990							
group as % of non-agr. LF	23.5	7.7	12.7	8.0	14.7	33.3	100.0
% female in group	57.5	26.9	85.8	59.6	76.5	19.6	49.1

Table 8.3. (contd.)

Region/country/area	Major Occupational Group						
	Professional & technical	Admin. and managerial	Clerical	Sales	Services	Production	Total non-agricultural
Italy 1981							
group as % of non-agr. LF	14.7	1.2	16.8	10.3	11.8	45.2	100.0
% female in group	46.8	13.9	43.7	40.5	44.7	19.5	32.6
Luxembourg 1991							
group as % of non-agr. LF	13.4	1.2	27.2	9.2	14.3	34.8	100.0
% female in group	36.5	11.6	48.9	53.3	72.5	6.7	35.9
Netherlands 1990							
group as % of non-agr. LF	25.6	4.8	20.0	11.0	13.3	25.3	100.0
% female in group	43.3	13.4	58.4	43.1	71.9	8.7	40.0
New Zealand 1986							
group as % of non-agr. LF	17.0	5.6	19.8	11.5	11.3	34.8	100.0
% female in group	48.5	17.6	74.4	46.9	63.1	16.6	42.3
Norway 1990							
group as % of non-agr. LF	24.7	5.8	10.9	11.9	15.0	30.7	100.0
% female in group	56.9	31.0	79.9	53.6	73.1	15.1	47.1
Spain 1990							
group as % of non-agr. LF	12.4	2.1	14.8	12.6	15.6	42.5	100.0
% female in group	46.2	9.2	47.8	43.7	57.2	12.3	32.7
Sweden 1991							
group as % of non-agr. LF	33.2	4.2	13.6	9.6	10.0	29.3	100.0
% female in group	61.1	33.9	80.0	48.9	64.9	18.3	49.0
United States 1991							
group as % of non-agr. LF	16.9	12.8	16.0	12.3	14.3	27.7	100.0
% female in group	51.2	40.7	79.8	49.5	59.6	18.2	46.3

OECD average							
group as % of non-agr. LF	19.8	5.7	16.8	10.9	13.5	33.4	100.0
% female in group	48.3	21.3	67.4	50.6	61.8	14.8	40.7
Middle East and North Africa							
Bahrain 1991							
group as % of non-agr. LF	15.8	6.3	9.9	5.0	26.7	37.3	100.0
% female in group	32.2	7.8	25.9	7.6	29.4	2.2	16.9
Egypt 1986							
group as % of non-agr. LF	22.1	1.4	14.7	9.2	11.9	40.8	100.0
% female in group	28.2	11.4	33.9	5.9	6.0	2.4	13.6
Iran, Islamic Rep. 1986							
group as % of non-agr. LF	16.7	0.7	5.8	12.0	7.2	57.6	100.0
% female in group	32.5	2.3	12.5	1.6	7.0	6.3	10.5
Jordan 1979							
group as % of non-agr. LF	13.8	2.4	5.9	8.6	7.5	61.8	100.0
% female in group	34.5	4.5	26.0	1.3	13.4	1.0	8.1
Kuwait 1985							
group as % of non-agr. LF	16.8	1.6	12.7	6.8	29.1	34.0	100.0
% female in group	33.3	3.7	23.8	2.7	38.0	0.2	20.0
Tunisia 1989							
group as % of non-agr. LF	11.0	2.1	8.3	9.7	11.1	57.9	100.0
% female in group	30.5	9.4	29.6	6.7	21.4	18.2	19.6
Middle East and North Africa average							
group as % of non-agr. LF	16.0	2.4	9.6	8.4	15.4	48.2	100.0
% female in group	31.9	6.5	25.3	4.3	19.2	5.1	14.8
Asia/Pacific							
China 1982							
group as % of non-agr. LF	18.1	5.6	4.7	6.4	7.9	57.4	100.0
% female in group	38.3	10.4	24.5	45.9	47.9	35.5	35.7

Table 8.3. (contd.)

Region/country/area	Major Occupational Group						
	Professional & technical	Admin. and managerial	Clerical	Sales	Services	Production	Total non-agricultural
Fiji 1986							
group as % of non-agr. LF	15.5	2.4	13.6	13.0	13.5	41.9	100.0
% female in group	39.7	9.1	47.1	29.1	48.3	9.5	27.1
Hong Kong 1991							
group as % of non-agr. LF	8.8	5.5	18.8	11.6	18.9	36.5	100.0
% female in group	45.5	27.0	63.7	36.7	43.0	23.5	37.9
India 1981							
group as % of non-agr. LF	10.5	3.5	10.9	15.1	10.0	50.0	100.0
% female in group	20.5	2.3	6.4	6.7	17.9	12.8	12.1
Japan 1990							
group as % of non-agr. LF	13.1	4.8	21.1	15.3	9.9	35.9	100.0
% female in group	39.6	8.8	60.1	36.9	56.0	27.3	39.3
Republic of Korea 1983							
group as % of non-agr. LF	7.8	1.3	14.8	22.0	12.5	41.6	100.0
% female in group	27.4	2.5	31.9	39.8	52.0	20.3	30.6
Malaysia 1980							
group as % of non-agr. LF	11.7	1.7	13.5	15.4	14.8	43.0	100.0
% female in group	38.2	8.3	43.3	24.8	32.1	22.0	28.3
Asia/Pacific average							
group as % of non-agr. LF	**12.2**	**3.5**	**13.9**	**14.1**	**12.5**	**43.8**	**100.0**
% female in group	**35.6**	**9.8**	**39.6**	**31.4**	**42.4**	**21.6**	**30.1**

Other Developing

Angola 1992							
group as % of non-agr. LF	17.6	0.3	13.2	24.8	10.1	33.9	100.0
% female in group	32.3	10.7	52.4	86.4	42.8	8.5	41.3
Costa Rica 1991							
group as % of non-agr. LF	12.7	5.0	9.7	13.2	19.3	39.6	100.0
% female in group	46.2	26.1	49.2	32.7	59.4	23.2	37.1
Ghana 1984							
group as % of non-agr. LF	10.4	0.8	6.0	35.2	6.1	41.6	100.0
% female in group	35.7	8.9	29.8	89.0	34.7	44.8	57.6
Haiti 1986							
group as % of non-agr. LF	9.9	0.9	1.6	48.7	11.0	27.9	100.0
% female in group	46.1	9.8	47.0	92.0	72.1	25.5	65.2
Mauritius 1990							
group as % of non-agr. LF	7.7	2.1	12.6	8.0	14.7	54.8	100.0
% female in group	38.9	17.8	36.7	23.7	40.1	27.9	31.1
Netherlands Antilles 1981							
group as % of non-agr. LF	13.9	2.0	24.1	1151	17.7	30.9	100.0
% female in group	48.9	9.1	52.1	58.2	64.0	3.1	38.5
Senegal 1988							
group as % of non-agr. LF	16.6	0.9	12.5	4.5	20.6	45.1	100.0
% female in group	23.8	7.3	43.8	27.7	45.2	6.3	22.8
Other Developing average							
group as % of non-agr. LF	**12.7**	**1.7**	**11.4**	**20.9**	**14.2**	**39.1**	**100.0**
% female in group	**38.8**	**12.8**	**44.4**	**58.5**	**51.2**	**25.6**	**42.0**

Notes: Values for group as % of non-agricultural LF sum up to 100.0 unless there is rounding error. They help to indicate the overall occupational structure of the labour market. Regional average is unweighted average of national values.
Sources: Study data.

OCCUPATIONAL SEGREGATION BY SEX BASED ON DETAILED OCCUPATIONAL DATA: INEQUALITY INDICES

9

The previous chapter analysed occupational segregation by sex around the world based on data for six major non-agricultural occupations. This analysis, which relied on simple statistics such as percentages and representation ratios, provided a broad picture of the general types of occupations held by men and women. However, as demonstrated in Chapter 6, one-digit occupational data do not provide the best basis for analysis of inequality statistics.

The present chapter, and all the remaining chapters in this book, expand the analysis of occupational segregation by sex in two major ways. First, **much more detailed two- and three-digit level data are used, with approximately 175 occupations per country on average,** from the unique ILO data set described in Chapter 4 which includes 41 countries or areas drawn from various regions: OECD (17), Transition Economies (4), Asia/Pacific (7), Middle East and North Africa (6), and Other Developing Countries and Areas (7). These data are reasonably up-to-date, as approximately 50 per cent of the national data are for the 1990s and 75 per cent are for 1985 or more recently.

Second, several different inequality statistics are used. Each statistic provides a different perspective on labour market inequality. The present chapter examines the index of dissimilarity (ID), the most commonly used indicator of occupational segregation by sex. Subsequent chapters in Part III analyse the extent to which the labour force is divided into what could be described as "male" or "female" occupations, and thus the extent to which occupations have become sex-stereotyped.

9.1 Index of dissimilarity (ID) and occupational segregation by sex in the world today

The index of dissimilarity is by far the most commonly used statistic in the research literature for analysing occupational segregation by sex. ID has a minimum value of 0 and a maximum value of 1.0. The higher is ID, the greater is occupational segregation by sex. Major advantages of the ID index are its simplicity and widespread usage.[1]

Table 9.1 presents reported national ID values for our 41 study countries and areas for the latest available year along with **ID values (ID75) that have been adjusted so that they are all based on 75 non-agricultural occupations, the number of non-agricultural occupations at the two-digit level in ISCO-68.** Figure 9.1 presents ID75 values for each country/area study. Table 9.2, then, summarizes unadjusted ID and adjusted ID values for our five study regions and divides study countries/areas into three roughly equal groupings with relatively low, middle or high ID75 values.

ID75 is estimated by taking into consideration the mathematical relationship between ID and the number of occupations on which ID is based (as estimated in Chapter 6). Readers are referred to Chapter 6 for an explanation of how national ID75 values are calculated, and Appendix 9.1, table 9.7 for these calculations. ID75 and ID differ, since the former are based on 75 occupations whereas the latter are based on varying levels of disaggregation in the occupational data (from 21 to 509 occupations for study countries/areas, see table 4.2 in Chapter 4). Indeed, the sensitivity of ID (as shown in Chapter 6) to the level of aggregation in the occupational data on which it is based has been one of the most important factors reducing comparability in earlier studies. Of course, our national ID75 values are not exactly comparable, as national classifications differ and the adjustments to ID are only approximate. Also, national ID75 values are only estimates, and consequently differences between national values (especially small differences) must be interpreted very cautiously.[2] On the other hand, ID75 has greater comparability across countries as compared to ID.

Study data indicate a high degree of occupational segregation by sex in the world. The (unweighted) average ID75 for our 41 study countries and areas is approximately .58.[3] And ID75 exceeds .50 for 34 of our 41 study countries/areas. These high levels of inequality are even more striking when one considers the relatively "low" level of detail on which ID75 is based (as 75 occupations are not really very many occupations for representing complex labour markets, even if they are greater than for previous cross-national studies). For example, as demonstrated in Chapter 6, ID tends to be approximately .07 higher when based on typical three-digit data (approximately 265 non-agricultural occupations) as compared to typical two-digit data (approximately 75 non-agricultural occupations).

A second striking aspect of these data are the large differences across regions (table 9.2 and figure 9.2). The Asian region has the lowest level of occupational segregation by sex. The Middle East and North Africa has the highest level of occupational segregation by sex, with the Other Developing region the next highest. The OECD and Transition Economy regions are similar, with average ID75 levels in between those in Asia/Pacific and Other Developing Economies. *ID75 ranges from approximately .48 in Asia/Pacific, to .56 in OECD and Transition Economies, to .63 in the Other Developing region and to .68 in the Middle East and North Africa.*[4]

Table 9.1. National ID and ID75 (i.e. ID adjusted to classification with 75 non-agricultural occupations), latest available year

Region/country/area	ID (unadjusted)	Number of non-ag. occup. (NOCC)	ID75 (i.e. ID adjusted to 75 non-ag. occup.)
OECD			
Australia	.615	279	.581
Austria	.597	64	.607
Canada	.509	44	.541[*]
Cyprus	.634	376	.570[*]
Finland	.673	264	.616
France[a]	.607	433	.556[*]
Germany (West)[a]	.600	268	.523[**]
Italy	.517	231	.449
Luxembourg	.586	71	.589
Netherlands	.588	150	.567
New Zealand	.618	281	.582
Norway	.646	291	.573
Spain	.570	77	.569
Switzerland	.654	452	.581
Sweden	.604	49	.630[*]
United Kingdom	.638	509	.567
United States	.548	461	.463[**]
OECD average (unweighted)	**.600**	**253**	**.563**
Asia/Pacific			
China	.443	277	.363[**]
Fiji	.600	75	.603
Hong Kong	.490	73	.493
India	.492	423	.446
Japan	.529	259	.502[*]
Korea, Republic of	.402	56	.432[*]
Malaysia	.490	76	.489
Asian average (unweighted)	**.492**	**177**	**.476**
Other Developing			
Angola	.652	67	.656
Costa Rica	.566	55	.598[*]
Ghana	.710	75	.710
Haiti	.669	75	.669
Mauritius	.586	70	.593
Netherlands Antilles	.645	76	.644
Senegal	.577	80	.573
Average (unweighted)	**.629**	**71**	**.635**
Transition Economies			
Bulgaria	.507	43	.541[*]
Hungary	.585	118	.558[*]

Table 9.1. (contd.)

Region/country/area	ID (unadjusted)	Number of non-ag. occup. (NOCC)	ID75 (i.e. ID adjusted to 75 non-ag. occup.)
Poland	.677	361	.592**
Former Yugoslavia	.602	206	.540**
Average (unweighted)	**.593**	**182**	**.558**
Middle East and North Africa			
Bahrain	.635	86	.627
Egypt	.586	74	.587
Iran, Islamic Rep.	.638	21	.681*
Jordan	.769	61	.776
Kuwait	.743	268	.733
Tunisia	.663	55	.695*
Average (unweighted)	**.672**	**94**	**.683**
Total average (unweighted)	**.597**	**179**	**.577**

Notes: * One asterisk indicates when the adjustment for ID75 is relatively large (between 0.02 and 0.049). ** Two asterisks indicates when the adjustment for ID75 is especially large (greater than 0.05).
[a] ID75 value is very similar to that reported in recent European Union (EU) publication (Rubery and Fagan, 1993) for France, West Germany, Luxembourg, Netherlands, Spain and the United Kingdom.
See table 9.7 in Appendix 9.1 for source of unadjusted ID as well as size and method of adjustment to derive ID75.
Source: Study data.

Third, **there is considerable similarity in national ID75 within each study region** (see figure 9.1) which is also demonstrated by dividing study countries and areas based on ID75 into three groups (relatively low, middle, high ID75 values) with roughly equal numbers in each group (table 9.2).[5] In each region, study countries/areas tend to fall into one of these three groups. OECD and Transition Economy countries tend to have middle levels of inequality, as 12 out of the 21 study countries in these regions are in the middle group with the remaining countries in these regions fairly evenly split among the low and high groupings. Asian countries/areas have relatively low levels of inequality, as all of the Asian study countries/areas except Fiji are in the relatively low group. Middle Eastern and North African countries have high levels of inequality, as 5 of these 6 countries are in the relatively high group. The Other Developing region tends to have relatively high ID75 values as 4 of the 7 study countries/areas in this region are in the relatively high ID75 grouping. This similarity in ID75 values within regions, with at the same time large differences in ID75 between regions (also indicated by the fact that the standard deviation for ID75 is much lower within each region as compared to the standard deviation for all countries/areas, as shown in table 9.2) implies that factors related to cultural, historical and social/legal systems play an important role in determining the extent of labour market segregation for men and women.

Figure 9.1. National ID75 values (i.e. ID adjusted to 75 non-agricultural occupations), latest available year

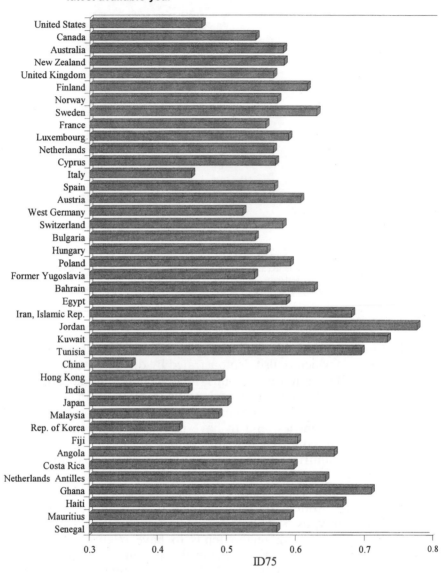

Note: Countries and areas arranged by region and by subregion for OECD countries.
Source: Table 9.1.

A fourth striking aspect of these data is the extent to which there is similarity in national ID75 values within OECD subregions (table 9.3 and figure 9.3). This is shown by the generally lower dispersion of values (as measured by the standard deviation) within OECD subregions as compared to that

GENDER AND JOBS

Table 9.2. Distribution of countries and areas by relative level (low, middle, high) for adjusted ID (i.e. ID75), latest available year, by region

Region	Low ID75 (<.55)		Middle ID75 (.55–.59)		High ID75 (>.60)		Mean[a] (x) Std deviation (σ)
	No.	Countries/areas	No.	Countries/areas	No.	Countries/areas	
OECD	4	Italy (.449*) United States (.463*) Germany (West) (.523*) Canada (.541*)	10	France (.556) Netherlands (.567) United Kingdom (.567) Spain (.569) Cyprus (.570) Norway (.573) Australia (.581) New Zealand (.582) Switzerland (.581) Luxembourg (.589)	3	Austria (.607) Finland (.616) Sweden (.630*)	$x = .560$ $\sigma = .056$
Transition Economies	2	Yugoslavia (.540*) Bulgaria (.541*)	2	Hungary (.558) Poland (.592*)	0		$x = .558$ $\sigma = .024$
Asia	6	China (.363*) Korea, Rep. (.432) India (.446) Malaysia (.489) Hong Kong (.493) Japan (.502*)	0		1	Fiji (.603)	$x = .476$ $\sigma = .074$
Other Developing	0		3	Senegal (.573) Mauritius (.593) Costa Rica (.598)	4	Netherlands Antilles (.644) Angola (.656) Haiti (.669) Ghana (.710)	$x = .635$ $\sigma = .049$
Middle East and North Africa	0		1	Egypt (.587)	5	Bahrain (.627) Iran, Islamic Rep. (.681*) Tunisia (.695)	$x = .683$ $\sigma = .068$

Table 9.2. (contd.)

Region	Low ID75 (<.55)		Middle ID75 (.55–.59)		High ID75 (>.60)		Mean[a] (x) Std deviation (σ)
	No.	Countries/areas	No.	Countries/areas	No.	Countries/areas	
				Kuwait (.733)			
				Jordan (.776)			
	16	0.577	13	0.666	12	0.482	
				Total average (unweighted)			
				$x = .576 \ \sigma = .085$			

Notes: * Indicates when ID75 includes a relatively large adjustment factor (between .02 and .049). ** Indicates when ID75 includes an especially large adjustment factor (greater than .05). [a] Averages are unweighted averages of country values in region.
Dividing line values for low, middle and high ID75 ranges based on ad hoc considerations such as use of "round numbers" (i.e. .50, .55, .60) and an interest to obtain similar numbers of countries in each grouping.
Source: Table 9.1.

Figure 9.2. Regional ID75 averages, latest available year

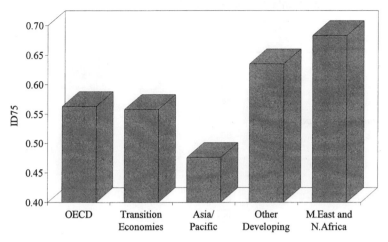

Source: Table 9.2.

for the OECD region as a whole (also see figure 9.1). The only seemingly heterogeneous OECD subregion is our southern European subregion which has a relatively high standard deviation of .10 (but with a relatively low average ID75 value of .51).[6] These results imply that cultural, historical and social/legal systems play a major role in determining labour market segregation by sex.

Since regional and national ID75 values are not always consistent with *a priori* expectations, some interesting and/or unexpected results are discussed below before a multi-variate regression analysis is presented in section 9.2.

Some interesting regional results

At the regional level, it is surprising that **Transition Economy (TE) countries prior to the fall of communism** had such high levels of occupational segregation by sex and that these were **similar to those in OECD countries** (figure 9.2). Earlier publications had (see, for example, United Nations, 1985a and Bodrova and Anker, 1985) concluded that labour market equality by sex was higher in communist Europe as compared to capitalist Europe.[7] The surprising result here might be partly due to data limitations, since (i) previous occupational classification systems in TE countries were conceptually different from those in OECD countries; (ii) ID75 for all four TE study countries is measured with less precision than usual, because of the relatively large adjustment factors included in ID75; and (iii) TE study countries are limited to only four countries. Despite these data limitations, we feel that we are observing a real phenomenon.

Table 9.3. OECD subregional averages and standard deviations for ID75, latest available year

OECD subregion/ country	ID75	Average[a]	Standard deviation
North America		.502	.055
Canada	.541*		
United States	.463**		
Other English-speaking		.577	.008
Australia	.581		
New Zealand	.582		
United Kingdom	.567		
Scandinavia		.606	.030
Finland	.616		
Norway	.573		
Sweden	.630*		
Western Europe		.571	.016
Netherlands	.567		
Luxembourg	.589		
France	.556*		
Southern Europe		.529	.070
Cyprus	.570*		
Italy	.449**		
Spain	.569		
Central Europe		.570	.043
Austria	.607		
Switzerland	.581		
Germany (West)	.523**		

Note: [a] Based on unweighted averages of country values from tables 9.1 and 9.2.
Recent ID estimates are also available for three additional European countries based on 80 occupations (including agriculture) from Rubery and Fagan (1993). Belgium had an ID of 0.47; Denmark had an ID of 0.59; and Portugal had an ID of 0.46.
* Indicates when ID75 includes a relatively large adjustment factor (between .02 and .049).
** Indicates when ID75 includes an especially large adjustment factor (greater than .05).
Source: Table 9.1.

There are several possible explanations for the similar ID75 values in OECD and TE countries. They can be explained in part by the greater progress made in many OECD countries over the past two decades in reducing occupational segregation by sex (see analysis on recent changes in Part IV), as analysts have probably been slow to appreciate both the changes going on in OECD countries as well as the stagnation in TE countries. Indeed, the entry of women into the non-agricultural labour force was more or less completed by 1970 in TE countries but still had a long way to go in 1970 in OECD countries. Another partial explanation is that analysts probably had

Figure 9.3. OECD subregional ID75 averages, latest available year

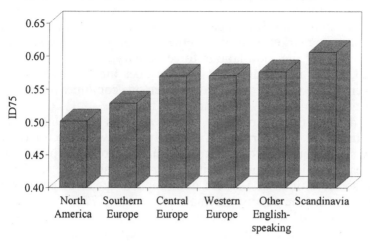

Source: Table 9.3.

a somewhat false earlier impression of the real situation in these former communist countries. A third possible explanation is that analysts undoubtedly did not sufficiently appreciate the long-lasting effects cultural and historical factors have on occupational segregation by sex.

In a related point, it is important to keep in mind that TE countries are neither homogenous in terms of their ID75 values nor in terms of their cultural, religious and historical foundations prior to communism. Indeed, the relatively high level of occupational segregation by sex in Poland is more similar to (yet slightly lower than) that found in Scandinavia; and levels in Hungary and Bulgaria are similar to, yet slightly lower than those found in capitalist Central Europe. Therefore, a more nuanced interpretation of ID75 values for Transition Economy study countries would be that communism did indeed help reduce occupational segregation by sex, but that this effect was weaker than many believed and had become relatively small by the fall of communism.[8]

It may also surprise many readers (especially Western readers) that **OECD countries tend to have rather average levels of occupational segregation by sex for the world** (see figure 9.2). They are definitely not among the lowest in the world. The fact is that OECD countries have very segmented labour markets based on sex, and this segmentation continues to exist in the face of high levels of female education, low male-female differentials in the number of years of schooling completed, high levels of female employment, high income levels, low fertility rates, and increasing popularity of feminist ideas of gender equity with women's participation in economic, political and social life.

One possibility is that analysts and laypersons may be combining into one impression different aspects of labour market inequality. For example, they may be combining (i) occupational segregation by sex for women who are in the labour market with (ii) whether or not women are excluded from the labour market (i.e. non-labour force activity). Readers are referred to section 9.3, where it is found that Europe does indeed have relatively low levels of gender inequality for the world when one combines these two aspects of labour market inequality into one index number.

In contrast, and unexpectedly, **Asian countries have relatively low ID75 values for the world.** Furthermore, a relatively low level of occupational segregation by sex is found throughout our Asian region (except in Fiji, which strictly speaking is in the South Pacific), despite considerable gender discrimination in society—in China where news reports speak of parents aborting pregnancies when the foetus is female (*New York Times,* 1994); in Japan and the Republic of Korea where male-female pay differentials are among the highest in the world (table 2.2) and news reports describe the difficulties women face in getting good jobs (Manpower, 1994); and in India where women comprise a very low percentage of the non-agricultural labour force and women are discriminated against in such basics as health care (Khan, Anker and Ghosh, 1989).

There are several possible explanations for Asia's relatively low ID75 levels. Of course, there might be major problems with Asian study data. My feeling after working closely with these data, however, is that they are of acceptable quality and that the lower level of occupational segregation by sex observed in Asia is a real phenomenon.[9]

One possibility is that Asia has a "favourable" occupational structure which "predisposes" Asian labour markets towards lower average ID75 values (i.e. by having a relatively high proportion of the non-agricultural labour force in occupations with relatively equal numbers of male and female workers). In fact, this does not appear to be the case, partly because Asia has a relatively high percentage of its non-agricultural labour force in production occupations, a set of occupations which tend to have relatively high levels of occupational segregation by sex (see Chapter 8).[10] Another possibility is that Asia's somewhat lower levels of female labour force participation as compared to the OECD might be allowing women to integrate into the labour market on a more equal basis through the inclusion of mainly the better educated women; yet this explanation has only weak support from the regression analysis discussed in section 9.2 which relates female education and labour force participation to occupational segregation by sex.

One (at least partial) explanation for Asia's unexpectedly low ID75 values is that occupational segregation by sex in Asia has to some extent a qualitatively different character. As compared to other regions, there is undoubtedly more *"vertical segregation"* in Asia, which is not picked up by two- or three-digit occupational classifications—whereby men and women are often in the same occupational group (for broad groups such as clerks, other clericals, and administrators) but in jobs with different grades/echelons, with women more likely to be in grades with lower pay and less authority, status and career advancement possibilities.[11] Obtaining jobs in a wider range of occupations is only part of the answer if women are to obtain higher paying jobs. It is also important for women to get jobs in the private sector, in larger and better paying private sector companies and to be promoted to higher grades within an occupation. In Japan, for example, many companies have two different types of jobs in terms of career promotion possibilities, with women being restricted to the set where promotion to a managerial positions is not possible.[12] Only recently has this system begun to break down somewhat in Japan (Lam, 1992).

Another reason why the relatively low level of occupational segregation by sex in Asia might appear surprising may be that analysts and laypersons are unconsciously thinking about levels of female labour force activity and whether or not women are in the labour force rather than occupational segregation by sex for those in the labour force. Indeed, when those two aspects of labour market inequality are combined into one index number (see section 9.3), it is found that East Asian countries have similar levels of occupational segregation by sex (and India a higher level) as compared to OECD countries.

Some interesting national and OECD subregional results

There are also some interesting, and surprising, national results worth pointing out and investigating further. It may surprise many readers to find that **Scandinavian countries** Finland and Sweden **have the highest ID75 values among OECD countries** (and Norway's ID75 is also relatively high),[13] and these values fall within our relatively high ID75 grouping. Yet, the general impression among laypersons is that Scandinavian countries have a relatively low level of occupational segregation by sex, since they have reasonably high female-male pay ratios (with women receiving on average approximately 90 per cent as much pay as men in Finland and Sweden—among the highest percentages in the world—according to data in the ILO *Yearbook of Labour Statistics* reported in table 2.2). They are also relatively egalitarian societies with a strong public policy commitment to gender-equality. Indeed, child-care expenditures absorb approximately 6 per cent of GDP in Sweden and much of this is supported by the government, since "functions which used to be carried out at home are now done in the public sector" (Denmark's finance minister Mogens Lykketoft quoted in *Economist*, 5 November 1994). This policy of providing support for working women not only helps women to be labour force participants; it also contributes to occupational segregation by sex, since women dominate these care-related labour force occupations. For example, in Sweden in 1990, women were 96.5, 73.5 and 89.2 per cent respectively of the following occupations: child-care minders, social workers, and other care-givers; and these three occupations, which are generally public sector supported, accounted for 14.7 per cent of all female non-agricultural employment.[14] Scandinavian countries have established separate but reasonably equal labour markets for men and women, but as discussed below in Chapters 10 and 12, it is questionable whether or not this model is transferable to other countries and if it is sustainable into the future in Scandinavia.

Among OECD countries, two **(Italy and the United States) have especially low ID75 values for this region.** The contrast between the United States and many European OECD countries both in the level and downward trend in occupational segregation by sex is particularly interesting (see Part IV for a discussion of recent changes).[15]

Among Middle Eastern and North African countries, Egypt has a relatively low ID75 for this region (which is none the less above average for the world). This cannot be attributed to higher female education levels, as Egypt does not have a relatively high level of female education for the region (see Chapter 7). One possible explanation could be that Egypt has relatively less traditional social values for the Middle Eastern region.[16]

Among Asia/Pacific countries, Fiji has an unusually high ID75. It is so different from other countries in the region as to imply that Fiji—a small island state in the South Pacific—more appropriately belongs in our Other Developing region in terms of occupational segregation by sex.

Among other Asian countries, we are particularly struck by the **low ID75 values for China and India.** One should not forget that China and India include over two billion people, and around 40 per cent of the world's population.

China has the lowest ID75 among our 41 study countries and areas. It would seem reasonable to hypothesize that this situation is caused in part by an ideological commitment of the Chinese government to gender equity. On the other hand, as noted above, former communist Transition Economy countries in Europe, which presumably had a similar ideological commitment to gender equity, did not have substantially lower ID75 values as compared to non-TE European countries. It is unclear why a presumably similar ideological commitment should be more effective in China than it was in Europe. One possible explanation could be that the non-agricultural sector was, and still is, much smaller in China and so communist China inherited less of a sexist tradition in non-agricultural sectors. Another possible explanation is that, just as there seems to have been a convergence over time in ID75 values in capitalist and communist European countries (see discussion on this in Part IV), perhaps the same thing is occurring in Asia. The increase in ID75 observed in China between 1982 and 1990 (see Part IV) could be indicative of such a process of convergence.[17]

India's relatively low ID75 is surprising in light of its low female non-agricultural labour force participation rate (which indicates a strong bias against women working at all), and the fact that gender biases in Indian society are known to be very large (reflected by, for example, the unusual phenomenon of a higher life expectancy in India for men as compared to women). India seems to be unique in the world—in that it has a relatively low ID75 while having at the same time very low female non-agricultural labour force participation rates and very few female-dominated occupations (see Chapter 12). Thus, it seems that Indian women face less occupational segregation by sex than in almost all other countries once they get into the non-agricultural labour force, even though they face considerable social and economic barriers to entering the non-agricultural labour force. It would be worthwhile analysing more recent 1991 Indian census data in part to observe recent changes and in part to see if the unusual combination of a low percentage female for the non-agricultural labour force and relatively low ID75 is a statistical artefact.

9.2 Socio-economic, labour market and regional determinants of occupational segregation (as measured by ID75)

An important issue is whether occupational segregation by sex in countries is related to national socio-economic and labour market conditions. For this reason, in this section we relate ID75 to some key socio-economic and labour market variables using OLS multiple regressions (tables 9.4 to 9.6). Regional binaries are also specified, in part to control for cultural and historical differences and in part to see if the regional differences in ID75 observed in section 9.1 can be attributed to differences in socio-economic and labour market conditions across regions.

Readers need to keep in mind that the following regression analysis is relatively simple as only a small set of explanatory variables are used. As a result, explanatory variables which are included in this regression analysis may "inappropriately capture" the effect of factors which are not included due to data limitations. In addition, all cross-national multivariate analyses are subject to important limitations such as high multi-colinearity among socio-economic variables, often making it difficult to estimate the separate effect of each explanatory variable.[18] For these reasons, the following regression analysis is kept fairly simple—more to provide insights than definitive answers.

A priori expectations are that occupational segregation by sex will decrease along with economic development and rising income levels, as women become: better prepared for labour force activity (indicated by improved female education levels), and less constrained by family responsibilities and traditional social values (as birth rates and traditional family-based roles for women weaken along with modernization).[19]

It is expected that occupational segregation by sex will be negatively related to female labour force activity. As women enter the labour market in increasing numbers, the duration and diversity of their labour-market experiences should increase, as should labour market commitment. Also, along with changes in women's labour force commitment, one would expect equity laws to become increasingly important and employers' opinions of women workers to become increasingly positive. These changes, should, in turn, encourage the entry of women into traditional male occupations. In any case, it seems logical that some of the increasing numbers of women workers entering the labour market would find employment in non-traditional occupations for women. It is difficult to predict how increases in the level of part-time employment should affect occupational segregation by sex. While on the one hand, part-time jobs tend to be highly clustered as regards occupation and this should help increase overall levels of occupational segregation, on the other hand, part-time employment allows many women to continue labour force activity even during the life-cycle period of family formation, thereby increasing women's human capital and chances of staying in non-traditional occupations for women.

Figures 9.4 and 9.5 provide scatterplots of ID75 with GDP per capita and education levels of adult women respectively. These figures indicate that there is no consistent relationship between ID75 and the level of socio-economic development across countries.

Regression results confirm that **differences in ID75 are not significantly related to any of the three socio-economic variables specified in table 9.4**[20] **when regional variables are also specified** (equations 2, 3, 4, and 6 in table

Figure 9.4. Scatterplot of ID75 and gross domestic product per capita (GDPPC), latest available year

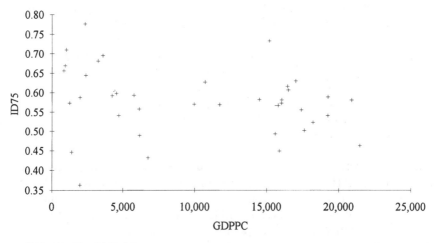

Sources: Tables 4.1–4.5 and table 9.8.

Figure 9.5. Scatterplot of ID75 and education level of adult women (EDF), latest available year

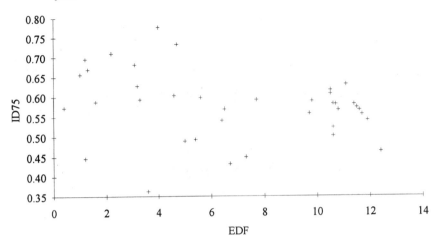

Sources: Table 4.1–4.5 and table 9.8.

9.4). Coefficients for all three socio-economic variables are small in magnitude, having elasticities less than 0.10 (based on equation 6), implying that a 10 per cent increase (over mean values) in GDPPC, PAG or EDF is associated with a change in ID75 of less than 0.005.

Regional variables, by themselves, account for over one-half of the variation in ID75. The R square (adjusted R square) is .61 (.56) based on equation 1 (table 9.4). Furthermore, estimated coefficients for three of the four study regions are significantly different from those in OECD (positive for the Other Developing region and Middle East/North Africa and negative for Asia/Pacific) and quite large at around .07 for Asia, +.07 for the Other Developing region and +.17 for Middle East/North Africa (equation 5, table 9.4). ID75 values for Transition Economy countries (TE) are again found to be similar to those for OECD countries (the "excluded" region in the regressions).

ID75 is not quite significantly related to PFEM (table 9.4).[21] The positive sign for PFEM is, however, at variance with *a priori* expectations as we expected increases in PFEM would be associated with decreasing occupational segregation.

To investigate this result further, additional regressions were estimated. PFEM was regressed on ID75 separately for: (i) each study region (table 9.5 and figure 9.6) and (ii) using a non-linear specification and different ranges of PFEM (table 9.6 and figure 9.7). For simplicity, only regional binaries and PFEM are specified in these regressions (in part because the socio-economic variables specified in table 9.4 were insignificant).

Table 9.4. Regression results (OLS) relating socio-economic and labour market variables to ID75 for latest available year (t statistics in brackets)

Independent variables	Equations						
	(1)	(2)	(3)	(4)	(5)	(6)	(7^z)
Constant	0.562 $(42.18)^a$	0.547 $(14.10)^a$	0.565 $(41.22)^a$	0.516 $(9.94)^a$	0.487 $(10.47)^a$	0.510 $(6.44)^a$	0.544 $(19.10)^a$
TE	−0.005 (0.16)	0.011 (0.26)	−0.002 (0.07)	0.012 (0.32)	−0.006 (0.21)	−0.026 (0.52)	x
ASIA	−0.087 $(3.53)^a$	−0.079 $(2.44)^c$	−0.072 $(2.38)^b$	−0.064 $(1.83)^c$	−0.066 $(2.46)^b$	−0.057 (1.56)	x
ME	0.121 $(4.62)^a$	0.130 $(3.70)^a$	0.127 $(4.68)^a$	0.154 $(3.45)^a$	0.169 $(4.40)^a$	0.169 $(3.24)^a$	x
OD	0.072 $(2.92)^a$	0.085 $(2.12)^b$	0.088 $(2.87)^a$	0.107 $(2.26)^b$	0.071 $(2.96)^a$	0.080 (1.56)	x
GDPPC	x	9.60×10^{-7} (0.42)	x	x	x	-3.18×10^{-6} (0.81)	x
PAG	x	x	4.72×10^{-4} (0.89)	x	x	6.71×10^{-4} (0.75)	x
EDF	x	x	x	0.005 (0.94)	x	0.003 (0.46)	x
PFEM	x	x	x	x	0.0018 (1.69)	0.0017 (1.37)	x
PTIME	x	x	x	x	x	x	0.0011 (0.67)
R^2	0.61	0.61	0.62	0.61	0.64	0.64	0.03

Adjusted R^2	0.56	0.55	0.56	0.55	0.58	0.55	−0.04
F value	13.89	10.56	11.21	10.35	12.25	6.69	0.447
Significance F	.001	.001	.001	.001	.001	.001	0.516
Degrees of freedom (residual)	36	34	35	33	35	30	13

Notes: ASIA is binary variable representing Asia/Pacific.
  ME is binary variable representing Middle East and North Africa.
  TE is binary variable representing Transition Economies.
  OD is binary variable representing the Other Developing region.
  The excluded region for the set of regional binaries is OECD.

GDPPC is GDP per capita adjusted for purchasing power parity.
PAG is percentage of labour force in an agricultural occupation.
EDF is the average number of years of education completed by adult women.
PFEM is the percentage of non-agricultural labour force which is female.
PTIME is the percentage of labour force in part-time job.

[a] Significant at the .01 level. [b] Significant at the .05 level. [c] Significant at the .10 level. [z] Data available for OECD only. x indicates that variable is not specified in equation.
Degrees of freedom somewhat differ across equations due to missing information for some equations: former Yugoslavia for GDPPC; former Yugoslavia and Netherlands Antilles for FED; Cyprus and Switzerland for PTIME.
When GDPPC, PAG, EDF and PFEM are specified in quadratic form in equations 2-6, both the square and linear terms are insignificant at the .10 level (unreported regressions).
Sources: For most socio-economic independent variables: UNDP's *Human Development Report, 1993* and other national study data. Years for these data correspond as much as possible to the year for study occupational data (see tables in Chapter 4). For dependent variable (ID75) and PFEM: study data.

Table 9.5. Regression results (OLS) for ID75 as a function of percentage female for non-agricultural labour force (PFEM), by region (t values in brackets)

Independent variables	OECD	Transition Economies	Middle East and North Africa	Asia/Pacific	Other Developing	Total	
						Without regional binaries	With regional binaries
Constant	0.4617	0.4910	0.7208	0.4846	0.5145	0.6012	0.487
	$(4.87)^a$	$(4.33)^a$	$(6.73)^a$	$(4.33)^a$	$(15.79)^a$	$(15.07)^a$	$(10.47)^a$
PFEM	0.0024	0.0016	−0.0025	−0.0003	0.0029	-6.72×10^{-4}	0.0018
	(1.07)	(0.59)	(0.37)	(0.09)	$(3.88)^b$	(0.63)	$(1.69)^c$
R^2	0.07	0.15	0.03	0.00	0.75	0.01	0.64
Adjusted R^2	0.01	−0.28	−0.21	−0.20	0.70	−0.02	0.58
F value	1.15	0.35	0.13	0.01	15.03	0.41	12.25
Significance F	0.301	0.614	0.732	0.936	0.001	0.527	0.001
N	17	4	6	7	7	41	41

Notes: [a] Significant at .01 level. [b] Significant at .05 level. [c] Significant at .10 level.
PFEM is the percentage of the non-agricultural labour force which is female.
Source: Study data.

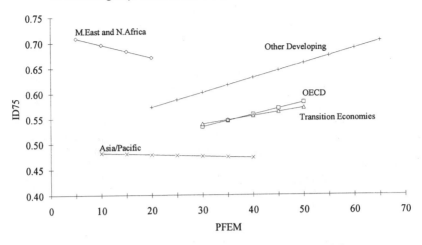

Note: Based on regression analysis where only PFEM is specified (i.e. region is not specified).
Source: Table 9.5.

When regional binaries are *not* specified, the regression results shown in tables 9.5–9.6 and figures 9.6–9.7 indicate that ID75 and PFEM tend to be negatively related when PFEM is low (up to around 35 per cent), as well as for regions (Asia/Pacific and Middle East/North Africa) with low to middle PFEM values. In contrast, ID75 and PFEM tend to be positively related for higher PFEM values (from around 35 per cent), as well as for regions (OECD, Transition Economies and Other Developing) with middle to high PFEM values. These results provide support, for the argument that increasing female labour force participation helps break down occupational barriers— but only when women comprise a relatively small percentage of the non-agricultural labour force.

When regional binaries, however, *are* specified and PFEM is specified in quadratic form (equation 2, top half of table 9.6), PFEM and ID75 are weakly (and insignificantly) related. Thus, the significant non-linear relationship observed in equation 1, top half of table 9.6 is mainly be due to PFEM proxying for average regional differences—and may simply reflect the fact that ID75 values are relatively low in our Asian region (where PFEM values tend to be around 35 per cent) as compared to Middle East and North African countries on the one hand (where ID75 is relatively high and PFEM relatively low) and OECD, Transition Economy and Other Developing countries/areas on the other hand (where PFEM tends to be greater than 35 per cent and ID75 tends to be average to high).[22]

In summary, the above relatively simple cross-section regression analysis at one point in time leads to the following conclusions. First, sex-segregation

Table 9.6. Regression results for ID75 as a function of percentage of non-agricultural labour force which is female (PFEM), by level of PFEM (t values in brackets)

Using quadratic form	For full sample $(N = 41)^d$	
	without regional binaries	with regional binaries
PFEM	−0.0132	−0.0017
	$(3.49)^a$	(0.43)
$(PFEM)^2$	1.877×10^{-4}	4.612×10^{-5}
	$(3.42)^a$	(0.90)
Constant	0.779	0.554
Implied Turning Point	35.2	18.4
Degrees of Freedom (residual)	38	34

Using PFEM ranges	For countries in specified PFEM range^{e,f}
<30	−0.0052
<35	$−0.0064^b$
>0.35	0.0050^b
>0.40	0.0050^b
35–49	0.0030
40–49	−0.0010

Notes: ^{a} Significant at .01 level. ^{b} Significant at .05 level. ^{c} Significant at .10 level. ^{d} PFEM is per cent of non-agricultural labour force with is female. ^{e} PFEM is specified in linear form when function is estimated for a PFEM range, since range is too small for non-linear relationship. (Note that unreported regressions indicate that PFEM and $(PFEM)^2$ are always insignificant when both are specified for each range.) ^{f} Regional binaries are not specified in this equation because of limitations on degrees of freedom in this respect.
Source: Study data.

levels in study countries are not related to either socio-economic development (proxied for by GDP per capita, average female education level and percentage of workers in agricultural occupations) or among OECD countries to the extensiveness of part-time employment. Second, women's share of non-agricultural employment in study countries and areas is found to be significantly or insignificantly related to occupational segregation by sex depending on the specification of the regression equation. When the region to which a study country belongs is specified, ID75 is found to be positively and almost significantly related to PFEM. When region is not specified, ID75 is found to be significantly related to PFEM in a non-linear way (negatively related for PFEM values up to around 35 per cent and positively related for PFEM values above 35 per cent). Third, the large regional differences

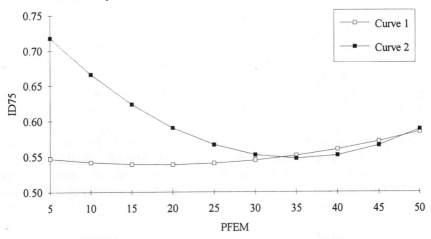

Notes: Curve 1 is estimated with regional binaries specified. Regional binaries are not specified for curve 2.
Source: Table 9.6, equations in top half of table.

observed in tables 9.1 and 9.2 cannot be explained away by differences in socio-economic levels or labour market conditions. This result provides empirical support for arguments presented in Chapters 1 and 2 that cultural, social, legal and historical factors are important determinants of occupational segregation by sex and that these effects persist for long periods of time, even in the face of economic development and the education of women. **Indeed, the regression results reported on in this section imply that cultural, social, legal and historical factors are probably the most important determinants of occupational segregation by sex around the world.**

9.3 Occupational segregation by sex if one assumed that one-half of the non-agricultural labour force is female and that supposedly non-working women are in fact working in a new occupation entitled "unpaid housepersons and care-givers"

It is possible to think of labour market inequality as consisting of two separate aspects: (i) women being left out of the labour market altogether (and assigned to so-called non-labour force activities of housework and care-giving); and (ii) occupational segregation by sex for women who are in the labour market. The latter is, of course, the focus of this book, while the former is ignored (except when we analyse the relationship between occupational segregation by sex and the percentage of the non-agricultural labour force which is female). In order to investigate how countries differ in regard to the combination of these two aspects, a new version of the ID index (which has been dubbed IDHALF because women are assumed to make up one-half of the non-agricultural labour force) is created in this section. IDHALF is calculated based on the assumption that there are equal numbers of men and women in the non-agricultural labour force and that women who are not in the officially measured non-agricultural labour force are working as "unpaid housepersons and care-givers".

The definition of the labour force implied by IDHALF is consistent with United Nations' recommendations that the value of unpaid household activities should be incorporated into an extended measure of GDP. Indeed, unpaid household work makes an extremely important contribution to welfare, with its value estimated to be between 25 to 50 per cent of currently measured GNP (Goldschmidt-Clermont, 1982 and UNDP, 1987). This definition is also consistent with suggestions in earlier ILO publications by the author (see for example, Anker, Khan and Gupta, 1987; and Dixon-Mueller and Anker, 1988) concerning the usefulness of a new "extended labour force" definition which includes many so-called non-labour force activities. It is also consistent with the focus of the 1995 UNDP *Human Development Report* as well as ILO posters for the 1995 Beijing World Conference on Women which stated that "All women are working women".

IDHALF is calculated in exactly the same manner as ID—but after a new occupational category "unpaid housepersons and care-givers" has been created. In order to simplify calculations, the number of women workers in this new occupation (and note that by assumption all workers in this occupation are women) is set equal to the difference between the number of male and female workers in the officially measured non-agricultural labour force. Although this assumption means that factors which affect the relative sizes of the male and female non-agricultural labour forces are ignored, (e.g. differences between men and women in retirement age, unemployment rate, migration rate and age at entry into the labour market), this assumption simplifies calculations.[23] Since IDHALF exceeds ID whenever women are less than 50 per cent of the official non-agricultural labour force, the difference between IDHALF and ID is greatest for countries with a low female labour force participation rate (for example for many of our Middle Eastern, North African, Asian and Other Developing Economies)—a good attribute for our purposes here.

Table 9.8 in Appendix 9.1 indicates national ID and IDHALF values along with an adjusted IDHALF where the level of disaggregation in the national occupational classification is taken into consideration (by utilizing the ratio between ID75 and ID). Table 9.9 in Appendix 9.1 presents average regional and relative (low, middle, high) adjusted IDHALF values.

Figure 9.8. Regional adjusted IDHALF averages, latest available year

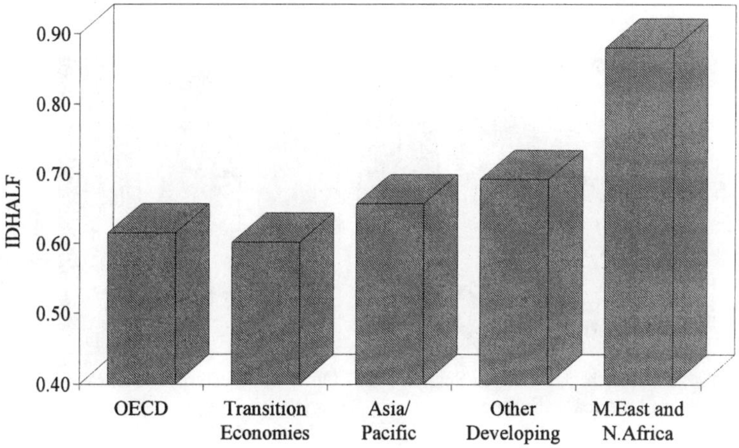

Source: Table 9.9.

Results for IDHALF are often qualitatively different from those for ID75. Indeed, several of the unexpected results discussed at the end of Chapter 9 disappear (figure 9.8). First, the Asia/Pacific and OECD regions now have similar inequality levels according to adjusted IDHALF, including East Asian countries. This contrasts with the lower adjusted ID75 values in Asia reported in section 9.1. Second, India has a relatively high level of sex inequality in the labour market according to adjusted IDHALF (as compared to a relatively low ID75 value). Third, inequality levels according to adjusted IDHALF are now very much higher in Middle Eastern and North African countries and areas (including Egypt) as compared to all other study countries. Fourth, the surprising result of relatively high ID75 values for Scandinavia is not observed for adjusted IDHALF (figure 9.9).

In short, **results for IDHALF lend support to the idea that many preconceived notions about occupational segregation by sex are consistent with a view which combines into one index number women's exclusion from the labour market with the sex segregation of occupations for women who are in the labour market.**

Nevertheless, some of the interesting or unexpected results discussed at the end of section 9.1 continue to exist. The relatively low levels of occupational segregation by sex for China and the United States (and to a lesser extent Japan) noted above based on ID75 remain according to adjusted IDHALF; also, levels of occupational segregation by sex remain similar in OECD and Transition Economy study countries according to both ID75 and adjusted IDHALF.

Figure 9.9.   OECD subregional adjusted IDHALF averages, latest available year

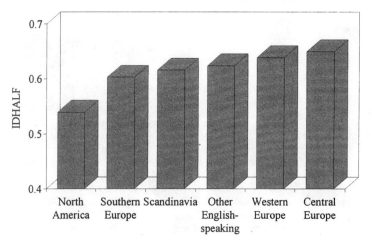

Source: Table 9.8.

Notes

[1] Another supposed advantage of ID is that it has an intuitively understandable meaning. Appendix 5.1, which investigates the intuitive interpretation and meaning of ID, reveals that there is a great deal of confusion and misinterpretation, in the research literature. ID is often said to be equal to the minimum proportion of female workers *or* male workers which would have to change occupations in order to bring about a situation where each occupation has the same percentage female (see, for example, Barbezat, 1994; Blau and Hendricks, 1979). However, as shown in Appendix 5.1, ID actually equals the proportion of women workers who would have to change occupation *plus* the proportion of male workers who would have to change occupation in order to bring about a situation where all occupations have the same percentage female. Unfortunately, this correct interpretation is not very intuitively meaningful.

[2] It is also true that observed cross-national differences based on two-digit data can differ somewhat from those based on three-digit data. Although this is unlikely to be a major problem (since as demonstrated in Chapter 7, national ID values are generally relatively insensitive to disaggregation in occupational data beyond two-digit classifications), it does mean that small differences in ID75 between countries should not be taken too seriously. One good example of this is found among Scandinavian neighbours Finland, Norway and Sweden. In 1990, based on almost completely comparable three-digit data of 183 non-agricultural occupations for these countries (Melkas and Anker, forthcoming), Finland is found to have the highest ID at .663 and Norway the lowest at .635, with Sweden's similar to Norway's at .641. Based on our estimated ID75, however, Sweden's value appears to be higher than Norway's—although Finland continues to have the highest value and Norway the lowest value in both cases.

[3] It is possible to calculate a weighted ID75 by using the size of the non-agricultural labour force as weights. This results in the following weighted average (and unweighted averages for comparison) for ID75: overall .47 (.57), OECD .51 (.56), Transition Economies .57 (.56), Asia .42 (.48), Middle East and North Africa .65 (.68), Other Developing region .64 (.61). Weighted values tend to be considerably lower than the unweighted values reported in the text due to the relatively low ID75 values found in the three most populous countries in the world (China, India and the United States). These weighted values imply that occupational segregation by sex for the average woman in the world is considerably lower than our unweighted values indicate. None the less, unweighted averages continue to be used in the text because weighted averages are so strongly influenced by a few large countries.

GENDER AND JOBS

[4] These regional differences are much more distinct for ID75 than for ID. This is due to the fact that adjustments made to ID in order to calculate ID75 are negative on average in the three regions with the lowest average ID values and positive on average in the two regions with the highest average ID values. This reflects the fact that the proportion of countries with more detailed occupational classifications, is much more common among OECD, Transition Economy and Asia/Pacific countries and areas (71, 75 and 43 per cent of study countries or areas have more than 100 non-agricultural occupations classified) as compared to countries or areas in the Other Developing and Middle Eastern/North African regions (17 and 0 per cent of study countries or areas, respectively). This is also indicated by the average number of non-agricultural occupations classified in study regions: 253, 182 and 177 in OECD, Transition Economies and Asia (and Pacific) respectively, as compared to 94 and 71 in Middle East/North Africa and Other Developing regions respectively.

[5] A relatively low ID75 is defined here as less than .55 and a relatively high ID75 as greater than .60. For simplicity, we used "round numbers" as dividing points (.55 and .60) which gave roughly equal numbers of countries in each ID75 (low, middle, high) relative grouping.

[6] Despite a relatively high degree of homogeneity within OECD subregions, there are none the less substantial differences in national ID75 values within some OECD subregions such as (West) Germany's lower value compared to Switzerland's and Austria's; and Italy's lower value compared to Spain's and Cyprus'.

[7] There is evidence that women were much more likely to be working in production occupations during communism. See, for example, Anker and Hein (1986) for evidence on Hungary where women comprised approximately 40 per cent of production workers and Quack (1992) for evidence on the German Democratic Republic.

[8] A similar conclusion—of only slightly lower levels of occupational segregation by sex in Transition Economies—was reached by Rubery and Fagan (1993) based on a comparison of data for Eastern and Western Germany.

[9] For example, the lower average ID75 observed in Asia as compared to the OECD does not appear to be due to the use of an ID statistic which has been adjusted to an occupational classification based on two-digit data (i.e. ID75). According to data in table 7.3, ID tends to increase just as quickly in Asian countries as compared to OECD countries when the occupational classification changes from a two-digit to a three-digit classification.

[10] To look at the effect this factor (occupational structure) has on ID values in Asia, we recalculated ID for China and Japan after assuming that each had the same distribution of occupations at the one-digit level as in OECD countries. It was found that China's ID decreased by .022 and Japan's increased by .017. This crude standardization for occupational structure is *not* consistent with the hypothesis that Asian countries have "favourable" occupational distributions that help reduce observed levels of occupational segregation by sex.

[11] Echelon segregation is undoubtedly important in a number of countries in the world, as indicated by the fact that, for example, a substantial percentage of women non-agricultural workers are reported to be in the broad occupational group entitled "Other general clerical workers". According to data presented in Chapter 11, this occupational group accounts for more than 10 (or more than 15) per cent of 5 (3) OECD, 4 (3) Asian, and 1 (1) Middle East study countries or areas—an occupation which is often important in public sector and large corporate bureaucracies where there are a number of grade or echelon levels.

Japan would appear to represent a country with an unusually high level of echelon segregation, since 21 per cent of Japanese non-agricultural women workers in 1990 are reported to be in the occupational group "General clerical workers" and an additional 9 per cent are reported to be in the occupational group "Accounting clerks". These are also large occupational groups for men as they account for 11 and 2 per cent respectively of all Japanese non-agricultural male workers. The percentage female in these occupational groups is 56 and 75 per cent respectively. To get a rough idea of how echelon segregation might be affecting measured levels of occupational segregation in Japan, we recalculated Japan's ID after dividing up the above two occupational groups into three echelons/grades, based on the assumptions that: (i) there is a pyramid shape to the workforce in these occupational groups with 60 per cent in grade 1, 30 per cent in grade 2 and 10 per cent in grade 3; (ii) percentage female is only 20 per cent in grade 3 for both occupational groups but is 75 per cent in grade 1 for general clerical workers and 90 per cent in grade 1 for accounting clerks. The recalculated ID for Japan is .034 higher as compared to the ID in table 9.1. These calculations for Japan seem to indicate that a substantial proportion of Japan's lower ID as compared to other industrialized countries is due to echelon segregation, which is hidden in Japan's occupational data.

On the other hand, the above calculations cannot explain away the lower levels of occupational segregation generally found in East and South Asia. First of all, Japan has a relatively high ID75 level for East and South Asia. Second, Japan appears to represent a situation where echelon segregation is especially high. Third, any comparisons to Asia would need to take into consideration that echelon segregation is also important in other countries in an extreme case (for example, 22 per cent of Austrian non-agricultural women workers are reported to be in an occupation entitled "Other clerical workers and other administrative workers").

[12] For example, in a recent survey of 744 career-track women in Japanese firms (where over 70 per cent of respondents planned to continue working long term), 60 per cent felt that they were treated unfairly in hiring, promotion and other aspects of corporate life (Manpower, 1994).

[13] The seemingly lower ID75 for Norway as compared to Sweden and Finland shown in table 9.1 is misleading. Based on almost completely comparable three-digit data for these three countries consisting of 183 non-agricultural occupations (Melkas and Anker, forthcoming), the following ID values are found: .635 (Norway), .641 (Sweden), and .663 (Finland). Thus, it would appear that Norway does not, in fact, have substantially lower occupational segregation by sex as compared to Sweden and Finland.

[14] To observe how these three occupations influence the level of occupational segregation by sex reported in tables 9.1 and 9.2, we recalculated Sweden's ID after excluding the child-care minders, social workers and other care-givers occupations. Although this caused Sweden's ID to decrease (by .016), its ID remained relatively high for Europe and the world. A similar conclusion is reached in Melkas and Anker (forthcoming) where a similar recalculation was done using comparable 1990 data with 183 non-agricultural occupations for Sweden, Norway and Finland, this time excluding four public sector occupations (child-care staff, social workers, municipal home-helps, assistant nurses and attendants); ID was reduced by between .013 for Finland to .029 for Sweden.

[15] The relatively low ID75 observed for Italy embodies an unusually large adjustment factor (see table 9.7 in Appendix 9.1), and is due (as noted in Chapter 10) to a relatively small number of female-dominated occupations.

[16] This explanation of relatively less traditional social values in Egypt should also apply to Tunisia; yet, Tunisia has a considerably higher ID75 value than Egypt in tables 9.1 and 9.2. With this in mind, we recalculated Tunisia's ID after deleting the "workers in textile" occupation—an occupation which includes over 40 per cent of all reported female non-agricultural workers in Tunisia—as it is possible that this large percentage is a peculiar aspect of the Tunisian labour force survey (that was not, but perhaps should have been, reported in other surveys and censuses in the region). Tunisia's re-estimated unadjusted ID is .561 (lowered by about .10), thereby making Tunisia's value similar to that in Egypt and so consistent with our hypothesis about the effect of traditional social values on occupational segregation by sex.

[17] Subsequent to finishing analysis in Part III of this book, 1990 census data for China were obtained. These newer data indicate that China's ID rose between 1982 and 1990, by about .04 (Chapter 13). In light of the very rapid economic growth and liberalization of labour markets in large parts of China since 1990, it is important to analyse even more recent data.

[18] For example, the correlation coefficient between the average female education level and the ratio of female to male education level in each of our 41 study countries and areas is 0.89 and highly significant. This means that it is not sensible for practical reasons to specify in the same equation both female education level and the ratio of female to male education level.

[19] A recent study of European Communities countries (Rubery and Fagan, 1993) found that ID was not significantly related to GDP per capita or female labour force participation rates. It is possible, however, for these same variables to be significantly related to ID when a different set of countries (with a wider range of experiences) are analysed, as in the present book.

[20] All three socio-economic variables are also insignificant when they are specified in quadratic form (unreported regressions).

[21] ID75 is not significantly related, however, to PPART among OECD study countries (table 9.4). Nor does the fit for PPART improve when it is specified in quadratic form. It is possible that this insignificant relationship is due to counterbalancing effects as noted in the text.

[22] Also notice that the significant positive slope estimated in the bottom of table 9.6 for countries where PFEM exceeds 35 per cent is mainly due to the inclusion of two study countries where PFEM exceeds 50 per cent (Haiti and Ghana).

[23] Because of the way IDHALF is calculated, a problem arises when women non-agricultural workers outnumber male non-agricultural workers, as this would imply a negative number of "unpaid housepersons and care-givers". Such a situation can arise where many men migrate to other countries, or where many men remain in the agricultural sector and many women migrate to the cities. In such situations (which occur in two study countries, Ghana and Haiti), we assume that no women are working exclusively as "unpaid housepersons and care-givers".

Appendix 9.1. Estimation of adjusted ID (i.e. ID75)

Table 9.7. Adjusting national ID values to classification with 75 non-agricultural occupations (i.e. ID75) by taking into consideration degree of disaggregation in national occupational classification

Region/country/area	Data used to estimate unadjusted ID		Source of data[a]	Adjustment to estimate ID75		ID75 (adjusted to 75 non-ag. occup.)
	ID (unadjusted)	No. of non-ag. occup. (NOCC)		Factor used[b]	Size of adjustment to 75 non-ag. occup.	
OECD						
Australia	.581[b]	71	research literature	NA	NA	.581
Austria	.597	64	basic data	.061	.010	.607
Canada	.509	44	basic data	.061	.033	.541[*]
Cyprus	.604	104	reaggregated data	.103	−.034	.570
Finland	.606	64	reaggregated data	.061	.010	.616
France	.585	119	reaggregated data	.061	.028	.556[*]
Germany (West)	.600	268	basic data	.061	−.078	.523[**]
Italy	.517	231	basic data	.061	−.069	.449[**]
Luxembourg	.586	71	basic data	.061[c]	.003	.589
Netherlands	.556	63	reaggregated data	.061	.011	.567
New Zealand	.583	77	reaggregated data	.061	−.002	.582
Norway	.564	65	reaggregated data	.061	.009	.573
Spain	.570	77	basic data	.061	−.002	.569
Sweden	.604	49	basic data	.061	.026	.630[*]
Switzerland	.573	66	reaggregated data	.061[c]	.008	.581
United Kingdom	.570[b]	80	research literature	NA	NA	.567
United States	.548	461	basic data	.061[d]	−.085	.463[**]
Average (unweighted)	**.574**	**128**		.061[d]	**−0.14**	**.563**
Asia/Pacific						
China	.293	38	reaggregated data	.103	.070	.363[**]
Fiji	.603	75	basic data	.061	.000	.603
Hong Kong	.490	73	basic data	.103	.003	.493
India	.457	83	reaggregated data	.103	−.010	.446
Japan	.458	49	reaggregated data	.103	.044	.502[*]

Korea, Republic of	.402	56	basic data	.103	.030	.432*
Malaysia	.490	76	basic data	.103	−.001	.489
Average (unweighted)	**.456**	**64**			**.019**	**.476**
Other Developing						
Angola	.652	67	basic data	.034	.004	.656
Costa Rica	.566	55	basic data	.103	.032	.598*
Ghana	.710	75	basic data	.061	.000	.710
Haiti	.669	75	basic data	.034	.000	.669
Mauritius	.586	70	basic data	.103	.007	.593
Netherlands Antilles	.645	76	basic data	.061	−.001	.644
Senegal	.577	80	basic data	.061	−.004	.573
Average (unweighted)	**.629**	**71**			**.005**	**.635**
Transition Economies						
Bulgaria	.507	43	basic data	.061	.034	.541*
Hungary	.585	118	basic data	.061	−.028	.558*
Poland	.677	361	basic data	.061[a]	−.085	.592**
Former Yugoslavia	.602	206	basic data	.061	−.062	.540**
Average (unweighted)	**.593**	**182**			**−.035**	**.558**
Middle East and North Africa						
Bahrain	.635	86	basic data	.061	−.008	.627
Egypt	.586	74	basic data	.034	.001	.587
Iran, Islamic Rep.	.638	21	basic data	.034	.043	.681*
Jordan	.769	61	basic data	.034	.007	.776
Kuwait	.733	75	reaggregated data	.061	.000	.733
Tunisia	.663	55	basic data	.103	.032	.695*
Average (unweighted)	**.671**	**62**			**.012**	**.683**
Total average (unweighted)	**.579**	**103**			**−.003**	**.577**

Notes: * One asterisk indicates that the size of the adjustment is relatively large (between 0.02 and 0.049). ** Two asterisks indicates that the size of the adjustment is especially large (greater than .05). [a] Preferred data source (when available) is roughly two-digit level data, from either basic data set (see Chapter 4) or the data set which was aggregated for analysis in Chapter 6. When roughly two-digit level data are not available from either of these data sources, ID estimates from research literature are used when available (Australia and United Kingdom) and three-digit data from basic data set when not available (West Germany, Italy, United States, Poland and Yugoslavia). [b] Multiplier factor used is the relevant estimated coefficient from equations 4–6 in table 6.6. This factor is multiplied by the value of [ln(75) - ln (NOCC)] to calculate the adjustment. [c] Factor used for Italy and Switzerland is 0.061 even though it should be .103 strictly speaking, since their IDs based on one-digit level data are below 0.30 (0.28 and 0.29 respectively). A factor of .061 was used to be consistent with that for other OECD countries, since Italy's and Switzerland's ID values based on one-digit data are quite close to 0.30. [d] Computed as if ID (before adjustment) is based on 300 occupations.
NA indicates not applicable, since country's ID75 is based on data from research literature.
Source: Study data.

Table 9.8. Unadjusted and adjusted IDHALF (which assumes that one-half of non-agricultural labour force is female), latest available year

Region/country/area	Unadjusted ID	Unadjusted IDHALF	Unadjusted IDHALF – Unadjusted ID	Adjusted IDHALF[a]
OECD				
Australia	.615	.671	.056	.634
Austria	.597	.645	.047	.655
Canada	.509	.551	.042	.586
Cyprus	.634	.703	.069	.633
Finland	.673	.679	.006	.621
France	.607	.660	.054	.606
Germany (West)	.600	.682	.082	.594
Italy	.517	.647	.129	.502
Luxembourg	.586	.691	.106	.695
Netherlands	.588	.684	.096	.659
New Zealand	.618	.672	.054	.633
Norway	.646	.665	.019	.590
Spain	.570	.676	.106	.674
Sweden	.604	.610	.006	.637
Switzerland	.654	.718	.064	.644
United Kingdom	.638	.679	.041	.604
United States	.548	.583	.035	.493
Average (unweighted)	**.600**	**.660**	**.060**	**.615**
Transition Economies				
Bulgaria	.507	.551	.044	.588
Hungary	.585	.608	.023	.579
Poland	.677	.712	.035	.623
Former Yugoslavia	.602	.689	.087	.618
Average (unweighted)	**.593**	**.640**	**.047**	**.602**
Middle East and North Africa				
Bahrain	.635	.839	.204	.828
Egypt	.586	.844	.258	.845
Iran, Islamic Rep.	.638	.883	.245	.943
Jordan	.769	.916	.147	.924
Kuwait	.743	.869	.126	.857
Tunisia	.663	.858	.195	.900
Average (unweighted)	**.672**	**.868**	**.196**	**.883**
Asia/Pacific				
China	.443	.608	.165	.499
Fiji	.600	.760	.160	.764
Hong Kong	.490	.603	.113	.607
India	.492	.870	.378	.789
Japan	.529	.590	.061	.559
Korea, Republic of	.402	.646	.244	.694
Malaysia	.490	.691	.201	.689
Average (unweighted)	**.492**	**.681**	**.189**	**.657**

Table 9.8. (contd.)

Region/country/area	Unadjusted ID	Unadjusted IDHALF	Unadjusted IDHALF – Unadjusted ID	Adjusted IDHALF[a]
Other Developing				
Angola	.652	.701	.049	.600
Costa Rica	.566	.688	.122	.727
Ghana[b]	.710	.710	.000	.710
Haiti[b]	.669	.669	.000	.669
Mauritius	.586	.720	.134	.728
Netherlands Antilles	.645	.696	.051	.695
Senegal	.577	.792	.215	.713
Average (unweighted)	**.629**	**.711**	**.082**	**.692**
Overall average (unweighted)	**.597**	**.701**	**.104**	**.673**

Notes: [a] Adjusted IDHALF is equivalent to an IDHALF which has been adjusted, in a rough sense, for level of disaggregation in the national occupational classification. It is calculated by multiplying a country's unadjusted IDHALF by its ratio of ID75 to unadjusted ID. [b] It is assumed that all adult women are already working in Ghana and Haiti, since women are reported to comprise more than one-half of the non-agricultural labour force in these countries. Therefore, it is assumed that no women are exclusively "unpaid housepersons and care-givers" in these countries, and consequently IDHALF and ID are equal.
Source: Study data.

Table 9.9. Distribution of countries by relative level (low, middle, high) for adjusted IDHALF, by region, latest available year, by region

Region	Relative adjusted IDHALF[a] (number of countries)			Average adjusted IDHALF
	Low (<.65)	Middle (.65–.69)	High (>.70)	
OECD	13	4	–	.615
Transition Economies	4	–	–	.602
Middle East and North Africa	–	–	6	.887
Asia/Pacific	3	2	2	.657
Other Developing	–	2	5	.692
Total	**20**	**8**	**13**	**.673**

Notes: [a] Ranges are set equal to ranges in table 9.2 plus .10 (which is the approximate average difference between unadjusted ID and unadjusted IDHALF). Note that the difference between unadjusted and adjusted IDHALF differs quite substantially across regions, ranging from about .06 in Transition Economies and OECD regions to about .20 in Asia/Pacific and Middle East and North Africa regions. These regional differences are mainly due to regional differences in female labour force participation rates.
Source: Based on data from table 9.8.

OCCUPATIONAL SEGREGATION BY SEX BASED ON DETAILED OCCUPATIONAL DATA: EXTENT TO WHICH OCCUPATIONS ARE MALE-DOMINATED OR FEMALE-DOMINATED

10

The previous chapter analysed occupational segregation by sex based on inequality indices, where variations in the distributions of male and female workers across all occupations are combined into one index number. Yet as indicated in Chapter 5, indices provide an incomplete picture, which is often difficult to understand intuitively and sometimes even misleading. By their nature, index numbers are just too simple to provide complete and fully satisfactory information on occupational segregation in the labour market.

This chapter presents a different perspective by analysing the extent to which the labour force consists of occupations which are sex-stereotyped to such an extent that they could be considered as "male" or "female" occupations. **"Male" and "female" occupations are defined here as occupations where at least 80 per cent of the workers are of one sex** (and so there is at least a 4 to 1 ratio of males to females or females to males).[1,2] Readers are referred to Chapter 5 where there is an extensive discussion of this measure of occupational segregation and its sensitivity to the level of detail in the occupational data on which it is based. Readers are also referred to Appendix 10.2 which provides data on the extensiveness of gender-dominated occupations in study countries and areas using a relative concept to measure gender-domination; and to Chapter 5 for a detailed discussion of the rationale and attributes of this statistic and the relative concept underlying it.

Seen from the point of view of the excluded sex, "male" and "female" occupations are occupations where the excluded gender has an unequal chance of getting or holding a job. (No judgement is made about whether or not this virtual exclusion from an occupation is due to societal or attitudinal biases prior to labour market entry, or to discrimination once in the labour market, or to "choice"/self-discrimination.) Seen from the perspective of the dominant sex, these are occupations where the dominant sex is protected to a large extent from competition from the other sex. Such occupations could be either valuable havens, or ghettos where the dominant sex is relegated to poor quality jobs.

The existence of labour market segmentation based on sex has important negative implications for economic efficiency and labour market flexibility as discussed in Chapter 1. In addition, of course, there are important negative implications for gender equity and equality of opportunity in employment for men and women. When men or women are more or less excluded from particular occupations, this reduces occupational mobility and labour market flexibility, and this, in turn, reduces economic growth and national incomes.

While this form of occupational segregation by sex is known to greatly affect women, it seems that in recent years it is also increasingly affecting men as well because of the shift in job growth away from traditional "male" occupations (such as in the production sector) towards traditional "female" occupations (such as in the sales and services sectors). Indeed, occupational segregation by sex may help to explain in part why prime-age men in industrialized countries are experiencing decreasing labour force participation rates; as retrenchment occurs in production sector jobs, men may be dropping out of the labour force rather than taking (or perhaps never being offered) "female" jobs.

10.1 Extensiveness of gender-dominated occupations based on unadjusted study data

Tables 10.1 and 10.2 present national study data on the extent to which the female, male and total non-agricultural labour forces are segregated into gender-dominated occupations based on unadjusted national data where the number of occupations classified varies across countries. Also, Chapter 11 presents data on the feminization and masculinization of 17 typical "female" and "male" occupations as well as for the largest female-dominated occupations in study countries and areas.

There are several general points we would like to make based on tables 10.1 and 10.2. First, **male-dominated occupations are much more common than female-dominated occupations.** This predominance of male-dominated occupations is due partly to the nature of the labour market and occupational segregation by sex, partly to higher labour force participation rates for men as compared to women and partly to the fact that occupational classifications are more detailed for the types of occupations men tend to hold, as compared to those which women tend to hold (for discussion on the latter point, see Chapters 4 and 6). It is clear that men have a much better choice of occupations where they have little or no competition from women, as compared to women who have many fewer of "their own" occupations. There are, on average, *approximately seven times as many male-dominated occupations as female-dominated occupations* reported for our 41 study countries and areas.

Second, there are *large regional differences in the ratio of the number of male-dominated to female-dominated occupations* (figure 10.1), which goes

Table 10.1. Percentage of female and male non-agricultural labour forces in gender-dominated occupation, unadjusted national data, latest available year

Region/country/area	Year	No. of occup. classified	% fem. of non-ag. LF (PFEM)	Female non-ag. LF (%)			Male non-ag. LF (%)		
				in FDOM occ.	in MDOM occ.	in either FDOM or MDOM occ.	in MDOM occ.	in FDOM occ.	in either FDOM or MDOM occ.
OECD									
Australia	1990	279	41.7	29.6	5.2	34.9	56.0	1.6	57.7
Austria	1990	64	40.8	12.6	5.5	18.1	59.6	1.6	61.3
Canada	1990	44	45.9	31.4	4.2	35.6	39.8	2.7	42.5
Cyprus	1989	376	37.3	31.4	5.2	36.6	62.9	1.2	64.1
Finland	1990	264	49.1	60.9	4.3	65.2	59.1	4.5	63.7
France	1990	433	42.6	44.9	4.2	49.2	54.6	3.5	58.1
Germany (West)	1989	268	41.7	35.4	4.3	39.7	59.9	2.7	62.6
Italy	1981	231	32.6	20.6	10.3	30.9	59.5	1.4	60.9
Luxembourg	1991	71	35.9	36.5	7.2	43.7	63.4	1.7	65.1
Netherlands	1990	151	39.1	36.8	5.4	42.2	60.6	2.2	62.8
New Zealand	1986	281	42.3	46.3	5.8	52.1	56.9	4.6	61.5
Norway	1990	291	47.1	48.4	4.9	53.3	60.1	3.6	63.7
Spain	1990	77	32.7	14.4	6.5	20.9	60.6	0.7	61.3
Sweden	1991	49	49.2	49.2	6.1	55.3	54.6	5.5	60.2
Switzerland	1980	452	36.7	33.5	4.8	38.3	67.6	2.2	69.8
United Kingdom	1990	509	44.0	31.3	5.4	36.7	60.7	1.6	62.3
United States	1991	461	46.5	46.0	4.2	50.2	43.9	4.5	48.4
Average (unweighted)		**253**	**41.5**	**35.8**	**5.5**	**41.4**	**57.6**	**2.7**	**60.4**
Transition Economies									
Bulgaria	1985	43	45.6	13.8	2.6	16.4	26.1	1.2	27.3
Hungary	1990	118	45.6	32.8	5.1	37.9	57.4	2.9	60.3
Poland	1988	361	44.2	63.2	4.6	66.9	65.0	5.9	70.9
Former Yugoslavia	1981	206	33.3	18.3	8.2	26.6	66.1	1.4	67.6
Average (unweighted)		**182**	**42.2**	**32.2**	**5.2**	**37.2**	**53.7**	**2.8**	**56.5**

Middle East and North Africa

Bahrain	1991	86	16.9	0	17.9	80.8	0	80.8
Egypt	1986	74	13.6	0	21.6	79.7	0	79.7
Iran, Islamic Republic of	1986	21	10.5	0	27.8	89.8	0	89.8
Jordan	1979	61	8.1	5.7	19.8	88.6	0.12	88.7
Kuwait	1985	268	20.0	7.2	19.8	86.8	0.03	86.9
Tunisia	1989	55	19.6	44.3	61.9	83.9	2.21	86.2
Average (unweighted)		**94**	**14.8**	**9.5**	**28.1**	**84.9**	**0.39**	**85.3**

Asia/Pacific

China	1980	277	35.7	15.0	22.3	43.4	0.6	44.1
Fiji	1986	75	27.1	26.4	36.4	70.1	0.6	70.6
Hong Kong	1991	73	37.9	14.7	20.2	42.5	0.7	43.2
India	1981	423	12.1	3.1	44.3	85.8	0.1	85.8
Japan	1990	259	39.3	16.9	22.8	53.8	1.3	55.1
Korea, Rep. of	1983	56	30.6	0	3.4	39.5	0	39.5
Malaysia	1980	76	28.2	9.8	19.9	55.8	0.3	56.1
Average (unweighted)		**177**	**30.1**	**12.2**	**24.2**	**55.8**	**0.5**	**56.3**

Other Developing

Angola	1992	67	41.3	52.1	53.3	60.4	2.4	62.8
Costa Rica	1991	55	37.1	45.6	49.9	53.4	4.2	57.6
Ghana	1984	75	57.6	77.2	79.3	60.3	10.4	70.8
Haiti	1986	75	65.2	76.3	76.9	58.8	11.3	70.1
Mauritius	1990	70	31.1	13.6	23.2	66.4	0.5	66.9
Netherlands Antilles	1981	76	38.5	32.4	36.8	66.8	1.6	68.5
Senegal	1988	80	22.8	29.5	47.6	75.8	2.1	77.8
Average (unweighted)		**71**	**41.9**	**46.7**	**52.4**	**63.1**	**4.6**	**67.8**
Average overall (unweighted)		**179**	**35.8**	**29.4**	**37.9**	**61.8**	**2.3**	**64.2**

Note: Gender-dominated occupations are defined as those where at least 80 per cent of the workers are either male or female. FDOM refers to female-dominated occupations. MDOM refers to male-dominated occupations. Either column is calculated by summing values for MDOM and FDOM columns.
Source: Study data.

Table 10.2. Number of gender-dominated occupations and percentage of total non-agricultural labour force in a gender-dominated occupation, unadjusted national data, latest available year

Region/country/area	Year	No. of occ. classified	% fem. of non-ag. LF (PFEM)	Total non-ag. LF No. occ.			% of non-ag. LF		
				FDOM occ.	MDOM occ.	in either FDOM or MDOM occ.	in FDOM occ.	in MDOM occ.	in either FDOM or MDOM occ.
OECD									
Australia	1990	279	41.7	24	142	166	13.3	34.9	48.2
Austria	1990	64	40.8	4	27	31	6.1	37.5	43.6
Canada	1990	44	45.9	4	14	18	15.9	23.5	39.3
Cyprus	1989	376	37.3	33	214	247	12.5	41.4	53.9
Finland	1990	264	49.1	52	93	145	32.2	32.2	64.4
France	1990	433	42.6	36	198	234	21.2	33.1	54.3
Germany (West)	1989	268	41.7	23	157	180	15.1	38.8	53.9
Italy	1981	231	32.6	12	115	127	7.7	43.5	51.2
Luxembourg	1991	71	35.9	9	38	47	14.2	43.2	57.4
Netherlands	1990	151	39.1	16	87	103	15.8	38.6	54.3
New Zealand	1986	281	42.3	28	143	171	22.4	35.1	57.5
Norway	1990	291	47.1	29	124	153	24.7	34.1	58.8
Spain	1990	77	32.7	4	40	44	5.2	43.1	48.2
Sweden	1991	49	49.2	7	18	25	27.0	30.8	57.7
Switzerland	1980	452	36.7	45	250	295	13.7	44.6	58.3
United Kingdom	1990	509	44.0	40	292	332	14.7	36.3	51.0
United States	1991	461	46.5	55	195	250	23.8	25.5	49.2
Average (unweighted)		**253**	**41.5**	**25**	**126**	**151**	**16.8**	**36.2**	**53.0**
Transition Economies									
Bulgaria	1985	43	45.6	4	7	11	6.9	15.4	22.4
Hungary	1990	118	45.6	16	36	52	16.3	33.6	49.9
Poland	1988	361	44.2	55	114	169	31.2	38.3	69.5
Former Yugoslavia	1981	206	33.3	8	94	102	7.1	46.8	53.9
Average (unweighted)		**182**	**42.2**	**21**	**63**	**84**	**15.4**	**33.5**	**48.9**

	Year								
Middle East and North Africa									
Bahrain	1991	86	16.9	0	64	64	0	70.2	70.2
Egypt	1986	74	13.6	0	59	59	0	71.8	71.8
Iran, Islamic Republic of	1986	21	10.5	0	18	18	0	83.3	83.3
Jordan	1979	61	8.1	1	53	54	0.6	82.5	83.1
Kuwait	1985	268	20.0	5	199	204	1.5	72.0	73.5
Tunisia	1989	55	19.6	1	39	40	10.4	71.0	81.4
Average (unweighted)		**94**	**14.8**	**1**	**72**	**73**	**2.1**	**75.1**	**77.2**
Asia/Pacific									
China	1980	277	35.7	14	77	91	5.8	30.5	36.3
Fiji	1986	75	27.1	4	47	51	7.6	53.8	61.4
Hong Kong	1991	73	37.7	3	28	31	5.9	28.5	34.5
India	1981	423	12.1	3	376	379	0.4	80.4	80.8
Japan	1990	259	39.3	23	115	138	7.4	35.0	42.4
Korea, Rep. of	1983	56	30.6	0	24	24	0	28.5	28.5
Malaysia	1980	76	28.2	2	36	38	3.0	42.9	45.9
Average (unweighted)		**177**	**30.1**	**7**	**100**	**107**	**4.3**	**42.8**	**47.1**
Other Developing									
Angola	1992	67	41.3	4	33	37	22.9	36.0	58.9
Costa Rica	1991	55	37.1	4	28	32	19.5	35.2	54.7
Ghana	1984	75	57.6	6	43	49	48.9	26.8	75.7
Haiti	1986	75	65.2	9	39	48	53.7	20.9	74.6
Mauritius	1990	70	31.1	2	42	44	4.6	48.7	53.3
Netherlands Antilles	1981	76	38.5	4	47	51	13.5	42.8	56.3
Senegal	1988	80	22.8	2	61	63	8.4	62.5	70.9
Average (unweighted)		**71**	**41.2**	**4**	**42**	**46**	**24.5**	**39.0**	**63.5**
World average (unweighted)		**179**	**35.7**	**14**	**93**	**107**	**13.7**	**43.2**	**56.9**

Notes: Percentage of total non-agricultural labour force in female-dominated occupations is calculated as: PFEM/100 * % female non-ag. LF in female-dominated occupations + (1-%PFEM) * % male non-ag. LF in female-dominated occupations. For percentage in male-dominated occupations, it is calculated as: PFEM/100 * % female non-ag. LF in male-dominated occupations + (1-%PFEM/100) * % male non-ag. LF in male-dominated occupations.
Either column is calculated by summing values from the FDOM and MDOM columns.
Gender-dominated occupations are defined as those where at least 80 per cent of the workers are either male or female. FDOM occ. refers to female-dominated occupations. MDOM occ. refers to male-dominated occupations.
Source: Table 10.1.

Figure 10.1.   Ratio of number of male-dominated to female-dominated non-agricultural occupations, by region

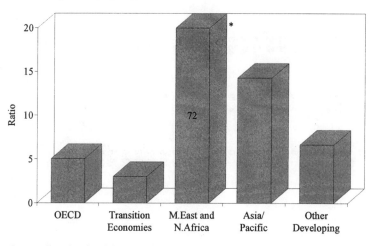

Notes: Based on unadjusted national data.
* Value for Middle East and North Africa is actually 72.
Male-dominated and female-dominated occupations are defined as occupations where at least 80 per cent of workers are male or female respectively.
The number of male-dominated and female-dominated non-agricultural occupations observed in national data are affected by the level of detail in national occupational classification. However, it is uncertain how much this affects the *ratio* of the number of male-dominated to female-dominated non-agricultural occupations, as both numerator and denominator should increase along with increasing disaggregation of an occupational classification (although there should be some tendency for this ratio to increase since disaggregation in an occupational classification tends to be greater for male-dominated types of occupations as compared to female-dominated types of occupations).
Source: Table 10.2.

from about three to one in Transition Economy study countries, to about five to one in OECD study countries, ten to one in the Other Developing region, 14 to one in Asia/Pacific study countries and areas and up to 70 to one in Middle Eastern and North African study countries.

Third, *only a small percentage of men and women workers in the world work in an occupation dominated by the other sex*. The unweighted average for our 41 study countries and areas indicates that only about 9 per cent of female non-agricultural workers and 2 per cent of male non-agricultural workers work in a non-agricultural occupation dominated by the other sex (when one excludes countries from the Middle East and North Africa, averages are only about 5 and 3 per cent respectively). Such low percentages would seem to be self-evident, since by definition these occupations are dominated by the other sex. This result is not, however, definitionally preordained, especially in countries with low female labour force participation rates. For example, in study countries where women comprise less than 25 per cent of the non-agricultural labour force, approximately 21 per cent of women non-agricultural workers are working in a male-dominated occupation; in India (where we have data on 423 non-agricultural occupations), 41 per cent of the female non-agricultural labour force is in a male-dominated occupation. The non-agricultural labour market is such a male world in countries with low female participation rates that a sizeable proportion of women workers in such countries find themselves working in a "male" occupation.

10.2 Adjusting national data to increase cross-national comparability

To increase the cross-national comparability of study data, we estimated adjusted national values by taking into consideration the level of detail in national occupational classifications. This is especially important for the proportion of female workers in female-dominated non-agricultural occupations (and to a lesser extent the proportion of the total non-agricultural workforce in gender-dominated occupations), since as shown in Chapter 6, this proportion is quite sensitive to the level of aggregation in the occupational classification. Interested readers are referred to Chapter 6 where this adjustment process is described in detail and to Appendix 10.1 where the adjustment process and adjustment factors are presented in tabular form.

These **adjusted national data are used in the remainder of the discussion and analysis in the present chapter.** Table 10.3 presents these adjusted national values. Tables 10.4 to 10.6 divide these adjusted national values into three relative groupings containing roughly equal numbers of countries and areas (with relatively low, middle and high values). The adjustment process is in many ways similar to that used in Chapter 9 for ID,[3] except that adjustments here rely on interpolation based on observed national and regional values whereas adjustments for ID rely on relationships estimated based on regression analysis.

Most adjustments here are small. There are only 11, 2 and 12 study countries or areas where the adjustment factor is greater than 5 percentage points for the female, male and total non-agricultural labour forces, respectively (and 6, 0 and 0 study countries have an adjustment factor greater than 10 percentage points). To assist readers, we have indicated such cases with asterisks in tables 10.3 to 10.6 as well as in tables 10.8 to 10.10 in Appendix 10.1.

Of course, even though our adjusted national values for gender-dominated occupations have greater comparability than unadjusted national values, *readers always need to remain cognizant of the fact that our adjusted national values are not fully comparable.* Cross-national comparability is affected by factors such as coding instructions, coding classifications, reporting errors, nature of the labour market, etc. (see Chapter 4 for detailed discussion of these points). Readers also need to be reminded that the extent to which the female non-agricultural labour force (and to a lesser extent the total non-agricultural labour force) is observed to be working in gender-dominated occupations depends partly on whether this observation is based on a two-digit or three-digit occupational classification. Although two- and three-digit data generally provide similar results whereas one- and two-digit data often provide different results (see Chapter 6), the fact remains that two- and three-digit data do not always indicate the same relative ranking of countries on the extent to which the female non-agricultural labour force (and to a lesser extent the male and total non-agricultural labour forces) is in gender-dominated occupations. For example, as shown in Chapter 6, the percentage of the female (total) non-agricultural labour force observed to be in a gender-dominated occupation increases by just zero (two) percentage points in India and two (one) percentage points in Cyprus based on two-digit occupational data as compared to three-digit occupational data. This is very different than the observed increases of 19 (10) and 26 (12) per cent for France and New Zealand. This means that three-digit data and two-digit data sometimes indicate different relative rankings of countries. While generally this should not cause a major problem, as shown in Chapter 6, it can be important for particular countries.

One other possibly important aspect of reduced cross-national comparability for the analysis in this chapter is the use of a single cut-off point for defining gender-dominance (i.e. at least 80 per cent of one sex). This means that it is possible for a particular national value to be greatly affected by having one or a few large occupations where the percentage female or male is just above or just below the 80 per cent cut-off point. In such situations, only a small difference in percentage male or female for one or a few occupations (perhaps due to some measurement error) could have a major effect on observed national values and therefore cross-national comparability. Yet, one would not want to draw conclusions from an observed difference between countries A and B that is due to country A having say 10 per cent of its female non-agricultural labour force in a very large occupation where women comprise 80.1 per cent of workers.

While it is not possible to "correct" for such occurrences, it is possible to warn readers when this may be an important factor. With the above in mind, Appendix 10.3 provides data on the percentage of the female non-agricultural labour force, male non-agricultural labour force and total non-agricultural labour force having reasonably large occupations[4] where the percentage female or male is within 5 per cent of our 80 per cent cut-off point (i.e. between 77.50–79.99 and 80.00–82.49 per cent). Based on these data, it is indicated in tables 10.3 to 10.6 when there is a substantial imbalance between the proportion of the relevant labour force just above the cut-off point as compared to the proportion just below the cut-off point. To indicate this, a D or U is placed (to indicate substantial downward or upward tendency) next to the national value.[5] Overall, there is little tendency for the total non-agricultural labour force to be "biased" upwards or downwards because of our fixed 80 per cent cut-off point, implying that larger occupations are reasonably evenly spread over the 77.5 to 82.5 per cent male or female range. However, whereas there are no national examples of a substantial tendency for the male non-agricultural labour force and only three examples for the total non-agricultural labour force, there are eight examples for the female non-agricultural labour force. Again, precision is lower for measuring the percentage female in female-dominated occupations as compared to the equivalent information for the male non-agricultural labour force.

10.3   Male workers and male-dominated occupations

We now turn our attention to an analysis of the male non-agricultural labour force and male-dominated occupations. This discussion relies mainly on table 10.3 (which contains the basic national data) and table 10.4 (which separates national values into relatively low, middle and high groups). It should be noted that this analysis and discussion are not greatly affected by differing levels of disaggregation in the national occupational data nor by a clustering of occupations just above or just below the somewhat ad hoc cut-off point of 80 per cent male which is used to define male-dominated occupations. For example, as indicated in Chapter 6, the percentage of the male non-agricultural labour force in a male-dominated occupation is, on average, only approximately 2 to 3 per cent higher when based on two-digit data as compared to three-digit data.

There is a **reasonably high degree of consistency across regions in the degree to which male workers are working in male-dominated non-agricultural occupations** (table 10.3 and figure 10.2). This percentage is approximately 60 per cent overall. Approximately 55 per cent of male non-agricultural workers in our OECD, Transition Economy and Asian regions are in a male-dominated occupation. *The Middle East and North Africa region and to a lesser extent the Other Developing region stand out as having especially high MDOM75 values.* Approximately 84 per cent of male non-agricultural workers in the ME region and 64 per cent in the OD region work in a male-dominated occupation.

There is also **considerable similarity in MDOM75 across OECD subregions** (table 10.7 and figure 10.3), as indicated by the fact that five of the six OECD study subregions have average values within a range of only about six percentage points of each other (approximately 55 to 61 per cent). It is noteworthy, however, that *MDOM75 in North America is much lower than in the other OECD subregions* (about 43 per cent compared to about 58 per cent for other OECD study countries). At the same time, there is variation among the Transition Economy countries, as MDOM75 is much lower in Bulgaria than in the other three study countries in this region.

Table 10.3. Adjusted national values for percentage of female, male and total non-agricultural labour force working in gender-dominated occupations, latest available year, by region

Region/country/area	Year	% fem. for non-ag. LF (PFEM)	Adjusted values (%)		
			FDOM75	MDOM75	TDOM75
OECD					
Australia	1990	41.7	17.4*	55.1	41.6*
Austria	1990	40.8	14.3	60.5	44.9
Canada	1990	45.9	37.2*D	42.9	43.6*
Cyprus	1989	37.3	25.6	54.8*	47.3*
Finland	1990	49.1	55.4	56.0	62.3
France	1990	42.6	22.0	50.7	42.1
Germany (West)	1989	41.7	23.6*U	59.0	47.5*
Italy	1981	32.6	10.2*D	58.7	45.6*
Luxembourg	1991	35.9	37.3D	63.7	57.9
Netherlands	1990	39.1	31.4	59.2	51.7
New Zealand	1986	42.3	19.5	58.1	45.9
Norway	1990	47.1	35.0	51.8	48.1
Spain	1990	32.7	14.2	60.6	48.1
Sweden	1991	49.2	53.8	57.1	61.2
Switzerland	1980	36.7	17.3	62.7	49.6
United Kingdom	1990	44.0	13.5*D	59.3	41.4*
United States	1991	46.5	29.2*	42.6	40.1*
Average (unweighted)		**41.5**	**26.9**	**56.0**	**48.2**
Transition Economies					
Bulgaria	1985	45.6	19.8*D	29.3	26.9*D
Hungary	1990	45.6	28.6	57.1	47.6
Poland	1988	44.2	48.6*	63.9	61.7*
Former Yugoslavia	1981	33.3	8.9*	65.4	48.9*
Average (unweighted)		**42.2**	**26.5**	**53.9**	**46.3**
Middle East and North Africa					
Bahrain	1991	16.9	0.0	79.6	69.1
Egypt	1986	13.6	0.0	79.8	71.8
Iran, Islamic Rep.	1986	10.5	0.0	90.0	83.3
Jordan	1979	8.1	6.2	88.9	83.4
Kuwait	1985	20.0	7.2	84.2	73.5D
Tunisia	1989	19.6	45.6[a]	83.5	81.9
Average (unweighted)		**14.8**	**9.8**	**84.3**	**77.2**
Asia/Pacific					
China	1980	35.7	10.5	41.8	32.8
Fiji	1986	27.1	26.4	70.1	61.4
Hong Kong	1991	37.7	14.8	42.8	34.8
India	1981	12.1	0.0	87.3	83.3
Japan	1990	39.3	7.7	52.4	38.4
Republic of Korea	1983	30.6	1.0	42.6	32.1
Malaysia	1980	28.2	9.8	55.5	45.7D
Average (unweighted)		**30.1**	**10.0**	**56.1**	**46.9**

Table 10.3 (contd.)

Region/country/area	Year	% fem. for non-ag. LF (PFEM)	Adjusted values (%)		
			FDOM75	MDOM75	TDOM75
Other Developing					
Angola	1992	41.3	52.1	60.7	58.9
Costa Rica	1991	37.1	52.0*	60.9*	62.3
Ghana	1984	57.6	77.2	60.3	75.7
Haiti	1986	65.2	76.3	58.8	74.6
Mauritius	1990	31.1	14.0	68.2	54.7
Netherlands Antilles	1981	38.5	32.2	66.7	56.2
Senegal	1988	22.8	28.8D	75.2	70.5
Average (unweighted)		**41.9**	**47.5**	**64.4**	**64.7**
Average overall		**35.8**	**25.0**	**61.4**	**54.9**

Notes: Gender-dominated occupations are defined as occupations where at least 80 per cent of workers are male or female. FDOM is the percentage of the female non-agricultural labour force in a female-dominated occupation. MDOM is the percentage of the male non-agricultural labour force in a male-dominated occupation. TDOM is the percentage of the total non-agricultural labour force in a male-dominated or female-dominated occupation. FDOM75, MDOM75, and TDOM75 refer to national values which have been adjusted so as to be roughly comparable for an occupational classification with 75 non-agricultural occupations.
* indicates when FDOM75, MDOM75 or TDOM75 is estimated with lesser precision as the adjustment factor included in it is greater than 5.0 percentage points (see Appendix 10.1).
D indicates a marked tendency for FDOM75, MDOM75 or TDOM75 to be "biased" downwards due to a clustering of larger occupations at just below the 80 per cent cut-off point (i.e. 77.5–79.9) as compared to just above the 80 per cent cut-off point (i.e. 80.0–82.5). A "D" is placed next to a national value when this net "downward" tendency is greater than 10 percentage points (see Appendix 10.3).
U indicates a marked tendency for FDOM75, MDOM75 or TDOM75 to be "biased" upwards due to a clustering of larger occupations at just above the 80 per cent cut-off point (i.e. 80.0–82.5) as compared to just below the 80 per cent cut-off point (i.e. 77.5–79.9). A "U" is placed next to a national value when this net "upward" tendency is greater than a 10 percentage points (see Appendix 10.3).
[a] Tunisia has one occupation (textile workers) which comprises 44.3 per cent of the female non-agricultural labour force. This is obviously due to measurement non-compatibility with other countries in the region. In this regard, note that Tunisia's female share of the total non-agricultural labour force would be similar to that found in Egypt and the Islamic Republic of Iran if this one occupation were similarly enumerated in these three countries.
Sources: Appendix 10.1, tables 10.9 to 10.11.

When sorted according to their MDOM75 value (table 10.4 and figure 10.4), it is found that only six study countries or areas have less than 50 per cent of male non-agricultural workers in a male-dominated occupation. This includes both of our North American countries, Canada and the United States; the transition economy Bulgaria; and three Far Eastern countries or areas, China, Hong Kong and the Republic of Korea. All of these also have relatively low adjusted ID75 values as observed in Chapter 9.

At the other extreme (i.e. countries with a relatively high percentage of their male non-agricultural labour force in a male-dominated occupation, defined as above 65 per cent) are 12 study countries and areas. This includes all six countries from the Middle East and North Africa region, none from the OECD, one Transition Economy country (former Yugoslavia) which has a value just above 65 per cent (i.e. 65.4 per cent), two Asia/Pacific countries

Figure 10.2.   Percentage of male non-agricultural labour force in male-dominated occupation (MDOM75), latest available year, by region

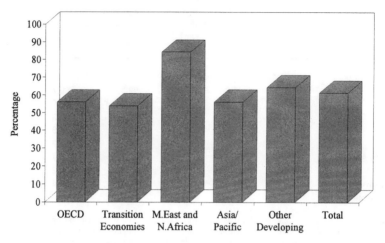

Note: Male-dominated occupations are defined as occupations where at least 80 per cent of workers are men.
Source: Table 10.3.

(India and Fiji) and three Other Developing countries and areas (Netherlands Antilles, Mauritius and Senegal). It is interesting to note that only two of these 12 cases has a relatively low adjusted ID75 value.

Several general conclusions can be drawn from the above analysis of male-dominated occupations and the extent to which male non-agricultural

Figure 10.3.   Percentage of male non-agricultural labour force in male-dominated occupation (MDOM75), latest available year, by OECD subregion

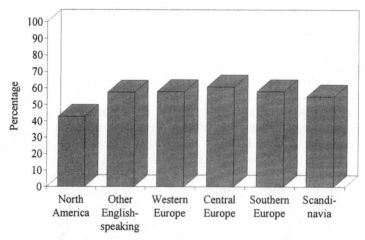

Note: Male-dominated occupations are defined as occupations where at least 80 per cent of workers are men.
Source: Table 10.7.

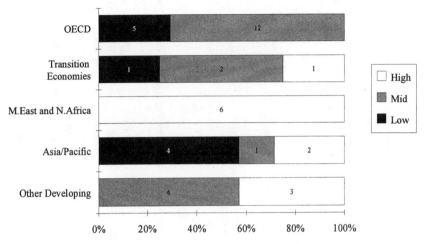

Figure 10.4. Distribution of countries and areas by relative level (low, middle, high) for percentage of male non-agricultural labour force (MDOM75) working in male-dominated occupation, latest available year, by region

Notes: Numbers inside bars indicate number of study countries and areas.
Male-dominated occupations are defined as occupations where at least 80 per cent of workers are men.
Source: Table 10.4.

workers work in such occupations. First, a **majority of male non-agricultural workers in the world** (approximately 61 per cent based on an unweighted average for 75 non-agricultural occupational groups and approximately 56 per cent based on a weighted average using the size of the male non-agricultural labour force as weights) **work in a non-agricultural occupation which could be described as "male-dominated"**. This high degree of occupational segregation means that most male workers have it easy in the sense that they do not face much if any competition from women. This advantage is especially valuable, since "male" occupations tend to have higher pay as compared to "female" occupations (see Chapters 2 and 11). Second, this situation is typical for all regions, as the lowest unweighted regional average is approximately 54 per cent.

Third, there is some regional variation, although the OECD, TE and Asia/Pacific regions have similar unweighted MDOM75 averages (approximately 55 per cent). The Middle East and North Africa region (at about 84 per cent) and Other Developing region (at about 64 per cent) have much higher percentages. Fourth, within the OECD, Transition Economy and Asia/Pacific regions, a few study countries and areas stand out as having unusually low MDOM75 values (below 50 per cent): Bulgaria, the United States, Canada, China, the Republic of Korea and Hong Kong.

Fifth, especially low levels of occupational segregation by sex indicated by MDOM75 are generally associated with low values of ID75. All six

Table 10.4. Distribution of countries/areas by relative level (low, middle, high) for percentage of male non-agricultural labour force working in male-dominated[a] occupations (MDOM75), latest available year, by region

Region	<55.0 (MDOM75)		55.0–65.0 (MDOM75)		>65.0 (MDOM75)		Mean (x) Std dev. (σ)
	No.	Countries/areas	No.	Countries/areas	No.	Countries/areas	
OECD	5	United States (42.6) Canada (42.9) France (50.7) Norway (51.8) Cyprus (54.8)*B	12	Australia (55.1) Finland (56.0) Sweden (57.1) New Zealand (58.1) Italy (58.7)B Germany (West) (59.0) United Kingdom (59.3) Netherlands (59.2) Austria (60.5) Spain (60.6) Switzerland (62.7) Luxembourg (63.7)	0		x = 56.0 σ = 6.1
Transition Economies	1	Bulgaria (29.3)	2	Hungary (57.1) Poland (63.9)	1	Former Yugoslavia (65.4)B	x = 53.9 σ = 16.8
Middle East and North Africa	0		0		6	Bahrain (79.6) Egypt (79.8) Tunisia (83.5) Kuwait (84.2) Jordan (88.9) Iran, Islamic Rep. (90.0)	x = 84.3 σ = 4.4
Asia/Pacific	4	Rep. of Korea (42.6) Hong Kong (42.8) Japan (52.4) China (41.8)	1	Malaysia (55.5)	2	Fiji (70.1) India (87.3)	x = 56.1 σ = 17.1

Other Developing	0		4	Haiti	(58.8)	3	Netherlands Antilles	(66.7)	$x = 64.4$
				Ghana	(60.3)		Mauritius	(68.2)	$\sigma = 5.9$
				Angola	(60.7)		Senegal	(77.0)	
				Costa Rica	(60.9)				

Notes: [a] Per cent of the male non-agricultural labour force working in male-dominated occupations (MDOM) is adjusted so as to be for an occupational classification with 75 non-agricultural occupations (MDOM75) in order to increase cross-national comparability.

* indicates when MDOM75 is estimated with lesser precision as the adjustment factor included in MDOM75 is greater than 5.0 percentage points (see Appendix 10.1).

B indicates when the net tendency for MDOM75 is to be "biased" downward or upward due to a clustering of relatively large occupations at just below the 80 per cent cut-off point (i.e. 77.5–79.9) as compared to just above the 80 per cent cut-off point (i.e. 80.0–82.5) which causes the national value for MDOM75 to "shift" over the borderline to another low, middle or high relative grouping (see Appendix 10.3).

Regional averages are unweighted averages of national values.

Source: Based on national values in table 10.3.

study countries/areas with MDOM75 values below 50 per cent also have relatively low ID75 values. Sixth, at the same time, the relationship between the percentage of the male non-agricultural labour force in a male-dominated occupation (MDOM75) and ID75 is far from perfect. For example, countries outside of the Middle East and North Africa region with relatively high MDOM75 values do not always have a relatively high adjusted ID75 value. It is obviously possible to have a relatively large proportion of men working in occupations "reserved" for them even when an overall measure of occupational segregation, such as ID75, is not relatively high. It seems that men can enjoy having large portions of the non-agricultural labour market sheltered from female competition in countries where the overall level of occupational segregation by sex tends to be relatively low; as will be shown in Chapter 12, "female" occupations tend to be small in such countries.

10.4 Female workers and female-dominated occupations

To begin with, it is important to re-emphasize the point made above about **the relative lack of female-dominated occupations.** Of the approximately 7300 occupations in our study data set for the latest available year, there are only about 700 examples of female-dominated occupations (compared to about 3800 male-dominated examples); among our 20 Asian, Middle Eastern and Other Developing study countries and areas, there are only 84 examples of female-dominated occupations; among the 16 with two-digit data, there are only 39 examples. These represent only about 8, 1 and 0.5 per cent respectively of all occupations in our study data set in these regions.

For readers interested in jumping ahead, tables 11.4 and 11.5 list for each study country or area the five largest female-dominated non-agricultural occupations in terms of employment. When viewed in this way, the choice of occupations "reserved" for women is seen to be small indeed, as we find only 38 "different" female-dominated occupations across all 41 study countries and areas; and even a number of these are closely related occupations (such as registered nurse, nurses' aide, trained midwife; ayah, housekeeper, maid, cleaner).

Despite the small number of female-dominated occupations, *approximately 25 per cent of female non-agricultural workers in the world on average* (based on an unweighted average of national values)[6] *are in a female-dominated occupation* (approximately 20 per cent for study countries/areas with a two-digit classifications and approximately 30 per cent for study countries/areas with a three-digit classification). This percentage is much higher than the percentage of occupations which are "female" occupations (about 10 per cent of all occupations are female-dominated). This difference is mainly due to the relatively large size of female occupations (due in part to occupational classification schemes which are less detailed for occupations where women tend to dominate as compared to the occupations where men tend to dominate). Differences in these percentages can be very large indeed (for example, 10 and 1 per cent respectively on average for the Middle East and North Africa region; 48 and 6 per cent respectively for the Other Developing region).

The **percentage of women non-agricultural workers in a female-dominated occupation varies greatly across regions as well as across OECD subregions** (table 10.5 and figures 10.5 to 10.7). The Middle East and North Africa region has the lowest percentage. Indeed, with the exception of Tunisia (where this is 44 per cent because women comprise 83 per cent of one very large occupation—workers in textiles), the average in this region is only about 3 per cent. Clearly, there is *virtually no separate female world of work in the Middle East and North Africa region.*

The Asia/Pacific region has the next lowest percentage, with an average FDOM75 of only about 10 per cent. Excluding Fiji (which, as noted in the previous analysis of ID in Chapter 9, is more similar to countries in the OD region than the Asian region), the highest national value in the Asian region is less than 15 per cent. And even the few "female" occupations available to Asian women often have relatively low pay, are often in highly "flexible" export-oriented sectors, and are often associated with traditional preconceptions about the types of work which are appropriate for women (see detailed discussion and tables 11.4 and 11.5 in the following Chapter 11).

The *Other Developing region* has, by far, the *highest regional average* for FDOM75 at approximately 48 per cent. This average, however, hides considerable variation within this heterogeneous set. Indeed, this is the only region where the standard deviation for the region is larger than the standard deviation for the world as a whole. Particularly worth noting are the unusually high percentages for Haiti and Ghana (at approximately 77 per cent), as these are over 20 percentage points higher than for any other study country; these unusually high percentages can be traced in part to the fact that women comprise over one-half of the non-agricultural labour force in these two countries. Despite the high percentage for FDOM75 in the Other Developing region, there is only a narrow range of (low paying) female-dominated non-agricultural occupations available, and these are *generally in the informal sector* (such as petty trader and food preparer).

FDOM75 values for the OECD and Transition Economy regions are in the middle for the world, just as they are for ID75. Approximately 27 per cent of the female non-agricultural labour force is in a female-dominated occupation in these regions. As with the Other Developing region, there is *considerable heterogeneity within the OECD and the Transition Economy regions*, where national FDOM75 values range from 9 to 55 per cent.[7] Table 10.7 and figure 10.6 present OECD subregional averages and standard deviations.

Table 10.5. Distribution of countries by relative level (low, middle, high) for per cent of female non-agricultural labour force working in female-dominated[a] occupations (FDOM75), latest available year, by region

Region	<10.0 (FDOM75) No.	Countries/areas	10.0–30.0 (FDOM75) No.	Countries/areas	>30.0 (FDOM75) No.	Countries/areas	Mean (x) Std dev. (σ)
OECD	0		11	Italy (10.2)*D	6	Netherlands (31.4)	x = 26.9
				United Kingdom (13.5)*D		Norway (34.0)	σ = 13.4
				Spain (14.2)		Canada (37.2)*	
				Austria (14.3)		Luxembourg (37.3)D	
				Switzerland (17.2)		Sweden (53.8)	
				Australia (17.4)*		Finland (55.4)	
				New Zealand (19.5)			
				France (22.0)			
				Germany (23.6)*U			
				Cyprus (25.6)			
				United States (29.2)*			
Transition Economies	1	Former Yugoslavia (8.9)*	2	Bulgaria (19.8)*D	1	Poland (48.6)*	x = 26.5
				Hungary (28.6)			σ = 16.8
Middle East and North Africa	5	Iran, Islamic Rep. of (0.0)	0		1	Tunisia (44.3)[b]	x = 9.8
		Bahrain (0.0)					σ = 17.8
		Egypt (0.0)					
		Kuwait (7.2)D					
		Jordan (6.2)					
Asia/Pacific	4	India (0.0)	3	China (10.5)	0		x = 10.0
		Korea, Rep. of (1.0)D		Hong Kong (14.8)			σ = 8.9
		Japan (7.7)		Fiji (26.4)			
		Malaysia (9.8)					

Other Developing	0	
	2	Mauritius (14.0)
		Senegal (28.8)D
	5	Netherlands Antilles (32.2)
		Costa Rica (52.0)*
		Angola (52.1)
		Haiti (76.3)
		Ghana (77.2)
		x = 47.5
		σ = 24.0

Notes: [a] Percentage of female non-agricultural labour force working in female-dominated occupations (FDOM) is adjusted so as to be for an occupational classification with 75 non-agricultural occupations (FDOM75).

* indicates when FDOM75 is estimated with lesser precision as the adjustment factor included in FDOM75 is greater than 5.0 percentage points (see Appendix 10.1).

B indicates when the net tendency for FDOM75 is to be "biased" downward or upward due to a clustering of relatively large occupations at just below the 80 per cent cut-off point (i.e. 77.5–79.9) as compared to just above the 80 per cent cut-off point (i.e. 80.0–82.5) which causes the national value for FDOM75 to "shift" over the borderline into another low, middle or high relative grouping (see Appendix 10.3).

[b] Tunisia has one occupation (textile workers) which comprises 44.3 per cent of the female non-agricultural labour force. This is obviously due to measurement non-compatibility with other countries in the region. In this regard, note that Tunisia's female share of the total non-agricultural labour force would be similar to that found in Egypt and the Islamic Republic of Iran and if this one occupation were similarly enumerated in these three countries.

Regional averages are unweighted averages of national values.

Source: Based on national values in table 10.3.

Figure 10.5. Percentage of female non-agricultural labour force in female-dominated occupation (FDOM75), latest available year, by region

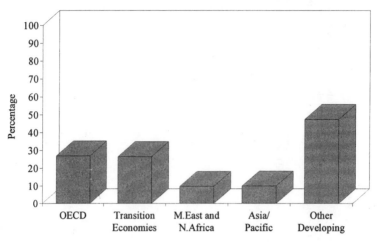

Note: Female-dominated occupations are defined as occupations where at least 80 per cent of workers are female.
Source: Table 10.3.

Notice that the standard deviations for all six OECD subregions are lower than for OECD as a whole. Once again, OECD subregions are found to be distinctly different from each other.

At one extreme in the OECD region are *Scandinavian countries*, which all have relatively high FDOM75 values (approximately 48 per cent on average).

Figure 10.6. Percentage of female non-agricultural labour force in female-dominated occupation, latest available year (FDOM75), by OECD subregion

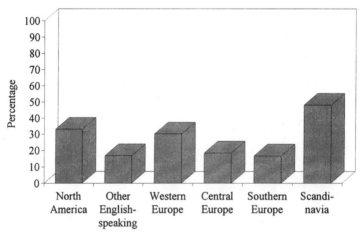

Note: Female-dominated occupations are defined as occupations where at least 80 per cent of workers are female.
Source: Table 10.5.

Figure 10.7. Distribution of countries and areas by relative level (low, middle, high) for percentage of female non-agricultural labour force (FDOM75) working in female-dominated occupation, latest available year, by region

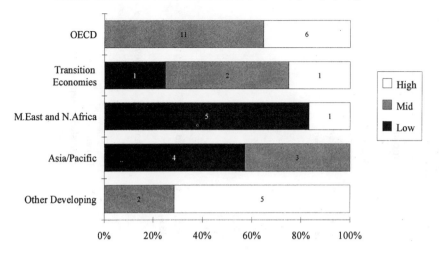

Notes: Numbers inside bars indicate number of study countries and areas.
Female-dominated occupations are defined as occupations where at least 80 per cent of workers are female.
Source: Table 10.5.

Scandinavian countries have created a labour market with very high female labour force participation rates (approximately one-half of the labour force is female) and relatively equal pay for men and women—in large part by creating separate but somewhat equal (in terms of pay) worlds of work for men and women. Also, countries in North America and Western Europe (as well as Poland) tend to have relatively high FDOM75 values.

At the other extreme in the OECD and TE regions, with relatively low FDOM75 values, are former Yugoslavia, English-speaking countries outside of North America as well as Southern and Central European countries. Approximately 10 to 20 per cent of the female non-agricultural labour force is in a female-dominated occupation in these countries.

10.5   Total non-agricultural labour force and gender-dominated occupations

The discussion now turns to the total non-agricultural labour force and the extent to which it is comprised of gender-dominated occupations (TDOM75). This statistic provides a good indicator of labour market segmentation and consequently of labour market barriers and inefficiencies due to gender inequalities. Table 10.3 and figure 10.8 present adjusted

Table 10.6. Distribution of countries/areas by relative level (low, middle, high) for percentage of total non-agricultural labour force working in gender-dominated[a] occupations (TDOM75), latest available year, by region

Region	<45.0 (TDOM75)		45.0–60.0 (TDOM75)		>60.0 (TDOM75)		Mean (x) Std dev. (σ)
	No.	Countries/areas	No.	Countries/areas	No.	Countries/areas	
OECD	6	Australia (41.6)	9	Italy (45.6)*B	2	Sweden (61.2)	x = 48.2
		United States (40.1)		New Zealand (45.7)B		Finland (62.0)	σ = 6.7
		United Kingdom (41.4)		Cyprus (47.3)*			
		France (42.1)		Germany (West) (47.5)*B			
		Canada (43.6)*B		Spain (48.1)			
		Austria (44.9)		Norway (48.1)			
				Switzerland (49.6)			
				Luxembourg (57.9)			
				Netherlands (51.7)			
Transition Economies	1	Bulgaria (26.9)	2	Hungary (47.6)	1	Poland (61.7)*B	x = 46.3
				Former Yugoslavia (48.9)*			σ = 14.4
Middle East and North Africa	0		0		6	Bahrain (69.1)	x = 77.2
						Egypt (71.8)	σ = 6.4
						Kuwait (73.5)	
						Tunisia (81.9)	
						Iran, Islamic Rep. of (83.3)	
						Jordan (83.4)	
Asia/Pacific	4	Korea, Rep. of (32.1)	1	Malaysia (45.7)	2	Fiji (61.4)	x = 64.7
		China (32.8)				India (83.3)	F = 19.0
		Hong Kong (34.8)					
		Japan (38.4)					

Other Developing	0			
	3	Mauritius	(54.7)	
		Netherlands Antilles	(56.2)	
		Angola	(58.9)	
	4	Costa Rica	(62.3)	x = 64.7
		Senegal	(70.5)	σ = 8.8
		Ghana	(75.7)	
		Haiti	(74.6)	

Notes: [a] Percentage of the total labour force working in a gender-dominated occupation (TDOM) is adjusted so as to be for an occupational classification with 75 non-agricultural occupations (MDOM75) in order to increase cross-national comparability.

* indicates when TDOM75 is greater than 5 percentage points (see Appendix 10.1).

B indicates when the net tendency for TDOM75 is "biased" downward or upward due to a clustering of relatively large occupations at just below the 80 per cent cut-off point (i.e. 77.5–79.9) as compared to just above the 80 per cent cut-off point (i.e. 80.0–82.5) which causes the national value for TDOM75 to "shift" over the borderline into another low, middle or high relative grouping (see Appendix 10.3).

"Round numbers" (e.g. .45 and .60) were chosen for defining the low, middle and high groups which resulted in roughly equal numbers of countries/areas in each grouping. Note that the low (and high) cut-off point for TDOM75 is roughly equal to the summation of: (1) [the low (high) value for FDOM75 plus the average percentage female in male-dominated occupations] times the average percentage women in the non-agricultural labour force plus (2) [the low (high) value for MDOM75 plus the average percentage male in female-dominated occupations] times the average percentage men in the non-agricultural labour force. These calculations give .44 and .56 compared to our actual cut-off points of .45 and .60.

Regional averages are unweighted averages of national values.

Source: Based on national values in table 10.3.

national values and regional averages for TDOM75. Table 10.6 and figure 10.9 sort study countries according to whether they have relatively low, middle and high values in a similar manner as in previous sections for the female-dominated and male-dominated labour forces.

Levels of occupational segregation by sex as measured by TDOM75 are extremely high. On average (unweighted) *approximately 55 per cent of workers in our 41 study countries/areas work in an occupation where at least 80 per cent of workers are either male or female* (based on a classification with 75 non-agricultural occupations).[8] Yet this already high percentage is even higher in the real world, since it is known (see Chapter 6) that TDOM tends to increase (by about 6 per cent on average we estimate) when the occupational data on which it is based are disaggregated from the two-digit level to the three-digit level (i.e. from approximately 75 to 265 non-agricultural occupations). It is obvious that economic efficiency in the world is significantly reduced by this high level of labour market segmentation based on the sex of the worker.

There are also **large regional differences in TDOM75.** *The Middle East and North Africa region stands out as having very highly segmented labour markets*, as approximately 80 per cent of non-agricultural workers in this region are in an occupation where one sex dominates (figure 10.8). Furthermore, all six study countries in the ME region are located in our relatively high TDOM75 category (figure 10.9). These very high TDOM75 values for the ME region can only partly be attributed to low rates of female labour force participation; as shown in Chapter 9 and as will be shown in Appendix 10.2 and subsequently in Chapter 11, the ME region has very high levels of occupational segregation by sex on all of the inequality measures used in this book. It is interesting to note that the somewhat lower level of occupational segregation by sex for Egypt which we observed in Chapter 9 based on ID75 is not observed here for TDOM75.

Countries in *the Other Developing region also stand out as having relatively high TDOM75 values* (figures 10.8 and 10.9). While values are lower than in the ME region, they are none the less much higher than in our other three study regions. Approximately 65 per cent of the total nonagricultural labour force in the OD region is, on average, in a genderdominated occupation, with the lowest national value in this region (55 per cent in Mauritius) only about average for the world. These high TDOM75 values in the OD region reflect quite well the high level of occupational segregation by sex in this region, since high values cannot be "blamed" on low female labour force participation rates.

It is surprising to find that TDOM75 for Asia and the Pacific is, on average, similar to that for the OECD (table 10.6 and figure 10.8). This similarity is, however, misleading, since this average is greatly influenced by high values for India and Fiji. Indeed, *average TDOM75 is lower in Asia as compared to the OECD when India is excluded* (at 40.8 per cent); it is even

Figure 10.8. Percentage of total non-agricultural labour force in gender-dominated occupation (TDOM75), latest available year, by region

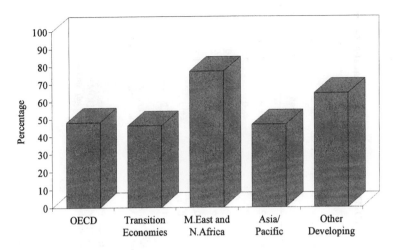

Notes: Gender-dominated occupations are defined as occupations where at least 80 per cent of workers are either men or women.
Average for five study countries and areas in East Asia (i.e. excluding India and Fiji) is considerably lower at 36.7 per cent.
Source: Table 10.3.

Figure 10.9. Distribution of economies by relative level (low, middle, high) for percentage of total non-agricultural labour force (TDOM75) working in gender-dominated occupation, latest available year, by region

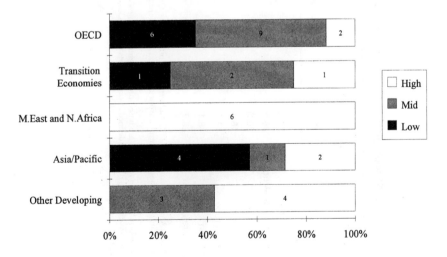

Notes: Numbers inside bars indicate number of study countries and areas.
Source: Table 10.6.

Table 10.7. OECD subregional averages and standard deviations for FDOM75, MDOM75 and TDOM75, latest available year

OECD subregion	FDOM75		MDOM75		TDOM75	
	Mean	Standard deviation	Mean	Standard deviation	Mean	Standard deviation
North America	33.2	5.7	42.8	0.2	41.9	2.5
Other English-speaking	16.8	3.0	57.5	2.2	43.0	2.5
Western Europe	30.2	7.7	57.9	6.6	50.6	8.0
Central Europe	18.4	4.8	60.7	1.9	47.3	2.4
Southern Europe	16.7	8.0	58.0	3.0	47.0	1.3
Scandinavia	48.1	11.3	55.0	2.8	57.2	7.9
OECD (overall)	26.9	13.5	56.0	6.1	48.2	6.7

Notes: North America is comprised of Canada and the United States; Other English-speaking of Australia, New Zealand and the United Kingdom; Western Europe of France, the Netherlands and Luxembourg; Central Europe of Austria, West Germany and Switzerland; Southern Europe of Cyprus, Italy and Spain; and Scandinavia of Finland, Norway and Sweden.

Regional and subregional averages are based on unweighted averages of national values.

Gender-dominated occupations are defined as occupations where at least 80 per cent of workers are male or female. FDOM is the percentage of the female non-agricultural labour force in a female-dominated occupation. MDOM is the percentage of the male non-agricultural labour force in a male-dominated occupation. TDOM is the percentage of the total non-agricultural labour force in a male-dominated occupation. FDOM75, MDOM75 and TDOM75 refer to national values which have been adjusted so as to be roughly comparable for an occupational classification with 75 non-agricultural occupations.

Source: Based on national values in table 10.3.

lower when Fiji is also excluded (at 36.7 per cent). This tendency for lower TDOM75 values in Asia is also reflected in the fact that a majority of Asian economies are found in our relatively low TDOM75 grouping (figure 10.9). Indeed, China, Japan, the Republic of Korea and Hong Kong are in the relatively low groups for both TDOM75 and ID75 (and Malaysia nearly so).

Regional averages for OECD and TE regions are almost identical at approximately 47 per cent. This similarity between TE and OECD regions parallels earlier results for ID75, FDOM75 and MDOM75. Once again, we find that (i) these regions tend to have very similar levels of occupational segregation by sex; (ii) values tend to be rather average for the world; and (iii) there is substantial variation within these regions.

As regards OECD subregions, it is found that four of the six OECD subregions have much lower standard deviations for TDOM75 as compared to the standard deviation for the OECD region as a whole (table 10.7). Once again, there is considerable similarity for countries within OECD subregions. Also once again, *Scandinavia has the highest average TDOM75 among OECD subregions* (figure 10.10) and *North America has the lowest average TDOM75* among OECD subregions. An interesting difference from results based on ID75 is that Other English-speaking countries have relatively low values for TDOM75 but not for ID75; this difference can be traced to differences in the relative sizes of FDOM75 and MDOM75. Among TE countries, Bulgaria has a relatively low TDOM75 value (similar to values in

Figure 10.10. Percentage of total non-agricultural labour force in gender-dominated occupation, latest available year (TDOM75), by OECD subregion

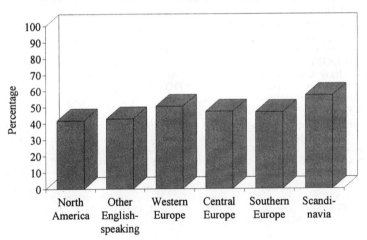

Note: Gender-dominated occupations defined as occupations where at least 80 per cent of workers are either men or women.
Source: Table 10.7.

North America) and Poland a relatively high value (similar to values in Scandinavia).

Notes

[1] This definition of "male" and "female" occupations uses the same 80 per cent cut-off point for all countries, regardless of whether they have high or low female labour force participation rates.

[2] Since use of a single dividing line for defining "male" and "female" occupations (here 80 per cent of one sex) can cause national values to be sensitive to one or a few large occupations where percentage male or female is just above or just below this 80 per cent dividing line, Appendix 10.3 presents national data on the percentage of the male and female non-agricultural labour forces working in occupations where 77.5 to 82.5 per cent of workers are either male or female. In addition, it is indicated in table 10.3 to 10.6 when the existence of large occupations near to the 80 per cent dividing line has an important effect on national values for the size of the male- or female-dominated non-agricultural labour forces.

[3] In both cases: the adjustment is made to 75 occupations (the number of non-agricultural occupations at the two-digit level in ISCO-68, the most common classification scheme in the world); the adjustment is positive (negative) when the relevant national data have less (more) than 75 occupations; the further from 75 occupations are national data, the greater is the adjustment; the marginal effect of the adjustment in the national data is a decreasing function of the number of occupations classified (as a log functional form was utilized for the adjustment). See Chapter 7 for a discussion of this procedure and Appendix 10.3 for the calculations.

[4] These calculations are restricted to occupations which contain at least 1 per cent of the relevant non-agricultural labour force, because we are mainly concerned with situations where small changes in one or a few occupations might have a major effect on observed national values.

[5] The letter B is placed next to the national value in tables 10.4–10.6 when the net tendency could have affected whether a country was placed in the relatively low, middle or high grouping. There are seven national examples for FDOM75, three examples for MDOM75 and eight examples for TDOM75. The reason for this relatively large number of examples is mainly due to the fact that a number of countries have FDOM75, MDOM75 and TDOM75 values which are close to the borderline value for a relative group (e.g. 10, 30, 40 per cent for FDOM75).

[6] Based on a weighted (by size of female non-agricultural labour force) average of national values, approximately 19 per cent of women workers in the world are in a female-dominated occupation (for countries with a two-digit classification).

[7] While FDOM75 is only about 10 per cent in Italy and former Yugoslavia, these national values have lesser precision than for most other countries due to the relatively large adjustment factors they embody. Also, Italy's FDOM75 value is "biased downward" because of an unusually high concentration of occupations with 77.5 to 79.9 per cent female (see Appendix 10.3).

[8] Global and regional averages in the text are unweighted averages of national values. Although it is possible to calculate weighted averages using the size of the labour force (i.e. number of workers) as weights, this is not done in the text, because values for a few very large countries (such as China, the United States and India) would too greatly dominate results. When weighted averages are calculated, it is found that TDOM75 is smaller than that indicated by the unweighted average; this comes about because two of the largest study countries (China and the United States) have relatively low TDOM75 values. The weighted (and unweighted averages) for TDOM75 are as follows: World, 46.1 (54.8); OECD 43.1 (48.2); TE 52.3 (46.3); Asia 40.0 (46.9); ME 77.6 (77.2); OD 69.9 (64.7).

Appendix 10.1. Estimation of adjusting national values to percentage of female non-agricultural labour force in female-dominated occupations (FDOM75), male non-agricultural labour force in male-dominated occupations (MDOM75) and total non-agricultural labour force in gender-dominated occupations (TDOM75) by taking into account the level of disaggregation in national occupational classifications

Table 10.8. Adjusting national MDOM values (i.e. percentage of male non-agricultural labour force in male-dominated occupations) to 75 occupations by taking into account the level of disaggregation in national occupational classifications

Region/country/area	MDOM unadjusted	NOCC	Adjustment factor		Adjusted MDOM75[b]
			Type[a]	Amount	
OECD					
Australia	56.0	279	OECD 2→3	−0.9	55.1
Austria	59.6	64	OECD 1→2	0.9	60.5
Canada	39.8	44	OECD 1→2	3.1	42.9
Cyprus	62.9	376	N 1→2		
	61.3	104		−6.5	54.8*
	4.7	6			
Finland	59.1	264	N 1→2		
	55.6	64		0.4	56.0
	52.6	6			
France	54.6	433	N 1→2		
	51.9	119		−1.2	50.7
	43.4	5			
Germany (West)	59.9	268	OECD 2→3	−0.9	59.0
Italy	59.5	231	OECD 2→3	−0.8	58.7
Luxembourg	63.4	71	N 1→2	0.2	63.7
	52.3	6			
Netherlands	60.6	151	N 2→3		
	58.8	63		0.4	59.2
	45.4	6			
New Zealand	56.9	281	N 1→2		
	58.1	77		−0.0	58.1
	59.8	6			

Table 10.8. (contd.)

Region/country/area	MDOM unadjusted	NOCC	Adjustment factor Type[a]	Amount	Adjusted MDOM75[b]
Norway	60.1	291	N 2→3		
	50.9	65		0.9	51.8
	49.3	6			
Spain	60.6	77	OECD 2→3	−0.0	60.6
Sweden	54.6	49	OECD 1→2	2.5	57.1
Switzerland	67.6	452	N 2→3		
	62.4	66		0.3	62.7
	36.0	8			
United Kingdom	60.7	509	OECD 2→3	−1.4	59.3
United States	43.9	461	OECD 2→3	−1.3	42.6
Average (unweighted)				**−0.3**	**56.05**
Transition Economies					
Bulgaria	26.1	43	OECD 1→2	3.2	29.3
Hungary	57.4	118	OECD 2→3	−0.3	57.1
Poland	65.0	361	OECD 2→3	−1.1	63.9
Former Yugoslavia	66.1	206	OECD 2→3	−0.7	65.4
Average (unweighted)				**−0.3**	**53.9**
Middle East and North Africa					
Bahrain	80.8	86	N 1→2	−1.2	79.6
	56.5	6			
Egypt	79.7	74	N 1→2	0.1	79.8
	70.4	6			
Iran, Islamic Rep. of	89.8	21	ME 1→2	0.2	90.0
Jordan	88.6	61	N 1→2	0.3	88.9
	85.4	6			
Kuwait	84.2	75	N 1→2	0.0	84.2
	51.4	6			
Tunisia	83.9	55	N 1→2	0.4	83.5
	81.2	6			
Average (unweighted)				**0.0**	**84.3**
Asia/Pacific					
China	43.4	277	N 2→3	0.9	41.8
	40.9	38			
	7.8	6			
Fiji	70.1	75	N	0.0	70.1
	55.1	6			
Hong Kong	42.5	73	Asia 1→2	0.3	42.8
India	85.8	423	N 1→2		
	87.2	83		0.1	87.3
	90.5	6			

Table 10.8. (contd.)

Region/country/area	MDOM unadjusted	NOCC	Adjustment factor		Adjusted MDOM75[b]
			Type[a]	Amount	
Japan	53.8	259	N 2→3		
	51.9	49		0.5	52.4
	7.2	6			
Republic of Korea	39.5	56	Asia 1→2	3.1	42.6
	1.8	6			
Malaysia	55.8	76	N 1→2	−0.3	55.5
	2.2	6			
Average (unweighted)				**0.7**	**56.1**
Other Developing					
Angola	60.4	67	N 1→2	0.3	60.7
	53.3	6			
Costa Rica	53.4	55	N 1→2	7.5	60.9*
	0.0	6			
Ghana	60.3	75	N	0.0	60.3
	1.6	6			
Haiti	58.8	75	N	0.0	58.8
	2.4	6			
Mauritius	66.4	70	N 1→2	1.8	68.2
	2.0	6			
Netherlands Antilles	66.8	76	N 1→2	−0.1	66.7
	51.6	6			
Senegal	75.7	80	N 1→2	−0.5	75.2
	57.4	6			
Average (unweighted)				**1.3**	**64.4**

Notes: MDOM is defined as the percentage of the male non-agricultural labour force working in a male-dominated occupation (i.e. an occupation where at least 80 per cent of the workers are men).
NOCC is the number of non-agricultural occupations classified in the national data.
[a] Adjustment is done by interpolation between 1- and 2-digit (i.e. 1→2) data or between 2- and 3-digit data (i.e. 2→3). Adjustment in MDOM values based on either national (N) or regional (i.e. OECD, Asia/Pacific, ME or OD) relationships.
[b] The adjusted MDOM (i.e. MDOM75) is adjusted to classification with 75 non-agricultural occupations by adding adjustment amount to unadjusted MDOM.
* indicates when an adjustment is greater than 5.0 percentage points and so the adjusted MDOM75 is measured with relatively less precision.

Table 10.9. **Adjusting national FDOM values (i.e. percentage of female non-agricultural labour force in female-dominated occupations) to 75 occupations by taking into account the level of disaggregation in national occupational classifications**

Region/country/area	FDOM unadjusted	NOCC	Adjustment factor		Adjusted FDOM75[b]
			Type[a]	Amount	
OECD					
Australia	29.6	279	OECD 2→3	−12.2	17.4*
Austria	12.6	64	OECD 1→2	1.7	14.3
Canada	31.4	44	OECD 1→2	5.8	37.2*
Cyprus	31.4	376	N 1→2		
	28.9	104		−3.3	25.6
	0.0	6			
Finland	60.9	264	N 1→2		
	54.7	64		0.7	55.4
	22.3	6			
France	44.9	433	N 1→2		
	25.8	119		−3.8	22.0
	0.0	5			
Germany (West)	35.4	268	OECD 2→3	−11.8	23.6*
Italy	20.6	231	OECD 2→3	−10.4	10.2*
Luxembourg	36.5	71	N 1→2	0.8	37.3
	0.0	6			
Netherlands	36.8	151	N 2→3		
	30.1	63		1.3	31.4
	0.0	6			
New Zealand	46.3	281	N 1→2		
	19.7	77		−0.2	19.5
	0.0	6			
Norway	48.4	291	N 2→3		
	33.6	65		1.4	35.0
	0.0	6			
Spain	14.4	77	OECD 2→3	−0.2	14.2
Sweden	49.2	49	OECD 2→3	4.6	53.8
Switzerland	33.5	452	N 2→3		
	16.1	66		1.2	17.3
	0.0	8			
United Kingdom	31.3	509	OECD 2→3	−17.8	13.5*
United States	46.0	461	OECD 2→3	−16.8	29.2*
Average (unweighted)				**−3.5**	**26.9**
Transition Economies					
Bulgaria	13.8	43	OECD 1→2	6.0	19.8*
Hungary	32.8	118	OECD 2→3	−4.2	28.6
Poland	63.2	361	OECD 2→3	−14.6	48.6*
Former Yugoslavia	18.3	206	OECD 2→3	−9.4	8.9*
Average (unweighted)				**−5.6**	**26.5**

Table 10.9.   (contd.)

Region/country/area	FDOM unadjusted	NOCC	Adjustment factor Type[a]	Amount	Adjusted FDOM75[b]
Middle East and North Africa					
Bahrain	0.0	86	N 1→2	−0.0	0.0
	0.0	6			
Egypt	0.0	74	N 1→2	0.0	0.0
	0.0	6			
Iran, Islamic Rep. of	0.0	21	ME 1→2	0.0	0.0
Jordan	5.7	61	N 1→2	0.5	6.2
	0.0	6			
Kuwait	7.2	75	N 1→2	0.0	7.2
	0.0	6			
Tunisia	44.3	55	ME 1→2[c]	1.3[c]	45.6
	0.0	6			
Average (unweighted)				**0.3**	**9.8**
Asia/Pacific					
China	15.0	277	N 2→3	2.3	10.5
	8.2	38			
	0.0	6			
Fiji	26.4	75	N	0.0	26.4
	0.0	6			
Hong Kong	14.7	73	Asia 1→2	0.1	14.8
India	3.1	423	N 1→2		
	0.0	83		0.0	0.0
	0.0	6			
Japan	16.9	259	N 2→3		
	4.5	49		3.2	7.7
	0.0	6			
Republic of Korea	0.0	56	Asia 1→2	1.0	1.01
	0.0	6			
Malaysia	9.8	76	N 1→2	−0.1	9.8
	0.0	6			
Average (unweighted)				**0.9**	**10.0**
Other Developing					
Angola	52.1	67	N 1→2	0.09	52.1
	51.9	6			
Costa Rica	45.6	55	N 1→2	6.4	52.0*
	0.0	6			
Ghana	77.2	75	N	0.0	77.2
	54.3	6			
Haiti	76.3	75	N	0.0	76.3
	68.7	6			
Mauritius	13.6	70	N 1→2	0.4	14.0
	0.0	6			

Table 10.9.   (contd.)

Region/country/area	FDOM unadjusted	NOCC	Adjustment factor		Adjusted FDOM75[b]
			Type[a]	Amount	
Netherlands Antilles	32.4	76	N 1→2	−0.2	32.2
	0.0	6			
Senegal	29.5	80	N 1→2	−0.7	28.8
	0.0	6			
Average (unweighted)				**0.9**	**47.5**

Notes: FDOM is defined as the percentage of the female non-agricultural labour force working in a female-dominated occupation (defined as an occupation where at least 80 per cent of the workers are women).
NOCC is the number of non-agricultural occupations classified in the national data.
[a] Adjustment is done by interpolation between 1- and 2-digit data (i.e. 1→2) or 2- and 3-digit data (i.e. 2→3) .
Adjustment in FDOM values based on either national (N) or regional (i.e. OECD, Asia, ME or OD) relationships. [b] The adjusted FDOM (i.e. FDOM75) is adjusted to classifications with 75 non-agricultural occupations by adding adjustment amount to unadjusted FDOM. [c] For Tunisia it was assumed that the adjustment relationship is as for the ME region in order to keep this adjustment factor similar to that other countries in the region.
[*] indicates when an adjustment is greater than 5.0 percentage points, and so when the adjusted FDOM75 is measured with relatively less precision.

Table 10.10. Adjusting national TDOM values (i.e. percentage of total non-agricultural labour force in gender-dominated occupation) by taking into account the level of disaggregation in national occupational classifications

Region/country/area	TDOM unadjusted	NOCC	Adjustment factor Type[a]	Adjustment factor Amount	Adjusted TDOM75[b]
OECD					
Australia	48.2	279	OECD 2→3	−6.6	41.6*
Austria	43.6	64	OECD 1→2	1.3	44.9
Canada	39.3	44	OECD 1→2	4.4	43.6*
Cyprus	53.9	376	N 1→2		
	53.0	104		−5.7	47.3*
	3.0	6			
Finland	64.4	264	N 1→2		
	62.0	64		0.3	62.3
	46.0	6			
France	54.3	433	N 1→2		
	44.0	119		−1.9	42.1
	31.0	5			
Germany (West)	53.9	268	OECD 2→3	−6.4	47.5*
Italy	51.2	231	OECD 2→3	−5.6	45.6*
Luxembourg	57.4	71	N 1→2	0.5	57.9
	36.0	6			
Netherlands	54.3	151	N 2→3		
	51.0	63		0.7	51.7
	30.0	6			
New Zealand	57.5	281	N 1→2		
	46.0	77		−0.1	45.9
	41.0	6			
Norway	58.8	291	N 2→3		
	47.0	65		1.1	48.1
	31.0	6			
Spain	48.2	77	OECD 2→3	−0.1	48.1
Sweden	57.7	49	OECD 1→2	3.5	61.2
Switzerland	58.3	452	N 2→3		
	49.0	66		0.6	49.6
	25.0	8			
United Kingdom	51.0	509	OECD 2→3	−9.6	41.4*
United States	49.2	461	OECD 2→3	−9.1	40.1*
Average (unweighted)				**−1.9**	**48.2**
Transition Economies					
Bulgaria	22.4	43	OECD 1→2	4.5	26.9*
Hungary	49.9	118	OECD 2→3	−2.7	47.6
Poland	69.5	361	OECD 2→3	−7.8	61.7*
Former Yugoslavia	53.9	206	OECD 2→3	−5.0	48.9*
Average (unweighted)				**−2.8**	**46.3**

Table 10.10.   (contd.)

Region/country/area	TDOM unadjusted	NOCC	Adjustment factor		Adjusted TDOM75[b]
			Type[a]	Amount	
Middle East and North Africa					
Bahrain	70.2	86	N 1→2	−1.2	69.1
	49.0	6			
Egypt	71.8	74	N 1→2	0.1	71.8
	63.0	6			
Iran, Islamic Rep. of	83.3	21	ME 1→2	0.0	83.3*
Jordan	83.1	61	N 1→2	0.3	83.4
	80.0	6			
Kuwait	73.5	75	N 1→2	0.0	73.5
	41.0	6			
Tunisia	81.4	55	N 1→2	0.5	81.9
	78.0	6			
Average (unweighted)				−0.1	**77.2**
Asia/Pacific					
China	36.3	277	N 2→3	1.8	32.8
	31.0	38			
	0.0	6			
Fiji	61.4	75	N	0.0	61.4
	44.0	6			
Hong Kong	34.5	73	Asia 1→2	0.3	34.8
India	80.8	423	N 1→2		
	83.0	83		0.3	83.3
	90.0	6			
Japan	42.4	259	N 2→3		
	37.0	49		1.4	38.4
	5.0	6			
Republic of Korea	28.5	56	Asia 1→2	3.6	32.1
	1.0	6			
Malaysia	45.9	76	N 1→2	−0.2	45.7
	2.0	6			
Average (unweighted)				1.0	**46.9**
Other Developing					
Angola	58.9	67	N 1→2	0.0	58.9
	59.0	6			
Costa Rica	54.7	55	N 1→2	7.6	62.3*
	0.0	6			
Ghana	75.7	75	N	0.0	75.7
	36.0	6			
Haiti	74.6	75	N	0.0	74.6
	50.0	6			
Mauritius	53.3	70	N 1→2	1.4	54.7
	2.0	6			

Table 10.10. (contd.)

Region/country/area	TDOM unadjusted	NOCC	Adjustment factor Type[a]	Amount	Adjusted TDOM75[b]
Netherlands Antilles	56.3	76	N 1→2	−0.1	56.2
	33.0	6			
Senegal	70.9	80	N 1→2	−0.4	70.5
	53.6	6			
Average (unweighted)				**1.2**	**64.7**

Notes: TDOM is defined as a percentage of the total non-agricultural labour force in a gender-dominated occupation (defined as an occupation where at least 80 per cent of the workers are either male or female).
NOCC is the number of non-agricultural occupations classified in the national data.
[a] Adjustment is done by interpolation between 1- and 2-digit data (i.e. 1→2) or 2- and 3-digit data (i.e. 2→3). Adjustment in TDOM values based on either national (N) or regional (i.e. OECD, Asia/Pacific , ME or OD) relationships. [b] The adjusted TDOM (i.e. TDOM75) is adjusted to classification with 75 non-agricultural occupations by adding adjustment amount to unadjusted TDOM.
* indicates when an adjustment is greater than 5.0 percentage points and so when the adjusted TDOM75 is measured with relatively less precision.

Appendix 10.2. Extent to which occupations are gender-concentrated, gender-integrated and gender-underrepresented using a *relative* concept of gender dominance

Table 10.11. Number of female-concentrated, gender-integrated and female-underrepresented non-agricultural occupations and percentage of women in such occupations using a *relative* concept of female-concentration, latest available year, by region

Region/country/area	Year	Women's share of non-ag. LF (%)	Total number of non-ag. occupations classified	Female-concentrated occupations		Gender-integrated occupations		Number of female underrepresented occupations
				Number	% female non-ag. LF	Number	% female non-ag. LF	
OECD								
Australia	1990	41.7	279	55	72.9	77	25.3	147
Austria	1990	40.8	64	14	78.6	23	17.6	27
Canada	1990	45.9	44	10	51.2	17	43.9	17
Cyprus	1989	37.3	376	71	63.0	94	30.2	211
Finland	1990	49.1	264	58	63.6	100	27.5	106
France	1990	42.6	433	63	61.2	161	34.3	209
Germany (West)	1989	41.7	268	51	71.7	62	25.4	155
Italy	1981	32.6	231	52	55.3	76	35.9	103
Luxembourg	1991	35.9	71	15	57.2	19	34.6	37
Netherlands	1990	39.1	151	29	71.1	36	28.3	86
New Zealand	1986	42.3	281	51	70.7	84	26.4	146
Norway	1990	47.1	291	49	66.7	108	29.1	133
Spain	1990	32.7	77	16	69.4	26	24.3	35
Sweden	1991	49.2	49	9	57.0	20	36.2	20
Switzerland	1980	36.7	452	107	78.5	97	16.7	248
United Kingdom	1990	44.0	509	71	73.4	134	21.5	304
United States	1991	46.5	461	85	56.2	170	41.0	206
Average (unweighted)		**41.3**	**253**	**47**	**65.8**	**77**	**29.3**	**129**

	Year							
Transition Economies								
Bulgaria	1985	45.6	43	13	55.5	22	52.0	8
Hungary	1990	45.6	118	28	48.2	53	40.6	37
Poland	1988	44.2	361	97	71.6	149	25.3	115
Former Yugoslavia	1981	33.3	206	50	64.7	73	26.3	83
Average (unweighted)		**42.2**	**182**	**47**	**60.0**	**74**	**36.0**	**61**
Middle East and North Africa								
Bahrain	1991	16.9	86	18	77.6	20	15.5	48
Egypt	1986	13.6	74	15	78.4	19	20.7	40
Iran, Islamic Republic of	1986	10.5	21	3	72.2	7	15.4	11
Jordan	1979	8.1	61	13	87.5	8	7.5	40
Kuwait	1985	20.0	268	36	82.8	40	15.8	192
Tunisia	1989	19.6	55	9	74.5	25	18.6	21
Average (unweighted)		**14.8**	**94**	**16**	**78.8**	**20**	**15.6**	**59**
Asia/Pacific								
China	1980	35.7	277	72	47.2	138	47.5	67
Fiji	1986	27.1	75	16	66.5	27	27.3	32
Hong Kong	1991	37.7	73	10	63.1	34	36.9	28
India	1981	12.1	423	52	60.3	112	37.6	259
Japan	1990	39.3	259	52	47.0	93	40.8	114
Republic of Korea	1983	30.6	56	7	47.6	27	48.8	22
Malaysia	1980	28.2	76	22	67.4	27	25.3	27
Average (unweighted)		**30.1**	**177**	**73**	**57.0**	**65**	**37.7**	**79**
Other Developing								
Angola	1992	41.3	67	6	63.1	28	34.9	33
Costa Rica	1991	37.1	55	9	60.2	19	39.1	27
Ghana	1984	57.6	75	4	76.7	22	20.4	49
Haiti	1986	65.2	75	4	0.9	20	75.9	51
Mauritius	1990	31.1	70	11	69.1	26	25.5	33
Netherlands Antilles	1981	38.5	76	12	72.0	20	21.8	44
Senegal	1988	22.8	80	12	62.1	25	23.3	45
Average (unweighted)		**41.9**	**71**	**8**	**57.7**	**23**	**34.4**	**40**

Table 10.11. (contd.)

Region/country/area	Year	Women's share of non-ag. LF (%)	Total number of non-ag. occupations classified	Female-concentrated occupations		Gender-integrated occupations		Number of female under-represented occupations
				Number	% female non-ag. LF	Number	% female non-ag. LF	
Average (overall)		35.8	179	33	64.2	57	30.2	88

Notes: Female-concentrated occupations are defined as occupations where the percentage female is greater than 1.5 times the average percentage female for the non-agricultural labour force as a whole.
Female-underrepresented occupations are defined as occupations where the percentage female is less than 0.5 times the average percentage female for the non-agricultural labour force as a whole.
Gender-integrated occupations are defined as occupations where the percentage female is between 0.5 and 1.5 times the average percentage female for the non-agricultural labour force as a whole.
Source: Study data.

Appendix 10.3. Percentage of male, female and total non-agricultural labour forces with occupations having between 77.50 and 82.49 per cent of workers either males or females

Table 10.12. Percentage of the female, male and total non-agricultural labour forces with occupations having between 77.50 and 82.49 per cent of its workers either females or males (i.e. within 2.5 per cent of 80 per cent cut-off point used to define gender-dominance)[a], latest available year, by region

Region/country/area	Female non-ag. LF[b]			Male non-ag. LF[b]			Total non-ag. LF[b]		
	77.5–79.9% female (1)	80.0–82.5% female (2)	Net tendency in FDOM (3)=(2)–(1)	77.5–79.9% male (4)	80.0–82.5% male (5)	Net tendency in MDOM (6)=(5)–(4)	77.50–79.9% (7)	80.0–82.5% (8)	Net tendency in TDOM (9)=(8)–(7)
OECD									
Australia	1.6	1.2	–0.3	5.8	0	–5.8	3.4	0	–3.4
Austria	2.6	0	–2.6	1.2	2.0	0.8	1.4	1.5	0.1
Canada	10.4	0	–10.4*	6.8	4.4	–2.4	10.7	2.9	–7.8
Cyprus	4.9	0	–4.9	4.7	0	–4.7	6.1	0	–6.1
Finland	1.1	3.2	2.1	1.9	3.2	1.3	1.2	2.4	1.2
France	4.0	3.2	–0.8	0	0	0	1.5	1.7	0.2
Germany (West)	0	13.7	13.7*	2.6	0	–2.6	2.1	6.4	4.3
Italy	0	3.0	3.0	0	4.9	4.9	0	5.2	5.2
Luxembourg	11.3	0	–11.3*	1.0	3.9	2.9	4.3	3.1	–1.2
Netherlands	0	4.8	4.8	0	2.4	2.4	0	4.1	4.1
New Zealand	5.7	13.5	7.1	3.0	0	–3.0	4.1	7.1	2.9
Norway	0	0	0	0	0	0	0	0	0
Spain	8.0	4.6	–3.3	3.1	1.0	–2.1	5.0	1.9	–3.2
Sweden	1.8	0	–1.8	0	3.6	3.6	1.1	2.3	1.2
Switzerland	3.2	0	–3.2	0	0	0	1.5	0	–1.5
United Kingdom	12.5	0	–12.5*	1.8	2.7	0.9	7.6	0	–7.6
United States	1.6	7.1	5.5	2.1	1.7	–0.4	1.4	4.5	3.1
Average (unweighted)	**4.0**	**3.2**	**–0.8**	**2.0**	**1.7**	**–0.3**	**3.0**	**2.5**	**–0.5**

Table 10.12. (contd.)

Region/country/area	Female non-ag. LF[b]			Male non-ag. LF[b]			Total non-ag. LF[b]		
	77.5–79.9% female (1)	80.0–82.5% female (2)	Net tendency in FDOM (3)=(2)−(1)	77.5–79.9% male (4)	80.0–82.5% male (5)	Net tendency in MDOM (6)=(5)−(4)	77.50–79.9% (7)	80.0–82.5% (8)	Net tendency in TDOM (9)=(8)−(7)
Transition Economies									
Bulgaria	21.4	0.0	−21.4*	0.0	0.0	0.0	12.4	0.0	−12.4*
Hungary	3.9	2.7	−1.3	0.0	3.4	3.4	0.0	1.3	1.3
Poland	0.0	7.6	7.6	1.4	0.0	−1.4	0.0	3.3	3.3
Former Yugoslavia	0.0	3.1	3.1	0.0	1.8	1.8	0.0	2.8	2.8
Average (unweighted)	**6.3**	**3.3**	**−3.0**	**0.3**	**1.30**	**1.0**	**3.1**	**1.8**	**−1.3**
Middle East and North Africa									
Bahrain	0.0	0.0	0.0	0.0	3.5	3.5	1.0	3.6	2.6
Egypt	1.6	0.0	−1.6	2.4	0.0	−2.4	2.6	0.0	−2.6
Iran, Islamic Rep. of	0.0	0.0	0.0	0.0	0.0	0.0	0.0	0.0	0.0
Jordan	0.0	5.7	5.7	0.0	0.0	0.0	0.0	0.0	0.0
Kuwait	48.8	0.0	−48.8*	0.0	1.3	1.3	12.6	1.3	−11.3*
Tunisia	0.0	0.0	0.0	0.0	1.1	1.1	0.0	1.1	1.1
Average (unweighted)	**8.4**	**0.9**	**−7.5**	**0.4**	**1.0**	**0.6**	**2.7**	**1.0**	**−1.7**
Asia/Pacific									
China	3.6	0.0	−3.6	3.2	0	−3.2	4.3	0.0	−4.3
Fiji	0.0	0.0	0.0	0.0	0	0.0	0.0	0.0	0.0
Hong Kong	0.0	0.0	0.0	0.0	0	0.0	0.0	0.0	0.0
India	0.0	0.0	0.0	1.3	0	−1.3	1.5	0.0	−1.5
Japan	0.0	3.2	3.2	1.2	0	−1.2	0.0	1.6	1.6
Republic of Korea	10.5	0.0	−10.5*	5.7	0	−5.7	9.1	0.0	−9.1
Malaysia	6.4	0.0	−6.5	9.5	0	−9.5	10.9	0.0	−10.9*
Average (unweighted)	**2.9**	**0.5**	**−2.5**	**3.0**	**0**	**−3.0**	**3.7**	**0.2**	**−3.4**

Other Developing

Angola	0.0	0.0	0.0	2.1	0.0	-2.1	1.6	0.0	-1.6
Costa Rica	0.0	1.3	1.3	5.2	4.2	-1.0	4.2	3.2	-1.0
Ghana	0.0	0.0	0.0	4.2	0.0	-4.2	2.2	0.0	-2.2
Haiti	0.0	0.0	0.0	0.0	0.0	0.0	0.0	0.0	0.0
Mauritius	0.0	0.0	0.0	0.0	5.3	5.3	0.0	4.4	4.4
Netherlands Antilles	6.8	0.0	-6.8	1.1	1.7	0.5	2.7	1.3	-1.4
Senegal	6.6	28.1	21.6*	0.0	3.3	3.3	1.9	11.1	9.2
Average (unweighted)	**1.9**	**4.2**	**2.3**	**1.8**	**2.1**	**0.3**	**1.8**	**2.9**	**1.1**
Overall average (unweighted)	**4.4**	**2.6**	**-1.8**	**1.7**	**1.3**	**-0.4**	**2.9**	**1.9**	**-1.0**

Notes: [a] Restricted to reasonably large occupations which comprise at least 1 per cent of the relevant labour force.
[b] Net upward (downward) tendency/bias in FDOM, MDOM and TDOM is defined here as the sum of the relevant labour force with 80.0–82.49 per cent female (and/or per cent male as relevant) minus the percentage with 77.50–79.99 per cent female (and/or per cent male as relevant). This measures whether the clustering of larger occupations near our 80 per cent cut-off point biases FDOM, MDOM and TDOM in that direction, since a small difference in percentage male or female for one or a few largest occupations could have a measurable effect on FDOM, MDOM and TDOM. This information is useful for cross-national comparisons of the current situation as well as analysis of national time trends.
* Indicates when the net bias is greater than 10 percentage points for FDOM, MDOM or TDOM.
Source: Study data.

OCCUPATIONS TYPICALLY HELD BY MEN AND WOMEN

11

Previous chapters demonstrated that there are high levels of occupational segregation by sex around the world. Based on crude data for six broad non-agricultural occupational categories (see Chapter 8), women are relatively concentrated in clerical and services occupations and, to a lesser degree, in professional occupations. In contrast, women are greatly underrepresented in administrative and managerial occupations, as well as in production occupations. Sales occupations present a mixed picture, with women greatly overrepresented in some regions and underrepresented in other regions of the world.

The present chapter reviews the extent to which occupations are feminized and masculinized, this time based on detailed two- and three-digit occupational information for our 41 study countries and areas. The **main issues addressed in the present chapter are:** (i) *whether a wide range of specific occupations tend to be sex-stereotyped around the world,* (ii) *the extent to which sex-stereotyping of specific occupations is common across countries and regions* and, (iii) *whether observed patterns in the sex-stereotyping of occupations correspond to typical preconceived beliefs of female and male abilities and appropriate roles.*

Expectations are as follows. First, in light of results from Chapter 10 that gender-dominated occupations comprise over one-half of the non-agricultural labour force, it is expected that many narrowly defined specific occupations are dominated by one sex, becoming in essence "male" or "female" occupations. Second, it is expected that there is substantial variation across regions and countries in the specific occupations which are "reserved" for males and females because of differences in cultural values, traditions and socio-economic development.

Third, it is expected that sex-stereotyping of specific occupations will be consistent to a significant degree with typical socially prescribed gender roles and preconceived notions of gender-related abilities. In Chapter 2 and in an earlier publication by the author (Anker and Hein, 1986), it was argued that employers and society at large often believe that women and men have different traits, experiences, abilities and preferences. These are summarized in table 2.1. There are "positive" characteristics for women, such as a caring nature (supposedly making women better nurses, doctors, social workers, nannies, teachers); greater manual dexterity (supposedly good for weaving, knitting, sewing, typing, microelectronics work); greater skill and experience in household activities (supposedly making women better cooks, launderers, hairdressers, cleaners, maids, etc.); greater honesty (supposedly making women better bookkeepers, salespersons and cashiers); and more pleasant physical appearance/attractiveness (supposedly making women better receptionists and salespersons). There are also "negative" traits, as it is often believed that women are physically weaker (supposedly making men better blacksmiths, toolmakers, miners, drillers, masons, construction workers, etc.); less able to do maths or science (supposedly making men better mathematicians, architects, engineers, physical scientists); and less able to supervise others (presumably making men better managers, supervisors, executives and legislators); less willing to travel (supposedly making men better airline pilots, ship's officers, transport drivers, technical salespersons and commercial travellers); less willing to face physical danger or use physical force (supposedly making men better fire-fighters, police officers, security guards, miners). Although there is very little which is biological in nature in these lists, especially when one takes into consideration the great degree of overlap in the distribution of physical traits of men and women, such stereotyping none the less is expected to have a powerful influence on the types of occupations men and women hold.

To investigate the above issues, this chapter is divided into three sections. Section 11.1 examines the percentage female and percentage male for 17 specific occupations—occupations which have a reputation among most laypersons in Western industrialized countries as being typical "male" or "female" occupations. Section 11.2 looks at the five most important female-dominated occupations in terms of employment in each study country. Section 11.3 looks at the five largest occupations for women workers in study countries—regardless of whether or not they are female-dominated.

Before presenting results in this chapter, readers need to be cautioned that the comparability of specific occupations across countries (and therefore the comparability of how feminized are these occupations) is always somewhat questionable due to a number of factors. First, coding quality differs across countries, sometimes resulting in unnecessarily large occupational "dump" categories, such as is often observed for the "other" and "not elsewhere classified" occupational groups. Second, the quality of data collection differs. This can cause large numbers of women, especially those working in family enterprises or in the informal sector as petty traders, to be enumerated as workers in one country but not in another. Third, national occupational classifications sometimes differ substantially from the widely used ISCO-68 classification that is the basis for many of the occupational classifications used in study countries (see discussion in Chapter 4 on this). This affects the comparability of occupational categories across countries. Fourth, national occupational data are at different levels of aggregation. For example, medical doctor, dentist, nurse, veterinary surgeon, etc. are separate occupations in the ISCO-68 three-digit classification but aggregated into one occupational group in the ISCO-68 two-digit classification. Fifth, occupations with the same title will often involve different work activities in countries at different levels of economic development (e.g. salespersons and cashiers may not do the same work in the United States and Ghana due to the greater use of electronic cash registers and scanning machines in the United States; nor do owner-proprietors do quite the same work in industrialized countries as in developing countries because of the differing size of the informal sector).

Since all five of the above factors affect comparability of specific occupations across countries, we made various efforts to help increase comparability and especially tried to take into account factors 3 and 4 noted above.[1] When we felt that we could not identify a sufficiently comparable occupational category in a country, we excluded this country's data from the analysis. Also, in order to assist readers, notes are provided at the bottom of tables 11.1 to 11.7 to indicate: (i) when national occupational titles for specific occupations are felt to be somewhat different from usual; and (ii) when the aggregation of three-digit occupational group data into a two-digit occupational group appears to be different from usual. Despite these caveats (and so the need to treat national values for specific occupations very cautiously), we feel that the data and analysis in this chapter on occupational segregation of specific occupations is very useful for understanding occupational segregation by sex.

11.1   Seventeen typical "male" and "female" occupations

This section presents data on **17 specific occupations chosen to represent relatively important occupations which have a reputation among laypersons in Western industrialized countries as being typical "male" or "female" occupations.** These 17 occupations were also chosen to ensure roughly equal representation in each of the six ISCO-68 one-digit major non-agricultural occupational groups, with roughly equal numbers of supposedly "male" and "female" occupations.

These 17 occupations include (with expected gender-domination indicated in brackets):[2] (i) three professional and technical occupations: nurses (female), teachers (female) and architects, engineers and related technicians (male); (ii) the only administrative and managerial occupations: legislative officials and government administrators (male) and managers (male); (iii) two clerical occupations: stenographers and typists (female) and bookkeepers, cashiers and related workers (female); (iv) two sales occupations: salespersons and shop assistants (female) and sales supervisors and buyers (male); (v) four service occupations: cooks, waiters and bartenders (female), maids and related housekeeping services workers (female), hairdressers, barbers, beauticians and related workers (female) and protective service workers (male); and (vi) four production occupations: tailors, dressmakers, sewers and upholsterers (female), production supervisors and foremen (male), blacksmiths and tool-makers (male), bricklayers, carpenters and other construction workers (male).

We feel that this list of 17 specific occupations represent a good cross-section of "male" and "female" occupations as it includes (i) approximately one-fifth of the 75 non-agricultural occupations classified in ISCO-68, (ii) between 20 and 45 per cent of the male and female workers in countries as diverse as the United States (43.6 per cent), Costa Rica (33.5 per cent) and India (22.3 per cent), and (iii) occupations from all major occupational groups. At the same time, readers need to keep in mind three aspects of this list which affects the following analysis. First, as the selected occupations were chosen so as to represent typical "male" and "female" occupations, they are not a random cross-section of occupations. Second, two-digit occupational data are sometimes insufficiently disaggregated to observe the gender-domination of occupations, as several two-digit occupational groups are themselves heterogeneous composites. For example, teachers is a two-digit occupation comprised of special education, pre-primary, primary, secondary and university teachers; and each of these teacher occupations tends to have a substantially different percentage female.

Data are presented in tables 11.1–11.3 for 35 of our 41 study countries or areas. Excluded are our four Transition Economy countries (because in the past, their classification schemes were not comparable to those used in capitalist countries) in addition to two OECD countries, Sweden and the United Kingdom, for various reasons.[3]

Table 11.1 presents data on the percentage female for the nine selected occupations expected to be highly feminized, while table 11.2 presents results on the eight occupations expected to be highly masculinized. In order to assist readers in interpreting these data, an "x" is used in table 11.2 to indicate when an occupation is *not "male-dominated"* (defined as an occupation where less than 80 per cent of workers are male); in table 11.1 an "x" denotes when an occupation *is not a female-concentrated occupation* in a relative sense (defined, as in Chapter 5, as an occupation where the female share of workers is less than 0.5 times the average percentage female for the non-agricultural labour force as a whole). This relative measure of gender concentration for women is used in table 11.1 to increase comparability across study countries by taking into account the greatly different female shares of non-agricultural employment found in study countries. If the absolute definition of gender-dominance of 80 per cent were used for defining "female" occupations, countries with low female labour force participation rates (such as India where the female share of non-agricultural employment is only about 12 per cent) would clearly have few "female" occupations, even though many occupations might have a relatively high concentration of women workers. Finally, tables 11.3A and B summarize results for each occupation for each study

Table 11.1. Percentage female for nine typical "female" occupations

Occupation	Country/area and percentage women in comparable occupational group								
	Australia 1990	Austria 1990	Canada 1990	Cyprus 1989	Finland 1990	France 1990	Germany (West) 1989	Italy 1981	Luxembourg 1991
OECD countries									
Nurses	90.5	n/a	90.4	78.3[a]	94.1[a,u]	87.1[a]	82.3[a]	66.5[a]	n/a
Teachers (all levels)	64.3	64.7	62.6(x)	54.8(x)	63.6(x)	65.4	57.1(x)	72.7	52.6(x)
Stenographers, typists, etc.	98.6	n/a	98.3	97.1	96.1	97.1	97.4	84.0	91.9
Bookkeepers, cashiers and related workers	83.6	70.8	n/a	55.4	93.4	83.5	76.7	53.8	56.4
Salespersons, shop assistants, etc.	67.4	66.9[b]	n/a	52.7(x)	70.6(x)	76.7	80.8	46.2(x)	79.3
Cooks, waiters, bartenders, etc.	72.0	67.6[c]	n/a	25.7(x)	87.2[c]	46.2(x)	66.0(x)	44.1(x)	52.9(x)
Maids and related housekeeping services workers	100.0[e]	n/a	n/a	86.7	99.5	99.0	95.2	92.3	97.1
Hairdressers, barbers, beauticians and related workers	85.8	82.7	n/a	73.0	97.4	85.2	85.7	60.8	77.7
Tailors, dressmakers, sewers, upholsterers, etc.	73.6[n]	n/a	n/a	87.5	90.9	76.3	89.1	75.0	89.3

Occupation	Country/area and percentage women in comparable occupational group					
	Netherlands 1990	New Zealand 1986	Norway 1990	Spain 1990	Switzerland 1980	United States 1991
OECD countries (cont.)						
Nurses	85.2	93.9	93.4[u]	n/a	89.8	95.0
Teachers (all levels)	47.3(x)	64.6	48.4(x)	58.8	49.9[z](x)	68.9(x)
Stenographers, typists, etc.	99.9	98.4	95.8	94.5	n/a	98.4
Bookkeepers, cashiers and related workers	56.1(x)	77.1	77.7[y]	37.0(x)	48.3(x)	85.5

Occupation	Bahrain 1991	Egypt 1986	Iran, Islamic Rep. 1986	Jordan 1979	Kuwait 1985	Tunisia 1989
Salespersons, shop assistants, etc.	59.3	66.1	75.2	55.4	83.5	66.9(x)
Cooks, waiters, bartenders, etc.	58.3(x)[c]	75.2	77.2[c]	41.4(x)	60.9	58.3(x)
Maids and related housekeeping services workers	95.8	87.9	96.7	97.4	93.6	89.7
Hairdressers, barbers, beauticians and related workers	85.7	86.2	90.4	79.5	77.6	81.4
Tailors, dressmakers, sewers, upholsterers, etc.	65.6	79.8	82.6	80.7	77.8	62.8(x)

Occupation	Country/area and percentage women in comparable occupational group					
	Bahrain 1991	Egypt 1986	Iran, Islamic Rep. 1986	Jordan 1979	Kuwait 1985	Tunisia 1989
Middle East and North Africa						
Nurses	64.1	n/a[q]	n/a	n/a	97.9	43.7[a]
Teachers (all levels)	45.4	39.9	44.7	50.1	56.6	30.4
Stenographers, typists, etc.	74.5[i]	65.5	n/a	76.0	58.0	54.5
Bookkeepers, cashiers and related workers	25.0[k](x)	35.7	n/a	9.9(x)	13.1(x)	20.6(x)
Salespersons, shop assistants, etc.	7.5(x)	8.1(x)	2.2[f](x)	3.4(x)	3.7(x)	3.3(x)
Cooks, waiters, bartenders, etc.	7.4(x)	3.6(x)	n/a	3.4(x)[p]	7.9(x)	4.7(x)
Maids and related housekeeping services workers	85.6[m]	78.6	n/a	81.1[g]	77.5	68.1
Hairdressers, barbers, beauticians and related workers	28.4	3.6(x)	n/a	19.0	22.4(x)	29.8
Tailors, dressmakers, sewers, upholsterers, etc.	19.5(x)	14.6(x)	n/a	26.2	4.7(x)	82.9[h]

Table 11.1. (contd.)

Asia/Pacific

Occupation	Country/area and percentage women in comparable occupational group						
	China 1982	Fiji 1986	Hong Kong 1991	India 1981	Japan 1990	Republic of Korea 1983	Malaysia 1980
Nurses[w]	94.7	n/a	89.4[a]	93.1	96.5	n/a	n/a
Teachers (all levels)	39.1(x)	53.1	61.4	28.2	43.4(x)	36.0(x)	45.7
Stenographers, typists, etc.	86.3	93.7	94.0	27.9	93.3	n/a	90.9
Bookkeepers, cashiers and related workers	70.4[o]	43.4	70.3	6.8(x)	75.6[s]	n/a	49.4
Salespersons, shop assistants, etc.	51.6(x)	34.5(x)	43.8(x)	6.6(x)	64.6	65.4	30.3(x)
Cooks, waiters, bartenders, etc.	47.5(x)	44.1	n/a	10.7(x)	63.1	n/a	45.9
Maids and related housekeeping services workers	n/a	95.8	91.4	53.2	97.4	n/a	93.9
Hairdressers, barbers, beauticians and related workers	26.0[j](x)	40.9	35.5(x)	0.9(x)	69.1	54.0	60.1
Tailors, dressmakers, sewers, upholsterers, etc.	86.4[d]	71.2	65.5	11.0(x)	80.4	62.1	79.9

Other Developing

Occupation	Country/area and percentage women in comparable occupational group						
	Angola 1992	Costa Rica 1991	Ghana 1984	Haiti 1986	Mauritius 1990	Netherlands Antilles 1981	Senegal 1988
Nurses	n/a	n/a	n/a[t]	n/a	59.0	n/a	46.1[a]
Teachers (all levels)	39.7(x)	73.4	40.1(x)	64.2(x)	50.4	63.3	23.9(x)
Stenographers, typists, etc.	70.9	89.5	70.9(x)	100.0	84.9	95.1	77.7
Bookkeepers, cashiers and related workers	49.9(x)	45.7(x)	26.4(x)	73.7(x)	43.3(x)	61.7	23.0[l]

Occupation							
Salespersons, shop assistants, etc.	47.3(x)	39.4(x)	30.1(x)	92.9	27.2(x)	71.1	29.0[l]
Cooks, waiters, bartenders, etc.	59.9(x)	n/a	69.2(x)	94.1	23.4(x)	42.6(x)	15.5[l]
Maids and related housekeeping services workers	29.3[r]	87.8	63.9(x)	86.2	97.0	96.9	65.6[l]
Hairdressers, barbers, beauticians and related workers	100.0	81.0	91.3	15.3(x)	38.3(x)	69.5	n/a
Tailors, dressmakers, sewers, upholsterers, etc.	54.3(x)	84.0	69.9(x)	64.1(x)	62.0	56.9(x)	8.7[l]

Notes: n/a indicates that no comparable occupation was available for comparison.
(x) indicates an occupation which is not female-concentrated (defined as an occupation where the percentage female is less than 1.5 times the female share for the non-agricultural labour force as a whole).
* Classification of occupational group is only very roughly comparable with ISCO-68 classification.
[a] For Finland and France, psychiatric nurses are classified with nurses. For West Germany, Tunisia, Senegal, Hong Kong and Cyprus, midwives are classified with nurses. For Italy, data refer to nurses and related workers. [b] For Austria, buyers are included with salespersons and shop assistants. [c] For Austria, Finland, Norway and the Netherlands, kitchen assistants are specifically included with cooks. [d] For China, includes only embroiderers, sewing machine operators and textile machine operators. [e] Data refer to housekeepers only (maids not mentioned) for Australia. [f] Data for the Islamic Republic of Iran refer to salesmen only. [g] Data for Jordan for maids and related housekeeping include cooks. [h] Data refer to workers in textile; therefore this undoubtedly includes spinners and weavers and related workers which would help explain the very high per cent female for Tunisia. [i] Stenographers not included for Bahrain. [j] For China, the category refers only to hairdressers. [k] For Bahrain, data refer to cashiers only. [l] For Senegal, data refer to 1976 since there is no comparable occupation in the 1988 classification. [m] Data for Bahrain refer to housemaids only. [n] For Australia, 1980, data are used as the occupational classification in 1980 refers to tailor, dressmakers, sewers, upholsterers, etc. There are no comparable data for 1990. [o] For China, there is no reference to bookkeepers, only cashiers. [p] For Jordan, data include waiters and bartenders only and does not mention cooks. [q] For Egypt, Moghadam (1995) indicates that nurses are 68 per cent female. This percentage is typical for the Middle East and North African region. [r] For Angola, the occupation building caretakers, charworkers, cleaners and related workers is 77.0 per cent female. Taking this occupation together with the maids and related housekeeping service workers occupation, the percentage female becomes 64.1, which would make this a female-concentrated occupation. [s] For Japan, data referred to accounting clerks and there is no mention of cashiers. [t] Data from ILO (1994f) indicate that nurses are 91.7 per cent female in Ghana in 1991. This percentage is high for the Other Developing region but not for the world. [u] Data for Finland and Norway includes institutional child-care staff. Data from ILO (1994f) indicate that the percentage female for nurses is 89.4 per cent for England and 91.1 per cent for Scotland in 1990 and 96.4 per cent for Denmark in 1989 — all rather typical values for OECD countries. [w] Data from ILO (1994f) indicate that nurses are 95.4 per cent female in the Philippines in 1987. This is a typical percentage for the Asian region. [y] For Norway, accountants and bookkeepers form one occupation group. [z] Data for Switzerland include child-care crèches because this occupation is included together with kindergarten teachers in one occupation.
OECD countries not included in this table are the United Kingdom whose classification scheme is substantially different, Sweden, which has too few occupations classified and Japan. (Note that considerably more detailed data became available later for Sweden for analysis in Part IV. These data indicate quite similar percentages as for Finland and Norway). Also, Canada has many missing values, since so few occupations are classified, thereby making even rough by comparable occupations often very difficult to identify.
Source: Study data.

Table 11.2. Percentage male for nine typical "male" occupations

Occupation	Country/area and percentage men in comparable occupational group								
	Australia 1990	Austria 1990	Canada 1990	Cyprus 1989	Finland 1990	France 1990	Germany (West) 1989	Italy 1981	Luxembourg 1991
OECD countries									
Architects, engineers and related technicians	94.1	93.3	89.6	78.6(x)	85.0	87.2	95.3	95.4	94.5
Legislative officials and government administrators	93.9	74.3[f] (x)	64.8(x)	97.8[e]	58.3[a] (x)	n/a	78.9(x)	87.6[a]	93.6
Managers	83.3	86.1	59.5(x)	91.2	75.3(x)	85.8	78.4(x)	65.2(x)[b]	87.6
Sales supervisors and buyers	81.1	n/a	n/a	91.1[d]	n/a	n/a	n/a	n/a	85.6
Protective service workers	92.0	98.8	83.2	94.3	90.4	93.6	96.7	98.5	96.8
Production supervisors and general foremen	n/a	n/a	n/a	87.5	n/a	n/a	n/a	n/a	98.8
Blacksmiths, toolmakers, etc.	98.9	99.2	94.5	98.8	97.0	97.9	n/a	85.6	98.2
Bricklayers, carpenters and other construction workers	98.8	98.5	98.2	99.9	97.3	99.9	n/a	98.3	99.3

Occupation	Country/area and percentage men in comparable occupational group					
	Netherlands 1990	New Zealand 1986	Norway 1990	Spain 1990	Switzerland 1980	United States 1991
OECD countries (cont.)						
Architects, engineers and related technicians	95.4	91.7	87.8	92.9	98.5	88.1
Legislative officials and government administrators	n/a	84.7	54.2(x)	86.2	94.0	54.5(x)
Managers	86.6	82.4	82.8[c]	91.0	94.2	53.9(x)
Sales supervisors and buyers	79.2[i] (x)	76.3(x)	72.1(x)[l]	89.1	67.9(x)	65.7(x)[m]

Occupation	Bahrain 1991	Egypt 1986	Iran, Islamic Rep. 1986	Jordan 1979	Kuwait 1985	Tunisia 1989
Protective service workers	100.0	93.9	81.0	96.7	92.4	84.8
Production supervisors and general foremen	94.4	84.1	n/a	95.4	n/a	96.8
Blacksmiths, toolmakers, etc.	97.4	92.2	90.2	96.4	98.1	96.6
Bricklayers, carpenters and other construction workers	100.0	99.1	97.4	98.6	99.9	99.0

Occupation	Country/area and percentage men in comparable occupational group					
	Bahrain 1991	Egypt 1986	Iran, Islamic Rep. 1986	Jordan 1979	Kuwait 1985	Tunisia 1989
Middle East and North Africa						
Architects, engineers and related technicians	96.1	94.4	95.8	98.8	97.9	86.8
Legislative officials and government administrators	93.0	88.5	87.5	95.6	95.9	89.8
Managers	95.1[c]	88.6	100.0	95.5[c]	96.3	90.9
Sales supervisors and buyers	n/a	92.1	n/a	n/a	96.8	n/a
Protective service workers	99.6	99.6	99.3	98.9	99.8	98.0
Production supervisors and general foremen	n/a	97.4	n/a	n/a	100.0	89.6
Blacksmiths, toolmakers, etc.	99.8	99.3	n/a	99.7	100.0	98.4
Bricklayers, carpenters and other construction workers	99.9	99.7	99.2	100.0	100.0	99.3

Table 11.2 (contd.)

Occupation	Country/area and percentage men in comparable occupational group						
	China 1982	Fiji 1986	Hong Kong 1991	India 1981	Japan 1990	Republic of Korea 1983	Malaysia 1980
Asia/Pacific							
Architects, engineers and related technicians	82.3	95.1	96.3	98.4	97.6	98.3	92.2
Legislative officials and government administrators	n/a	68.1(x)	92.3	98.2	98.3	n/a	80.3
Managers	89.7	77.1(x)	90.6	97.6	90.8	n/a	93.2
Sales supervisors and buyers	94.9[k]	56.9(x)[j]	81.6	97.4	n/a	78.4(x)	84.4
Protective service workers	93.7	93.4	97.1	99.2	97.2	99.3	97.6
Production supervisors and general foremen	n/a	85.6	94.0	97.8	n/a	97.1	88.2
Blacksmiths, toolmakers, etc.	67.8(x)	87.9	91.8	97.3	95.2[h]	93.6	88.4
Bricklayers, carpenters and other construction workers	93.9	96.9	99.4	93.3	95.4	97.1	94.5

Occupation	Country/area and percentage men in comparable occupational group						
	Angola 1992	Costa Rica 1991	Ghana 1984	Haiti 1986	Mauritius 1990	Netherlands Antilles 1981	Senegal 1988
Other Developing							
Architects, engineers and related technicians	91.5	96.2	97.8	95.3	94.2	97.5	92.8
Legislative officials and government administrators	77.2(x)	74.0	87.2	100.0	89.2	88.0	90.4
Managers	100.0	73.9(x)	92.3	88.2	81.9	91.1	93.9
Sales supervisors and buyers	100.0	n/a	58.2(x)	100.0	77.7(x)	74.3(x)	92.2[g]

Protective service workers	96.7	99.4	96.9	100.0	97.5	97.8	95.4
Production supervisors and general foremen	n/a	n/a	93.0	100.0	80.8	98.7	99.7
Blacksmiths, toolmakers, etc.	100.0	99.6	98.1	100.0	95.2	100.0	95.1
Bricklayers, carpenters and other construction workers	100.0	97.5	98.4	97.2	99.7	99.7	97.1

Notes: n/a indicates no comparable occupation was available for comparison.

(x) indicates an occupation which is not male-dominated (i.e. occupation where less than 80 per cent of the workers are male).

* Classification of occupational group is only very roughly comparable with ISCO-68 classification.

[a] For Finland and Italy, data refer to government administrators and there is no mention of legislators. [b] For Italy, data for managers include managers and directors in public/private enterprises in addition to administrative employees with managerial functions. [c] For Norway, Bahrain and Jordan, data for managers include working proprietors. [d] For Cyprus, data for 1991 referred to buyers only. [e] For Cyprus, 1989 data refer only to senior government legislators and administrators. [f] For Austria, data referred to *"mandataires politique"* only. [g] For Senegal, data are for 1976. No comparable data are available for 1988. Therefore, 1976 data used. [h] For Japan, the closest occupational category is forgers and hammermen, and these data are used here. [i] For Netherlands, branch managers and sales managers are included with buyers; sales supervisors do not appear to be included. [j] For Hong Kong, data include commercial travellers and technical salesmen. [k] For China, data refer to buyers only; there is no mention of sales supervisors. [l] For Norway, data refer to buyers only (and do not include sales supervisors). [m] For the United States, data refer to supervisors and proprietors and not to buyers.

OECD study countries not included in this table are the United Kingdom whose classification schemes is substantially different, and Sweden, which has too few occupations classified. (Note that considerably more detailed data became available later for Sweden for analysis in Part IV. These data indicate quite similar percentages as for Finland and Norway). Also, Canada has many missing values, since so few occupations are classified (see table 4.2), thereby making even roughly comparable occupations often very difficult to identify.

Source: Study data.

Table 11.3A. Summary for nine typical "female" occupations: percentage female and whether female-concentrated, latest available year, by region

Occupations	Region									
	OECD (N = 15)		Middle East/North Africa (N = 6)		Asia/Pacific (N = 7)		Other Developing (N = 7)		Total (N = 35)	
	x/y	Mean	x/y	Mean	x/y	Mean	x/y	Mean	x/y	Mean
Nurses	12/12	87.2	3/3	68.6	4/4	93.4	2/2	52.6	21/21	82.4
Teachers (all levels)	6/15	59.7	6/6	44.5	4/7	43.8	3/7	50.7	19/35	49.6
Stenographers, typists	13/13	96.0	5/5	65.7	6/6	80.4	6/7	84.1	30/31	85.4
Bookkeepers, cashiers and related workers	11/14	68.2	1/5	20.9	5/6	52.6	2/7	46.2	19/32	53.1
Salespersons, shop assistants, etc.	10/14	67.6	0/6	4.7	2/7	42.4	3/7	48.1	15/34	42.3
Cooks, waiters, bartenders, etc.	6/14	59.5	0/5	5.4	3/5	42.3	2/6	50.8	11/30	45.9
Maids and related housekeeping service workers	13/13	94.7	5/5	78.2	5/5	86.3	5/7	76.1	28/30	86.2
Hairdressers, barbers, beauticians and related workers	14/14	82.1	3/5	20.6	4/7	40.9	4/6	65.9	25/32	60.4
Tailors, dressmakers, sewers, upholsterers, etc.	12/13	79.3	2/5	29.6	6/7	65.2	3/7	57.1	23/32	63.6
Percentage female in non-agricultural labour force		40.1		15.6		30.1		41.2		34.3

Note: x/y: x – indicates number of countries where occupation is a "female-concentrated" (i.e. per cent female is at least 1.5 times the per cent female for the non-agricultural labour force as a whole). y – indicates the total number of countries in the region with relevant data.
Mean is the unweighted average of national values.
See notes at the bottom of table 11.1 for indications of when national data are less comparable.
Source: Table 11.1.

Table 11.3B. Summary for eight typical "male" occupations: percentage male and whether male-dominated, latest available year, by region

Occupations	Region									
	OECD (N = 15)		Middle East/North Africa (N = 6)		Asia/Pacific (N = 7)		Other Developing (N = 7)		Total (N = 35)	
	x/y	Mean	x/y	Mean	x/y	Mean	x/y	Mean	x/y	Mean
Architects, engineers and related technicians	14/15	91.2	6/6	95.0	7/7	94.3	7/7	95.1	34/35	93.2
Legislative officials and government administrators	7/13	78.7	6/6	91.7	4/5	87.4	5/7	86.6	22/31	84.4
Managers	10/15	80.2	6/6	94.4	5/6	89.8	6/7	88.8	27/34	86.2
Sales supervisors and buyers	4/9	78.7	2/2	94.4	4/6	82.3	3/6	83.7	13/23	82.3
Protective service workers	15/15	92.8	6/6	99.2	7/7	96.8	7/7	97.7	35/35	95.7
Production supervisors and general foremen	6/6	92.8	3/3	95.7	5/5	92.5	5/5	94.4	19/19	93.6
Blacksmiths, toolmakers, etc.	14/14	95.8	5/5	99.4	6/7	88.9	7/7	98.3	32/33	95.6
Bricklayers, carpenters and other construction workers	14/14	98.9	6/6	99.7	7/7	95.8	7/7	98.5	34/34	98.3
Percentage male in non-agricultural labour force		59.9		84.4		69.9		58.8		65.7

Note: x/y: x – indicates number of countries where occupation is a "male-dominated" (i.e. at least 80 per cent of workers are men). y – indicates the total number of countries in the region with relevant data.
Mean is the unweighted average of national values.
See notes at bottom of table 11.2 for indications of when national data are less comparable.
Source: Table 11.2.

region; it indicates the (unweighted) average percentage male or female among study countries and regions along with the number of study countries where an occupation is female-concentrated or male-dominated.

Figures 11.1 and 11.2 present results graphically by region for the eight typical "male" and the nine typical "female" occupations.

a. Professional and Technical Occupations

As discussed in Chapter 8, professional and technical occupations are a large share of the non-agricultural labour force, ranging from approximately 12 per cent on average in Asia/Pacific study countries and areas to approximately 19 per cent, on average, in the OECD region. Analysis of this Major Group in Chapter 8 revealed that women tend to be overrepresented in the professional and technical occupational group when compared to their overall share in the non-agricultural labour force. Women are especially overrepresented in this Major Group in the Middle East and North Africa. However, as we will see below, **women tend to cluster within a very narrow range of professional and technical occupations, primarily in the teaching and medical/nursing professions.**

(i) Architects, engineers and related technicians
This is **a male-dominated set of occupations** in 34 of 35 study countries with data (with the "exception" having "only" 78.6 per cent of these workers men). On average, over 90 per cent of architects, engineers and related technicians in the world are men, and this is true in each study region (figure 11.1). It seems that the perception that men are better in the sciences is one which is held throughout the world.

(ii) Nurses
Under ISCO-68 guidelines, nursing is classified as a three-digit occupation (the only three-digit occupation reviewed in this section) and is included within the two-digit Medical, Dental, Veterinary and Related Workers occupation. Nursing is truly **a "female" occupation,** as roughly 82 per cent of nurses in study countries or areas are women. Nursing is a female-concentrated occupation in all 21 countries with data.[4] Furthermore, women comprise over 80 per cent of nursing professionals in 15 of the 21 study countries or areas with data. This sex-stereotyping of nursing is consistent with the universal perception that women are better care providers compared to men.

On the other hand, it is important to point out that *male nurses are reasonably common in non-Asian Third World countries.* Indeed, approximately one-half of nurses are men according to study data for Senegal and Tunisia and approximately one-third are men in Bahrain and Mauritius.

It is also important to point out that physician is often a "male" occupation around the world. For example, 79.8 per cent of physicians are men in the United States, 70.6 per cent in the Netherlands, and 70.5 per cent in France.

Figure 11.1. Percentage male for eight typical male occupations, latest available year, by region

Architects, engineers and related technicians

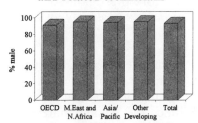

Legislative officials and government administrators

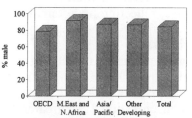

Managers

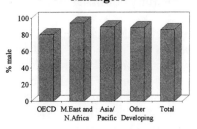

Sales supervisors and buyers

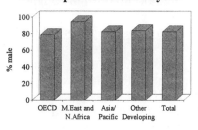

Protective services workers

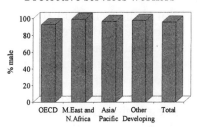

Production supervisors and general foremen

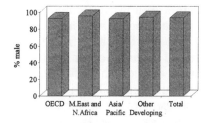

Blacksmiths, toolmakers, etc.

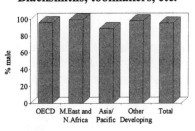

Bricklayers, carpenters and other construction workers

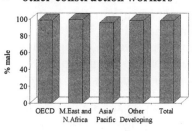

Source: Table 11.3.

This is a good example of how the clustering of men and women along different career tracks both greatly influences and is influenced by an occupation's status and earning potential. The career tracking of women as nurses and men as physicians accounts for much of the male/female earnings gap among medical workers. Furthermore, physician is a more prestigious occupation than nurse, reflecting male/female power relationships in society at large.

(iii) Teachers

Although teaching is an occupation in which women tend to be concentrated, this is at a lower level of concentration than in almost all of the other typical female occupations selected for this chapter. Using our relative measure of female-concentration (i.e. greater than 1.5 times the female share for the non-agricultural labour force as a whole), teaching is found to be a female-concentrated occupation in roughly one-half of study countries or areas with data (19 of 35).

Basically, **teaching has a fairly equal mix of male and female teachers.** *Roughly one-half of teachers in study countries are men and one-half are women.* Furthermore, there are no examples where teacher is a female-dominated or a male-dominated occupation, and the percentage female is between approximately 30 and 70 per cent in almost all study countries. Indeed, the lowest percentages are 23 and 28 per cent in Senegal and India respectively, while the highest percentages are approximately 73 per cent in Italy and Costa Rica.

There are, however, some noticeable regional differences in the extent to which teaching is a female-concentrated occupation (figure 11.2). The Middle East and North African region stands out, as teacher is a female-concentrated occupation in all six study countries in this region. Indeed, teaching is one of the few non-agricultural occupations acceptable for women in this region. This is strikingly demonstrated by the fact that 23, 38 and 48 per cent of all women working in non-agricultural occupations are teachers in Egypt, the Islamic Republic of Iran and Jordan respectively according to study data. Part of the reason for this result in Middle Eastern and North African countries may be that separate schools for boys and girls are common and this helps create a demand for women teachers for girls' schools.

Part of the reason why teaching is observed to be less of a female-concentrated occupation than expected is due to the fact that *two-digit data on teachers hide considerable gender segregation.* When three-digit data on teachers are looked at, it is found that men are likely to be concentrated in secondary or higher education while women are likely to be concentrated in nursery and primary school. The United States, where women comprised 68.9 per cent of teachers in 1991, provides an example for an industrialized country. Whereas 85.9 per cent of elementary school teachers are women, they represent only a slight majority in secondary schools (54.7 per cent)

Figure 11.2. Percentage female for nine typical female occupations, latest available year, by region

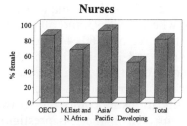

Nurses

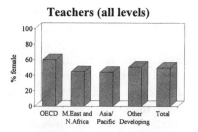

Teachers (all levels)

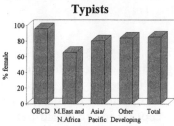

Typists

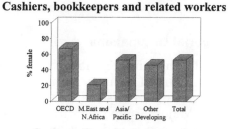

Cashiers, bookkeepers and related workers

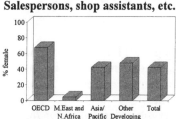

Salespersons, shop assistants, etc.

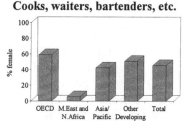

Cooks, waiters, bartenders, etc.

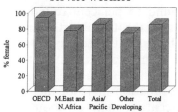

Maids and related housekeeping service workers

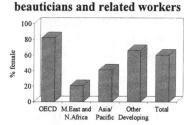

Hairdressers, barbers, beauticians and related workers

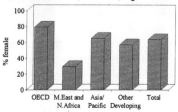

Tailors, dressmakers, sewers, upholsterers etc.

Source: Table 11.3.

and a minority at the college and university level (40.8 per cent). Data from a recent ILO publication (ILO CAPA, 1990) provide examples for African developing country regions from the United Republic of Tanzania (Eastern), Botswana (Southern) and Ghana (Western); whereas 92, 93 and 50 per cent respectively are primary school teachers in these regions, 60, 44 and 23 per cent respectively are secondary school teachers and just 15, 3 and 18 per cent respectively are teachers in polytechnics. Again, as with the case of nurses and doctors, the degree of gender concentration is much more pronounced in three-digit occupational classifications as compared to two-digit classifications, with again women concentrated in the less prestigious and less well-paid occupational subgroups.

b. Managerial Occupations

Managerial occupations, although comprising a small share of total employment, are important. Managers wield significant influence and control over social and economic decisions, and the high level of female underrepresentation in this Major Group seems to reflect a perception in the world that men make better managers and decision-makers.

(i) Legislative officials and government administrators
This is **a male-dominated occupational group** (figure 11.1). Approximately 84 per cent of legislative officials and government administrators in the world are men, and at least 80 per cent of these workers are men in 22 of the 31 study countries or areas for which we have data.[5]

Relatively speaking, there is *somewhat less male dominance of this group among OECD countries,* as men comprise less than 80 per cent of legislative officials and government administrators in 6 of the 13 OECD countries with data (with relatively low percentages, at around 55 per cent found in two Nordic countries of Finland and Norway and the two North American countries of Canada and United States)—although it needs to be pointed out that there is no study country where men comprise less than 50 per cent of these workers.

In contrast, this is a male-dominated occupation in 15 of the 18 non-OECD countries or areas, with a mean percentage male of about 89 per cent; even the lowest value here is as high as 68 per cent male.

(ii) Managers
As with the above occupational group, **managers is a predominantly male occupation** (figure 11.1). On average, approximately 86 per cent of this occupational group is male, and the lowest national value is as high as 54 per cent. As with legislative officials and government administrators, there is *somewhat less male dominance among OECD countries and relatively greater male dominance among Middle Eastern and North African countries.* Thus, this

is not a male-dominated occupation in 5 of 15 OECD study countries (with the two North American countries standing out as having relatively low percentages at less than 60 per cent male). In contrast, more than 80 per cent of managers are men in 17 of 19 Asian, Middle Eastern, Transitional and Other Developing countries or areas with data, with the average percentage male about 90 per cent (and even the two "exceptions" have percentages close to 80 per cent male, at 77 and 74 per cent).

c. Clerical Occupations

As described in Chapter 8, women are greatly overrepresented in this Major Group in most regions of the world, particularly in OECD countries. Furthermore, clerical jobs are a major source of employment for women. In New Zealand in 1986 for example, 30.0 per cent of women in the non-agricultural labour force worked in five clerical occupations: stenographers and typists (5.7 per cent), telephone operators (1.0 per cent), computer operators (1.7 per cent), bookkeepers and cashiers (7.7 per cent) and other clerical workers (14.0 per cent). In Egypt in 1986, 32.2 per cent of female non-agricultural employment was concentrated in three clerical occupational groups: stenographers and typists (7.5 per cent), bookkeepers and cashiers (7.8 per cent) and other clerical workers (16.9 per cent). In Hong Kong in 1991, these same three occupations included approximately 29 per cent of women working outside of agriculture.

(i) Stenographers and typists

This is **a female-concentrated occupation in virtually all countries reviewed** (the "exception" of Ghana is due to the very high female share of the non-agricultural labour force, as even here women comprise approximately 71 per cent of stenographers and typists). On average, approximately 85 per cent of stenographers and typists in the world are women (figure 11.2). Indeed, women comprise more than 80 per cent of stenographers and typists in 22 of 31 study countries or areas with data, and India provides the only example where the percentage female is less than 50 per cent.

All examples of where typists and stenographers is *not* a female-dominated occupation are in non-OECD countries; six of these have very low overall female non-agricultural labour force participation rates (Bahrain, Egypt, Jordan, Kuwait, Tunisia and India) and three are in Africa (Angola, Ghana and Senegal). So while stenographer and typist is a female-concentrated occupation in the world, and often a female-dominated occupation, this *tendency is strongest and most consistent in OECD countries, with male secretaries much more common outside of the OECD region.* In the OECD region, in fact, this occupation is so sex-stereotyped that it is at least 90 per cent female in 12 of 13 OECD study countries with data; the only "exception" is Italy with "only" 84 per cent female.

(ii) Bookkeepers and cashiers

Women comprise just over one-half of workers in this occupation, which is a female-concentrated occupation in 19 of the 30 study countries or areas with data. Compared to almost all of the other specific occupations analysed in this section, there is much greater **variation in the world in terms of women's share of employment among bookkeepers and cashiers.** We feel that most of this variation is real and only part is due to some non-comparability of these data due to differences in national occupational classifications (see earlier discussion on this in this chapter and in Chapter 4).

Much of this *variation is regional in nature* (table 11.2). This is a female-concentrated occupation in 16 of 20 OECD and Asian study economies with data. Spain is the only OECD country where less than 50 per cent of cashiers and bookkeepers are women and India is the only Asian example where this percentage is less than 40 per cent.[6]

In contrast, this is a female-concentrated occupation in only 3 of the 12 study countries or areas in our Middle East/North Africa and Other Developing regions.[7] In some of these countries (especially Middle East/North Africa), this lower percentage female is undoubtedly related to the fact that such jobs are not always seen as socially acceptable for women because public contact with men is usually required.

It is interesting to note that, although women are often concentrated in clerical occupations, they generally do not predominate among clerical supervisors. Several examples illustrate this. Whereas women account for almost two-thirds (64 per cent) of clerical workers in Hong Kong, only about one in three clerical supervisors is a woman. In the Netherlands, women comprise 58 per cent of clerical workers but only 30 per cent of clerical supervisors. In the United States, 59 per cent of clerical supervisors are women whereas women account for 80 per cent of clerical workers. Thus, *even in countries where clerical work is a female-concentrated occupation, women generally have restricted opportunities for career advancement and better pay.*

d. Sales Occupations

Sales work throughout much of the world is another area where women workers are likely to be concentrated. However, as the earlier analysis by Major Group in Chapter 8 indicated, there are some notable regional differences. For example, sales occupations are often highly masculinized in the Middle East and North Africa, because they require public contact between men and women.

(i) Sales supervisors and buyers

This is **a male-dominated occupation** in the world as approximately 83 per cent of sales supervisors and buyers are men (table 11.1). In 16 of the 25 study countries/areas with data, men comprise over 80 per cent of these workers.

In no study country is the percentage of men less than 50 per cent, and there are only three examples where it is less than 70 per cent. This situation of *a male-dominated occupation within a female-concentrated Major Occupational Group is a particularly pernicious example of low female pay and status.* Sales supervisor or buyer is a more prestigious and better remunerated occupation compared to other sales jobs, making it more attractive and socially acceptable for men, thereby putting men into positions of authority and power over women.

(ii) Salespersons and shop assistants

This group presents **a mixed picture as regards feminization.** This is definitely not a female-dominated occupation throughout the world, as the percentage female share exceeds 80 per cent in only 3 study countries. Just under 50 per cent of these workers in the world are women.

There are large regional differences, as regional averages range from approximately 5 per cent in the Middle East and North Africa to 68 per cent in OECD (figure 11.2). Large regional differences are also found in the frequency with which this is a female-concentrated occupation. Thus, this is a female-concentrated occupation in 10 out of 14 OECD countries, whereas in contrast, there are very few women in this occupation in the Middle East and North Africa region. The Asia/Pacific and the Other Developing regions present a mixed picture. For example, this is a female-concentrated occupation in two Far Eastern countries (Japan and the Republic of Korea) but not in the five other Asia/Pacific countries/areas (Fiji, China, Hong Kong, India and Malaysia).

Salespersons, shop assistants and related workers (which includes street vendors) is *an extremely important occupation for women in sub-Saharan African and Caribbean countries*—attested by the fact that a very high percentage of urban women workers in these countries work in the informal sector as petty traders. Thus, 68 per cent of female non-agricultural workers are located here in Haiti and 49 per cent in Angola. For Ghana, while this appears to be a relatively small occupation, the occupational classification scheme used in Ghana probably helps explain this low proportion, since 54 per cent of female non-agricultural workers in Ghana are owner proprietors and another 21 per cent are food and beverage preparers; both of these occupations probably imply informal sector petty trading.[8]

One explanation for the very large regional variation in percentage female is that salespersons and shop assistants is *a less socially acceptable role for women in some countries, because of the public contact with men which is required.* That Malaysia, where the majority of the population is Muslim, follows the same pattern as in the Middle East supports this hypothesis. A similar explanation could apply to India as this would be consistent with the widespread observance of purdah and Indian society's views of what is and is not acceptable work for women.

e. Services Occupations

As shown in Chapter 8, women are overrepresented in this Major Group in all study regions. Furthermore, services occupations account for a considerable share of total non-agricultural employment, ranging from about 11 per cent in the OECD to about 15 per cent in the Middle East and North Africa.

(i) Protective service workers

This group—comprising police officers, fire-fighters and other security personnel—is **a highly masculinized occupation** around the world, with men comprising approximately 96 per cent of protective service workers in the world (figure 11.1). This is a male-dominated occupation in all 35 countries or areas for which we have data. The perception that men are physically and mentally better able to undertake the hardships and risks associated with protective service work appears to be a worldwide belief helping to sex-stereotype these occupations.[9]

(ii) Maids and related housekeeping personnel

This is **a "female" occupation** (figure 11.2). On average, 85 per cent of maids and housekeeping personnel in the world are women. Indeed, this is a female-concentrated occupation in all but two of the 30 study countries/areas with data,[10] and it is female-dominated in 22 of them.

The perception that maid and housekeeping functions are an extension of the home environment stereotypes such jobs as more appropriate for women. As this is a strongly held belief around the world, it is not surprising to find that maids and related household personnel is a "female" occupation around the world. This is *especially marked in OECD countries* where the lowest national value is 87 per cent female.

On the other hand, it is interesting that *male maids and housekeepers are fairly common in several non OECD-countries.* Perhaps one-half of maids and housekeeping personnel are men in Angola and India, approximately one-third in Tunisia, Ghana and Senegal and about one-quarter in Egypt and Kuwait.

(iii) Hairdressers and barbers

This tends to be **a female-concentrated occupation.** On average, approximately 60 per cent of these workers are female, and this is a female-concentrated occupation in 25 of the 32 study countries or areas with data.

At the same time, however, there *is considerable variation in the feminization of this occupation, especially across regions* (figure 11.2). Whereas this is very much a female-concentrated occupation in the OECD region with females comprising over 80 per cent of hairdressers and barbers in the region on average (and the lowest national percentage in the OECD region is as high as 61 per cent, in Italy), the picture is mixed in the remainder of the world. Among non-OECD study countries and areas, the average percentage female is only about 44 per cent; and, this is a female-concentrated occupation in only 11 of our 18 non-OECD study countries and areas. Indeed, women comprise less than 50 per cent of these workers in 11 of the 18 non-OECD study countries and areas. It is worth pointing out that hairdressers and barbers is not a female-concentrated occupation in the two most populous countries in the world (India and China).

We can think of two factors which help to explain much of the regional and national variations in the degree of feminization of this occupational group. First, due to the need to avoid direct contact with men, it would generally be unacceptable for women do men's hair in certain countries (such as in the Middle East, North Africa and often in the Indian subcontinent). Second, there is a great deal of variation in the world in the extent to which women and men go to hairdresser shops and pay for their hair to be done. In many settings, especially in lower income countries, most women have their hair done in a home setting by friends and family on the basis of unpaid (or possibly paid) reciprocity. In such situations, much if not most hairdressing would not enter into the official labour force statistics, as unpaid hairdressing would not often be considered to be a labour force activity and paid home-based hairdressing would often go unrecorded in labour force statistics. This, in turn, would decrease the observed feminization of this occupation. Even given these two explanations, there clearly is still a considerable degree of unexplained national and regional variation in the degree of feminization of this occupational group.

(iv) Cooks and waiters
There is a weak tendency in the world for cooks and waiters to be a female-concentrated occupation.[11] On average, women comprise slightly less than one-half of these workers (46 per cent). Of the 30 study countries/areas for which data are available, this is a female-concentrated occupation in 11 and a female-dominated occupation in only 2.

There is **considerable regional variation in the feminization of this occupation** (figure 11.2). Whereas the percentage female is 60 per cent on average in OECD countries, it is only 34 per cent on average in non-OECD countries. It is as low as 5 per cent in the Middle East and North Africa region and 10 per cent in India. In non-OECD countries in addition, the heterogeneous nature of this occupation in terms of its feminization undoubtedly relates in large part to the type of contact and interaction required between men and women (especially important for India and the Middle East/North Africa).

Another reason why the cooks and waiters occupation is a mixed occupational group in terms of feminization can be traced to differences in its two main occupational sub-groups. *Cooks are more likely to be male, while waiters and waitresses are more likely to be female.* For 10 study countries or areas where we were able to identify cooks and waiters separately,[12] the percentage female is 47 per cent on average for cooks and 64 per cent on average for waiters, and is higher for 8 of these 10 study countries or areas (the exceptions being Finland, where both occupations are approximately 80 per cent female and Italy, where 50 per cent of cooks are female whereas 41 per cent of waiters are female). In Japan and the United States, for example, women comprise about 80 per cent of waiters and waitresses as compared to about 50 per cent of cooks. In the Netherlands and China, women comprise about 40 per cent of cooks as compared to about 70 per cent of waitresses and waiters. Here is another example of men and women often being slotted into related occupations which differ in terms of skill and pay, with *men tending to concentrate in the better paid of these related occupations.*

f. Production Occupations

Women are not generally found in large numbers in production occupations. According to data presented in Chapter 8, **women are underrepresented in the production sphere** in 54 of the 56 countries or areas reviewed, the only exceptions being India and Pakistan.

(i) Production supervisors and general foremen; Blacksmiths, toolmakers, etc.; Bricklayers, carpenters and other construction workers
These three production occupational groups are **excellent examples of the extraordinary consistency with which production occupations are male-dominated in the world** (figure 11.1). These three occupations are male-dominated in 85 of the 86[13] country/area examples presented in tables 11.2 and 11.3. Indeed, the male share is above 90 per cent most of the time (in 76 of our 86 country/area examples). For example, over 95 per cent of bricklayers, carpenters and other construction workers are men in 31 of 34 study countries/areas, the only "exceptions" have "only" 93 to 94 per cent male.[14]

The male dominance of these production occupations is all the more striking when one stops to consider that these are, in fact, reasonably heterogeneous occupational groups. The bricklayers, carpenters and construction workers occupation in ISCO-68, for example, consists of eight sub-occupations (bricklayers, stonemasons and tile setters; reinforced concreters, cement finishers and terrazzo workers; roofers; carpenters, joiners and parquetry workers; plasterers; insulators; glaziers; construction workers not elsewhere classified). This means that the very high degree of male dominance observed for the composite group is almost surely present for each subgroup.

Since the three "male" production occupations discussed above are large occupations (5.4, 10.8 and 7.6 per cent of workers are in these three occupational groups in countries as diverse as the United States, China, and India respectively), this virtual exclusion of women from many relatively well-paid production occupations has important implications for female–male pay differentials as well as allocative efficiency of the labour market.

There is one small difference among countries for these three "male" production occupations worth mentioning. Five of the six study countries where the male share is less than 90 per cent for production supervisors are countries with large textile sectors (which are export-oriented) where there are many women workers. That as many as 10 to 20 per cent of production supervisors in these countries are women can be seen as encouraging or discouraging for those interested in gender equality—encouraging if one focuses on the non-negligible percentage here or discouraging if one focuses on the fact that this percentage is not higher in light of the large numbers of women working in production occupations in textiles in these countries.

(ii) Tailors, dressmakers, sewers, upholsters, etc.
This is one of the few production occupations with a concentration of female workers in a number of study countries (textile weavers, spinners and weavers is another). As discussed in Chapter 2, women are often found in these occupations presumably because the principal tasks involved (such as garment making) are seen as building on women's supposed experiences and roles in the home, as well as requiring manual dexterity/nimble fingers which is usually viewed as a female trait.[15] In addition of course, as textiles is a fiercely competitive industry with worldwide competition, this means that producers seek out low wage workers which often implies women workers.

Still, there is also **considerable variation in the world in the feminization of this occupation**. While, on average, approximately 64 per cent of workers in this occupation are female in the 32 study countries/areas with data, this is a female-concentrated occupation in only 22 of these 32 countries/areas; and the female share is less than 50 per cent in 4 study countries.

The OECD and Asia/Pacific regions have the highest averages (figure 11.2). Approximately 80 and 65 per cent of this occupational group is female in the OECD and Asian regions. This is a female-concentrated occupation in 12 of the 13 OECD and 6 of the 7 Asia/Pacific study countries/areas with data. India, with only 11 per cent female, and the United States with 68 per cent female are the only exceptions in these two regions.

In contrast, tailors, dressmakers, sewers and upholsterers is *often not* a female-concentrated occupation in non-Asian and non-OECD countries. It is a female-concentrated occupation in only 5 of the 12 study countries in these regions with an average female share of only about 45 per cent.

Part of the reason for some variation in the OECD region in the feminization of this occupational group is due to the somewhat heterogeneous nature of this occupational group, with tailors and upholsterers more likely to be male and dressmakers and sewers more likely to be female. For example, for the four OECD study countries where it is possible to identify separate occupational groups for (i) sewers and machine operators and (ii) upholsterers, it is found that the former is 96 per cent female on average whereas the latter is 30 per cent female on average. Another reason for observed differences across countries is probably due to measurement error and the underreporting of what is often a home-based, informal sector or grey market activity.[16]

Thus, there are major national and regional differences in the sex-stereo-typing of this occupation as male tailors and sewers predominate in the Middle East, North Africa and India and are common in many developing countries. In contrast, male tailors are fairly unusual in industrialized countries.

In summary, analysis in this section indicates that **there is a considerable degree of similarity around the world in the sex-stereotyping of the eight typical "male" occupations represented here.** Percentage male in these occupations is uniformly high throughout the world. In contrast, **there is a fair degree of variation in the female share for the nine occupations chosen to represent typical "female" occupations.**

11.2   Five largest female-dominated occupations

The previous section looked at 17 specific occupations which have a reputa-tion among laypersons in Western industrialized countries as being predomi-nantly "female" or "male" occupations. The present section broadens this discussion by looking at the five largest female-dominated occupations in each of our 37 non-Transition Economy study countries/areas, using our usual definition of female-dominated (i.e. occupations where women comprise at least 80 per cent of the workers).

Study data are presented in tables 11.4 and 11.5. In all, there are 137 entries. Note that this number is far less than the 185 entries which would result if each study country/area had five entries, because 18 of these 37 study countries/areas have four or fewer female-dominated occupations reported (see notes at bottom of table 11.4 for details on this). Since our national study occupational data are at different levels of aggregation, for purposes of exposition we have arranged the data in tables 11.4 and 11.5 so that similar occupations could be bracketed together. This helps increase com-parability across study countries and makes it easier to observe the types of female-dominated occupations found around the world.[17]

Data in tables 11.4 and 11.5 confirm many of our earlier hypotheses and discussions. First, the **range of female-dominated occupations in the world is quite small.** Three occupational groups (nurse/midwife; secretary/typist; maid/housekeeper/domestic) are responsible for approximately one-half of the entries in tables 11.4 and 11.5, and six occupational groups (also including bookkeeper/cashier; building caretaker/cleaner; tailor/sewer) are responsible for approximately three-quarters of the entries.

Second, **the female-dominated occupations listed in tables 11.4 and 11.5 are very consistent with typical gender stereotypes about women** and the

Table 11.4. Five largest female-dominated[b] non-agricultural occupations in study countries or areas (based on number of female workers), latest year, by region (per cent female in occupation in brackets)

Occupation	Region/country/area[a]			
	OECD	Asia/Pacific	Middle East and North Africa	Other Developing
Professional/Technical				
Professional nurses (3 digit)	Australia (90.5) Canada (90.4) Finland (96.1) Germany (West) (82.3) Netherlands (89.1) New Zealand (94.4) Norway (93.2) Sweden (85.0) United Kingdom (91.6) United States (94.8)	China (94.7) Hong Kong (89.4) India (93.1) Japan (96.7)	Kuwait (100.0)	
Nursing aides, orderlies and attendants (3 digit)	France (91.6) Switzerland (99.9)			
Nursing personnel n.e.c. (3 digit)	Norway (95.2)		Kuwait (88.1)	
Professional midwives (3 digit)		India (83.6)	Kuwait (100.0)	
Midwifery personnel n.e.c. (3 digit)			Kuwait (100.0)[d]	
Elementary school teachers and related workers (3 digit)	Italy (88.5) United States (86.0)			
Teachers n.e.c. (3 digit)			Kuwait (100.0)	

Table 11.4. (contd.)

Occupation	Region/country/area[a]			
	OECD	Asia/Pacific	Middle East and North Africa	Other Developing
Clerical				
Stenographers and typists and card punching machine operators (2 or 3 digit)	Australia (98.7) Canada (98.3) Cyprus (99.4) Germany (97.9) Luxembourg (91.9) New Zealand (98.8) Norway (96.0) Spain (94.5) United Kingdom (98.9)	Fiji (93.7) Hong Kong (94.0) Malaysia (90.9)		Costa Rica (89.5) Haiti (100.0) Mauritius (84.9) Netherlands Antilles (95.1)
Secretaries and receptionists (3 digit)	Australia (91.7) Cyprus (99.6) Finland (95.9) France (97.7) Netherlands (100.0) United Kingdom (97.3) United States (99.0)			
Bookkeepers, cashiers and related workers (2 and 3 digit)	Australia (91.1) Canada (88.1) France (83.5) New Zealand (85.3) Sweden (92.1) United States (86.2)[e]			
Other clerical workers n.e.c. (3 digit)	Norway (89.9) Finland (92.0) France (81.2) New Zealand (81.1)			

Occupation				
Sales				
Working proprietors (wholesale and retail trade) (2 and 3 digit)				Ghana (90.4)
Salesmen, shop assistants and related workers (2 and 3 digit)	Germany (West) (81.5) Switzerland (85.5)			Haiti (92.9)
Sales workers n.e.c. (2 and 3 digit)				Angola (93.5)
Services				
Working proprietors (catering and lodging) (2 and 3 digit)				Ghana (81.0)
Cooks, waiters, bartenders and related workers (2 digit)	New Zealand (82.2)[c] United States (81.6)	Japan (80.3)		Haiti (94.1)
Superintendents, caretakers and related workers in social care (3 digit) NOC	Sweden (89.2)[d]			
Public sector workers (3 digit)				
Maids and related housekeeping service workers n.e.c. (2 and 3 digit)	Austria (85.5) Finland (99.5) Luxembourg (97.1) Netherlands (90.3) Spain (97.4) Switzerland (87.0)	Fiji (95.8) Malaysia (93.9)	Jordan (81.3)	Costa Rica (87.8) Haiti (86.2) Mauritius (97.0) Senegal (80.2) Netherlands Antilles (97.0)
Housekeeping and related service supervisors (2 and 3 digit)				Angola (100.0)
Domestic ayahs and babysitters (3 digit NOC)	Australia (92.6) France (99.7) Sweden (96.5)	Hong Kong (93.4) India (88.7)		
Domestic helpers and cleaners (3 digit)	Cyprus (99.8) Germany (West) (95.2) Italy (92.3) Switzerland (92.9) United Kingdom (98.7)			
Caretaking personnel n.e.c. (3 digit)	Netherlands (97.7)			

Table 11.4. (contd.)

Occupation	Region/country/area[a]			
	OECD	Asia/Pacific	Middle East and North Africa	Other Developing Economies
Building caretakers, charworkers, cleaners and related workers (2 digit)	Cyprus (88.1) Finland (92.6) Luxembourg (90.8) Netherlands (83.8) Norway (90.0) Sweden (87.0) Switzerland (87.0)			Netherlands Antilles (85.6)
Launderers, dry-cleaners and related workers (2 and 3 digit)	Austria (86.2) Spain (83.6)			Angola (100.0) Haiti (93.6) Netherlands Antilles (80.4)
Hairdressers, barbers, beauticians and related workers (2 and 3 digit)	Austria (82.7) Germany (West) (84.5)	Japan (85.7)		Angola (100.0) Costa Rica (81.0) Ghana (91.3)
Personal, apparel and furnishing service (2 digit NOC)	Canada (87.1)			
Service workers n.e.c. (3 digit)	Luxembourg (89.5)			
Production and related workers				
Spinners and weavers, knitters, dyers and related workers (2 digit)		Fiji (92.8)	Tunisia (83.0)	
Fibre preparers (3 digit)		China (91.0)		
Tailors, dressmakers, sewers, upholsterers and related workers (2 digit)	Austria (82.9) Italy (84.4) Luxembourg (89.3) Spain (80.7)			Costa Rica (84.0)

Occupation						
Embroidery (3 digit)			China	(99.5)		
Machine operators-textile products (3 digit)			China	(87.0)		
Machine operators-sewing (3 digit)	Cyprus (99.2)	United Kingdom (93.4)	China	(92.3)		
Hosiers and shoemakers (3 digit NOC)	Italy (86.3)		Japan	(89.9)		
Paper and paper product makers (3 digit)			Fiji	(82.5)		
Food and beverages processors (2 digit)					Ghana	(92.5)
Package wrappers (3 digit NOC)			Japan	(87.9)		
Glass formers, potters and related workers (2 digit)					Ghana	(91.0)
Production and related workers n.e.c. (2 digit)					Senegal	(91.0)

Notes: [a] Countries in Transition Economies region are excluded from this table because in the past they used conceptually different occupational classifications. [b] Female-dominated occupations are defined as occupations where at least 80 per cent of the workers are women. Only the five largest female-dominated occupations from each country are included in this table (based on number of female workers). [c] Data are for waiters and bartenders only, and exclude cooks for this country. [d] This occupation was classified in the professional category for this country. [e] In the United States, both cashiers and bookkeepers, which are listed separately, are female-dominated occupations. NOC indicates use of a National Occupational Classification system. n.e.c. indicates not elsewhere classified.

Occupational classification for Australia, Cyprus, France, Finland, West Germany, the Netherlands, New Zealand, Norway, Italy, Switzerland, the United States, China, India, Japan and Kuwait are at the three-digit level of aggregation. The remainder of the countries and areas have two-digit data.

Four countries have no female-dominated occupations in the study data (Bahrain, Egypt, the Islamic Republic of Iran and the Republic of Korea); two countries have only one female-dominated occupation (Jordan and Tunisia); three countries have only two female-dominated occupations (Malaysia, Mauritius and Senegal); two countries/areas (Hong Kong and India) have only three female-dominated occupations; and seven have only four female-dominated occupations (Austria, Canada, Spain, Fiji, Angola, Costa Rica and Netherlands Antilles). All other study countries have at least five female-dominated occupations.

To some extent, the identification of female-dominated occupations is affected by the level of detail (i.e. disaggregated) in the national occupational classification. To assist readers, column 1 indicates the level of disaggregation at which occupation is found.

For the relevant notes on comparability of national occupational data, see tables 11.1 and 11.2.
Source: Study data.

Table 11.5.   Summary for five largest female-dominated non-agricultural occupations in study countries or areas (based on number of female workers), latest available year, by region and major occupational group

Major Occupational Group	Region[d]					Specific occupations[a,b]	
	OECD	Asia/Pacific	ME	OD	Total		
Professional/Technical	15 (18%)	5 (23%)	5 (71%)	0	25 (18%)	Nurses	(22)[c]
						Teachers	(3)
Administrative/Managerial	0	0	0	0	0		
Clerical	27 (33%)	3 (14%)	0	4 (15%)	34 (25%)	Stenographers, typists and secretaries	(24)
						Bookkeepers, cashiers	(6)
						Other clerical	(4)
Sales	2 (2%)	0	0	3 (12%)	5 (4%)	Salespersons, shop assistants	(3)
						Miscellaneous	(2)
Services	31 (38%)	6 (27%)	1 (14%)	15 (58%)	53 (39%)	Maids and related workers	(20)
						Building caretakers	(7)
						Launderers, dry cleaners	(5)
						Hairdressers, barbers	(6)
						Cooks, waiters	(4)
						Caretakers	(8)
						Miscellaneous	(3)
Production	7 (9%)	8 (36%)	1 (14%)	4 (15%)	20 (14%)	Tailors, dressmakers and sewers	(11)
						Spinners and weavers	(3)
						Miscellaneous	(6)[a]
Total	82 (100%)	22 (100%)	7 (100%)	26 (100%)	137 (100%)		

Note: [a] Miscellaneous occupational groups consist of occupations which have only one country entry in table 11.4. Miscellaneous occupations are as follows: For services: personal, apparel and furnishing service (Canada); service workers n.e.c. (Luxembourg); working proprietors in wholesale and retail trade (Ghana). For production: hosiers and shoemakers (Italy); food and beverage processors (Ghana); glass formers and potters (Ghana); package wrappers (Japan); paper and paper brand product makers (Fiji); production and related workers n.e.c. (Senegal). [b] For expositional purposes, almost all occupations represented in this table are at the two-digit classification level in ISCO-68. Therefore, in compiling these data, judgement was used to bracket closely allied occupations from two- and three-digit classifications for presentation in this table (but not for identifying important occupations to include here or in table 11.4). [c] For Sweden, the occupation included is health, nursing and veterinary work. [d] Four countries have no female-dominated occupation; two have one female-dominated occupation; three have two female-dominated occupations; two have three female-dominated occupations; and seven have four female dominated occupations. See notes at bottom of table 11.4 for detailed explanations for national data.
Source: Table 11.4.

types of work women are believed to be especially suited—as discussed in Chapter 2 and hypothesized in table 2.1.

Indeed, it is difficult to find many examples in tables 11.4 and 11.5 (or in tables 11.6 and 11.7 discussed in the next section which look at the largest occupations for women regardless of whether or not these occupations are female-dominated) which do not fall fairly neatly into the above schema of the sex-stereotyping of women shown in table 2.1. Some examples from Africa which might not appear to fit directly into this schema (e.g. working proprietors in catering and lodging; food and beverage processors) are undoubtedly poorly remunerated informal sector occupations in less developed labour markets. According to our interpretation of these data, the only possible exceptions in the 137 occupations noted in table 11.4 may be package wrappers in Japan, and paper and glass formers and potters in Ghana, but then again, a more detailed knowledge of these situations may provide good explanations.

Third, despite the small range of female-dominated occupations in the world, there are **some important regional differences** (figure 11.3). The *Middle Eastern and North African region has very few female-dominated occupations*. Only four show up in table 11.4 for the entire region: nurse, teacher, spinner/weaver and maid. This small range of female-dominated occupations can only partly be explained by low female labour force participation rates in these countries; for example, sales and service occupations, which require public interaction with men, are more or less ruled out for women in the Middle East and North Africa.

In the *Other Developing study region, the largest female-dominated occupations tend to be concentrated in services and sales occupations,* such as maids, housekeepers, launderers, hairdressers, working proprietors, salespersons. The absence of professional occupations for this region is partly due to the fact that the study countries/areas have only two-digit data, and this obfuscates the observation of some typical female-dominated three-digit professional occupations such as nurse and primary school teacher. Even so, inspection of much more detailed data which are available for Mauritius (381 occupations; see Chapter 4) reveal only three additional female-dominated occupations in that country over those observed based on two-digit data: textiles, garments and related workers; primary school teachers; nurses. These are again the same typical and traditional female stereotyped occupations.

The *Asia/Pacific region is unusual in having a relatively high proportion of their largest female-dominated occupations in the production* Major Group. Eight (36 per cent) of the 22 Asia/Pacific entries in table 11.4 are production occupations; the next highest regional percentage for production occupations is 16 per cent (for the OD region). These large female-dominated production occupations in Asia are *mainly concentrated in the textile sector:* spinners, weavers and knitters; fibre preparers; tailors and sewers; embroidery workers;

Figure 11.3. Percentage distribution of five largest female-dominated occupations, by major ISCO occupational group, latest available year, by region

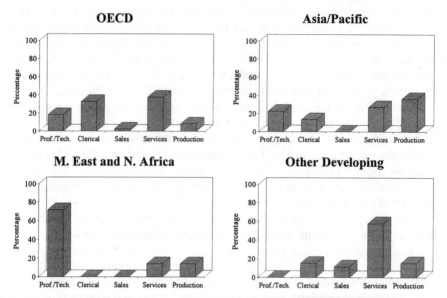

Notes: The five largest female-dominated occupations for each major occupational groups are:
Professional/Technical: Nurses (22), Teachers (3).
Administrative and Managerial: None.
Clerical: Stenographers, typists and secretaries (24), Bookkeepers, Cashiers (6), Other clerical (4).
Sales: Salespersons, shop assistants (3), Miscellaneous (2).
Services: Maids and related workers (20), Building caretakers (7), Launderers, dry cleaners (5), Hairdressers, barbers (6), Cooks, waiters (4), Caretaking (8), Miscellaneous (3).
Production: Tailors, dressmakers and sewers (11), Spinners and weavers (3), Miscellaneous (6).
Largest defined in terms of number of female workers.
Source: Table 11.5.

textile machine operators; sewing machine operators. These occupations appear in table 11.4 in part because they are typical "female" activities and in part because they employ large numbers of women, since textile products play an important role in the export-oriented development strategy followed by many Asian countries and areas.[18]

In the *OECD region, clerical occupations stand out as being relatively over-represented* in table 11.4. It is much more common in the OECD region, as compared to other regions, for secretaries/receptionists; typists; cashiers/book-keepers to be large female-dominated occupations. Although a bit repetitive, it is still worth noting that despite the larger number of entries for OECD countries in table 11.4 (approximately 60 per cent of all entries), there is hardly a wider range of large female-dominated occupations listed for OECD countries. For example, the only professional female-dominated occupations listed are nurse and teacher. Among services occupations, the most common large female-dominated occupations are domestic helper/cleaner; maid/housekeeper;

GENDER AND JOBS

ayah; building caretaker/cleaner; cook/waiter; hairdresser/barber; and launderer. Large female-dominated production occupations are restricted to the
textile industrial sector.

Fourth, *female-dominated occupations tend to have relatively low pay and
status.* For example, nurses and teachers are virtually the only two important
professional occupations for women in the world. Yet, nurses have lower
prestige and pay as compared to the allied medical profession of doctor
which tends to be a male occupation. Further, women teachers are much
more likely to be primary and pre-primary school teachers as compared to
male teachers who tend to be concentrated in secondary and higher education.
Among production occupations, another set of generally higher paid occupations, women are concentrated in the textile industry, a sector known for fierce
international competition and the seeking out of low labour-cost sites. In
clerical and sales occupations, the percentage female is generally much
lower for sales supervisors and buyers as compared to salespersons and
shop assistants as well as for clerical supervisors as compared to typists/
secretaries/receptionists or bookkeepers/cashiers. And quite tellingly, the
small, but influential managerial occupations of managers as well as legislative
officials and government administrators are generally male-dominated
occupations.

**In conclusion, women workers in the world have a rather limited set of
female-dominated occupations**—that is, occupations where they face little if
any competition from men. In addition, the value of these niches to women
is often of dubious value as these occupations tend to have relatively low
pay and status. Furthermore, despite some regional differences, there is a
great similarity around the world in the types of large occupations which
are female-dominated. This **strong worldwide pattern is consistent with typical
gender stereotypes such as those noted in table 2.1. There is clearly a significant
degree of sexism and sex-stereotyping in the world of work throughout the world.**

11.3 Five largest occupations for women

The present section looks at the most important occupations in the world in
terms of female employment. Although similar to the analysis in the previous
section, which looked at the five largest female-dominated occupations in each
study country or area, the present analysis differs in two major ways. First, all
occupations are eligible to be included in the present analysis and not just
female-dominated occupations as in the previous section. Consequently,
while all study countries/areas have, by definition, five largest occupations
for women; many study countries/areas do not have five female-dominated
occupations. Notice that whereas 185 occupations are identified in table 11.6
(five for each of the 37 non-Transition Economy study countries/areas),[19]

Table 11.6. Five largest non-agricultural occupations for women workers in study countries and areas (based on number of female workers) by major occupational group and region, latest available year

Major Occupational Group	Region (number and % countries and areas)					Specific occupations[a,b]
	OECD	Asia	ME	OD	Total	
Professional/Technical	15 (18%)	5 (14%)	13 (43%)	7 (20%)	40 (22%)	Nurses (15)[c,e] Teachers (22) Accountants (2) Physicians (1)
Administrative/Managerial	3 (4%)	0 (0%)	0 (0%)	0 (0%)	3 (2%)	Administrative and managerial (3)
Clerical	30 (35%)	9 (26%)	8 (27%)	6 (17%)	53 (29%)	Stenographers, secretaries and typists (20) Bookkeepers, cashiers (15)[g] Other clerical (17)[f]
Sales	15 (18%)	7 (20%)	0 (0%)	6 (17%)	28 (15%)	Salespersons and shop assistants (23) Working proprietors (3)
Services	18 (21%)	7 (20%)	5 (17%)	7 (20%)	37 (20%)	Maids, housekeeping personnel (16) Building caretakers (14) Childcare or other care-givers (5)[i] Cooks, waiters (2)[d]
Production	4 (5%)	7 (20%)	4 (13%)	9 (26%)	24 (13%)	Tailors, dressmakers, sewers, upholsterers and related workers (12) Spinners and weavers (4)[h] Food and beverages processors (2) Miscellaneous (6)[a]
Total	85 (100%)	35 (100%)	30 (100%)	35 (100%)	185 (100%)	

Notes: [a] Miscellaneous groups consist of occupations with only one country entry. [b] For expositional purposes, almost all occupations represented are at 2-digit classification level in ISCO-68. Therefore, in compiling these data, judgement was used to bracket closely allied 2-and 3-digit occupations for presentation in this table (but not for purposes of identifying important occupations to be included in this table). For China, a sixth most important occupation was added because two of its five largest occupations were within the same two-digit occupational group (tailors, dressmakers, sewers and related workers). [c] For countries with two-digit data, the occupational category is medical, dental and veterinary workers; this includes nurses. This is so for Bahrain, Egypt, the Islamic Republic of Iran, Jordan, and Ghana where this occupation is among the five largest for women workers. We included this under nurses as we believed that most of these medical workers would be nurses. [d] Specified as cooks in Japan and coffee service (waitress) in Switzerland. [e] For Sweden, includes health and veterinary as well as nurse. [f] For New Zealand, specified as corresponding and reporting clerk. For Italy, specified as administrative employees not elsewhere classified. [g] For Japan and Australia, specified as accounting clerk. [h] For Tunisia, specified as workers in textiles. [i] For Sweden, includes caretakers in social care.

Source: Study data.

only 137 occupations are identified in table 11.4. This difference is particularly important for the Middle East and North African region which has 30 entries in table 11.6 as compared to only 7 entries in table 11.4. Second, it is common for large occupations (such as salespersons/shop assistants; clerical workers not elsewhere classified; and teachers) to be very important in terms of female employment while at the same time not being female-dominated.[20]

Since results for the present analysis are similar to results for the previous section, the following discussion concentrates on differences between these analyses. This discussion proceeds by major occupational group. Figure 11.4 indicates for each study region the percentage distribution of the five largest occupations for women according to the six Major ISCO Occupational Groups.

Nurses and teachers stand out as being the pre-eminent professional occupations for women workers. They are just about the only professional occupations identified in table 11.6 for our 37 non-Transition Economy

Figure 11.4. **Percentage distribution of five largest occupations for women according to six major non-agricultural groups, latest available year, by region**

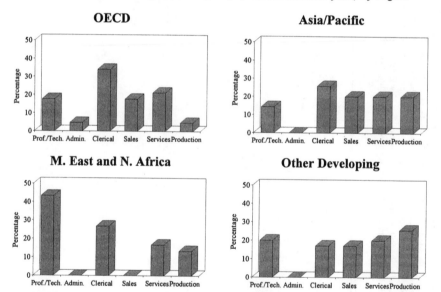

Notes: Five largest female occupations in each major occupational groups are:
Professional/Technical: Nurses (15), Teachers (22), Accountants (2), Physicians (1).
Administrative and Managerial: Administrative and Managerial (4).
Clerical: Stenographers, typists and secretaries (20), Bookkeepers, Cashiers (15), Other clerical (16).
Sales: Salespersons, shop assistants (23), Working proprietors (3).
Services: Maids and related workers (16), Building caretakers (14), Launderers, dry cleaners (5), Child and other care givers (5), Cooks, waiters (2).
Production: Tailors, dressmakers, sewers, upholsterers and related workers (12), Spinners and weavers (4), Food and beverages processors (2), Miscellaneous (6).
Largest defined in terms of number of female workers.
Source: Table 11.6.

study countries or areas; the only other professional occupations identified are in the Middle East and North African region: accountant (in the Islamic Republic of Iran and Egypt) and physician (in Jordan).

These results contrast with earlier ones for the five largest female-dominated non-agricultural occupations in two interesting ways. First, teacher is much more important in table 11.6 as compared to table 11.4 (22 entries as compared to 3 entries), because teaching is *not* often a female-dominated occupation unless one looks at specializations within the broader teaching occupation (such as pre-primary teacher) and each of these sub-occupations is much smaller in size as compared to all teachers as one occupational group. Second, the *Middle East and North Africa region stands out as having a high concentration of their largest non-agricultural occupations in the professional grouping;* this would seem to be due to cultural values which consider a few professional occupations among the only occupations acceptable for women. For example, 48 per cent of all women non-agricultural workers are teachers in Jordan, 38 per cent in the Islamic Republic of Iran and 23 per cent in Egypt. These percentages are lower, but still large, in the other countries in this region as about 15 per cent of all female non-agricultural workers in Bahrain and Kuwait and 8 per cent in Tunisia are teachers. Nurses or other medical professionals generally account for around an additional 5 to 10 per cent of female non-agricultural workers in this region.

The *Administrative and Managerial Major Group of Occupations* has only three country examples in table 11.6. Once again, we find that this important set of occupations in terms of influence, responsibility and status *is not a place where many women workers are found.* This result differs slightly from that observed for female-dominated occupations where there are no examples. All three examples are found in OECD countries (Cyprus, the United States and Canada). This is a good sign for these countries as it indicates that many women in these countries are in occupations with decision-making authority and responsibility. One must not get too excited about these results, however, since the occupational categories identified here are relatively broad in scope being for such administrative and managerial workers as those not elsewhere classified; or other such workers; or other related workers—implying that a relatively broad range of workers are included here as compared to other countries.

Results for clerical and production occupations are similar to those reported in the previous section which analysed important female-dominated occupations. There *are relatively few production occupations in the world which employ many women*—and the few which do exist are concentrated in the low paying textile sector where women's supposed greater manual dexterity and willingness to accept low remuneration are prized. *Among clerical occupations, lower paying occupations* (such as secretaries/typists, bookkeepers/cashiers and other clerical workers not elsewhere classified) *are important sources of jobs for women all around the world.*

Two sales occupations—salespersons/shop assistants or working proprietors—are found to be one of the five largest non-agricultural occupations for women workers in virtually all study economies outside of the Middle East and North Africa (27 of 31). These results differ from those reported above for the most important female-dominated non-agricultural occupations. Whereas there were only a few country examples of large female-dominated sales occupations, there are many country examples of large sales occupations for women workers. Obviously, sales occupations in many countries are large enough in size to be very important sources of employment for female workers even when they are not highly feminized occupations. *In some developing countries, a majority of women non-agricultural workers are in sales occupations as petty traders in the informal sector.* For example, 54 per cent of female non-agricultural workers in Ghana are reported to be working proprietors in retail or wholesale trade; and 67 and 49 per cent of female non-agricultural workers in Haiti and Angola respectively are reported to be salespersons or shop assistants.

Service occupations is the only major non-agricultural occupational group which has fewer entries in table 11.6 as compared to table 11.4. This is due to the fact that launderers and hairdressers (which are sometimes large female-dominated occupations) are not one of the five largest employers of women workers in any study country, even though these are important occupations for women workers (e.g. employing around 1 per cent of all female non-agricultural workers in each of these occupations in the 10 country examples where these are female-dominated occupations). *The female-dominated service occupation of maids and housekeepers is one of the most important employment areas for women workers all around the world,* employing as many as 49 per cent of female non-agricultural workers in Kuwait, 39 per cent in Bahrain and 23 per cent in Costa Rica.

Another indication of the restricted occupational choice available to women working in non-agricultural occupations is indicated by data in table 11.7 on the largest female occupation (shown in figure 11.5). At least 15 per cent of women workers (i.e. approximately 1 in 6 to 7) are in one occupational group in 24 of our 37 non-Transition Economy study countries or areas. This is especially important in non-Asian, non-OECD study countries[21] as over 25 per cent of women non-agricultural workers in these study countries or areas are in one occupational group in 11 of these 13 study non-Asian, non-OECD countries and over 35 per cent in 8 of these study countries. Another striking indication of the restricted occupational choice available for women workers in the world is that the *largest non-agricultural occupation in in each of our 37 non-Transition Economy study countries or areas includes only 9 different occupations* (table 11.7) and these tend to be concentrated in one major occupational group in each study region.

The broad picture of the world of work for women described in this section—based on the five largest non-agricultural occupations in each

Table 11.7. Largest female non-agricultural occupation in study countries or areas (based on number of female workers), latest available year, by region (percentage of female non-agricultural labour force in occupation in brackets)

Major Occupational Group	Specific occupations	Region			
		OECD	Asia/Pacific	Middle East and North Africa	Other Developing
Professional and Technical	Teachers			Jordan (48) Iran, Islamic Rep. (38)	
Clerical	Stenographers, typists and secretaries	Germany (West) (24)c France (8) United States (7)			
	Bookkeepers and cashiers	Canada (10) Sweden (15)			
	Other clerical	Austria (22)c Finland (8) Italy (8)d Luxembourg (16) New Zealand (10) Spain (16) United Kingdom (14)	Rep. of Korea (15) Hong Kong (16) Japan (21) Malaysia (12)	Egypt (24)	
Sales	Salespersons and shop assistants	Australia (10) Cyprus (12) Netherlands (9) Norway (10) Switzerland (25)c			
	Working proprietors in trade				Netherlands Antilles (16) Haiti (68) Angola (49) Ghana (54)

Table 11.7. (contd.)

Major Occupational Group	Specific occupations	Region			
		OECD	Asia/Pacific	Middle East and North Africa	Other Developing
Services	Maids and related housekeeping service workers		Fiji (15)	Kuwait (49) Bahrain (39)	Costa Rica (23) Senegal (28)
Production	Tailors, sewers, upholsterers, and related workers		China (7)[b]	Tunisia (44)[a]	Mauritius (25)
	Bidi (local cigarette) makers		India (11)		

Notes: There are four examples where the second largest occupation is also very large, employing between 1 in 7 (about 15 per cent) and 1 in 4 (about 25 per cent of women workers): the Islamic Republic of Iran, spinners and weavers (26 per cent); Ghana, food and beverages preparers (21 per cent); Egypt, teachers (23 per cent); Jordan, bookkeepers and cashiers (17 per cent); Mauritius, spinners and weavers (17 per cent); Netherlands Antilles, other clerical workers (16 per cent); and Senegal, petty traders (21 per cent). [a] For Tunisia, the occupation refers to workers in textiles (which includes spinners/weavers and sewers/tailors). [b] For China, two occupations (embroidery workers and sewing machine operators) have been merged for presentational purposes in this table, because these are allied occupations in a three-digit occupational classification. [c] For West Germany, occupation refers to office clerks. We took this to mainly represent secretaries and typists, since there are separate occupations for bookkeepers, other clerical workers and stenographers but not for secretaries/typists. [d] For Austria, occupation refers to other office clerks and other administrative workers. [e] For Italy, occupation refers to administrative employees not elsewhere classified. [f] For Switzerland, Austria and West Germany, occupation refers to sales clerk and office clerk. [g] For Sweden, occupation refers to "bookkeepers, cashiers, clerical and related work" based on a classification with 49 non-agricultural occupations. However, according to a much more detailed classification with 261 non-agricultural occupations, secretaries comprise 12.2 per cent of the female non-agricultural labour force.
Source: Study data.

Figure 11.5. **Percentage of largest occupation for women falling within six major non-agricultural occupations, latest available year, by region**

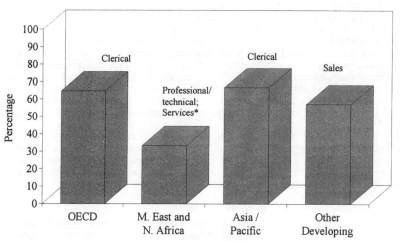

Note: Largest defined in terms of number of women workers.
* For the Middle East and North Africa region the professional/technical and the service major occupational groups are equal at 29 per cent for each.
Largest occupation in each major occupational group is:
Professional and Technical: Teachers (2); only in the Middle East and North Africa.
Administrative and Managerial: Administrative and managerial (1); only in Italy.
Clerical: Stenographers, typists and secretaries (3): only in OECD. Bookkeepers and cashiers (2): only in OECD. Other clerical (12); none in Other Developing.
Sales: Salespersons and shop assistants (8): none in Asia or the Middle East and North Africa. Working proprietors (1): only in Ghana. *Services*: Maids and related workers (5): none in OECD.
Production: Tailors, sewers and related workers (3): none in OECD. Bidi (local cigarette) makers, only in India.
Source: Table 11.7.

study country in terms of female employment—is one of **limited options.** Women all around the world tend to be working in a small set of occupations—and in addition these occupations tend to have *lower pay, lower status and less decision-making authority* than the types of occupations in which male workers tend to be located. Furthermore, the main occupations in which women work have characteristics which are **consistent with the types of stereotyped traits often attributed to women as described in table 2.1,** such as a supposedly caring nature; greater honesty; greater manual dexterity, especially with fingers; more experience and skill at typical household tasks; greater willingness to be subservient and take orders; less physical strength; less ability in maths and science. **Clearly, the pernicious sex stereotyping of all women regardless of their individual abilities or interests needs to be changed if women are to enter into new non-traditional occupations, and the world is to move towards gender equality in the labour market.**

Notes

[1] Given that study data from non-OECD countries generally use two-digit classifications, we decided to examine specific occupations primarily at this level of aggregation. However, we

chose to include nurses (which is at the three-digit level) for two reasons. First, it is a very important female occupation; secondly, it is clearly specified in a number of national occupational classification systems, including China's.

In countries with three-digit data, we aggregated these data into a two-digit classification as necessary. In some instances, identifying the appropriate three-digit occupations for aggregating into comparable ISCO-68 two-digit groups required judgement on our part. This was particularly true for Australia, France, West Germany, Switzerland, Japan and China which have their own national occupation classification schemes that differ substantially from ISCO-68. Data presented for China in this section should be viewed with special caution. Although its classification system is similar to ISCO-68 at the one-digit level, two-digit subgroups frequently involve a different "mix" of occupations than in ISCO-68. Despite this reduced level of comparability with other countries, China is included in the analysis here because of its size and importance.

For a few of these 17 occupations, sometimes there is confusion in particular national classifications in the placing of workers into these occupations. This sometimes occurs for the tailors, dressmakers and sewers occupation with regard to the spinners and weavers occupations; for the stenographers, typists and card and tape punching machine operations occupation with regard to the clerical workers not elsewhere classified occupation; and for the maids and related housekeeping service workers not elsewhere classified occupation with regard to the building caretakers, charworkers, cleaners and related workers occupation.

[2] Note that the somewhat unequal distribution of "male" and "female" occupations across one-digit ISCO-68 occupational groups reflects the relative concentrations of "male" and "female" occupations across these groups.

[3] Sweden was excluded because the data available when this chapter was written had relatively few occupations classified (only 44). The United Kingdom was excluded because of the difficulty we had in aggregating occupations into a classification which would be somewhat similar to ISCO-68. Subsequently, three-digit data for Sweden for 1990 were obtained; percentage female for the 17 specific occupations analysed in this chapter is generally similar to that found in Sweden's two Scandinavian neighbours Norway and Finland (see Melkas and Anker, forthcoming).

[4] After completing this chapter, non-study data on nursing for six additional "countries" came to my attention. They indicate very similar percentages as in the study data. The percentage female is 89.4 (1990) in England, 91.1 (1990) in Scotland, 96.4 (1989) in Denmark, 95.4 (1987) in the Philippines, 91.7 (1991) in Ghana, as reported in ILO (1994f) and 68 per cent (1986) in Egypt as reported in Moghadam (1995).

[5] According to the UNDP's *Human Development Report 1995*, women represented about 10 per cent of the world's parliamentarians in mid-1994, ranging from 4 per cent in Arab States to about 35 per cent in Nordic countries. In 55 countries, women comprised less than 5 per cent of parliamentarians. The UNDP report mainly attributes this lack of political opportunities for women to cultural and social constraints as well as economic development level.

[6] In the case of India, this situation may be due in part to the historical context in which the bookkeeping and cashier occupation developed. Beginning with the British colonial period and the establishment of a national system of administration and record-keeping, clerks and bookkeepers have traditionally been men. This early stereotyping of these occupations has probably contributed to keeping women out of these occupations.

[7] In *Job queues and gender cues*, Reskin and Roos (1990) note that the feminization of many occupations is tied to levels of automation. Occupations appear to become more feminized as the degree of automation increases. The deskilling of an occupation reduces pay and makes it less attractive to men. In the case of bookkeepers and cashiers, a relatively low level of female concentration among developing countries could be related to the fact that it remains a largely unautomated, somewhat skilled and reasonably well-paid occupation and, therefore, valued by many men.

[8] Although percentages are lower for the other two African or Caribbean study countries/areas, they are still high. Thus, 21 per cent and 5 per cent of female non-agricultural workers in Senegal work as sales workers not elsewhere classified and as salespersons, shop assistants and related workers respectively. In the Netherlands Antilles, 16 per cent of female non-agricultural workers are salespersons, shop assistants and related workers.

[9] It is interesting to look in more detail at the only three study countries where percentage male is less than 90 per cent. Norway and the United States (more detailed Canadian data are not available) display very similar patterns with some variation in percentage male among the occupational subgroups. Approximately 99 per cent of fire-fighters, 90 per cent of police and 80 per cent of prison guards are men in both countries. Somewhat different in these two countries is: (1) customs officers in Norway (which is an occupation with a substantial number of workers in Norway and so is specified as a separate occupation in Norway but not in the American classification) is only 68 per cent male; and (2) other protective services workers in Norway are only 68 per cent male and non-public guards and police in the United States, the largest other protective services workers sub-occupation in the country, are 84 per cent male.

[10] In Angola, a similar occupation (building caretakers, charworkers, cleaners and related workers) is much more highly feminized at 77.0 per cent female. As there may have been some confusion in the placing of workers between this occupation and the maids and related housekeeping service workers occupation, it is interesting that the female share for the two occupations taken together is 64.1 per cent. This is a similar figure to that found in Ghana and still represents a situation where men comprise a sizeable proportion of the workers.

[11] There is also some noticeable degree of non-comparability across countries for this occupational group because of differences in national occupational classifications (see Chapter 5 for further discussion on this point). For example, cooks are not included for Bahrain, Australia and Jordan; waiters and bartenders are not included for Austria; and kitchen helpers are explicitly mentioned and included for the Netherlands, Finland, Austria and Norway. Our feeling is that, despite such examples of non-comparability, average values for regions and broad groups of countries are useful for drawing general conclusions.

[12] The related occupations of kitchen assistants and waiters in bars were ignored whenever they were classified separately. For the United States, a separate occupation of short order cooks (27 per cent female) was ignored.

[13] The one exception is China, where men comprise "only" 68 per cent of the blacksmiths, toolmakers, etc. occupational group. A closer examination of the sub-occupations here indicates that this unusually low percentage male is due to the fact that: (1) the largest sub-occupation (which comprises approximately 50 per cent of the workers in this occupational group)— setters, polishers and sharpeners—is only approximately 56 per cent male; and (2) a relatively low percentage male is found for most sub-occupations, as three of the five sub-occupations are less than 80 per cent male (and a fourth sub-occupation is approximately 80 per cent male). In short, census data for China indicate that the relatively low percentage male for this occupational group is a phenomenon that extends across its sub-occupations.

[14] In India, the "relatively high" percentage female (11 per cent) for the bricklayers, carpenters and other construction workers occupational group (the highest percentage observed in our data set), is at the same time surprisingly low to the author. Anyone who has observed construction sites in India knows that there is considerable female participation in construction activities. Women are frequently seen carrying loads of earth at construction sites. I suspect that the 11 per cent figure reported in the Indian census is a substantial underestimate, perhaps because construction activity in India is often done by families on a subcontract basis.

[15] These occupations can be quite important for women. In Malaysia and the Republic of Korea, for example, over 9 per cent of all women in the non-agricultural labour force are reported to work in either the tailor, dressmaker, sewer, upholsterer occupation or in the weaver, spinner, knitter occupation.

[16] The very high percentage female for Tunisia might be due to its occupational classification which has an occupation entitled "workers in textiles", as this probably combines two occupations (spinners and weavers along with tailors and sewers) which are enumerated separately in ISCO-68 and most national classifications. Inspection of Tunisian data from 1975, which includes separate occupational categories for tailors/sewers and for spinners/weavers, indicates that spinners/weavers outnumber tailors/sewers by about three to one, but the female share is similar for both occupational groups (89 and 77 per cent respectively).

[17] National results reported here are affected by the level of disaggregation in a country's occupational classification. The more detailed a national classification, the more likely it is that

female-dominated occupations will be observed; but at the same time, the smaller these observed female-dominated occupations will tend to be.

[18] According to a recent ILO report (ILO, 1994e), clothing exports in 1992 comprised more than 10 per cent of all exports for the following study countries/areas: China (20 per cent), Hong Kong (33 per cent), India (16 per cent), Mauritius (51 per cent), Tunisia (37 per cent). Available data indicate this was less than 10 per cent for 14 of our OECD or Transition Economy study countries and three other Asian study countries (Japan, the Republic of Korea and Malaysia).

[19] In identifying the five largest female occupations in each study country or area, we made sure that all five were from different two-digit occupations as found in ISCO-68. This means that if a country had among its five largest female occupations (as did China), embroidery workers as well as sewing machine operators (both of which appear within the same two-digit ISCO-68 occupational group of tailors, dressmakers, sewers and upholsterers), we included the sixth largest female occupation in this country in tables 11.6 and 11.7. This affected only France (which had among its five largest occupations both clerical workers in public sector as well as clerical workers in financial and accounting) and China (see above).

[20] As in the previous analysis in section 10.2, identification of the largest non-agricultural occupations for female workers in a particular country is affected by the level of disaggregation in a country's occupational classification. This can be particularly important for countries with three-digit data, especially for occupations where the occupational classification is much more disaggregated at the three-digit level as compared to the two-digit level. This may have affected results discussed in the present section, especially for the following somewhat heterogeneous two-digit occupational groups: medical/dental; teachers; stenographers, receptionists and typists; maids and related housekeepers and cleaners; tailors, dressmakers and sewers; cooks and waiters and waitresses; cashiers and bookkeepers. For example, teachers at the three-digit level in ISCO-68 is comprised of university teacher, secondary teacher, primary teacher and pre-primary teacher. Therefore, it is possible for teacher as a composite group to be one of the five largest occupations for women workers in a country without any of its sub-occupations being among the five largest.

[21] Only part of this tendency is due to the fact that data for OECD study countries are often disaggregated to the three-digit level, since six of 17 OECD study countries have two-digit data.

PATTERNS IN OCCUPATIONAL SEGREGATION BY SEX BASED ON COMBINATIONS OF DIFFERENT INEQUALITY STATISTICS

12

So far in this book we have analysed occupational segregation by sex using various inequality measures and statistics. Chapter 9 used indices of inequality—such as the index of dissimilarity (ID) and marginal matching index (MM)—which bring together into one index number the variations in the feminization and masculinization of occupations. Chapter 10 used statistics which measure the extent to which the female, male and total non-agricultural labour forces are segregated into occupations which have such a high percentage of male or female workers that they could be described as "male" or "female" occupations. Chapter 11 used statistics on the feminization of important specific occupations.[1] Throughout, the percentage of the non-agricultural labour force which is female has been used.

Different statistics have been used in the belief that one inequality statistic (or even one type of inequality statistic) is too simple to provide a complete or even satisfactory picture of occupational segregation by sex in the world. This being said, there are **a number of important issues regarding how these various statistics relate to each other and whether there are patterns in these relationships.** For example, it is important to know: (i) how inequality statistics are related to each other; (ii) whether they are statistically independent of each other; (iii) whether some inequality statistics are so highly related to each other that they represent, in essence, the same phenomenon; (iv) how many different and distinct dimensions of occupational segregation by sex they represent; (v) whether there are distinct patterns in occupational segregation statistics; and (vi) whether these patterns are specific to certain regions.

The issues noted in the previous paragraph are addressed in the remainder of this chapter. This analysis begins by looking at how the various inequality statistics used in this book are interrelated based on correlation matrices and factor analysis. Then, drawing on conclusions from these analyses the predominant patterns of occupational segregation by sex found in study regions are described, as indeed there are only a small number of distinct patterns in the world today.

12.1 Correlations between inequality statistics

Table 12.1 provides the correlation matrix for five important inequality statistics used in this book. Note that statistics on the feminization and masculinization of specific occupations (such as those presented in Chapter 11) are not included, since we are interested here in broad, general patterns and not specific occupations.

The first and perhaps most noticeable aspect of the correlation matrix (table 12.1) is the extent to which the various inequality statistics are related to each other. Seven of the ten correlations reported in table 12.1 are significantly different from zero at the .05 level and five of the ten correlations are significantly different from zero at the .01 level.

Second, despite the high degree of association between these inequality statistics, *FDOM75 is generally independent of the other inequality statistics*. Three of the four insignificant relationships based on a .01 significance level involve FDOM75. Indeed, FDOM75 is significantly and very strongly related only to PFEM. These results imply that FDOM75 represents a unique dimension of occupational segregation by sex—one that is independent of the other inequality statistics with the exception of PFEM.

Third, *MDOM75 and TDOM75 are highly related* as they have a correlation coefficient of .87. This is hardly surprising as TDOM75's most important component is MDOM75.

Fourth, while both ID75 and PFEM are significantly related to the other three inequality statistics included in table 12.1, ID75 and PFEM are not

Table 12.1. Correlation matrix for inequality statistics, latest available year ($N = 41$)

	FDOM75	PFEM	MDOM75	TDOM75	ID75
FDOM75	1.00				
PFEM	.68**	1.00			
MDOM75	−.19	−.72**	1.00		
TDOM75	.22	−.46**	.87**	1.00	
ID75	.37*	−.10	.56**	.68**	1.00

Notes:
FDOM75 Percentage of the female non-agricultural labour force in a "female-dominated" occupation for an occupational classification with 75 non-agricultural occupations.
PFEM Percentage of the non-agricultural labour force which is female.
MDOM75 Percentage of the male non-agricultural labour force in a "male-dominated" occupation for an occupational classification with 75 non-agricultural occupations.
TDOM75 Percentage of the total non-agricultural labour force in a "gender-dominated" occupation for an occupational classification with 75 non-agricultural occupations. A gender-dominated occupation is defined as an occupation where at least 80 per cent of the workers are male or female.
ID75 Index of dissimilarity (ID) for an occupational classification with 75 non-agricultural occupations.
* Significant at .05 level.
** Significant at .01 level.
Source: Study data.

significantly related to each other. This is interesting, because it implies that (i) both ID75 and PFEM are good general measures of sex inequality in the labour market but at the same time that (ii) each measures a different dimension. Both of these conclusions make intuitive sense, since PFEM measures women's exclusion from the non-agricultural labour force while ID75 is a general measure of sex segregation for women who are in the non-agricultural labour force. On the other hand, it is a little surprising that PFEM and ID75 are not significantly related to each other, as one would expect that the social-economic-cultural biases which keep women out of the labour force would also work against them when they are in the labour force (but this result is consistent with the regression analysis reported in section 9.2).

12.2 Factor analysis and patterns of inequality statistics

In order to observe if these statistics represent different dimensions, we undertook a factor analysis (based on principal components) using four of these inequality statistics—ID75, FDOM75, MDOM75 and PFEM. TDOM75 was not included, because it is basically the sum of FDOM75 and MDOM75 (which is weighted by PFEM and 1-PFEM). In any case, MDOM75 and TDOM75 are highly correlated; and the factor analysis (unreported) when TDOM75 is also included turns out to be qualitatively quite similar to that reported on below.

Two factors are identified in the factor analysis (table 12.2). FDOM75 and PFEM have the largest factor loadings for factor 1; in addition, these two variables load much more strongly into factor 1 as compared to factor 2.

Table 12.2. Factor analysis of inequality statistics, done separately for all study countries and areas and OECD study countries, latest available year

Inequality statistics	Factor loadings			
	Factor 1		Factor 2	
	All (N = 41)	OECD (N = 17)	All (N = 41)	OECD (N = 17)
FDOM75	.49	.48	.24	.15
MDOM75	−.20	−.28	.44	.57
ID75	.19	.20	.57	.67
PFEM	.45	.45	−.13	−.07

Notes: For definitions of inequality statistics, see table 12.1.
Source: Study data.

MDOM75 and ID75 have the largest factor loadings for factor 2; in addition, these two variables load much more strongly into factor 2 as compared to factor 1.

The *first factor seems to represent the female side of the labour market—* the extent to which women are in the non-agricultural labour force together with the extent to which women workers are in a female-dominated occupation. *The second factor seems to represent the male side of the labour market—*the extent to which male workers are working in a male-dominated occupation—*together with the overall level of occupational segregation by sex for all those in the labour market.* These results are consistent with discussion in the previous section based on correlations where it was observed that (i) FDOM75 is generally independent of the other inequality statistics except PFEM and (ii) that while PFEM and ID75 are not significantly correlated with each other, both are good general measures.

Figure 12.1 plots national factors scores from the factor analysis reported on above. In this graph, each letter-point represents a country or area from a particular region: o indicates an OECD country, e indicates a Transition Economy country, m indicates a Middle Eastern or North African country, a indicates an Asian/Pacific country or area, and d indicates an Other

Figure 12.1.   Factor scores based on factor analysis of inequality statistics, all study countries and areas

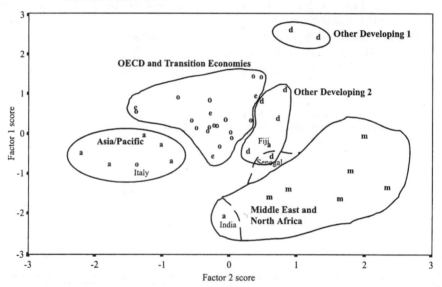

Notes: Letter indicates region of study country or area as follows: o: OECD, e: Transition Economies, m: Middle East and North Africa, a: Asia, d: Other Developing. Name of country indicated when it is located outside of its region. Freehand "circles" are drawn around groups of countries with similar factor scores. This is done for expositional purposes and some discretion is used (see text and footnotes). See notes for table 12.3.
Source: Based on results reported in table 12.2.

GENDER AND JOBS

Developing country/area. To assist readers, the name of certain countries is also indicated when the country is not near to other countries from its region. Notice that there is a very strong tendency for countries to cluster by region.

12.3   Regional patterns in inequality statistics

Since the above factor analysis, correlation matrix and figure indicate that **there are distinct regional patterns in how various inequality statistics relate to each other,** the following discussion proceeds on a region by region basis. Each region's pattern (as indicated by inequality statistics FDOM75, PFEM, ID75 and MDOM75) is presented in table 12.3 and discussed in this section.

Study countries in the Middle East and North Africa region are located in the bottom right-hand corner of figure 12.1. Women in these countries are disadvantaged both in terms of the extent to which women are in the

Table 12.3.   Stylized regional patterns in occupational segregation by sex based on four inequality statistics, latest available year ($N = 41$)

Region/subregion/ country	Factor 1[a]		Factor 2[b]	
	PFEM	FDOM75	ID75	MDOM75
1. Middle East and North Africa (+ Senegal)	Low	Low	High	High
1a. (+ possibly India)	(Low	Low	Low	High)
2. Asia (excluding India and Fiji) (+ Italy)	Mid	Low	Low	Low
3. OECD and Transition Economies	Mid-High	Mid	Mid	Mid
a. Europe and Australasia (− Italy and Scandinavia)	Mid-High	Mid	Mid	Mid
b. Scandinavia (+ Poland perhaps)	High	High	High	Mid
c. North America (+ Bulgaria perhaps)	High	High	Low	Low
4. Other Developing				
a. Other Developing 1[c]	Very High	Very High	High	High
b. Other Developing 2 (+ Fiji)	Mid-High	Mid-High	Mid-High	Mid-High

Notes: Levels of low, high and middle are used in a relative sense.
[a] Factor 1 appears to represent female side of labour market, as largest factor loadings are for FDOM75 and PFEM.
[b] Factor 2 appears to represent male side of labour market together with overall level of occupational segregation by sex, as largest factor loadings are for MDOM75 and ID75. [c] This group includes Ghana and Haiti (and possibly Angola). See table 12.1 for definition of inequality statistics PFEM, FDOM75, MDOM75 and ID75.
Source: Based on results of factor analysis reported in table 12.2.

non-agricultural labour force (PFEM) as well as in the extent to which those women who are working have a chance of being in a female-dominated occupation (FDOM75); this is factor 1. Countries in this region also have high scores on factor 2; both the overall level of occupational segregation by sex (ID75) as well as the extensiveness of male-dominated occupations (MDOM75) are relatively high. The only possible exception among study countries in the region to this distinct Middle Eastern and North African pattern might be Tunisia as it has a relatively high FDOM75 value—but this is probably a data artefact caused by the unusually high enumeration of many female spinners and weavers in the Tunisian census (who are reported to comprise approximately 44 per cent of Tunisia's non-agricultural labour force).

The only other study countries which have even a somewhat similar pattern to that found in the Middle East and North Africa are India and Senegal. It is interesting that both of these countries have socio-cultural milieus where public interaction between men and women is restricted for significant numbers of women; Senegal is largely a Muslim country, and many women in India are subject to purdah. While the various inequality statistics for Senegal are not as extreme as in the Middle East and North Africa region, Senegal appears to have the same general pattern, as it has relatively low values for PFEM and FDOM75[2] along with relatively high values for ID75 and MDOM75. India's pattern is similar to that in the Middle Eastern and North African region—except that India has a low overall level of occupational segregation by sex as measured by ID75. This combination of high MDOM75 and low ID75 is unique among our 41 study countries and areas as it is only found in India.

In summary, **Middle Eastern and North African countries have highly segmented labour markets based on sex, where male workers face little competition from women workers and where women workers are at a great disadvantage both in terms of getting jobs in the non-agricultural labour market as well as in having very few "female" occupations where working women are "sheltered" from male competition.**

The major East Asian study countries and areas (China, Japan, the Republic of Korea, Malaysia and Hong Kong) are located in the low-middle/left hand side of figure 12.1. They have relatively low overall levels of occupational segregation by sex for those in the non-agricultural labour force (ID75) and male workers have a relatively small segment of the non-agricultural labour force (MDOM75) "reserved" for them (factor 2). At the same time, the percentage of women working in female-dominated occupations (FDOM75) is relatively low while the female participation in the labour force (PFEM) has middle values (factor 1). The only other study country in the world which might fit this Asian pattern is Italy (although one needs to be cautious about Italy, since its FDOM75 and ID75 estimates include relatively large adjustment factors). In summary, **the pattern found** in **East Asian study countries and areas is one of relatively low levels of occupational segregation by sex—consisting of labour markets with relatively small male-dominated and female-dominated segments.**

The two Asia/Pacific study countries outside of East Asia have different patterns. Fiji's pattern is similar to that in the Other Developing region (see discussion below on this). India (as indicated above) has its own unique pattern; while similar to that found in the Middle Eastern and North African region (high FDOM75, high MDOM75, high ID75 and low PFEM), India has a low, rather than a high level of occupational segregation by sex for the non-agricultural labour force as a whole (indicated by India's relatively low ID75 value).

In the Other Developing region, there are mid to high values for both factors 1 and 2. Ghana and Haiti (and possibly Angola), however, have a qualitatively distinct pattern—as they have unusually high values for PFEM and FDOM75—in large part because Ghana and Haiti are the only two study countries where women comprise more than 50 per cent of the non-agricultural labour force. Such a situation occurs when there is a very large agricultural sector and more men than women work in agriculture (either because more women than men migrate to urban areas, as in Ghana and/or there is a high level of male migration to other countries, as in Haiti). This predominance of female non-agricultural workers does not mean, however, that women dominate positions of power and decision-making; indeed, the majority of working women in non-agricultural employment in these countries are in the informal sector—attested to by the fact that approximately 54 per cent of such women workers in Ghana are reported to be working proprietors in sales and 67 per cent of such working women in Haiti are reported to be salespersons, shop assistants or petty traders. In any case, one must remain somewhat cautious about drawing too strong a distinction between these two countries and our other study developing countries and areas, since data collection peculiarities regarding enumeration of women in the informal sector may help account for observed differences. In summary, the **Other Developing region tends to have relatively high levels of gender inequality in the labour market, with both relatively large male-dominated and female-dominated segments.** While inequality statistics in the Other Developing region are not always the highest among study countries and areas, they are never among the lowest.

OECD and Transition Economy countries are located in the middle of figure 12.1. They have average values for both factors 1 and 2. Values are average for the three inequality statistics measuring occupational segregation by sex for those in the non-agricultural labour force (FDOM75, MDOM75, ID75) and middle to high for women's participation in the labour force (PFEM). Basically, **OECD and Transition Economy countries tend to be rather average for the world in terms of their level and pattern of gender inequality in the labour market.**

12.4 OECD subregional patterns in inequality statistics

In order to help us observe if there are different results and/or patterns between OECD countries and subregions—differences which might be substantial when comparing countries within the OECD region but relatively small when comparing countries across the world—we did a factor analysis of the same four inequality statistics (FDOM75, MDOM75, ID75 and PFEM) for only OECD study countries. Results are reported in table 12.2 and figure 12.2. Also, in Appendix 12.1, the percentage of TDOM which is attributable to FDOM and MDOM is reported, as this also provides a simple—but insightful—way of understanding the somewhat independent influences FDOM and MDOM have on occupational segregation by sex.

Results for the factor analysis of OECD countries are very similar to those for all study countries and areas (table 12.2). Two factors with similar factor loadings are identified in each analysis. Again, factor 1 represents mainly the situation for women (as PFEM and FDOM75 have the largest factor loadings); and factor 2 again represents mainly the overall level of segregation by

Figure 12.2. Factor scores based on factor analysis of inequality statistics, OECD study countries

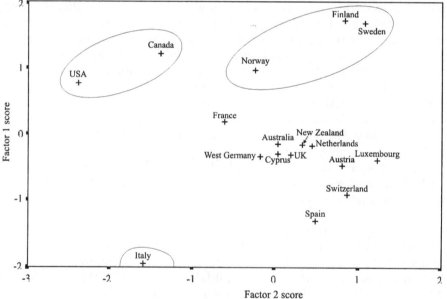

Note: Freehand "circles" are drawn around groups of countries with similar factor scores. This is done for expositional purposes and some discretion is used (see text and footnotes). See notes for table 12.3.
Source: Table 12.2.

sex as well as the male side of the labour market (as ID75 and MDOM75 have the largest factor loadings).

Figure 12.2 plots national factor scores based on the factor analysis of OECD study countries. **There are several distinct patterns among OECD study countries** (see table 12.3).

Scandinavian study countries (Finland, Norway and Sweden) represent one pattern. They have relatively high scores on both factor 1 and factor 2.[3] Women in Nordic countries have a relatively strong labour market position in the sense that (i) most adult women are labour force participants (with women workers comprising close to one-half of the non-agricultural labour force); and (ii) a relatively high percentage of the women workers are in a female-dominated occupation (just over one-half of women workers in Sweden and Finland) where they do not face much competition from men. At the same time, Scandinavian countries have relatively high overall levels of occupational segregation by sex (although MDOM75 is more or less average for the OECD region).

These results help shed some light on the distinctive nature of sex segregation in Scandinavia. *The relatively high level of sex segregation found in Scandinavian countries as measured by ID75 is largely attributable to a relatively high FDOM75.* Consequently, it is unclear whether or not the relatively high levels of occupational segregation by sex found in Scandinavian countries as compared to other OECD countries are worse or better for Scandinavian women. While it is clear that higher levels of occupational segregation and labour market segmentation based on sex are bad for economic efficiency and equality of opportunity, it is not clear if the existence of numerous and large female-dominated occupations is bad for women. This depends on the types of occupations women dominate—whether these are satisfactory occupations which are relatively well paying, have opportunities for advancement and are growing in importance. There does seem to be a reasonable outcome for Scandinavian women, since "women's" occupations in Scandinavia have reasonably good pay, attested to by the fact that women non-agricultural workers in Sweden receive about 90 per cent as much pay as men on average (table 2.2).

An important issue for those who might favour this Scandinavian "solution" (highly segregated labour markets comprised of separate but reasonably equal male and female segments) is that this "solution" may not be sustainable in the future in Scandinavia or transferable to other countries. For example, it may not be possible to institute or maintain the very low wage dispersion across occupations that is a hallmark of Scandinavian labour markets at present. It may not be possible to hire and retain the relatively large public sector employment (where there is greater gender equality) found in Scandinavian countries at present. It may not be possible to maintain the same generous social services (such as child care and social work) found in Scandinavian countries, something which both provides many reasonably well-paid female-dominated jobs and helps other working women to shoulder the double burden of their productive and reproductive roles. Consequently, it would be timely for policy-makers in Scandinavia to think about policies to help speed up the process of reducing occupational segregation by sex (see Part IV for analysis of recent downward trends in Scandinavia).

The two *North American countries* (Canada and the United States) appear to form a second distinct pattern within the OECD region—although we must be a little cautious on this since two of the inequality statistics for these countries (ID75 and FDOM75) are estimated with less precision than usual as they include relatively large adjustment factors. Both Canada and the United States have high scores on factor 1 and low scores on factor 2.[4] This is a *relatively favourable combination for women and for labour market efficiency,* since it represents relatively low overall levels of segregation by sex in the labour market along with a relatively large separate segment of "female" occupations, one that is roughly the same size as for "male" occupations.

Italy represents a third pattern within the OECD region—consisting of low scores on both factors 1 and 2. This is similar to the pattern found in the Asian study region, as noted in the previous section. There is a relatively low level of occupational segregation by sex for the non-agricultural labour force as a whole, along with relatively low female labour force participation rates and a relatively small number of female-dominated occupations.

The remainder of the OECD and Transition Economy countries are generally similar in that they tend to have fairly average values for the OECD region.

Notes

[1] There are also derivative inequality statistics based on these four types of statistics (e.g. what we called IDHALF described in section 9.3, which combines ID and the percentage of the non-agricultural labour force which is female). IDHALF, however, is highly correlated with MDOM75 and TDOM75, as it has correlation coefficients with them of 0.94 and 0.84 respectively.

[2] Senegal's FDOM75 value of 29 per cent is in a way an overestimate, since approximately 25 per cent of Senegalese working women are in female-dominated occupations where 80.0–82.5 per cent of the workers are women.

[3] Poland appears to have a similar pattern to that found in Scandinavia. The two main components of factor 1 are similarly high in Poland and Scandinavia (PFEM is 44.2 in Poland compared to 48.5 for Scandinavia; FDOM75 is 48.6 compared to 48.1). Regarding factor 2, the overall level of occupational segregation by sex is similarly high (ID75 is .592 in Poland as compared to .606) and the size of MDOM75 is somewhat on the high side (63.9 in Poland as compared to 55.0 in Scandinavia).

[4] Bulgaria appears to have a somewhat similar pattern to that found in North America. For factor 1, both the female share of the non-agricultural labour force (45.6 for Bulgaria compared to 46.2 for North America) and the size of FDOM75 are relatively high (19.8, which has a large downward bias due to a clustering of large occupations having between 77.5 and 79.9 per cent female, for Bulgaria compared to 33.2 for North America). For factor 2, both ID75 (.541 compared to .502) and MDOM75 (29.3 compared to 42.8) are relatively low in both Bulgaria and North America.

Appendix 12.1. Extent to which gender-dominated occupations are comprised of male-dominated or female-dominated occupations

The factor analysis in the main text of this chapter indicated that there are two distinct factors or groups of inequality statistics. Factor 1 is mainly associated with the female side of the labour market, mainly the female share of non-agricultural employment (PFEM) and the extensiveness of female-dominated occupations (FDOM75). Factor 2 is mainly associated with an overall index of occupational segregation by sex (ID75) and the extensiveness of male-dominated occupations (MDOM75). Also, the correlation analysis of inequality statistics indicates that FDOM75 is generally statistically independent of other inequality statistics.

Both of these analyses imply that the percentage of the total non-agricultural labour force in a gender-dominated occupation (TDOM) attributable to FDOM should provide insight into differences across countries in occupational segregation by sex. This statistic should help represent, in part at least, somewhat independent phenomena represented by FDOM.

Table 12.4 provides data on the percentage of TDOM which is attributable to FDOM and MDOM, while table 12.5 divides study countries and areas into three relative groups (low, middle, high) based on FDOM's contribution to TDOM. Table 12.6, then, provides averages and standard deviations for study regions and OECD subregions.

First, notice that *most of the occupational segregation by sex in the world as measured by TDOM consists of men working in a male-dominated occupation* (figure 12.3). On average, approximately 74 per cent of TDOM is contributed by MDOM among study countries and areas.[1]

Second, *only a very small percentage of TDOM consists of men and women working in an occupation where the other sex dominates* (only 7 per cent on average for the world as a whole, figure 12.3), and there is little variation across countries (with a standard deviation of only 2.0, table 12.6).

Third, there is a *high degree of variation across study countries in FDOM's contribution to TDOM*. This is reflected in the fact that FDOM's mean value is only slightly greater than (approximately 1.2 times) its standard deviation.

Fourth, and in contrast to FDOM's contribution to TDOM, *MDOM's contribution displays relatively little variation across countries,* as its mean value is over four times its standard deviation (table 12.6).

Fifth, there is a *high degree of similarity in FDOM's contribution to TDOM within most study regions and OECD subregions* (excluding the heterogeneous OD region which displays considerable variation). Thus, the range of values is just 0–11 per cent for the ME region (and 0–2 per cent excluding Tunisia); 0–16 per cent for Asia/Pacific; 13–21 per cent for OECD Central Europe; 14–18 per cent for other English-speaking; 22–24 per cent for

Figure 12.3.   Percentage contributions made to TDOM by FDOM, latest available year, by region

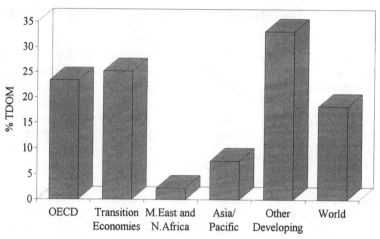

Source: Table 12.4.

Western Europe; 7–21 per cent for OECD Southern Europe; 33–39 per cent for OECD North America; 35–45 per cent for Scandinavia; and 6-34 per cent for TE (and 27–34 per cent excluding former Yugoslavia).

Sixth, *the large differences across regions* (figure 12.3 and tables 12.4–12.6) *and OECD subregions* (figure 12.4 and tables 12.5-12.6) in the percentage of TDOM attributable to FDOM are *similar to those observed in the factor analysis* shown in table 12.2 and figures 12.1–12.2—but less complicated. Thus, North America and Scandinavia, along with Bulgaria and Poland, form one distinct grouping as they are the only OECD and TE study countries where the percentage of TDOM attributable to FDOM exceeds 30 per cent; these same countries form two distinct OECD groups of countries according to the factor analysis of OECD data (see figure 12.2).

In terms of regional differences between results shown in tables 12.4–12.6 compared to the factor analysis in table 12.2, here Asia is similar to the Middle East and North Africa region in that most study countries in these regions have low values for FDOM's contribution to TDOM but these two regions have quite different patterns according to the factor analysis. A second noticeable difference is that four developing countries (Haiti, Ghana, Costa Rica and Angola) have high percentage contributions from FDOM (just as North America and Scandinavia), but a different pattern of occupational segregation by sex according to the factor analysis.

In summary, **FDOM's contribution to TDOM provides interesting insights into differences across countries in occupational segregation by sex— results which are similar to, but less complex in terms of groupings of countries than results from the factor analysis discussed in the main body of this chapter.**

Table 12.4. Percentage contributions to TDOM made by MDOM and FDOM, latest available year, by region

Region/country/area	% female in non-ag. LF (PFEM)	% TDOM from[a] FDOM	MDOM	Minority sex
OECD				
Australia	41.7	17.1	75.7	7.2
Austria	40.8	13.0	79.8	7.2
Canada	45.9	38.9	52.8	8.3
Cyprus	37.3	20.6	74.3	5.1
Finland	49.1	45.4	47.6	7.0
France	42.6	22.3	69.3	8.4
Germany (West)	41.7	20.7	72.3	7.0
Italy	32.6	7.1	84.0	9.0
Luxembourg	35.9	23.1	70.5	6.4
Netherlands	39.1	23.8	69.7	6.5
New Zealand	42.3	17.6	71.3	11.1
Norway	47.1	34.7	57.7	7.7
Spain	32.7	9.7	84.9	5.4
Sweden	49.2	43.0	47.1	9.8
Switzerland	36.7	13.0	81.1	6.0
United Kingdom	44.0	14.0	78.4	7.6
United States	46.5	33.5	56.1	10.4
Average (unweighted)	**41.5**	**23.4**	**69.0**	**7.6**
Transition Economies				
Bulgaria	45.6	33.4	59.0	7.6
Hungary	45.6	27.2	64.7	8.1
Poland	44.2	34.4	57.2	8.4
Former Yugoslavia	33.3	5.9	86.9	7.2
Average (unweighted)	**42.2**	**25.2**	**66.9**	**7.8**
Middle East and North Africa				
Bahrain	16.9	0.0	95.7	4.3
Egypt	13.6	0.0	95.9	4.1
Iran, Islamic Republic of	10.5	0.0	96.5	3.5
Jordan	8.1	0.6	97.9	1.5
Kuwait	20.0	2.0	94.5	3.5
Tunisia	19.6	11.0	82.6	6.4
Average (unweighted)	**14.8**	**2.3**	**93.9**	**3.9**
Asia/Pacific				
China	35.7	11.2	80.2	8.6
Fiji	27.1	11.7	83.2	5.2
Hong Kong	37.9	16.2	76.5	7.3
India	12.1	0.0	93.7	6.3
Japan	39.3	8.0	84.0	8.0

Table 12.4.   (contd.)

Region/country/area	% female in non-ag. LF	% TDOM from[a]		
	(PFEM)	FDOM	MDOM	Minority sex
Asia/Pacific				
Republic of Korea	30.0	0.0	96.4	3.6
Malaysia	28.2	6.1	87.2	6.7
Average (unweighted)	**30.1**	**7.6**	**85.9**	**6.5**
Other Developing				
Angola	41.3	36.4	60.3	3.2
Costa Rica	37.1	30.9	61.4	7.7
Ghana	57.6	58.8	33.8	7.4
Haiti	65.2	66.7	27.4	5.9
Mauritius	31.1	8.0	85.8	6.3
Netherlands Antilles	38.5	22.1	73.1	4.8
Senegal	22.8	9.3	82.6	8.1
Average (unweighted)	**41.9**	**33.2**	**60.6**	**6.2**

Notes: [a] Row percentages sums to 100 except for possible rounding errors. Percentages are based on reported FDOM (female workers in female-dominated occupations), MDOM (male workers in male-dominated occupations) and minority sex (workers in occupations where the other sex is dominant). Rough adjustments are made in percentages to take into account the degree of disaggregation in national occupational classification. This is done by using FDOM75/FDOM and MDOM75/MDOM ratios as adjustment factors. Regional averages are based on an unweighted average of national values. Female-dominated and male-dominated occupations are defined as occupations where at least 80 per cent of workers are female or male respectively.
Source: Study data.

Figure 12.4.   Percentage contributions made to TDOM by FDOM, latest available year, by OECD subregion

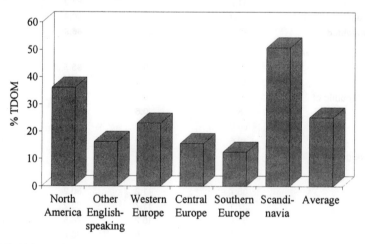

Source: Table 12.6.

Table 12.5. Distribution of countries/areas by relative level (low, middle, high) based on percentage contribution to TDOM made by FDOM, latest available year, by region

Region	<10.0% of TDOM from FDOM		10.0–24.9% of TDOM to FDOM		>25.0% of TDOM from FDCM	
	No.	Countries/areas	No.	Countries/areas	No.	Countries/areas
OECD	2	Italy (7.1) Spain (9.7)	10	Switzerland (13.0) Austria (13.0) United Kingdom (14.0) Australia (17.1) New Zealand (17.6) Cyprus (20.6) West Germany (20.7) France (22.3) Luxembourg (23.1) Netherlands (23.8)	5	United States (33.5) Norway (34.7) Canada (38.9) Sweden (43.0) Finland (45.4)
Transition Economies	1	Former Yugoslavia (5.9)	0		3	Hungary (27.2) Bulgaria (33.4) Poland (34.4)
Middle East and North Africa	5	Bahrain (0.0) Egypt (0.0) Iran, Islamic Rep. of (0.0) Jordan (0.6) Kuwait (2.0)	1	Tunisia (11.0)		
Asia/Pacific	4	India (0.0) Rep. of Korea (0.0) Malaysia (6.1) Japan (8.0)	3	China (11.2) Fiji (11.7) Hong Kong (16.2)	0	

Table 12.5. (contd.)

Region	<10.0% of TDOM from FDOM			10.0–24.9% of TDOM to FDOM			>25.0% of TDOM from FDOM		
	No.	Countries/areas		No.	Countries/areas		No.	Countries/areas	
Other Developing	2	Mauritius	(8.0)	1	Netherlands Antilles	(22.1)	4	Costa Rica	(30.9)
		Senegal	(9.3)					Angola	(36.4)
								Ghana	(58.8)
								Haiti	(66.7)

Note: "Round numbers" (e.g. 10 and 25) chosen as cut-off points to define relatively low, middle and high groupings which would result in roughly equal numbers of countries in each grouping.
Source: Based on national values in table 12.4.

Table 12.6. Regional and subregional means and standard deviations for percentage contributions to TDOM made by FDOM and MDOM, latest available year, by region

Regions/subregions	% from FDOM		% from MDOM		% from minority sex	
	Mean	Std. Deviation	Mean	Std. Deviation	Mean	Std. Deviation
OECD	23.4	11.7	69.0	12.3	7.6	1.7
N. America	36.2	3.8	54.5	2.4	9.4	1.5
Other English-speaking	16.2	1.9	75.2	3.6	8.6	2.2
W. Europe	23.1	0.7	69.8	0.6	7.1	1.1
C. Europe	15.6	4.5	77.7	4.7	6.7	0.7
S. Europe	12.5	7.2	81.1	5.9	6.5	2.2
Scandinavia	50.8	6.0	41.0	5.6	8.2	1.5
Transition Economies	25.2	13.3	66.9	13.7	7.8	0.5
Middle East and North Africa	2.3	4.4	93.9	5.6	3.9	1.6
Asia/Pacific	7.6	6.1	85.9	7.1	6.5	1.7
Other Developing	33.2	22.8	60.6	22.7	6.2	1.8
Average (overall)	**19.4**	**16.3**	**73.9**	**17.2**	**6.7**	**2.0**

Note: Regional and subregional averages based on unweighted average of national values.
Source: Based on data in Appendix table 12.4.

Note

^{1} TDOM can be more or less defined as the weighted average of the percentage of females and the percentage of males working in gender-dominated occupations, with the proportion of the female non-agricultural labour force (PFEM) and the male non-agricultural labour force (1.0-PFEM) as weights:

TDOM = (FDOM + percentage of females in male-dominated occupations) * (PFEM)

   + (MDOM + percentage of males in female-dominated occupations)

   * (1.0 − PFEM)

Rearranging terms:

TDOM = [FDOM * PFEM] + [MDOM * (1.0-PFEM)]

   + [(percentage of males in female-dominated occupations) * (1.0 − PFEM)

   + (percentage of females in male-dominated occupations) * PFEM]

The first term in the above equation indicates the contribution which FDOM makes to TDOM; the second term indicates the contribution made by MDOM; and the third term indicates the contribution made by males and females who work in an occupation which is dominated by the other sex.

This equation for TDOM does not exactly apply to TDOM75, since TDOM75 embodies an adjustment factor. Since, as shown in Chapter 6, FDOM is more sensitive to disaggregation in the occupational data as compared to MDOM, the size of the contribution to TDOM of FDOM relative to MDOM is in part a function of the level of aggregation in the national occupational data. This is taken into account in a rough sense by using the ratios FDOM75/FDOM and MDOM75/MDOM as adjustment factors.

OCCUPATIONAL SEGREGATION BY SEX AROUND THE WORLD—CHANGES IN PAST TWO DECADES

Part III analysed differences in occupational segregation by sex across the world for a recent year, generally around 1990. Part IV analyses recent changes in occupational segregation by sex for the 1970–1990 period.[1] The 32 study countries and areas included here form a reasonably good cross-section of our study set, and of countries in the world. Included are 16 of our 17 OECD study countries, all 4 of our Transition Economy study countries, 5 of our 6 Middle East and North African study countries, 4 of our 7 Asia/Pacific study countries or areas and 3 of our 7 Other Developing study countries/areas.[2]

The national data for 27 of the 32 study economies analysed in this chapter are comparable in the sense that the number of occupations classified are the same, or almost the same, in each data year.[3] For the five study countries where the number of occupations classified differ substantially in different data years, it is our feeling that this reduced comparability should not cause a major difficulty, in part because these national occupational classifications are at a relatively high level of aggregation where inequality statistics tend to be fairly insensitive to further disaggregation, and in part because approximate adjustments are made for these five countries in order to increase data comparability over time.[4]

Analysis in the present Part IV on changes over the past two decades in occupational segregation by sex proceeds in a similar fashion to the analysis in Part III. Analysis begins with inequality indices in Chapter 13 (such as ID, the index of dissimilarity). It continues with the extent to which the non-agricultural labour force is divided into gender-dominated occupations (Chapter 14), and finishes with the extent to which 17 specific typically "male" and "female" occupations are feminized (Chapter 15). Throughout this analysis, data are presented for individual countries as well as for regions and OECD sub-regions.[5]

As always, readers need to keep in mind that national data are of differing quality and comparability over time—due to factors such as differences over time in data collection methods and techniques, coding quality and instructions, comparability of occupational classifications, as well as the changing nature of occupations with the same title. Readers should also note that the following analysis of changes over time is based on the implicit assumption that the degree of disaggregation in a study country's occupational classification has no effect on observed *changes* in inequality statistics, that is, observed changes are utilized regardless of whether national data are classified at the two-digit or three-digit level. Evidence in Chapter 7 generally supports this assumption, since all national data are disaggregated to at least the two-digit level.[6,7]

Notes

[1] Fifteen study countries or areas have data for three study years, i.e. around 1970, 1980 and 1990; 17 study countries or areas have data for two years. There is some regional difference here, as OECD countries comprise 10 of the 15 study countries with data for three years. Readers are referred to Chapter 5 for details.

[2] Subsequent to completion of the cross-section analysis in Part III, additional data became available for two important study countries. More recent data became available for China (for 1990 whereas analysis in Part III uses data for 1982). Also, considerably more disaggregated data became available for Sweden (261 occupations for 1970, 1980 and 1990 whereas analysis in Part III uses data for only 49 occupations for 1990). These "newer" data are not incorporated into the empirical analyses in Part III because of the amount of work this would have involved. These newer data, however, are used in the present part of the book, because the analysis of recent changes had not yet been completed. It should be noted that inequality statistics based on these newer data for China and Sweden are not qualitatively different from those reported in Part III. China still has an unusually low level of occupational segregation by sex as measured by the index of dissimilarity (still the lowest observed for our 41 countries or areas, although somewhat higher in 1990 as compared to 1982); and Sweden still has a relatively high level of occupational segregation by sex for an OECD country (although the adjusted ID75 value for 1990 is somewhat lower based on the more disaggregated data). When appropriate, we have added footnotes in earlier chapters to indicate these differences.

[3] In 12 study countries, the original data supplied by the national statistical agency are fully comparable over time. In another eight countries, we adjusted ("mapped") the national data so that they have the same occupational classification in each data year (readers are referred to Chapter 4 where this mapping procedure is explained). In seven other study countries and areas, the number of occupations classified are almost the same in each data year. For example, the United States has 455, 460 and 461 occupations for 1970, 1980 and 1990 respectively. The United Kingdom has 502 and 509 occupations for 1981 and 1990 respectively. Based on regression results relating the sensitivity of ID to the number of occupations classified (see Chapter 6), this would imply an upward bias in ID75 over time in both the United States and United Kingdom of less than .001. Also, for Bulgaria (42, 43 occupations); China (277 and 270 occupations); Hong Kong (43, 46 and 45 occupations); Senegal (45 and 46 occupations); and Finland (274, 274 and 264 occupations), there are only small differences across years in the number of occupations classified. For these seven countries or areas, this aspect of non-comparability over time is ignored in Part IV.

[4] The five study countries where the number of occupations differs substantially (by more than 5 percent across reporting years) are: Australia (61, 64 and 279 occupations), Cyprus (243 and 376 occupations), Poland (270 and 361 occupations), Kuwait (236 and 268 occupations) and Bahrain (58, 58 and 86 occupations). Below, the likely upward bias over time in ID75 due to increased disaggregation in the occupational data is estimated by using regression results from equations in Chapter 6 in the manner described in Chapter 6 (although the estimate for Australia has been adjusted to take into account information from other published sources, which indicate that ID is relatively insensitive in Australia to disaggregation from 71 to 371 occupations). The following estimates of upward bias over time in the observed ID75 (due to increased disaggregation of the occupational data) are used to adjusted observed changes over time in ID75 values for these countries. A similar exercise was followed for adjusting statistics on changes in the percentage of workers who are segregated into gender-dominated

occupations (FDOM75, MDOM75, TDOM75), and this is indicated in a subsequent footnote in Chapter 14.

	1970s	1980s
Australia	.0004	.0338
Cyprus	x	.0217
Poland	x	.0060
Bahrain	.0000	.0240
Kuwait	x	.0077

[5] To increase comparability across countries, all observed national changes are converted into changes for an equivalent ten-year period. For example, if a country has data for 1982 and 1990 (as does China), then all observed changes for such a country would be multiplied by 1.25 (i.e. 10/8) to account for the fact that changes occurred over 8 years rather than over ten years. There are four country examples where there are less than 8 years in the 1970s or the 1980s. It is only four years for West Germany in the 1970s (1976–1980); five years for New Zealand in the 1980s (1981–1986) and Spain in the 1970s (1975–1980); and six years for Netherlands in the 1970s (1973–1979). Interested readers are referred to Chapter 5 for the data years for each country.

[6] Still, it is possible for there to be a relationship between the observed change in an inequality statistic (e.g. ID) and the number of occupations classified, if for no other reason than that the fact that inequality statistics (such as ID) tend to be higher *ceteris paribus* when the number of occupations classified is higher. As a result, the absolute size of changes in inequality statistics such as ID might be greater the higher is ID itself (perhaps simply because there is greater scope for this fall). For example, if ID75 were .58 on average (as it is roughly, see Chapter 9) and ID based on 265 non-agricultural occupations were about .07 higher (as it is roughly, see Chapter 7), then ID based on typical three-digit data might be approximately 12 per cent higher than ID based on typical two-digit data (i.e. about .65/.58). If this order of magnitude were also found for changes over time, this would imply an average overestimation of change per decade in ID75 of about .003 (i.e. 0.12 times −.025, the approximate average decade change, see Chapter 13) for countries with three-digit data as compared to countries with typical two-digit data. Since the existence of such a bias is uncertain, no adjustment for this is made in any of the text or tables contained in Part IV.

[7] Strictly speaking, the evidence on changes for indices in Chapter 13, gender-dominated occupations in Chapter 14 and important specific "female" occupations in Chapter 15 relate to observed national changes which are not adjusted for the level of disaggregation in the national occupational classification. To reduce confusion with discussion in Part III (which used adjusted inequality statistics), however, discussion in Part IV also generally refers to adjusted inequality statistics such as ID75, FDOM75, and MDOM75. Note that as the number of occupations classified in each study country/area is the same at the beginning and at the end of each time period (or adjusted for when different, see footnote 4 above), the size of the adjustment to 75 non-agricultural occupations for a study country can not affect observed national change—unless the type of adjustment factor used (see Appendices 9.1 and 10.1) should have differed for the beginning and end of the time period being observed. To get an idea of whether or not this latter phenomenon could be important, we looked at results in Chapter 13 for study countries with a clear change in ID for the 1970s or 1980s and an adjustment to ID75 greater than .01 (see Appendix 9.1)—in order to get a rough idea of how important this phenomenon could have been. The only countries where a possible change in adjustment factor might have caused a possible bias greater than .005 in ID75 change over a decade were Bahrain 1980s (a possible bias of around −.006) and the three Scandinavian countries (possible biases of about −.006 for Norway, −.007 for Finland and −.018 for Sweden per decade).

RECENT CHANGES IN OCCUPATIONAL SEGREGATION BY SEX BASED ON INEQUALITY INDICES

13

13.1 Recent changes in occupational segregation by sex as measured by the adjusted index of dissimilarity (ID75)[1]

Table 13.1 and figures 13.1 and 13.2 present changes in national ID75 values for the 1970s and the 1980s. Table 13.2 summarizes these changes according to region and OECD subregion. **Occupational segregation by sex in the world has very clearly decreased in recent decades.** This is true for the 1980s as well as the 1970s. On average, *ID75 has been decreasing by about .02 to .03 per country per decade around the world.* This average decrease is quite sizeable for a ten-year period, especially in light of the fact that many workers remain in the same occupation for long periods of time (which means that measures of occupational segregation such as those used in this book are not prone to major changes over relatively short periods of time).

There are very few country examples in the past two decades where ID75 clearly increased over a roughly ten-year period.[2] During the 1970s and 1980s, only approximately 10 per cent of study countries (2 in the 1970s and 3 in the 1980s) seemed to have experienced a clear increase in ID75. In contrast, approximately 60 per cent displayed a clear decrease in ID75 in both the 1970s and the 1980s (12 in the 1970s and 17 in the 1980s). A similar result is observed for the 15 study economies with data for both decades, as only one of these (Hong Kong) displayed a clear increase in ID75 over these two decades, whereas 10 of these countries displayed a clear decrease.

There are, however, important regional and subregional differences in recent ID trends. These are so marked in fact that the general conclusion noted above of decreasing occupational segregation by sex around the world is misleading, as **this decrease in ID75 is *not* observed in all study regions or all OECD subregions.**[3] This uneven picture of progress in reducing occupational segregation is described below.

Asia stands out as the region with the worst record as regards recent changes in ID75 (figures 13.3, 13.4 and 13.5). Excluding Fiji (which as noted in previous chapters is more similar to countries in our Other Developing region in terms of occupational segregation by sex than the highly populated

Table 13.1. Change in ID75 for the 1970s and 1980s, by region and OECD subregion[a]

Region/subregion/country/area	Change in ID75[b,c,d,e]	
	1970s	1980s
OECD		
North America[f]		
United States	−.085	−.041
Other English-speaking		
Australia	−.042	−.050
New Zealand		−.048
United Kingdom		−.051
Average (unweighted)		**−.050**
Scandinavia		
Finland	−.021	−.041
Norway	−.025	−.073
Sweden	−.044	−.047
Average (unweighted)	**−.030**	**−.054**
Western Europe		
France		−.037
Luxembourg	−.089	−.074
Netherlands	−.029	−.060
Average (unweighted)	**−.059**	**−.057**
Southern Europe		
Cyprus		.004
Italy	−.041	
Spain	.025	−.001
Average (unweighted)	**−.008**	**.002**
Central Europe		
Austria	.051	−.011
Germany (West)	−.043	−.005
Switzerland	−.013	
Average (unweighted)	**−.002**	**−.008**
OECD average (unweighted)	**−.030**	**−.038**
Transition Economies		
Bulgaria		−.033
Hungary		−.031
Poland		.008
Former Yugoslavia	−.005	
Average (unweighted)		**−.018**
Middle East & North Africa		
Bahrain	−.022	−.091
Egypt		.042
Jordan	−.013	

Table 13.1. (contd.)

Region/subregion/country/area	Change in ID75[b,c,d,e]	
	1970s	1980s
Kuwait		−.009
Tunisia		−.042[d]
Average (unweighted)	**−.017**	**−.025**
Asia/Pacific		
China		.038
Fiji		−.046
Hong Kong	.018	.068
Japan	.003	.000
Average (unweighted)	**.010**	**.015**
Other Developing		
Costa Rica	−.029	−.005
Mauritius	−.057	−.033
Senegal		−.056[d]
Average (unweighted)	**−.043**	**−.029**
Overall Average (unweighted)	**−.024**	**−.026**

Notes: [a] Table includes all study countries and areas which have data for two or more years (for approximately 1970 and 1980; or for 1980 and 1990; or for 1970, 1980 and 1990). [b] Observed change for five countries is adjusted in order to take into consideration substantially greater number of occupations classified at the end of the period (and therefore higher ID due to this greater disaggregation in later year). The following adjustments are subtracted from the observed changes for 1980s for Australia (.034), Cyprus (.022), Poland (.006), Bahrain (.024) and Kuwait (.008) to obtain the changes reported in this table. For other countries, no such adjustments are required because the number of occupations classified is the same in the beginning and at the end of each time period. [c] Observed changes adjusted so as to represent change for an equivalent ten-year period by taking into consideration that the time periods over which national changes are observed are not always ten years (see Chapter 4). [d] Considerable judgement was required to obtain comparable occupational classifications for the two data years for two countries (Senegal and Tunisia) where the occupational classification changed from ISCO-68 to a national classification. Therefore, trend data for these countries must be treated with considerable caution. [e] Regional and subregional averages are unweighted averages of national values. An average is not reported when data are available for only one country in a region (or OECD subregion) for a particular time period, with the exception of North America. [f] In Canada, ID fell by −.063 based on data for about 300 occupations between 1971 and 1981 according to Fox and Fox (1987).
Source: Study data.

countries of Asia), there are no Asian examples where ID75 clearly decreased in the 1970s or 1980s. Of the three large Asian economies with time series data, occupational segregation by sex clearly increased in Hong Kong and China in the 1980s, and there was basically no change in Hong Kong in the 1970s or in Japan in the 1970s or 1980s.

Evidence on recent changes in occupational segregation by sex in the Middle East and North Africa region is inconclusive. While the

Figure 13.1. Change in ID75 by country or area, for the 1970s

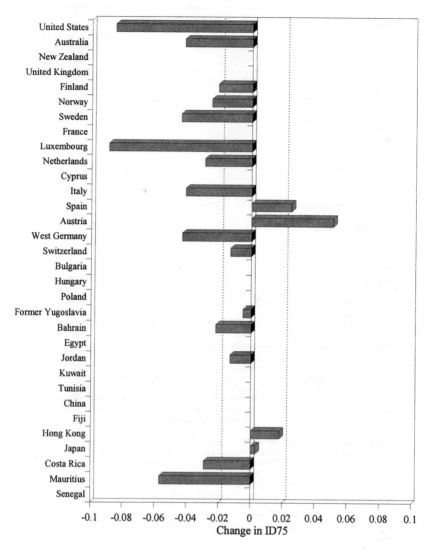

Notes: Dotted vertical line is drawn at +0.02 and −0.02 to help indicate clear changes (i.e. changes greater than +0.02 or −0.02).

Change is adjusted to be for a ten-year equivalent period. See table 4.1 for the exact data years for each country/area. Countries and areas arranged by region and for OECD countries by subregion.
Source: Table 13.1.

average change in ID75 for the region reported in tables 13.1 and 13.2 indicates a decrease in occupational segregation by sex for the region, closer examination of the national data leads to an inconclusive interpretation. Indeed, the only clear national decreases observed in the region are for

GENDER AND JOBS

Figure 13.2. Change in ID75 by country or area, for the 1980s

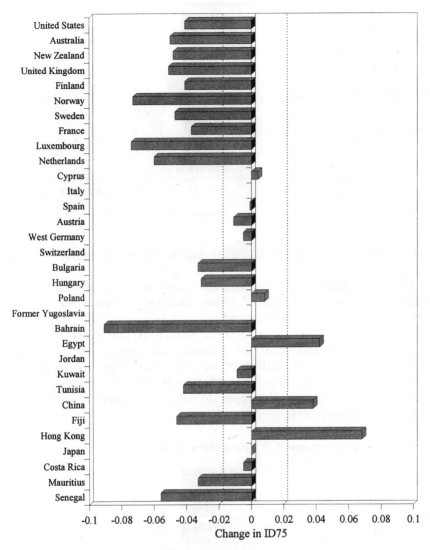

Notes: Dotted vertical line is drawn at +0.02 and −0.02 to help indicate clear changes (i.e. changes greater than +0.02 or −0.02)
Change is adjusted to be for a ten-year equivalent period. See table 4.1 for exact data years.
Countries and areas arranged by region and for OECD countries by subregion.
Source: Table 13.1.

Bahrain for both the 1970s and 1980s and for Tunisia for the 1980s (although Tunisia's data are less comparable over time than those for other countries). Analysis in subsequent chapters reinforces the interpretation that the *integration of male and female workers within occupations has not changed*

Figure 13.3.   Change in average ID75 for the 1970s, by region

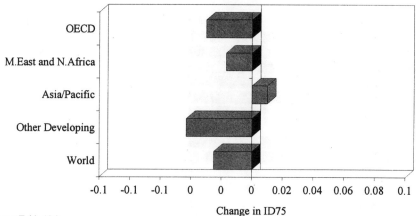

Change in ID75

Source: Table 13.2.

substantially throughout the Middle East and North Africa region in the past two decades.

There is evidence that occupational segregation by sex has recently decreased in our small sample of Other Developing countries with time series data (Mauritius, Costa Rica and Senegal as well as Fiji). It seems that women in small countries such as Fiji, Mauritius and Costa Rica have benefited in terms of reductions in occupational segregation by sex from export-oriented policies. Whether or not this reduction in occupational segregation by sex has translated into improvements in the relative pay of women as compared to men is a separate issue that deserves study and the attention of policy-makers.

Figure 13.4.   Change in average ID75 for the 1980s, by region

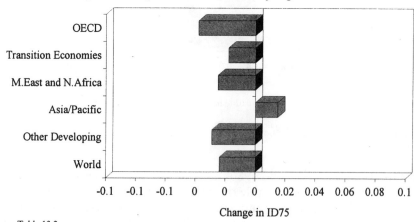

Change in ID75

Source: Table 13.2.

Figure 13.5. Average ID75 for 1970, 1980 and 1990, by region

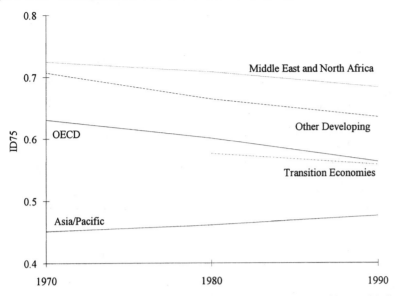

Notes: For expositional purposes, regional values for 1970, 1980 and 1990 are connected by a straight line.
Regional average is not indicated for 1970 for Transition Economies since data are available for only one study country in the region for change in the 1970s.
See notes for table 13.3.
Source: Table 13.3.

Among OECD subregions, Central Europe and Southern Europe have the worst records recently (figure 13.6–13.7; tables 13.1–13.3). On average, ID75 values are more or less unchanged in these OECD subregions for both the 1970s and the 1980s. Furthermore, all seven examples among OECD

Figure 13.6. Change in average ID75 for the 1970s and 1980s, by OECD subregion

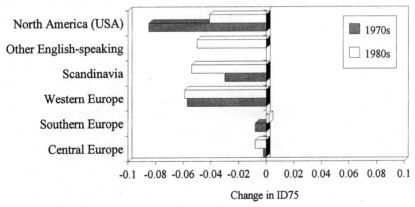

Note: 'Other English-speaking' excluded for 1970s as only one country value is available.
Source: Table 13.2.

Figure 13.7. Average ID75 for 1970, 1980 and 1990, by OECD subregion

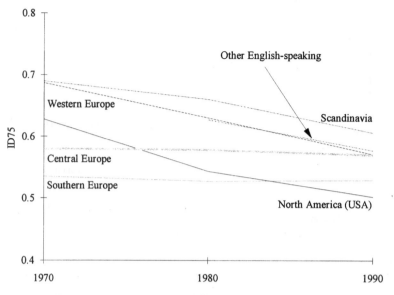

Notes: See notes for figure 13.5.
In interpreting figure 13.7, readers need to keep in mind that OECD subregions had quite different experiences in the 1970 to 1990 period as regards the reasons for changes in ID75 (see figures 13.10 and 13.11). While most of the observed decrease in ID75 for Scandinavia and North America is due to an increased integration of men and women within occupations, over one-half of the observed decrease in ID75 in Western Europe is due to shifts in the occupational structure of the labour market.
Source: Table 13.3.

countries of either no change or a clear increase in ID75 in the 1970s or in the 1980s are from our Southern European or Central European OECD subregions. It is particularly worth noting that both Austria and Spain had a large increase in ID75 in the 1970s and are the only two non-Asian study countries with data for the entire two decades where ID75 clearly increased over this period.

In contrast, ID75 decreased substantially in all the other OECD study subregions in both the 1970s and 1980s—with the average change in these subregions always greater than −.04 per ten-year period.[4] Indeed, ID75 has fallen so dramatically over the past two decades in OECD study countries outside of our Southern and Central Europe OECD subregions according to our estimates, that the level of occupational segregation by sex among OECD countries in 1970 had been fairly similar to that found today in the Other Developing study region (table 13.3 and figure 13.5). Thus, ID75 for around 1970 (estimated by adding average changes for 1970s and 1980s to average ID75 for latest available year) is estimated to have been approximately: .53 in North America (based on trend data), .67 in Other English-speaking countries (United Kingdom, New Zealand, Australia), and .69 in

GENDER AND JOBS

Table 13.2. Trends in ID75 for the 1970s and 1980s, by region and OECD subregion

Region/subregion	1970s				1980s			
	INC	DEC	Neutral[a]	Average change[b]	INC	DEC	Neutral[a]	Average change[b]
OECD	2	9	1	-.030	0	10	4	-.038
North America (United States)	0	1	0	-.085	0	1	0	-.041
Scandinavia	0	3	0	-.030	0	3	0	-.054
Other English-speaking	0	1	0	–	0	3	0	-.050
Western Europe	0	2	0	-.059	0	3	0	-.057
Southern Europe	1	1	0	-.008	0	0	2	+.002
Central Europe	1	1	1	-.002	0	0	2	-.008
Transition Economies	0	0	1	–	0	2	1	-.018
Middle East and North Africa	0	1	1	-.017	1	2	1	-.024
Asia/Pacific	0	0	2	-.010	2	1	1	-.015
Other Developing	0	2	0	-.043	0	2	1	-.029
Total	**2**	**12**	**5**	**-.024**	**3**	**17**	**8**	**-.026**

Notes: [a] Neutral (i.e. no clear trend) is defined as a change between −.02 and +.02 over an equivalent ten-year period. [b] Average change is the unweighted average of countries in the region or OECD subregion. The regional or OECD subregional average is not reported when data are available for only one country in the region or OECD subregion for a particular time period (except for North America).
Source: Table 13.1.

Table 13.3.   Estimated average adjusted ID (i.e. ID75) for approximately 1970, 1980 and 1990, by region and OECD subregion

Region/subregion	ID75[a,b]		
	1970	1980	1990
OECD	.631	.601	.563
North America (United States)	.628	.543	.502
Other English-speaking	–	.627	.577
Scandinavia	.690	.660	.606
Western Europe	.687	.630	.571
Southern Europe	.535	.527	.529
Central Europe	.580	.578	.570
Transition Economies	–	.576	.558
Middle East and North Africa	.725	.708	.683
Asia/Pacific	.451	.461	.476
Other Developing	.707	.664	.635
World	**.627**	**.603**	**.577**

Notes: [a] ID75 values are based on regional and OECD subregional averages. The 1990 values are drawn from tables 9.1 and 9.3 in Chapter 9 and are in fact unweighted averages of national values for latest available year. The 1980 values are estimated by subtracting from 1990 values in last column the average change for the region or OECD subregion for the 1980s as reported in table 13.2. The 1970 values are estimated by subtracting average changes for the 1970s and 1980s from the 1990 values.
– Average is not indicated when there is only one country observation for change in 1970s or 1980s, with the exception of North America (which uses change for the United States).
Sources: Tables 13.2, 9.1 and 9.3.

Scandinavia (Finland, Norway, Sweden) and in Western Europe (France, Luxembourg, Netherlands). Most of these ID75 values are similar to average ID75 values found today in the Middle East and North Africa (.68) and Other Developing (.63) regions according to study data. In short, *many OECD countries have come quite far in reducing the sex segregation of occupations. But since many began with such an unequal situation, they still have very far to go.*

This dramatic decrease in ID75 in some but not other regions, as well as in some but not other OECD subregions (together with the fact that decreases have tended to occur in regions and OECD subregions with relatively high ID75 values in 1970 and 1980) has resulted in a **convergence in ID75 values in much of the world in recent years.** This means that the clustering of ID75 values in the world currently at approximately .55 to .60 (as observed in Chapter 9) is a recent phenomenon.

Only time will tell whether future changes in occupational segregation by sex will be influenced more by a country's present level or its recent experience. That is a matter of whether the phenomenon of convergence and a country's current ID75 (whereby countries with relatively high ID75 values have relatively large decreases, and countries with relatively low ID75 values have relatively small decreases or even increases), or the fact of the trend itself will be a better predictor of future changes in ID. The author's expectation is that decreases in occupational segregation by sex in the future will be greatest in countries which have experienced decreases in recent decades; in other words, improvement will breed improvement. Thus, speculating about future trends in occupational segregation by sex for countries with similar levels of occupational segregation at present, but which reached this point from two quite different paths (for example, Scandinavia which experienced very large improvements in recent decades and Central and Southern OECD Europe where there has been little change in recent years), **we would expect occupational segregation by sex to decrease more in the future in countries which have experienced improvements recently** (for example, Scandinavia). In the author's opinion, attitudes and social values about gender roles are so strongly held in all societies that it is difficult to start the process of change. Consequently, our feeling is that once traditional attitudes start breaking down and occupational segregation by sex starts to decrease, such trends will tend to continue into the future.

13.2 Extent to which changes in ID are due to changes in the feminization of occupations or changes in the occupational structure of employment

An important issue to which we now turn is the extent to which the observed decrease in occupational segregation by sex in the world noted above is due to a more equal integration of women and men across occupations, or a change in the occupational structure of employment. This is an important issue to investigate, since most analysts and policy-makers consider that greater integration of the sexes indicates movement toward greater gender equality and lower occupational segregation by sex.

Table 13.4 presents results for the 1970s and 1980s based on a typical standardization technique suggested by Blau and Hendricks (1979) where observed changes in ID are separated into those due to changes in the: (i) feminization of occupations (SEX), (ii) distribution of occupations (OCC) and (iii) residual (RES).[5,6] Readers are referred to Chapter 5 where this standardization technique is described. Also Appendix 13.1 presents results for another standardization technique described in Chapter 5 and Jacobs (1989).

Results indicate that **both SEX and OCC have contributed to the general decrease in ID75 observed in both the 1970s and the 1980s.** If we make the ad

Table 13.4. Changes in ID for the 1970s and 1980s attributable to: (i) changes in sex composition of occupations (SEX), (ii) changes in size distribution of occupations (OCC) and (iii) residual (RES) based on standardization techniques[a], by region and country/area

Region/country/area	1970s			1980s		
	Change attributable to			Change attributable to		
	SEX	OCC	RES	SEX	OCC	RES
OECD						
Australia	−.024	−.019	.000			
Austria	.034	.022	−.005	.008	−.016	−.003
Cyprus						
Finland	−.022	−.004	.006	−.037	−.003	−.001
France				−.031	−.008	.002
Germany (West)	−.019	−.031	.007	−.003	−.001	−.003
Italy	−.009	−.041	.009			
Luxembourg	−.059	−.052	.022	−.028	−.050	.004
New Zealand				−.034	−.004	−.010
Netherlands	−.016	−.033	.021	−.010	−.020	−.030
Norway	−.009	−.028	.011	−.049	−.019	−.005
Spain	.039	−.011	−.003	.014	−.022	.007
Sweden	−.079	.018	.017	−.036	−.004	−.008
Switzerland	−.010	−.004	.001			
United States[b]	−.064	−.014	−.007	−.021	−.017	−.003
Average (unweighted)	**−.012**	**−.016**	**.007**	**−.021**	**−.015**	**−.005**
Transition Economies						
Bulgaria				−.029	−.005	.004
Hungary				−.009	−.014	−.009
Poland						
Former Yugoslavia	−.008	−.012	.014			
Average (unweighted)				**−.019**	**−.009**	**−.002**
Middle East and North Africa						
Bahrain	.022	−.001	−.044			
Egypt				.020	.025	−.003
Jordan	−.008	.009	−.014			
Kuwait						
Tunisia				−.016	−.009	−.017
Average (unweighted)	**.007**	**.004**	**−.029**	**.002**	**.008**	**−.010**
Asia/Pacific						
China				.034	.018	−.008
Fiji				−.027	−.027	.008
Hong Kong	−.012	.010	.019	.056	.012	.000
Japan	.002	−.005	.005	.011	−.009	−.002
Average (unweighted)	**−.005**	**.003**	**.012**	**.018**	**−.002**	**−.001**

Table 13.4.   (contd.)

Region/country/area	1970s			1980s		
	Change attributable to			Change attributable to		
	SEX	OCC	RES	SEX	OCC	RES
Other Developing						
Costa Rica	−.048	.026	−.007	−.003	.014	−.016
Mauritius	−.060	−.020	.022	−.049	.062	−.046
Senegal				−.057	−.020	.022
Average (unweighted)	**−.054**	**.003**	**.008**	**−.036**	**.019**	**−.014**
Overall average (unweighted)	**−.018**	**−.010**	**.004**	**−.013**	**−.005**	**−.005**

Notes: [a] For details on standardization technique recommended by Blau and Hendricks (1979), see Chapter 5. [b] In Canada between 1971–1981, SEX fell by −.053 and OCC by −.004 according to Fox and Fox (1987).
All values adjusted so as to represent change for an equivalent ten-year period.
Regional averages based on an unweighted average of national values. Regional average is not reported when only one country value is available for time period.
Source: Study data.

hoc assumption that a SEX or OCC value less than −.015 or greater than +.015 indicates a clear change and that a value between −.015 and +.015 indicates no change (tables 13.5 and 13.6)[7], we find that there are only a few country examples of clear increases for either the 1970s or 1980s. There are only six examples for both SEX and OCC (three each for the 1970s and 1980s). In contrast, there are 21 and 16 examples of clear decreases for SEX and OCC respectively.

It is important to note that *SEX tends to be more important than OCC in determining decreases in ID75*. First of all, negative values are approximately twice as large on average for SEX as compared to OCC (tables 13.5 and 13.6). Second, *trends in SEX and ID75 are very similar on a country by country basis*. In 36 of the 41 country-time periods represented in table 13.4, ID75 and SEX have the same clear trend (with the same sign for four of the five exceptions). In contrast, OCC and ID75 have different clear trends in 17 out of the 41 country-time periods shown in table 13.4.[8]

In terms of regional differences, results for SEX indicate a similar pattern to those for ID75 (tables 13.4–13.6 and figures 13.8 and 13.9). Thus, Asia is the worst performing region in recent decades according to both SEX and change in ID75. And again, the OECD and Other Developing study regions as a whole performed well in recent decades according to results for both SEX and change in ID75.

There are, however, some examples of qualitative differences in the regional and OECD subregional results for ID75 and SEX. *The decrease in*

Table 13.5. Summary of trends in ID for the 1970s attributable to change in the sex composition of occupations (SEX), change in size distribution of occupations (OCC) and residual (RES), by region

Region	1970s changes[b] attributable to											
	Sex				Occ				Residual			
	Inc	Dec	Neutral[a]	Average change[c]	Inc	Dec	Neutral[a]	Average change[c]	Inc	Dec	Neutral[a]	Average change[c]
OECD	2	7	3	−.012	2	7	4	−.016	3	0	9	.007
Transition Economies	0	0	1	−[d]	0	0	1	−[d]	0	0	1	−[d]
Middle East and North Africa	1	0	1	.007	0	0	2	.004	0	1	1	−.029
Asia/Pacific	0	0	2	−.005	1	0	2	.003	1	0	1	.012
Other Developing	0	2	0	−.054	1	1	0	.003	1	0	1	.008
Total	**3**	**9**	**7**	**−.018**	**3**	**8**	**9**	**−.010**	**5**	**1**	**13**	**.004**

Notes: [a] Neutral (i.e. no clear trend) is defined as a change between −.015 and +.015 for an equivalent ten-year period.
[b] Observed changes adjusted so as to represent changes for an equivalent ten-year period by taking into consideration that the number of years over which national changes are observed is not always ten years.
[c] Regional averages are unweighted averages of national values.
[d] Regional average is not reported when only one country value is available.
Source: Table 13.4.

Table 13.6. Summary of trends in ID for the 1980s attributable to change in the sex composition of occupations (SEX), change in the size distribution of occupations (OCC) and residual (RES), by region

Region	Sex				Occ				Residual			
1980s changes[b] attributable to	Inc	Dec	Neutral[a]	Average change[c]	Inc	Dec	Neutral[a]	Average change[c]	Inc	Dec	Neutral[a]	Average change[c]
OECD	0	7	4	-.021	0	6	5	-.015	0	1	10	-.005
Transition Economies	0	1	1	-.019	0	0	2	-.009	0	0	2	-.002
Middle East and North Africa	1	1	0	.002	1	0	1	.008	0	1	1	-.010
Asia/Pacific	2	1	1	.018	1	1	2	-.002	0	0	4	-.001
Other Developing	0	2	1	-.036	1	1	1	.019	1	2	0	-.014
Total	**3**	**12**	**7**	**-.013**	**3**	**8**	**11**	**-.005**	**1**	**4**	**17**	**-.005**

Notes: [a] Neutral (i.e. no clear trend) is defined as a change between -.015 and +.015 for an equivalent ten-year period.
[b] Observed changes adjusted so as to represent changes for an equivalent ten-year period by taking into consideration that the number of years over which national changes are observed is not always ten years.
[c] Regional averages are unweighted averages of national values.
Source: Table 13.4.

Figure 13.8.   Changes in ID for the 1970s attributable to changes in sex composition of occupations (SEX) and size distribution of occupations (OCC), by region

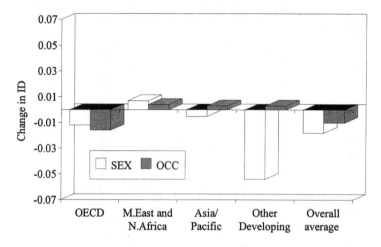

Notes: Transition Economies region is not shown, because the average is not provided for 1970s, as SEX and OCC are calculated for only one country in this region for 1970s.
The residual for 1970s is 0.007, −0.029, 0.012, 0.008 and 0.004 for OECD, Middle East and North Africa, Asia/Pacific, Other Developing and overall respectively.
Source: Table 13.4.

Figure 13.9.   Changes in ID for the 1980s attributable to changes in sex composition of occupations (SEX) and size distribution of occupations (OCC), by region

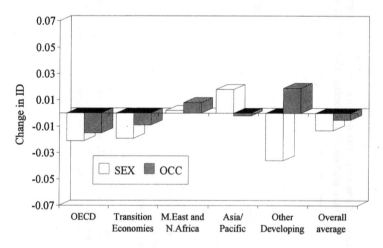

Note: The residual for 1980s is −0.005, −0.002, −0.010, −0.001, −0.004 and −0.005 for OECD, Transition Economies, Middle East and North Africa, Asia/Pacific, Other Developing and overall respectively.
Source: Table 13.4.

Figure 13.10. Changes in ID for the 1970s attributable to changes in sex composition of occupations (SEX) and size distribution of occupations (OCC), by OECD subregion

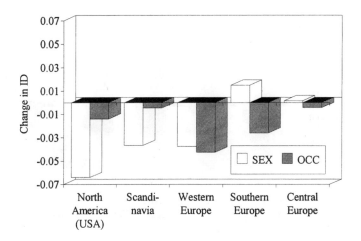

Note: Average for 'Other English-speaking' region is not provided, as SEX and OCC are calculated for only one country in this region.
Source: Table 13.4.

ID75 observed for the ME region is not attributable to improvements in SEX. On the other hand, the decrease in ID75 observed for four Other Developing Pacific countries with data (Fiji, Mauritius, Costa Rica, Senegal) is mainly due to improvements in SEX. These results indicate that there has been no progress in integrating male and female workers within occupations in Middle Eastern and North African countries in the past two decades, while progress in the few Other Developing countries with time series data sets— often small export-oriented economies—is striking.

In terms of OECD subregions, results for SEX reinforce observations made above based on ID75. While both OCC and SEX have contributed to reducing occupational segregation by sex in the OECD region, SEX has been considerably more important in certain OECD subregions (figures 13.10 and 13.11). Thus, the observed decrease in occupational segregation by sex is largely due to an increasingly equal distribution of male and female workers within occupations for the *North America* (based on data only for the United States)[9], *Scandinavia and other English-speaking OECD subregions.* This is what most policy-makers would consider *true improvement in gender equality and a reduction in occupational segregation by sex.* Somewhat in contrast, study data indicate that while substantial progress has been made in our *West European OECD* study subregion in recent decades, *approximately one-half of it has been due to changes in the occupational structure of employment.*

Figure 13.11. Changes in ID for the 1980s attributable to changes in sex composition of occupations (SEX) and size distribution of occupations (OCC), by OECD subregion

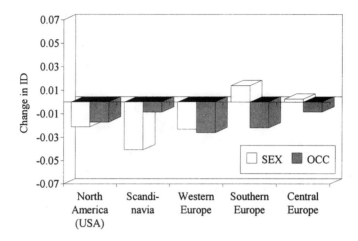

Note: Average for 'Other English-speaking' region is not provided, as SEX and OCC are calculated for only one country in this region.
Source: Table 13.4.

For the Southern European and Central European OECD subregions, results for SEX reinforce earlier conclusions that there has been little progress in these subregions in the integration of male and female workers within occupations in the past two decades. Thus, of the eight country-time periods with data for these two OECD subregions, there is only one example of a seemingly clear decrease for SEX (West Germany in the 1970s, and even this example is somewhat suspect, as it is based on a four-year period where the value for SEX was just $-.0075$). In addition, in the only other country-time period example in these OECD subregions where ID75 decreased (Italy 1971–1981), this improvement is mainly due to changes in the occupational structure of employment, with little improvement in the integration of men and women within occupations.

In summary, **while changes in the integration of men and women within occupations as well as changes in the occupational structure of the labour force have both contributed to the recent reduction in occupational segregation by sex in the world, it is the increasing integration of men and women within occupations which is the more important factor.** It is particularly worth noting, however, that the increasing integration of male and female workers within occupations is *not* observed in all parts of the world—including the Middle East and North Africa region, the Asia/Pacific region and Southern and Central OECD subregions.

GENDER AND JOBS

13.3 Recent changes in occupational segregation by sex as measured by the marginal matching index (MM)

We now turn to the marginal matching (MM) index. This index and how it differs from ID is explained in Chapter 5, and in particular how MM attempts to control for changes over time in the level of female labour force participation.

Results for MM (Appendix 13.2, table 13.12) are very similar to those for ID and SEX in terms of the general picture they paint of recent trends in occupational segregation by sex. Just as for ID and SEX, MM indicates that occupational segregation by sex has decreased in the world in the past two decades. Of the 47 country-time periods with data, there are only 5 examples where MM (or ID) increased by at least $+.02$ over an equivalent ten-year period. In contrast, MM decreased by more than $-.02$ in approximately 50 per cent of the country-time period examples (similar to the approximately 60 per cent for ID and 50 per cent for SEX).

There are, however, some notable examples where results for MM and SEX differ substantively. There are five cases where MM and SEX differ from each other by more than .03 and do not display the same clear trend (as defined above in table 13.2). Three are developing countries with low female labour force participation rates; another is Spain which has a relatively low female labour force participation rate for Europe. These differences between trends for MM and SEX, we feel, are probably due to the fact (as observed in Chapter 5) that MM and ID often differ substantially when female participation rates are low.[10]

13.4 Recent changes in occupational segregation by sex as measured by IDHALF

In this section, we analyse how IDHALF (a new inequality index which we developed and analysed in section 9.3 where women are assumed to comprise one-half of all non-agricultural workers) has been changing in the past two decades. IDHALF provides an interesting perspective on sex segregation as it combines into one inequality index two different aspects of labour market inequality faced by women—(i) occupational segregation for women who are in the labour force (as measured by ID), and (ii) the extent to which women are in or out of the non-agricultural labour force (as measured by the female share of the non-agricultural labour force, PFEM).

A priori expectations are that IDHALF has decreased around the world in the past two decades, since trends in both of IDHALF's underlying components should have been contributing to this. National data are presented in table 13.7 and a summary of regional trends are presented in

Table 13.7. Changes in IDHALF[a] for the 1970s and 1980s, by region and OECD subregion

Region/subregion/ country/area	Change in IDHALF[b,c]	
	1970s	1980s
OECD		
North America		
United States	−.101	−.059
Other English-speaking		
Australia	−.041	−.015
New Zealand		−.155
United Kingdom		−.126
Average (unweighted)		**−.098**
Scandinavia		
Finland	−.034	−.048
Norway	−.048	−.083
Sweden	−.065	−.065
Average (unweighted)	**−.049**	**−.065**
Western Europe		
France		−.048
Luxembourg	−.077	−.070
Netherlands		−.030
Average (unweighted)		**−.049**
Southern Europe		
Cyprus		−.017
Italy	−.090	
Spain	−.032	−.071
Average (unweighted)	**−.061**	**−.044**
Central Europe		
Austria	.028	−.022
Germany (West)	−.055	−.006
Switzerland	−.020	
Average (unweighted)	**−.016**	**−.014**
OECD overall average (unweighted)	**−.049**	**−.058**
Transition Economies		
Bulgaria		−.036
Hungary		−.046
Poland		−.008
Former Yugoslavia	−.033	
Average (unweighted)		**−.030**
Middle East and North Africa		
Bahrain	−.047	−.055
Egypt		−.056
Jordan	−.016	

Table 13.7.   (contd.)

Region/subregion/ country/area	Change in IDHALF[b,c]	
	1970s	1980s
Kuwait		−.042
Tunisia		−.018
Average (unweighted)	**−.031**	**−.043**
Asia/Pacific		
China		−.020
Fiji		−.068
Hong Kong	−.002	.000
Japan	−.018	−.012
Average (unweighted)	**−.010**	**−.025**
Other Developing		
Costa Rica	−.036	−.078
Mauritius	−.061	−.101
Senegal		−.080
Average (unweighted)	**−.048**	**−.086**
Overall Average (unweighted)	**−.041**	**−.051**

Notes: All study countries or areas are included which have data for two or more years (for approximately: 1970 and 1980; or for 1980 and 1990; or for 1970, 1980 and 1990). [a] IDHALF is computed in the same manner as ID but after assuming that all women are working women and consequently that women comprise one-half of the non-agricultural labour force (see section 9.3). [b] Observed changes adjusted so as to represent change for an equivalent ten year period by taking into consideration that the time periods over which national changes are observed are not always ten years (see Chapter 4). [c] Regional and subregional averages are unweighted averages of national values. Regional (and subregional) average not reported when only one country value is available except for North America (the United States).
Source: Study data.

table 13.8. Figures 13.12 and 13.13 display these results graphically for study regions and OECD subregions.

IDHALF has, indeed, decreased in the past two decades in the world, and this downward trend was strong in both the 1970s and the 1980s. Most of the country-time periods shown in tables 13.7 and 13.8 (35 of 46) indicate decreases of more than −.02 for an equivalent ten-year period, and there are only two country/area-time periods where IDHALF has a positive sign (Austria for 1971–80 and Hong Kong for 1981–91). In terms of magnitude, the *average change in IDHALF is approximately twice that for ID75*, being approximately −.04 to −.05 per equivalent ten-year period for the full set of study countries and areas.

Most, but not all, of the regional and OECD subregional differences for ID75 are also observed for IDHALF (figures 13.12 and 13.13). Thus, *Asia is*

Table 13.8. Trends in IDHALF[a] for the 1970s and 1980s, by region

Region	1970s				1980s			
	INC	DEC	Neutral[b]	Average change[c,d]	INC	DEC	Neutral[b]	Average change[c,d]
OECD	1	10	0	–.0485	0	11	3	–.0582
Transition Economies	0	1	0	–[e]	0	2	1	–.0300
Middle East and North Africa	0	1	1	–.0312	0	3	1	–.0425
Asia/Pacific	0	0	2	–.0101	0	2	2	–.0249
Other Developing	0	2	0	–.0482	0	3	0	–.0864
Total	**1**	**14**	**3**	**–.0414**	**0**	**21**	**7**	**–.0512**

Notes: [a] IDHALF is defined in section 9.3. It is calculated in the same manner as ID but after assuming that all women are working women, and consequently that women comprise one-half of the non-agricultural labour force. [b] Neutral (i.e. no clear trend) is defined as a change between –.02 and +.02 for a ten-year equivalent period. [c] Observed changes adjusted so as to represent change for an equivalent ten-year period by taking into consideration that the period over which national changes are observed is not always ten years. [d] Regional averages are unweighted averages of national values. [e] Regional average is not reported when only one country value is available. Source: Table 13.7.

Figure 13.12. Average change in IDHALF for the 1970s and 1980s, by region

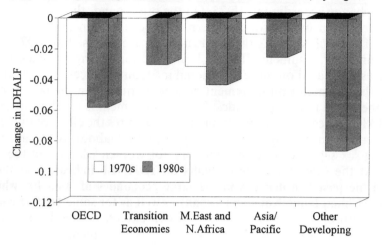

Source: Table 13.7.

the only region without a clear downward trend in IDHALF and ID75 (based on the experiences of the large Asian economies with time series data—China, Hong Kong and Japan). In the Middle Eastern and North African region, occupational segregation by sex has clearly decreased according to IDHALF whereas results are inconclusive according to ID75 and SEX.

Among OECD subregions, North America, Other English-speaking, Scandinavia and Western Europe all experienced major decreases in occupational segregation by sex according to both IDHALF and ID75. For OECD

Figure 13.13. Average change in IDHALF for the 1970s and 1980s, by OECD subregion

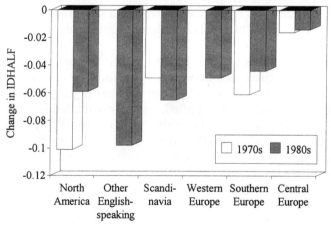

Source: Table 13.7.

Central Europe, there has been only a weak decrease according to IDHALF and little change according to ID75. On the other hand, the trend in occupational segregation by sex for Southern Europe has been clearly downward based on IDHALF whereas there was no clear trend based on ID75.

In summary, results for IDHALF provide convincing evidence supporting conclusions based on more traditional inequality indices (such as ID) that there has been a major improvement in gender equality in the labour market around the world in recent decades. This improvement is much more striking for IDHALF, since this new inequality index captures the effect of two distinct recent trends—increasing female entry into the labour force as well as decreasing sex segregation of occupations for women who are in the labour market. At the same time, **these results for IDHALF indicate that the poor record in the past two decades in the large economies of Asia for which we have data (China, Hong Kong and Japan) as well as for some OECD countries of Central Europe (Austria, and to a lesser extent, Switzerland and West Germany) remains strikingly different from trends in the remainder of the world.**

13.5 Regression analysis of the relationship between changes in ID and labour market variables

This section investigates whether or not two labour market aspects discussed above are significantly related (in a statistical sense) to recent changes in occupational segregation: (1) whether the increasing entry of women into the labour force (evidenced by rising female share of employment) is associated with reduction in occupational segregation by sex; and (2) whether the convergence in national ID75 values over time noted earlier in this chapter is statistically significant (i.e. whether ID75 values fell significantly faster in countries with relatively high ID75 values compared to countries with relatively low ID75 values).[11]

Cross-national analysis of the present situation presented in Chapter 9 indicated that the relationship between ID75 and the female share of the non-agricultural labour force (PFEM) is non-linear in nature and significant when regional variables are not specified, negatively related for PFEM values up to around 30 to 35 per cent and positively related to PFEM values beyond 35. When region is specified, ID75 and PFEM are positively related. It was also found that the extensiveness of part-time employment is not significantly related to ID75 for OECD countries.

Regression results for changes in the past two decades are presented in tables 13.9 and 13.10. The same explanatory labour market variables are used as in Chapter 9. Different from the earlier regression analysis is that: (i) *two dependent variables* are used here (change in ID75 and SEX);

Table 13.9. Regression results (OLS) relating labour market variables to change in index of dissimilarity (ID75) for the 1970s and 1980s (t values in brackets)

Independent variables	1970s					1980s				
	(1)	(2)	(3)	(4)	(5)	(6)	(7)	(8)	(9)	(10)
ΔPFEM	-.0077[c] (3.18)	-.0140[b] (3.47)	x	-.0066[b] (2.40)	-.0132[c] (2.96)	-.0027 (0.79)	-.0020 (0.34)	x	-.0020 (0.06)	-.0043 (0.94)
ΔPFEM* $\begin{bmatrix} 1\ \text{if PFEM} < 35 \\ 0\ \text{if PFEM} > 35 \end{bmatrix}$[d]	x	.0067[a] (1.92)	x	x	.0064[a] (1.81)	x	.0004 (0.09)	x	x	.0037 (1.08)
ID75 for 1970 or ID75 for 1980[e]	x	x	-.15[a] (1.94)	-.06 (0.82)	-.05 (0.70)	x	x	-.29[c] (4.93)	-.29[c] (4.78)	-.31[c] (4.92)
Constant	.01	.01	.07	.04	.04	-.02	-.02	.15	.17	.15
R^2	.37	.49	.18	.40	.51	.02	.02	.48	.51	.49
Adjusted R^2	.34	.43	.13	.32	.41	-.01	-.05	.46	.45	.45
F value	10.07[a]	7.69[c]	3.77[a]	5.27[b]	5.12[b]	0.62	0.30	24.30[c]	8.45[c]	12.02[c]
Degrees of freedom	17	16	17	16	15	26	25	26	24	25

Notes: x indicates variable is not specified in this equation.
[a] Significant at .10 level. [b] Significant at .05 level. [c] Significant at .01 level. [d] This ΔPFEM variable represents an interaction term as it equals zero when PFEM is greater than 35 and the value of PFEM when PFEM is less than 35. [e] Value for ID75 is value at beginning of time period being analysed (i.e. ID75 for approximately 1970 for 1970s equations or 1980 for 1980s equations).
ΔPFEM is percentage point change in PFEM (which is itself women's percentage share of the non-agricultural labour force).
To obtain estimated effect on ID75 of a 1 per cent change in PFEM for countries where PFEM is less than 35 per cent in the beginning of the time period (i.e. approximately 1970 or 1980), it is necessary to add coefficients of both ΔPFEM explanatory variables. For countries where PFEM is greater than 35, its effect is estimated by the coefficient for ΔPFEM.
Regional binaries are *not* specified because of the small degrees of freedom in each region.
Source: Study data.

Table 13.10. Regression results (OLS) relating labour market variables to change in sex composition of occupations (SEX), for the 1970s and 1980s (t values in brackets)

Independent variables	1970s					1980s				
	(1)	(2)	(3)	(4)	(5)	(6)	(7)	(8)	(9)	(10)
ΔPFEM	-.0050[a] (1.96)	-.0145[c] (3.65)	x	-.0042 (1.41)	-.0138[b] (3.18)	-.0030 (1.00)	-.0022 (0.42)	x	-.0028 (1.27)	-.0052 (1.39)
ΔPFEM* $\left[\begin{array}{l}\text{1 if PFEM} < 35 \\ \text{0 if PFEM} > 35\end{array}\right]$[d]	x	.0095[b] (2.84)	x	x	.0093[b] (2.71)	x	.0008 (0.20)	x	x	.0024 (0.81)
ID75 for 1970 or ID75 for 1980[e]	x	x	-.11 (1.51)	-.05 (0.63)	-.03 (0.45)	x	x	-.22[c] (4.34)	-.22[c] (4.34)	-.23[c] (4.40)
Constant	.00	.01	.05	.03	.03	-.35	-.50	.12	.12	.13
R^2	.18	.46	.12	.20	.47	.05	.05	.48	.53	.54
Adjusted R^2	.14	.39	.07	.10	.36	.00	-.05	.46	.48	.47
F value	3.83[a]	6.75[c]	2.27[a]	2.04[a]	4.34[b]	1.00	.50	18.82[c]	10.51[c]	7.10[c]
Degrees of freedom	17	16	17	16	15	20	19	20	19	18

Notes: x indicates variable is not specified in this equation.
[a] Significant at .10 level. [b] Significant at .05 level. [c] Significant at .01 level. [d] This ΔPFEM variable represents an interaction term as it equals zero when PFEM is greater than 35 and the value of PFEM when PFEM is less than 35. [e] Value for ID75 is value at beginning of time period being analysed (i.e. ID75 for approximately 1970 for 1970s equations or 1980 for 1980s equations).
ΔPFEM is percentage point change in PFEM (which is itself women's percentage share of the non-agricultural labour force).
To obtain estimated effect on ID75 of a 1 per cent change in PFEM for countries where PFEM is less than 35 per cent in the beginning of the time period (i.e. approximately 1970 or 1980), it is necessary to add coefficients of both ΔPFEM explanatory variables. For countries where PFEM is greater than 35, its effect is estimated by the coefficient for ΔPFEM.
Regional binaries are *not* specified because of the small degrees of freedom in each region.
Source: Study data.

(ii) here the dependent and independent variables measure *change* (as well as levels); and (iii) the regression analysis here is repeated for *two time periods* (1970s and 1980s). Also, of course, the sample included in these analyses differ, being all 41 study countries/areas for the cross-section analysis in Chapter 9 as compared to 19 study countries for the following time series analysis for the 1970s and 28 study countries for the 1980s.

Results for the 1970s and 1980s differ. **For the 1970s, changes in both ID75 and SEX are strongly and significantly related to changes in PFEM** (tables 13.9 and 13.10). An increase in PFEM of 4 per cent (approximately the average increase in PFEM observed for the decade) is associated with a change in ID75 of approximately −0.03 (and a change in SEX of about −0.02). This is quite a sizeable effect considering that the average change in ID75 for the 1970s was −0.024 and average ID75 was only about 0.60.

At the same time, *the relationship between change in PFEM and change in ID75 (also for SEX) differs significantly for different levels of PFEM in the 1970s* (tables 13.9 and 13.10; figures 13.14 and 13.15). This differential relationship for different ranges of PFEM is demonstrated by the statistical significance of the interaction between change in PFEM and PFEM range. Thus, the estimated effect of change in PFEM on change in ID75 is approximately −0.013 (and −0.014 for SEX) when PFEM is greater than 35 per cent as compared to −0.0068 for change in ID75 (and −0.0045 for SEX) when PFEM is less than 35 per cent (based on equation 5 in tables 13.9 and 13.10). Interestingly, however, the magnitude of the effect on ID75 for the 1970s predicted by the actual change in PFEM observed in the 1970s is similar

Figure 13.14. Change in ID75 as a function of increase in PFEM for the 1970s and 1980s

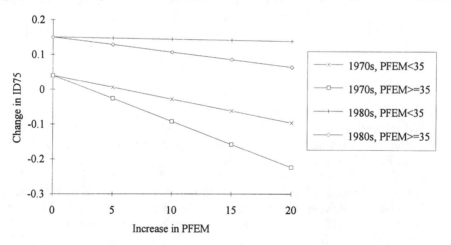

Note: Straight lines are based on regression equations where ID75 and change in PFEM are specified as explanatory variables.
Source: Table 13.9.

Figure 13.15. **Change in the sex composition of occupations (SEX) as a function of change in PFEM for the 1970s and 1980s**

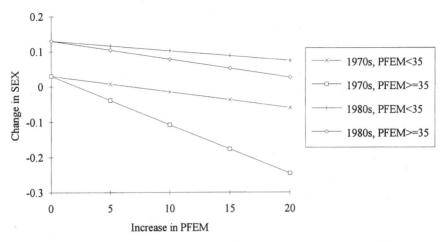

Note: Straight lines are based on regression equations where ID75 and change in PFEM are specified as explanatory variables.
Source: Table 13.10.

in relatively high and relatively low PFEM countries, because the average actual change in PFEM was greater for countries with lower PFEM levels (approximately five percentage points) as compared to countries with higher PFEM values (approximately three percentage points).

Whether or not the convergence of ID75 values noted above in sections 13.1 and 13.2 (whereby ID has tended to decrease more in countries with higher ID75 values as compared to countries with lower ID75 values) is statistically significant is tested in the regression equations reported in tables 13.9–13.10 and shown in figures 13.16 and 13.17. For the 1970s, change in ID75 is found to be significantly related to the ID75 level at the beginning of the period (and nearly significant for SEX) when ID75 is the only variable specified, with the estimated coefficient very large at −.15 (and −.11 for SEX). This relationship is, however, much weaker and statistically insignificant at the .10 level in the 1970s when change in PFEM is also specified (equation 5 in tables 13.9–13.10)—indicating that convergence in ID75 values is not a statistically significant phenomenon in the 1970s once change in PFEM is taken into consideration.

For the 1980s, regression results are reversed as compared to the 1970s in terms of significance for ID75 level and change in PFEM. **In the 1980s, change in ID75 (also for SEX) is not significantly related to change in PFEM.** On the other hand, **the ID75 level itself is very strongly and significantly related to change in ID75** (and SEX), and this is true whether or not change in PFEM is also specified in the regression equation. Indeed, the ID75 level by itself accounts for approximately 50 per cent of the variation in changes in ID75

Figure 13.16. Change in ID75 for the 1970s, by ID75 for 1970s value

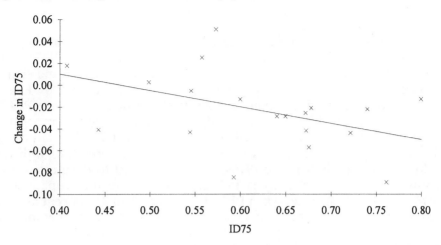

Note: Straight line is based on regression estimated in table 13.9, where only ID75 is specified as an independent variable. Source: Tables 13.1 and 13.9.

and SEX observed for the 1980s. Furthermore, the size of the ID75 coefficient is quite large as it implies that a difference in ID75 of .08 (approximately the difference in ID75 values between OECD and Other Developing regions in 1990) is associated with a change of about .023 in ID for a ten-year period, which is about the same as the average change in ID observed among study countries during the 1980s.

Figure 13.17. Change in ID75 for the 1980s, by ID75 for 1980s value

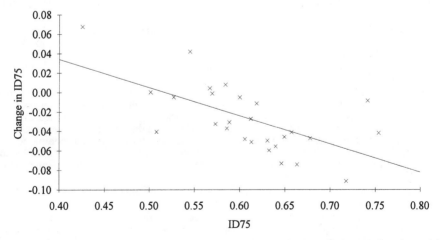

Note: Straight line is based on regression estimated in table 13.9, where only ID75 is specified as an independent variable. Source: Tables 13.1 and 13.9.

The above regression results of recent changes in ID75 and SEX reported in this section differ in important respects from the point-in-time cross-section analysis in Chapter 9 based on data for the latest available year.

The cross-section analysis indicates that the female share of the non-agricultural labour force (PFEM) is not significantly related to ID75 when a country's region is taken into consideration, and non-linearly and significantly related when region is not specified (negatively related for PFEM values up to around 35 per cent and positively related for higher PFEM values). In contrast, the time series analysis indicates a significant negative relationship between change in PFEM and change in ID75 (as well as for SEX) for countries with high PFEM values as well as countries with low PFEM values (especially in the 1970s). Also in contrast to the cross-section analysis, the time series analysis indicates that the relationship between PFEM and ID75 is stronger when PFEM is greater than 35 per cent as compared to when PFEM is less than 35 per cent. Second, the time series analysis indicates that there has been a significant convergence in ID values over the past two decades (an issue which could not be investigated in the cross-section analysis in Chapter 9), with this effect especially large and significant in the 1980s. It is difficult to know in which analysis to put more stock as regards the relationship between PFEM and ID75. My inclination is to put more credence in the time series analysis, since I feel that the relationship being investigated is mainly of a dynamic, time-related nature. On the other hand, both regression analyses are fairly simple and so all of these regression results need to be treated with caution.

Notes

[1] The adjusted ID is represented as ID75 because it is an ID value which has been adjusted in a rough way so as to be for a classification with 75 non-agricultural occupations (see Appendix 9.1).

[2] Table 13.2 is based on the assumption that a *clear trend* in a particular direction has been established *when ID75 changed by more than* $+.02$ *or* $-.02$ during an equivalent ten-year period. While this definition of a clear change is obviously ad hoc in nature, it helps considerably in the discussion as it avoids being overly influenced by small changes (and possible "noise" in the data).

[3] It is possible to calculate a weighted change in ID75 for the 1970s and the 1980s in the world using the size of the non-agricultural labour force as weights (and by so doing obtain an estimate for the average change for workers in the world). When such a weighted average is calculated, it is found that the average decrease in ID75 in study countries and areas is considerably greater for the 1970s ($-.042$) and slightly less for the 1980s ($-.022$) as compared to the unweighted averages used in the text ($-.024$ and $-.026$ respectively). The main reason for these differences is the experience of the largest study countries for the 1970s (United States) and the 1980s (China).

[4] A similar decrease in ID for the 1970s is reported for Canada in Fox and Fox (1987) of $-.063$ based on data for around 300 occupations.

[5] The number of study countries/areas included in the analysis in this section is somewhat smaller than for other analyses in this chapter. This occurs because it is only possible to calculate SEX, OCC and RES in a country when the number of occupations is identical in each data year; in contrast, it is possible to calculate ID for each data year regardless of the

number of occupations classified and then to make adjustments in ID for differences in numbers of occupations. We did not calculate SEX or OCC for 1980s for: Australia, the United Kingdom, Cyprus, Poland, Bahrain, Kuwait as the number of occupations differed substantially across data years. For most economies where the number of occupations across data years differed by only a few occupations (Bulgaria, Finland, China, Hong Kong, Senegal and the United States), we merged occupations when we felt we could in order to create data sets with identical numbers of occupations in each data year. This was not done for the United Kingdom even though there are similar numbers of occupations for 1980 and 1990 (502 and 509 respectively), because despite a difference of only seven occupations in the two data years, there are in actual fact, 16 examples of different occupations as several occupations, appeared or disappeared over time.

[6] The residual (RES) is defined as the difference between the observed change in ID minus values for SEX and OCC. RES should be more or less random, and this appears to be the case here. RES has a mean value for all study countries/areas of .004 for 1970s and −.005 for 1980s; also, RES has a value between −.015 and +.015 for 30 of the 41 country-time periods observed.

[7] A smaller band was chosen to indicate no change for SEX and OCC as compared to that for change in ID75, because the change in ID is comprised of changes in SEX and OCC. Although we could have chosen a value which is one-half of that for ID75 (i.e. .01), we decided to be somewhat cautious by choosing a slightly larger band (.015) for SEX and OCC.

[8] Also, SEX and OCC have different trends in many study countries. Indeed, using the same definition of change/trend as in tables 13.5 and 13.6, SEX and OCC display different trends in almost one-half of the 41 country-time periods shown in these tables (19 of 41), and have different signs in approximately one-third of the cases (12 of 41).

[9] Canada's experience in the 1970s appears to be similar to that in the United States according to Fox (1987) who report −.053 for SEX and −.004 for OCC based on data for 300 occupations for 1971–1981.

[10] There are 12 country-time period examples where changes in MM and ID differ qualitatively (by more than .03). Half of these are found in developing countries. Among OECD countries, the only clear differences between changes in MM and ID are that occupational segregation by sex clearly decreased according to ID but not according to MM for the Netherlands and Norway for 1970s and for Australia and New Zealand for 1980s. Also, the clear increases observed for 1970s for Spain and Austria based on ID are not observed based on MM.

[11] We also investigated whether the extensiveness of part-time employment (both its level as well as changes in it) among the 10 OECD study countries with relevant time series data is related to changes in ID75 and SEX. Regression results (unreported) indicate that these relationships are weak and statistically insignificant, regardless of whether ID75 and/or change in PFEM are or are not specified as explanatory variables.

Appendix 13.1.   Changes in size standardized ID due to changes in the sex composition of occupations (which assume that all occupations are the same size)

Another standardization methodology used in the research literature relies on the assumption that all occupations are of equal size (see Jacobs, 1989 and Chapter 5 for a description of this methodology). In this way, ID can only be affected by changes in the feminization of occupations, since the relative size/importance of all occupations remain unchanged over time (by definition).

Results based on this standardization methodology are not presented or discussed in the main text, partly for reasons of parsimony and partly because we feel this methodology is conceptually flawed, since changes in the feminization of small occupations count the same as changes in large occupations.

Despite our reservations with this standardization methodology, readers may be interested in results based on this methodology. For this reason, changes for the 1970s and 1980s based on this standardized ID are provided in this Appendix (table 13.11).

Results using this standardization methodology are not always the same as for ID75 or for SEX (the standardized ID used in the text). Of our 41 country-time periods for SEX and the size-standardized ID used in this Appendix, there are 27 clear trends for SEX and 32 clear trends for the size standardized ID used in this Appendix (using the same definition of a clear trend as a change greater than $+.015$ or less than $-.015$ for an equivalent ten-year period).

In terms of global trends, occupational segregation by sex is observed to be falling in the world as a whole based on this size-standardized ID, just as it is for ID75 and SEX. There are, however, some noteworthy regional differences. The OECD region shows little or no change in the 1970s based on this size-standardized ID, whereas the OECD region shows a substantial decrease based on ID75 and SEX. Asia/Pacific economies show a decrease in the 1970s and 1980s based on this size-standardized ID whereas they show little change or an increase based on ID75 and SEX. **These results imply that there are different trends in the integration of men and women into small occupations as compared to large occupations in these noted regions and time periods.**

Table 13.11. Changes in size-standardized ID due to changes in the sex composition of occupations (after assuming that all occupations are the same size) for the 1970s and 1980s, by region

Region/country/area[a]	Change[b] in size standardized ID due to changes in sex composition of occupations (which assumes that all occupations are the same size)	
	1970s	1980s
OECD		
Australia	.099	.003
Austria	.055	−.016
Cyprus		.016
Finland	.065	−.116
France		−.035
Germany (West)	−.031	−.018
Italy	−.047	
Luxembourg	−.038	−.051
New Zealand		−.031
Netherlands	−.049	−.022
Norway	−.031	−.052
Spain	−.022	−.059
Sweden	−.049	−.036
Switzerland	.044	
United Kingdom		−.039
United States	−.066	.016
Average (unweighted)	**−.006**	**−.031**
Transition Economies		
Bulgaria		−.083
Hungary		−.023
Poland		.011
Former Yugoslavia	−.027	
Average (unweighted)		**−.031**
Middle East and North Africa		
Bahrain	.010	−.088
Egypt		−.001
Jordan	−.026	
Kuwait		−.066
Tunisia		−.058
Average (unweighted)	**−.008**	**−.053**
Asia/Pacific		
China		−.014
Fiji		−.041

Table 13.11.   (contd.)

Region/country/area[a]	Change[b] in size standardized ID due to changes in sex composition of occupations (which assumes that all occupations are the same size)	
	1970s	1980s
Hong Kong	−.041	.063
Japan	−.018	−.014
Average (unweighted)	**−.029**	**−.001**
Other Developing		
Costa Rica	−.064	.079
Mauritius	−.061	−.056
Senegal		−.080
Average (unweighted)	**−.062**	**−.019**
Overall average (unweighted)	**−.012**	**−.029**

Notes: [a] Table includes all study countries and areas which have data for two or more years (for approximately 1970 and 1980; or for 1980 and 1990; or for 1970, 1980 and 1990). [b] Observed change adjusted so as to represent changes for an equivalent ten-year period by taking into consideration that the time period over which national change is observed is not always ten years (see Chapter 4).

Regional averages based on unweighted average of countries in the region. Regional average is not indicated when data are available for only one country in the region for the time period.

See Chapter 5 for description of standardization methodology which is drawn from Jacobs (1989).

Source: Study data.

Appendix 13.2.   Changes in Marginal Matching index

Table 13.12.   Changes in Marginal Matching (MM) index for the 1970s and 1980s, by region and OECD subregion[b,c]

Region/subregion/country/area[a]	1970s	1980s
North America		
United States	−.082	−.040
Other English-speaking		
Australia	−.046	.024
New Zealand		−.012
United Kingdom		−.034
Average (unweighted)		**−.007**
Scandinavia		
Finland	−.016	−.041
Norway	.008	−.064
Sweden	−.034	−.047
Average (unweighted)	**−.014**	**−.051**
Western Europe		
France		−.017
Luxembourg	−.076	−.079
Netherlands	.014	−.034
Average (unweighted)	**−.031**	**−.043**
Southern Europe		
Cyprus		.007
Italy	−.029	
Spain	−.028	−.012
Average (unweighted)	**−.029**	**−.003**
Central Europe		
Austria	.009	.016
Germany (West)	−.038	−.010
Switzerland	−.009	
Average (unweighted)	**−.012**	**.003**
OECD average (unweighted)	**−.027**	**−.025**
Transition Economies		
Bulgaria		−.023
Hungary		−.039
Poland		.009
Former Yugoslavia	−.001	
Average (unweighted)		**−.018**
Middle East and North Africa		
Bahrain	.047	−.015
Egypt		−.014
Jordan	−.063	

Table 13.12.   (contd.)

Region/subregion/country/area[a]	1970s	1980s
Kuwait		.041
Tunisia		−.076[d]
Average (unweighted)	**−.007**	**−.016**
Asia/Pacific		
China		.039
Fiji		−.039
Hong Kong	.006	.059
Japan	−.009	.007
Average (unweighted)	**−.001**	**.016**
Other Developing		
Costa Rica	−.032	−.009
Mauritius	.015	−.043
Senegal		−.047[d]
Average (unweighted)	**−.038**	**−.016**
Overall average (unweighted)	**−.022**	**−.016**

Notes: [a] Table includes all study countries or areas which have data for two or more years (for approximately: 1970 and 1980; or for 1980 and 1990; or for 1970, 1980 and 1990). [b] Changes adjusted in order to take into consideration greater number of occupations classified (and therefore higher MM due to this greater disaggregation) in later years as described in Chapter 6. For simplicity, the same adjustments are used as for ID and are subtracted from the observed MM changes for 1980s for: Australia (.034), Cyprus (.022), Poland (.006), Bahrain (.024) and Kuwait (.008) in order to obtain the changes reported in this table. [c] Observed changes adjusted so as to represent changes for an equivalent ten-year period by taking into consideration that the time period over which national change is observed is not always ten years (see Chapter 4). [d] Considerable judgement was used to obtain comparable occupational classifications for the two data years for two countries (Senegal and Tunisia). Therefore, trend data for these countries should be treated with considerable caution.
Regional and subregional averages are unweighted averages of national values. Averages are not indicated when data are available for only one country in the region (or subregion) except for North America.
See Chapter 5 for definition of marginal matching index.
Source: Study data.

RECENT CHANGES IN THE EXTENT TO WHICH MALE AND FEMALE NON-AGRICULTURAL LABOUR FORCES ARE IN GENDER-DOMINATED OCCUPATIONS

14

This chapter investigates changes in segregation into female-dominated and male-dominated occupations. As in Chapters 10, 11 and 12 in Part III, which investigated the current situation around the world, gender-dominated occupations are defined as those where at least 80 per cent of workers are male or female. For reasons of parsimony, there is no discussion in the text for the total non-agricultural labour force, and interested readers are referred to footnote 5 (page 370) for a brief discussion of recent changes.

A priori expectations are that the number of male-dominated non-agricultural occupations and the percentage of men working in male-dominated non-agricultural occupations have decreased over the past two decades—due to both the decreasing relative size of the male non-agricultural labour force and the decreasing sex segregation within occupations described in Chapter 13.

There are no *a priori* expectations as regards changes in the number and size of female-dominated non-agricultural occupations (FDOM75). While increases in female labour force participation rates should have helped to increase FDOM75, decreases in occupational segregation by sex should have had the opposite effect.

Tables 14.1 and 14.2 present national results. Tables 14.3 to 14.7 provide summaries for regions and subregions.[1,2] Figures 14.1 to 14.8 display these results graphically.

14.1   Recent changes for male-dominated non-agricultural occupations

As expected, **MDOM75 has very clearly decreased around the world in the past two decades** (figure 14.1). It decreased, *on average, by about 10 percentage points in the past two decades*—an average of 3.6 percentage points in the 1970s and a further 6.1 percentage points in the 1980s.[3] Furthermore, MDOM75 has a positive sign in only 3 of the 47 country/area-time periods reported in tables 14.2 and 14.4 (only in Austria 1971–1980, Hong Kong 1981–1991 and China 1982–1990).

Table 14.1. Changes in percentage of the female non-agricultural labour force working in female-dominated occupations (FDOM75) for the 1970s and 1980s, by region

Region/country/area	Latest value FDOM75[f] (approx. 1990)	Change in FDOM75[d] 1970s	1980s
OECD			
Australia	17.4	−9.3	−7.6[b]
Austria	14.3	6.8	−5.5
Cyprus	25.6		−0.8
Finland	55.4	2.8	−0.6
France	22.0		8.4
Germany (West)	23.6	−2.5	−1.3
Italy	10.2	4.8[c]	
Luxembourg	37.3	−1.0	−15.5[c]
New Zealand	19.5		−10.9[c]
Netherlands	31.4	7.1	−2.2
Norway	35.0	16.3	−7.9
Spain	14.2	−9.1	2.5
Sweden	53.8	7.4[c]	1.4
Switzerland	17.3	−4.2	
United Kingdom	13.5		−20.8[c]
United States	29.2	−8.0	−0.5
Average (unweighted)	**26.9**	**0.9**	**−4.4**
Transition Economies			
Bulgaria	19.8		−2.2
Hungary	28.6		−1.2
Poland	48.6		5.8[b]
Former Yugoslavia	8.9	5.7	
Average (unweighted)	**26.5**		**−0.1**
Middle East and North Africa			
Bahrain	0.0	0.0	0.0
Egypt	0.0		−7.1[c]
Jordan	6.2	3.1[c]	
Kuwait	7.2		−4.4
Tunisia	45.6		−17.7[a]
Average (unweighted)	**9.8**	**1.6**	**−7.3**
Asia/Pacific			
China	10.5		5.6
Fiji	26.4		−6.7
Hong Kong	14.8	−3.2	5.9
Japan	7.7	−0.9	−2.0
Average (unweighted)	**10.0**	**−2.0**	**0.7**

Table 14.1. (contd.)

Region/country/area	Latest value FDOM75[f] (approx. 1990)	Change in FDOM75[d]	
		1970s	1980s
Other Developing			
Costa Rica	52.0	4.8	−2.6
Mauritius[e]	14.0	−2.5	−37.5
Senegal	28.8		−10.7[a]
Average (unweighted)	**47.5**	**1.2**	**−16.9**
World (unweighted)	**25.0**	**1.0**	**−5.0**

Notes: [a] Considerable judgement was used for two countries to obtain comparable occupational classifications for the two data years. Therefore, trend data must be treated especially cautiously for these countries (Senegal and Tunisia). [b] Adjustments were made to take into account differences in the number of occupations classified in the two data years (since number of occupations differed substantially, by more than 10 per cent in the two data years). When the adjustment factor is relatively large (i.e. greater than 2.0 percentage points), trend data should be treated more cautiously than usual. This affects for 1980s: Poland with 2.7 and Australia with 13.7 for FDOM75. There were no relatively large adjustments for the 1970s. [c] FDOM75 can be substantially affected by changes in individual occupations being close to the 80 per cent cut-off point (i.e. 77.5–79.9 or 80.0–82.49 per cent female). When the net effect of occupations changing to or from 77.5 to 82.49 per cent female for FDOM75 is greater than +4.0 percentage points or less than −4.0 percentage points for the period under consideration, this is noted by a superscript c. This occurs for the 1970s for Sweden (−4.8), Italy (+5.1) and Jordan (+13.9); and for the 1980s for Luxembourg (−12.9), New Zealand (−4.0), UK (−16.0) and Egypt (−7.1). [d] Observed changes adjusted so as to represent change for an equivalent ten-year period by taking into consideration that the time period over which national changes are observed is not always ten years (see Chapter 4). [e] The large changes observed for Mauritius are greatly affected by changes in one occupation (spinners and weavers) where the percentage female went from 66.9 per cent female in 1972, to 90.0 per cent female in 1983 and back to 74.6 per cent female in 1990, while at the same time this occupation increased its share of non-agricultural employment from 0.6 per cent in 1972 to 4.2 per cent in 1983 and 13.0 per cent in 1990.
[f] Averages are the unweighted average of the latest national values for all study countries/areas as shown in table 10.3.
Female-dominated and male-dominated occupations are defined as occupations where at least 80 per cent of the workers are either female or male respectively.
Percentage point change is based on national data and does not take into account the number of occupations in the national classification unless these differ across data years (i.e. note b). The assumption is that observed change is unaffected by the level of disaggregation in the national classification, because all national classifications are reasonably detailed (see Chapter 6).
Averages are based on unweighted averages of national values. As a comparison, a weighted average of national values of the world (using size of the non-agricultural labour force as weights) indicates changes of −3.5 per cent for the 1970s and −1.8 per cent for the 1980s. Differences as compared to the unweighted world averages of +1.0 per cent and −5.0 per cent are largely due to experiences of the largest study country for each time period (the United States for the 1970s and China for the 1980s).
Regional averages are not indicated when only one country value is available.
Source: Study data.

Another indication of how quickly men have been losing their labour market advantage—of having their "own" occupations which are protected against female competition—is provided by recent changes in the numbers of male-dominated occupations (table 14.5). The number of male-dominated occupations fell by about 10 per cent in the 1970s and by approximately another 10 per cent in the 1980s—for a total of about 20 per cent or about 10 percentage points in the past two decades (from about 57 to about 47

Table 14.2. Changes in percentage of the male non-agricultural labour force working in male-dominated occupations (MDOM75) for the 1970s and 1980s, by region

Region/country/area	Latest value MDOM75[f] (approx. 1990)	Change in MDOM75[d]	
		1970s	1980s
OECD			
Australia	55.1	−8.4	−8.6
Austria	60.5	10.9	−7.6
Cyprus	54.8		−4.1
Finland	56.0	−5.5	−8.5
France	50.7		−9.1
Germany (West)	59.0	−6.5	−2.2
Italy	58.7	−4.2	
Luxembourg	63.7	−4.7	−7.9
New Zealand	58.1		−9.0
Netherlands	59.2	−6.6	−9.1
Norway	51.8	−6.7	−11.6
Spain	60.6	1.7	−0.9
Sweden	57.1	−6.7	−13.0
Switzerland	62.7	−2.0	
United Kingdom	59.3		−7.9
United States	42.6	−19.6	−7.0
Average (unweighted)	**56.0**	**−4.9**	**−7.6**
Transition Economies			
Bulgaria	29.3		−10.3
Hungary	57.1		−2.6
Poland	63.9		−1.2
Former Yugoslavia	65.4	−0.9	
Average (unweighted)	**53.9**		**−4.7**
Middle East and North Africa			
Bahrain	79.6	−0.5	−13.7[b]
Egypt	79.8		−6.0
Jordan	88.9	−2.9	
Kuwait	84.2		−5.4
Tunisia	83.5		−0.6[a]
Average (unweighted)	**84.3**	**−1.7**	**−6.4**
Asia/Pacific			
China	41.8		9.1[c]
Fiji	70.1		−4.0
Hong Kong	42.8	6.9	−2.9
Japan	52.4	−1.3	−0.5
Average (unweighted)	**56.1**	**2.8**	**0.4**

Table 14.2. (contd.)

Region/country/area	Latest value MDOM75[f] (approx. 1990)	Change in MDOM75[d] 1970s	1980s
Other Developing			
Costa Rica	60.9	−8.7	−0.3
Mauritius[e]	68.2	−3.5	−17.1
Senegal	75.2		−7.7[a]
Average (unweighted)	**64.4**	**−6.1**	**−8.4**
World (unweighted)	**61.4**	**−3.6**	**−6.1**

Notes: [a] Considerable judgement was used for two countries to obtain comparable occupational classifications for the two data years. Therefore, trend data must be treated especially cautiously for these countries (Senegal and Tunisia). [b] Adjustments were made to take into account differences in the number of occupations classified in the two data years (since number of occupations differed substantially, by more than ten per cent in the two data years). When the adjustment factor is relatively large (i.e. greater than 2.0 percentage points) for some countries and therefore these trend data should be treated more cautiously than usual. This affects for the 1980s Bahrain with adjustment of 3.6. There were no relatively large adjustments for the 1970s. [c] MDOM75 can be substantially affected by individual occupations being close to the 80 per cent cut-off point (i.e. 77.5−79.9 or 80.0−82.49 per cent male). When the net effect of occupations changing to or from 77.5 to 82.49 per cent male for MDOM75 is greater than +4.0 percentage points or less than −4.0 percentage points for the period under consideration, this is noted by a superscript c. This occurs only for China for 1980s (+5.0). [d] Observed changes adjusted so as to represent change for an equivalent ten-year period by taking into consideration that the time period over which national changes are observed is not always ten years (see Chapter 4). [e] The large changes observed for Mauritius are greatly affected by changes in one occupation (spinners and weavers) where the percentage female went from 66.9 per cent female in 1972, to 90.0 per cent female in 1983 and back to 77.6 per cent female in 1990, while at the same time this occupation increased its share of non-agricultural employment from 0.6 per cent in 1972 to 4.2 per cent in 1983 and 13.0 per cent in 1990. [f] Averages are the unweighted average of the latest national values for all study countries/areas as shown in table 10.3.
Female-dominated and male-dominated occupations are defined as occupations where at least 80 per cent of the workers are either female or male respectively.
Percentage point change is based on national data and does not take into account the number of occupations in the national classification unless these differ across data years (i.e. note b). The assumption is that observed change is unaffected by the level of disaggregation in the national classification, because all national classifications are reasonably detailed (see Chapter 6).
Averages are based on unweighted averages of national values. As a comparison, a weighted average of national values for the world (using size of the non-agricultural labour force as weights) indicates changes of −9.5 per cent for the 1970s and −4.5 per cent for the 1980s. Differences as compared to the unweighted world averages of −3.6 per cent and −6.1 per cent are largely due to experiences of the largest study country for each time period (the United States for 1970s and China for the 1980s).
Regional averages are not indicated when only one country value is available.
Source: Study data.

per cent of all the occupations in our data set).[4] A further indication of this downward trend in the number of male-dominated occupations is that while there are 37 country/area examples where the number of male-dominated occupations decreased in both the 1970s and the 1980s, there are only two examples (Austria 1971–1980; Spain 1980–1990) where the number of male-dominated non-agricultural occupations increased and only two examples where this number remained unchanged (Spain 1970–1980 and Hong Kong 1971–1981).

Figure 14.1. Average MDOM75 from 1970 to 1990, by region

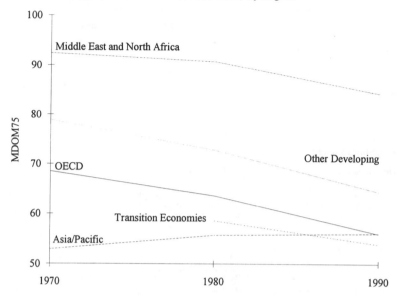

Notes: For expositional purposes, regional values for 1970, 1980 and 1990 are connected by straight line.
Regional average is not indicated if data for change in 1970s are available for only one study country in the region.
Values for 1990 are based on the average for the latest available year. Values for 1970 and 1980 are estimated by subtracting average changes in the 1970s and 1980s from the 1990 values.
Source: Table 14.2.

There are, however, some **important differences between regions as well as between OECD subregions** (figures 14.2 to 14.4)—differences that generally parallel those observed in Chapter 13 for recent changes in ID. Thus, *Asia/Pacific is the only region where MDOM75 increased on average* (a result which is even more striking when Fiji is excluded). There are no examples in Asia where MDOM75 *clearly* decreased, and two of the three examples in table 14.2 where MDOM75 clearly increased are found in Asia (Hong Kong for 1971–1981 and China for 1982–1990).

Within the OECD region, which has had a large decrease in MDOM75 on average, the Southern and Central European OECD subregions stand out as having experienced relatively little change in MDOM75 (figures 14.4 and 14.5). Thus, whereas the average percentage change was −8.3 and −9.2 for the 1970s and 1980s respectively for OECD countries outside of Southern and Central Europe, it was just −0.0 and −3.7 on average respectively for these decades in Southern and Central Europe. Furthermore, these OECD subregions contain the only non-Asian country examples where MDOM75 or the number of male-dominated non-agricultural occupations clearly increased (Austria for 1971–1980 and Spain 1980–1990); also MDOM75 clearly decreased in only 2 of its 8 country-time periods in contrast to 18 of the 19 country-time periods for the other OECD study countries. This is

GENDER AND JOBS

Table 14.3. Summary of regional trends in the percentage of the female non-agricultural labour force working in a female-dominated non-agricultural occupation (FDOM75) for the 1970s and 1980s, by region and OECD subregion

Region	1970s change[b]				1980s change[b]			
	Inc	Dec	Neutral[a]	Average change[c]	Inc	Dec	Neutral[a]	Average change[c]
OECD	4	3	5	0.9	1	6	7	-4.4
North America (United States)	0	1	0	-8.0	0	0	1	-0.5
Scandinavia	2	0	1	8.8	0	3	0	-13.1
Western Europe	1	0	1	3.1	0	1	1	3.1[e]
Southern Europe	0	1	1	-2.5	0	0	2	0.9
Central Europe	1	0	2	0.0	1	1	1	-3.4
Transition Economies	1	0	0	-[d]	0	0	3	-0.1
Middle East and North Africa	0	0	2	1.6	0	2	2	-7.3[e]
Asia/Pacific	0	0	2	2.0	2	1	1	0.7[e]
Other Developing	0	0	2	1.2	0	2	1	-16.9[e]
Total	**5**	**3**	**11**	**1.0**	**3**	**11**	**14**	**-4.9**

Notes: [a] Neutral (i.e. no clear trend) is defined as a change between −5.0 and +5.0 percentage points for a ten-year equivalent period. [b] Observed changes adjusted so as to represent change for an equivalent ten-year period by taking into consideration that the time over which national changes are observed is not always ten years (see Chapter 4). [c] Regional averages are unweighted averages of national values. Average regional changes for the 1970s are not fully comparable to those for the 1980s, since the countries with data (or even the total number of countries with data) in these two time periods are not the same. [d] Regional average is not reported when only one country value is available. [e] Observed change for one country in the region has a very large effect on the regional average. For the Other Developing region in the 1980s, the FDOM75 average change is −6.7 when Mauritius is excluded. For the Middle East/North Africa region in the 1980s, FDOM75 average change is −3.8 when Tunisia is excluded. For Asia in the 1980s, FDOM75 average change is +3.2 when Fiji is excluded. Western Europe average change for the 1980s is +3.1 when Luxembourg is excluded. Scandinavian average change for the 1980s is +0.4 when Norway is excluded.
Source: Table 14.1.

Table 14.4. Summary of regional trends in the percentage of the male non-agricultural labour force working in a male-dominated non-agricultural occupation (MDOM75) for the 1970s and 1980s, by region and OECD subregion

Region	1970s change[b]				1980s change[b]			
	Inc	Dec	Neutral[a]	Average change[c]	Inc	Dec	Neutral[a]	Average change[c]
OECD	1	7	4	-4.8	0	11	3	-7.6
North America (United States)	0	1	0	-19.6	0	1	0	-7.0
Scandinavia	0	3	0	-6.3	0	3	0	-11.0
Other English-speaking	0	1	0	_[d]	0	3	0	-8.5
Western Europe	0	1	1	-5.7	0	3	0	-8.7
Central Europe	1	1	1	0.8	0	1	1	-4.9
Southern Europe	0	0	2	-1.3	0	0	2	-2.5
Transition Economies	0	0	1	_[d]	0	1	2	-4.7
Middle East and North Africa	0	0	2	-1.7	0	3	1	-6.4
Asia/Pacific	1	0	1	2.8	1	0	3	0.4
Other Developing	0	1	1	-6.1	0	2	1	-8.4
Total	**2**	**8**	**9**	**-3.6**	**1**	**17**	**10**	**-6.1**

Notes: [a] Neutral (i.e. no clear trend) is defined as a change between -5.0 and +5.0 percentage points for a ten-year equivalent period. [b] Observed changes adjusted so as to represent change for an equivalent ten-year period by taking into consideration that the time over which national changes are observed is not always ten years. [c] Regional averages are unweighted averages of national values. Average regional changes for the 1970s and are fully comparable to those for the 1980s, since the countries with data (or even the total number of countries with data) in these two time periods are not the same. [d] Regional average is not reported when only one country value is available.
Source: Table 14.2.

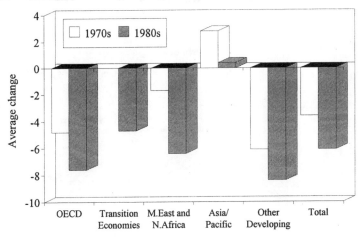

Source: Table 14.4.

another example of convergence of inequality statistics among OECD study countries and subregions, since according to study data, MDOM75 remained more or less unchanged in the Southern and Central OECD countries while falling rapidly in other OECD study countries.

In summary, in many countries and parts of the world, many men have been losing some of their labour market advantage of having occupations

Figure 14.3.   Average percentage change in number of male-dominated non-agricultural occupations for the 1970s and 1980s, by region

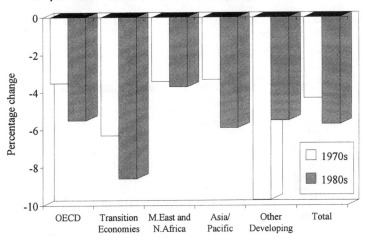

Note: Figure 14.3 differs from figure 14.2 in that here data refer to change in the *number* of different male-dominated non-agricultural occupations whereas in figure 14.2, data refer to change in percentage of male workers in male-dominated non-agricultural occupations.
Source: Table 14.5.

Figure 14.4. Average MDOM75 from 1970 to 1990, by OECD subregion

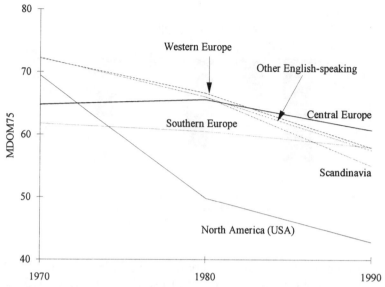

Note: See notes for figure 14.1.
Source: Table 14.6.

reserved more or less exclusively for them. This is good for labour market efficiency and gender equity, but this does not detract from the increased competitive pressure this has been exerting on male workers in the world. At the same time, there are important exceptions to this general trend, as men have

Figure 14.5. Average percentage point change in MDOM75 for the 1970s and 1980s, by OECD subregion

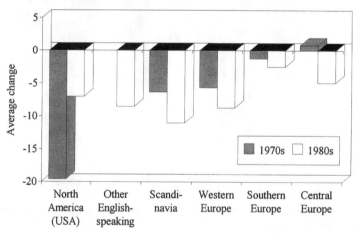

Source: Table 14.2.

GENDER AND JOBS

been holding on to their protected segments of the non-agricultural labour force in several large Asian economies (such as China, Hong Kong and Japan), in OECD countries located in Southern Europe and Central Europe (such as Spain, Switzerland, Austria and West Germany), in certain Transition Economy countries (such as Hungary, Poland and former Yugoslavia), as well as in certain Middle Eastern/North African countries (such as Jordan and Tunisia).

14.2 Recent changes for female-dominated non-agricultural occupations[5]

Changes in the past two decades in the extent to which female workers are working in female-dominated non-agricultural occupations (FDOM75) are quite different from those discussed above for MDOM75. There are also very different patterns for the 1970s and 1980s for changes in FDOM75.

In the 1970s, there was no discernible trend in the world as FDOM75 increased in about one-half and decreased in about one-half of the 17 study countries/areas with data for this time period; the average change in FDOM75 was only about one percentage point per country/area for the decade (tables 14.1 and 14.3).[6] Neither was there a discernible worldwide trend in the number of female-dominated occupations in the 1970s; this fell in seven study countries, rose in nine study countries and remained the same in three study countries (table 14.5).

Regional results for the 1970s indicate that the small change in FDOM75 observed for the world as a whole was also found in each region (figures 14.6 and 14.7). There were, however, important and striking differences found among OECD subregions (figure 14.8): Scandinavia stood out as having had a substantial increase in FDOM75 in the 1970s. Within the other OECD subregions, there was considerable variation in the 1970s in national experiences, although there were large decreases for the United States, Australia and Spain and large increases for Netherlands and Austria.

The 1980s were different.[7,8] **There was a worldwide tendency for FDOM75 to decrease.** On average, FDOM75 fell by about 5 percentage points per study country in this time period. And this fall in FDOM75 was found in the great majority of study countries, as a decrease is observed for 23 of the 28 study countries/areas with data for this time period. Even when only a "substantial" change is considered as a change (defined as at least 5 percentage points in an equivalent ten-year period), there are 11 clear decreases in the 1980s as compared to only 3 clear increases.

This decrease in FDOM75 for the world as a whole during the 1980s, however, was **not observed in all study regions or OECD subregions.** There

Figure 14.6. Average FDOM75 from 1970 to 1990, by region

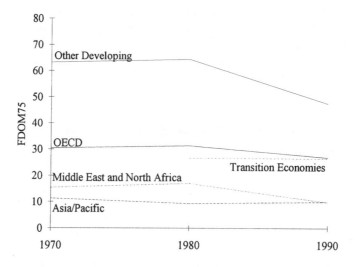

Note: See notes for figure 14.1.
Source: Table 14.7.

Figure 14.7. Average percentage point change in FDOM75 for the 1970s and 1980s, by region

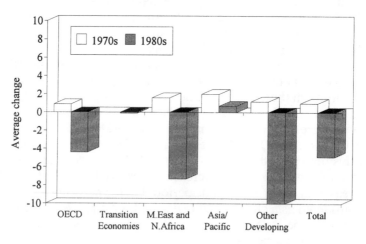

Note: Value for Other Developing region for the 1980s is −16.9; this is highly influenced by the value for Mauritius (−37.5). Excluding Mauritius, average would be −6.6.
Source: Table 14.3.

Figure 14.8.   Average percentage change in number of female-dominated non-agricultural occupations for the 1970s and 1980s, by region

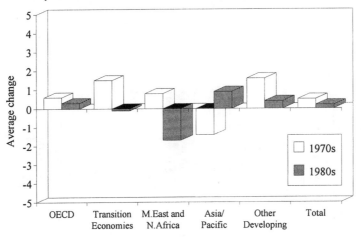

Note: Figure 14.8 differs from figure 14.7 in that here data refer to change in the *number* of different female-dominated non-agricultural occupations, whereas in figure 14.7 data refer to change in the percentage of women workers in female-dominated non-agricultural occupations.
Source: Table 14.5.

was *no discernible trend in FDOM in the Transition Economy region. And in the Asia/Pacific region, there was a slight upward bias,* as FDOM increased by about 5 percentage points in China and Hong Kong and showed little change in Japan.[9] Among OECD subregions, Southern Europe and North America as well as parts of other OECD subregions (e.g. France, West Germany and the Netherlands) showed little change or an increase in FDOM75 during the 1980s.

When we look at changes in the *number* of female-dominated non-agricultural occupations (table 14.5 and figure 14.8), it is found that female-dominated non-agricultural occupations (which are about 10 per cent of all non-agricultural occupations) increased only slightly from about 16.0 per study country in 1970 to about 16.5 per study country in 1990. In fact, virtually all of this small overall change in the number of female-dominated non-agricultural occupations in the world can be more or less traced to results for three study countries (Norway and Sweden for the 1970s and the United States for the 1980s).

This is an interesting result, because the large increase in female workers over the past two decades could easily have created many new female-dominated occupations. Rather, in the 1970s, it seems that existing female-dominated occupations expanded quickly enough to retain their relative importance for female workers. In the 1980s, however, it seems that the growth of already established female-dominated occupations absorbed most of the new female workers. **Instead, it seems that decreases in FDOM75**

Table 14.5. Change in number of non-agricultural occupations which are male-dominated and female-dominated for the 1970s and 1980s, by region

Region	Latest year (approx. 1990[d])			Average percentage point change in % occupations[a,b]			
	Average no. of non-ag. occupations classified	% of occups MDOM occup.[g]	% of occups FDOM occup.[g]	Male-dominated occupations		Female-dominated occupations	
				1970s[e]	1980s[f]	1970s[e]	1980s[f]
OECD	232	44.3	10.6	-3.5	-5.5	0.6	0.3
Transition Economies	81	23.4	11.4	-6.3	-8.6	1.5	-0.1
Asia/Pacific	162	41.8	5.7	-3.3	-5.9	-1.4	0.9
Middle East and North Africa	62	76.0	1.0	-3.4	-3.7	0.8	-1.7
Other Developing	57	60.2	4.8	-9.7	-5.5	1.6	0.4
Total	**169**	**46.8**	**8.3**	**-4.3**	**-5.7**	**0.5**	**0.2**

Notes: [a] Percentage point change represents net change (i.e. additions minus exits) as a percentage of all gender-dominated occupations (i.e. occupations that are male-dominated or female-dominated). [b] Another way to look at these results would be to calculate the approximate percentage change for male-dominated occupations by dividing the observed percentage point change for male-dominated occupations by 1990 MDOM75 value shown in column 3; similarly for female-dominated occupations, by dividing the observed percentage change for female-dominated occupations by 1990 FDOM75 value shown in column 4. [d] Averages here based on data for the 28 countries/areas with approximately 1990 data. [e] Countries included if data are available for 1970 and 1980 (19 countries). [f] Countries included if data are available for 1980 and 1990 (28 countries). [g] Percentage is affected by the number of occupations classified with more disaggregated classifications having higher percentages *ceteris paribus*. This implies that values in these columns are higher *ceteris paribus* in OECD and Asia/Pacific as compared to percentages for other regions.
There are a total of 32 different countries/areas with time series data included in this table. Of these, 15 countries/areas have data for 1970, 1980 and 1990. Therefore, the sample of countries/areas for 1970s and 1980s somewhat differ. Five countries with data for 1980s were excluded from this table, because the number of occupations classified differed substantially in 1980 and 1990 (see earlier notes on this).
Source: Study data.

in the 1980s are caused by women workers often entering into non-female-dominated non-agricultural occupations (and often male-dominated occupations).

This discussion leads us very nicely into Chapter 15 where we investigate how the 17 typical "male" and "female" occupations analysed in Chapter 11 have been changing in terms of their sex composition, and whether or not there are regional or OECD subregional patterns in these changes.

Notes

[1] In order to increase the comparability over time of national data, adjustments were made in national estimates of FDOM75, MDOM75 and TDOM75 for the same five countries as in Chapter 13 (i.e. countries where the number of occupations classified in national data differ by over 10 per cent across data years). These adjustment factors were calculated using the natural log relationship for these countries between number of occupations classified and FDOM, MDOM and TDOM based on data presented in Chapter 10.

The adjustment factors used in the present chapter to account for upward biases over time due to increases over time in the number of occupations classified are as follows for 1980s (with no adjustments required for 1970s):

	FDOM75	MDOM75	TDOM75
Australia	13.7	1.1	7.4
Cyprus	0.9	0.6	0.3
Poland	2.7	0.2	1.5
Bahrain	0.0	3.6	3.3
Kuwait	0.7	0.3	0.3

Notice that *adjustments are generally small*, being less than 2.0 percentage points except for: MDOM75 (Bahrain 1980s with 3.6); FDOM75 (Australia 13.7; and Poland 2.7); and TDOM75 (Australia 7.4; and Bahrain 3.3).

[2] To assist in the analysis, we looked into how changes over time in FDOM75 and MDOM75 may have been affected by occupations changing from being gender-dominated to being non-gender dominated or vice-versa by "just qualifying" (i.e. by having 80.0–82.49 per cent male or female) or by "just disqualifying" (i.e. having 78.5–79.99 per cent male or female). When the net effect of all such changes for a study country exceeded 4 per cent for an equivalent ten-year period, we made the ad hoc judgement that this effect was substantial and indicated this next to national values in tables 14.1 and 14.2.

While this net effect is small on average (e.g. +1.15 and −1.43 net biases for FDOM75 for the 1970s and 1980s respectively), and there are relatively few examples of values exceeding −4.0 or +4.0 (three examples for FDOM75 for 1970s and four for 1980s; no examples for MDOM75 for 1970s and one for 1980s), **there were several national examples of major net "biases".** Thus, for example, Jordan had one occupation (maids and related housekeeping not elsewhere classified) which employs approximately 14 per cent of female non-agricultural workers, which went from 67 to 81 per cent female between 1961 and 1979; Italy had one occupation (tailors and furriers) employing approximately 5 per cent of female non-agricultural workers, that went from 71 to 80 per cent female between 1971 and 1981; Luxembourg had one occupation (salesmen, shop assistants and related workers) employing approximately 13 per cent of female non-agricultural workers go from 84 to 79 per cent female between 1980 and 1990. There were *no* similar striking examples for MDOM involving one specific occupation, although in aggregate, China had a net bias of +5.0 per cent for MDOM for 1980s.

[3] This decrease observed in MDOM75 for the world for the 1970–1990 period is found to be even larger when a weighted average of national values (using size of non-agricultural labour

force as weights) is calculated at −14.0 per cent (compared to −9.7 per cent for unweighted world average). It is much higher for the 1990s, −9.5 per cent (compared to −3.6 per cent) but lower for the 1980s at −4.5 per cent (compared to −6.1 per cent). These differences between weighted and unweighted world averages are largely due to the experiences of the largest study countries in each time period (the United States for 1970s and China for 1980s).

[4] For these comparisons of changes over 10 years in the number of male-dominated occupations, we excluded country-examples where the number of occupations classified changed substantially over this period (i.e. Australia 1980–90; Cyprus 1981–89; Poland 1978–88; Bahrain 1981–91; Kuwait 1975–85).

[5] It is interesting to note that **the percentage of the total non-agricultural labour force working in a gender-dominated occupation (TDOM75) has been decreasing over time**. It decreased by an average of 2.9 percentage points in the 1970s and by a further 7.7 percentage points in the 1980s, based on an unweighted average of national values. A similar result for the entire 1970-1990 period is observed, a −12.0 percentage point change for the period (−7.8 per cent for the 1970s and −4.2 per cent for 1980s) when based on a weighted average of national values (using size of non-agricultural labour force as weights). Differences between the weighted average and unweighted world average is largely due to the experiences of the largest study country in each time period (the United States for 1970s and China for 1980s).

The decrease in TDOM75 in the 1970s was mainly due to falls in MDOM75, whereas in the 1980s falls in both MDOM75 and FDOM75 contributed to the fall in TDOM75. In general though, changes in TDOM75 and MDOM75 are highly related as they have correlation coefficients of 0.85 and 0.82 for the 1970s and 1980s respectively—implying that about 70 per cent of the recent changes in TDOM75 can be "explained" by recent changes in MDOM75 alone. In contrast, correlation coefficients for changes in FDOM75 and TDOM75 are 0.45 and 0.73 for the 1970s and 1980s respectively, implying that only about 20 and 50 per cent of changes in TDOM75 can be "explained" by changes in FDOM75 alone.

Also interesting is that even though TDOM and ID are both general measures of occupational segregation by sex, changes over time in ID75 and TDOM75 are not strongly correlated. (This is also true for the relationship between changes in TDOM75 and changes in ID attributable to the changing sex composition of occupations, what we called SEX in Chapter 13). Thus, based on study data for all available country-time periods, the correlation coefficient between changes in TDOM75 and changes in ID75 (changes in TDOM75 and changes in SEX) is only 0.57 (0.52) implying that only about 30 per cent of recent changes in TDOM75 or ID75 is "explainable" by changes in the other. These results indicate that *recent changes in TDOM75 and ID75 (or TDOM75 and SEX) have been independent of each other to a large extent* and so are due also in large part to other factors such as changes in female labour force participation.

[6] The same conclusion that there was no discernible worldwide trend in FDOM75 for the 1970s is drawn when we: (i) only considered substantial national changes in FDOM75 (defined as a change which is greater than a 5 percentage point change over an equivalent ten-year period); and/or (ii) excluded female-dominated occupations which changed to just being female-dominated (with 80.0–82.49 per cent female) or to just not being female-dominated (i.e. with 78.5–79.9 per cent female). The same conclusion, however, would not be drawn based on the weighted world average, largely because of the large decrease observed in the United States. The weighted world average change for FDOM75 for the 1970s is −3.5 per cent (compared to +1.0 per cent for the unweighted world average).

[7] For the 15 study economies with data for both the 1970s and 1980s, it is noteworthy that changes in FDOM75 were often qualitatively different in the 1970s as compared to the 1980s. For example, there were large changes in FDOM75 in Austria and Norway in both decades, but with opposite signs. Also, there were large changes in FDOM75 in Luxembourg, the Netherlands, Spain, Sweden, the United States, Hong Kong, Costa Rica and Mauritius in one decade and small changes in the other decade. It appears that because of the somewhat arbitrary nature of our definition of gender-dominated occupations (a yes or no definition with a single dividing point) that **a national trend in FDOM75 based on data for a ten-year time period can be misleading.** *More reliable, it appears to us, are average changes for groups of countries (for example, regions and subregions) for a ten-year period or changes for individual countries for a 20-year period.* Based on this perspective, we find that FDOM75 clearly changed

in the past two decades in 5 of the 15 study countries/areas with data for 1970–90. It clearly decreased in Australia, the United States and Mauritius while it clearly increased in Norway and Sweden. Luxembourg is not included as an example of a clear decrease for the 1970–1990 period, because almost all of the observed decrease in FDOM75 is due to results for one large occupation (which went from 83.6 per cent female in 1980 to 79.3 per cent female in 1991).

[8] It should be noted that a much weaker conclusion would be drawn for the 1980s based on a weighted world average (using size of non-agricultural labour force as weights) of national values. The weighted world average change for FDOM for the 1980s is −1.8 per cent (compared to −5.0 per cent for the unweighted world average) because of the large increase observed in China.

[9] Within OECD subregions, the Other English-speaking country subregion stands out as having had an especially large drop in FDOM75 during the 1980s. The magnitude of this drop is, however, exaggerated by results for one large occupation in United Kingdom (shop salesmen and assistants, went from 84.5 per cent female in 1981 to 78.0 per cent female in 1990).

RECENT CHANGES IN THE FEMINIZATION OF 17 IMPORTANT "MALE" AND "FEMALE" OCCUPATIONS

15

This chapter investigates changes in the past two decades in the feminization and masculinization of nine typically "female" occupations and eight typically "male" occupations. These are the same 17 occupations investigated in Chapter 11, where we analysed cross-national differences for a recent year, generally around 1990.

Table 15.1 presents country data on percentage point changes in percentage male and female for the 1970s and 1980s. Table 15.2 summarizes these data for study regions while figures 15.1 and 15.2 illustrate average changes for study regions. Table 15.3 indicates the extent to which these 17 occupations are male-dominated or female-concentrated for the earliest and latest available data years.

Readers need to keep in mind while interpreting these data that national occupational classifications for specific occupations sometimes differ over time for particular study countries. For this reason, we included national data only when we felt that the data are reasonably comparable over time. When we continued to have doubt about comparability, this is noted at the bottom of table 15.1 (e.g. nurses in country x may have included psychiatric nurses and/or professional midwives in one data year while there was no specific mention of these specializations in another year). Readers are also referred to notes at the bottom of tables in Chapter 11 for indications when an occupation in country x differs from that for other countries (e.g. an occupation may refer to cooks only in country x, whereas in country y this occupation might refer to cooks, waiters and waitresses).

We are generally agnostic as to *a priori* expectations regarding changes over the past two decades, simply wanting to observe recent changes in the feminization and masculinization of these 17 occupations and whether or not there are clear patterns to these changes. The only *a priori* expectation is that the percentage female should tend to increase along with the general increase in recent decades in female labour force participation rates for the non-agricultural labour force as a whole.

Figure 15.1. Average change in percentage male for eight typical "male" occupations for the1970s and 1980s, by region

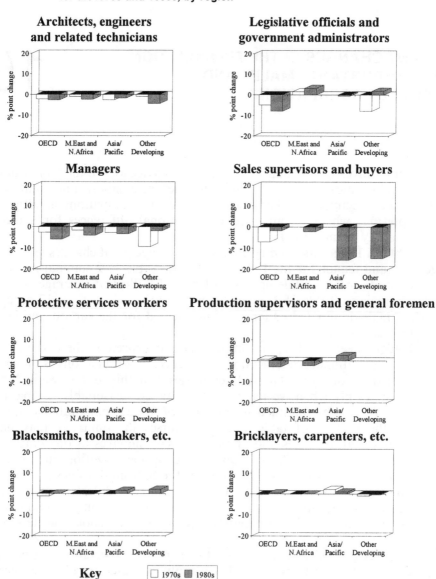

Notes: Percentage point changes reported are for an equivalent ten-year period.
Regional average is unweighted average of national values. Regional value is not reported when only one national value in the region is available for a time period.
Source: Table 15.2.

15.1 Changes in the feminization of eight typical "male" occupations

The eight specific "male" occupations analysed in Chapter 11 can be divided into two groups based on how the percentage male has changed in the past two decades. Just as in the cross-section analysis of the current situation in Chapter 11, there is considerable similarity across study countries, in how the percentage male has been changing recently.

"Male" occupations with little or no change in percentage female

Male percentage has remained more or less unchanged during the past two decades throughout the world in four of our eight typical "male" occupations. They represent striking examples of occupations which have been able to retain their masculine character despite increasing female labour force participation rates around the world.[1]

All three of the selected production sector occupations (production supervisors and general foremen; blacksmiths, toolmakers, etc.; bricklayers, carpenters, etc.) **along with the protective service workers occupation have remained very much "male" occupations during the 1970–90 period.** As indicated in table 15.2, percentage female changed by less than 5 percentage points per equivalent ten-year period in 47 out of 53 country examples for the 1970s and in 69 out of 75 country examples for the 1980s. Furthermore, the average decade change per study country for each of these four occupations was always less than 3 percentage points on average (and less than less than 1 percentage point in one-half of the country-time period examples). These are small changes in light of the increasing percentage female in the non-agricultural labour force as a whole (approximately 3 to 4 percentage points per decade). Partly because of this lack of change, these four occupations have remained male-dominated occupations throughout the world during the past two decades. As shown in table 15.3, these are male-dominated occupations in 83 out of our 85 country examples for the latest year.

Why these four occupations have remained so male-dominated throughout the world is an important issue, since these are often well paying. Clearly, this is an area of the labour market that needs increased gender sensitization to help speed the integration of women into these occupations—and *all three of the social partners (workers, employers and government) need to play a role in this sensitization, especially unions, as these are often highly unionized occupations.*

The nine country examples in tables 15.1 and 15.2 where percentage female increased by more than 5 percentage points over a ten-year equivalent period in one of these four "male" occupations could perhaps provide some insight into how it might be possible to integrate these occupations. For protective service workers, the United States and Norway stand out, as they

Table 15.1. Percentage point change in the feminization of nine typical "female" occupations and in the masculinization of eight typical "male" occupations for the 1970s and 1980s[a,b]

Occupation	Australia			Austria			Cyprus		
	1970s	1980s	Latest year value (%)	1970s	1980s	Latest year value (%)	1970s	1980s	Latest year value (%)
Typical "male" occupations									
Architects, engineers and related technicians	-5.4	10.6	94.1	2.9 (3.2)	-2.4	93.3		-1.8 (-2.3)	78.6
Legislative officials and government administrators	-.8	-5.3	93.9	11.3 (12.6)	-11.9	74.3		-.2[i] (-.3)	97.8
Managers	-2.4[j]	-2.5[j]	83.3	9.6 (10.7)	5.1	86.1		-.9 (-1.2)	91.2
Sales supervisors and buyers								4.5[k] (5.6)	91.1
Protective services workers	-3.5	-4.5	92.0	-1.1 (-1.2)	1.7	98.8		-1.6 (-2.1)	94.3
Production supervisors and general foremen								-1.7 (-2.1)	87.5
Blacksmiths, toolmakers, sharpeners and related workers	.3[m]	1.6[m]	98.9	-1.0 (-1.1)	.5	99.2		5.6 (7.1)	98.8
Bricklayers, carpenters and other construction workers	-1.7	.5	98.8	.1 (-.1)	.6	98.5		5.0 (6.3)	99.9
Typical "female" occupations									
Nurses	.1	-2.5	90.5					-1.0 (-1.2)	78.3
Teachers	1.8	3.3	64.3	2.2 (2.4)	3.1	64.7		7.7 (9.6)	54.8
Stenographers and typists	-.9	-.6	98.6		11.9[c]	25.7		-.6 (-.8)	97.1
Bookkeepers, cashiers and related workers	16.9	-6.6	72.2	11.4 (12.7)	4.0	70.8		8.2 (10.3)	55.4
Salespersons, shop assistants and related workers	-2.5	4.7	67.1	.8 (0.9)	1.9	66.9		-2.3 (-2.9)	52.7
Cooks, waiters, bartenders and related workers	-.8	9.6	79.2	-7.4 (-8.2)	-8.3	59.2		-7.0 (-8.8)	25.7
Maids and related housekeeping service workers				-5.2 (-5.8)	-3.0	78.2		-9.5 (-11.9)	86.7
Hairdressers, barbers, beauticians and related workers	.6	6.1	85.8	8.0 (8.8)	-1.6	82.7		11.7 (14.6)	73.0
Tailors, dressmakers, sewers, upholsterers, and related workers	-8.2		73.6					.9 (1.1)	87.5

Occupation	Finland			France			West Germany		
	1970s	1980s	Latest year value (%)	1970s	1980s	Latest year value (%)	1970s	1980s	Latest year value (%)
Typical "male" occupations									
Architects, engineers and related technicians	-3.9	-3.7	85.0		-6.1 (-7.6)	87.2	-.7 (-1.8)	-2.4 (-2.6)	95.3
Legislative officials and government administrators	-7.0	-10.4	58.3				-3.1 (-7.7)	-4.9 (-5.5)	78.9
Managers	-4.9	-11.9	75.3		1.2 (1.5)	85.8	-1.4 (-3.4)	-2.3 (-2.5)	73.4
Sales supervisors and buyers									
Protective services workers	-4.2	-2.5	90.9		-1.0 (-1.2)	93.6	-.1 (-.3)	-.2 (-.2)	96.7
Production supervisors and general foremen									
Blacksmiths, toolmakers, sharpeners and related workers	-1.2	-.2	97.0		-.5 (-.7)	97.9			
Bricklayers, carpenters and other construction workers	2.7	.8	97.3		.1 (.1)	99.9			
Typical "female" occupations									
Nurses	-1.6	-.7	94.1		1.3 (1.6)	87.1	-3.1 (-7.8)	-2.6 (-2.8)	82.3
Teachers	1.9	3.9	63.6		1.6 (2.0)	65.4	1.1 (2.7)	1.4 (1.6)	57.1
Stenographers and typists	-.5	.4	96.1		-.6 (-.8)	97.1	.2 (.4)	.4 (.4)	97.4
Bookkeepers, cashiers and related workers	2.4	-.4	93.4		5.6 (7.0)	83.5	1.7 (4.2)	1.4 (1.6)	76.7
Salespersons, shop assistants and related workers	-2.4	-1.9	70.6		-.1 (-.1)	76.7	1.5 (3.8)	-2.2 (-2.4)	80.8
Cooks, waiters, bartenders and related workers	-2.8	-4.3	87.2		-.8 (-1.0)	46.2	-1.5 (-3.8)	-5.9 (-6.6)	66.1
Maids and related housekeeping service workers	-.1	-.2	99.5		.7 (.9)	99.0	-1.3 (-3.4)	-2.0 (-2.2)	95.2
Hairdressers, barbers, beauticians and related workers	-.2	.9	97.4		-.5 (-.7)	85.2	4.0 (9.9)	3.3 (3.6)	85.7
Tailors, dressmakers, sewers, upholsterers, and related workers	2.5	-2.4	90.9		-.7 (-.8)	76.3	2.0 (5.1)	-1.5 (-1.7)	89.1

Table 15.1. (contd.)

Occupation	Italy			Luxembourg			New Zealand		
	1970s	1980s	Latest year value (%)	1970s	1980s	Latest year value (%)	1970s	1980s	Latest year value (%)
Typical "male" occupations									
Architects, engineers and related technicians	-2.9		95.4	-1.8 (-1.7)	-2.9	94.5		-2.8 (-5.6)	91.7
Legislative officials and government administrators	-.8		87.6	-4.3 (-3.9)	2.2	93.6		-5.4 (-10.9)	84.7
Managers	-12.3[f]		65.2[f]	4.0 (3.7)	-8.0	87.6		-8.8 (-17.7)	82.4
Sales supervisors and buyers				-8.1	5.7	85.6		-2.0 (-3.9)	76.3
Protective services workers	-1.1		98.5	-1.4 (-1.2)	-.6	96.8		1.6 (3.3)	93.9
Production supervisors and general foremen				-1.7 (-1.5)	.7	98.8		-5.6 (-11.2)	84.1
Blacksmiths, toolmakers, sharpeners and related workers	-4.6		85.4	-.2 (-.2)	-1.6	98.2		.1 (.2)	92.2
Bricklayers, carpenters and other construction workers	-1.0		98.3	-.3 (-.3)	-.4	99.3		-.4 (-.8)	99.1
Typical "female" occupations									
Nurses	-.6		66.5						
Teachers	6.1		72.7	2.7 (2.4)	-.2	52.6		2.0 (3.9)	64.6
Stenographers and typists	-6.7		84.0	-.4 (-.4)	-1.7	91.9		.2 (.3)	98.4
Bookkeepers, cashiers and related workers	8.2		53.8	15.9 (14.5)	5.4	56.4		6.4 (12.8)	77.1
Salespersons, shop assistants and related workers	-13.0		46.2	-1.5 (-1.3)	-4.3	79.3		.8 (1.6)	66.1
Cooks, waiters, bartenders and related workers	12.9		44.1	-6.6 (-6.0)	-6.7	52.9		.3 (.6)	75.2
Maids and related housekeeping service workers	-1.4		92.3	2.3 (2.1)	-2.1	97.1		-2.4 (-4.8)	87.9
Hairdressers, barbers, beauticians and related workers	14.6		60.8	16.1 (14.6)	.6	77.7		2.9 (5.9)	86.2
Tailors, dressmakers, sewers, upholsterers, and related workers	6.5		75.0	16.0 (14.5)	1.9	89.3		-.9 (-1.8)	79.8

Occupation	Netherlands			Norway			Spain		
	1970s	1980s	Latest year value (%)	1970s	1980s	Latest year value (%)	1970s	1980s	Latest year value (%)
Typical "male" occupations									
Architects, engineers and related technicians	-.2 (-.3)	-3.2 (-2.9)	95.4	-3.1	-5.1	87.8		-3.8	92.9
Legislative officials and government administrators	-3.6 (-6.1)	-6.3 (-5.8)		-16.6	-18.2	54.2	-6.3 (-12.5)	-7.6	86.2
Managers	-3.4 (-5.6)	-5.5 (-5.0)	86.6	-3.8	-6.1	82.8	.7 (1.3)	-5.8	90.9
Sales supervisors and buyers	-3.7 (-6.2)		79.2	-8.4	-10.2	72.1	-7.0 (-13.9)	1.6	89.1
Protective services workers	-2.5 (-4.2)	3.6 (3.3)	100.0	-7.7	-6.3	79.9	-.4 (-.9)	-1.1	96.7
Production supervisors and general foremen	1.3 (2.1)	-2.9 (-2.6)	94.4				1.6 (3.2)	-1.2	95.4
Blacksmiths, toolmakers, sharpeners and related workers	.5 (.8)	-2.3 (-2.1)	97.4	-5.4	-3.3	90.2	1.0 (1.9)	.1	96.4
Bricklayers, carpenters and other construction workers	-.3 (-.5)	.4 (.4)	100.0	-.9	-1.5	97.4	-.1 (-.3)	-.3	98.6
Typical "female" occupations									
Nurses	1.5 (2.4)	3.0 (2.7)	85.2	.1	.6	93.4			
Teachers	4.0 (6.7)	2.7 (2.4)	47.3	5.1	-4.1	48.4		-.8	58.8
Stenographers and typists	-.6 (-1.0)	3.1 (2.9)	99.9	7.6	6.4	95.8		3.0	94.7
Bookkeepers, cashiers and related workers	1.3 (2.2)	20.5 (18.7)	56.1	12.6	9.2	77.7		14.9	37.0
Salespersons, shop assistants and related workers	4.0 (6.6)	-10.9 (-10.0)	59.3	3.5	-3.3	75.2		-1.9	55.4
Cooks, waiters, bartenders and related workers	4.9 (8.2)	1.3 (1.2)	58.3	3.1	-5.4	77.2		-1.0	41.4
Maids and related housekeeping service workers	.4 (.6)	.3 (.3)	95.8	-1.6	-1.4	96.7		2.6	97.4
Hairdressers, barbers, beauticians and related workers	7.0 (11.6)	18.8 (17.1)	85.7	10.4	7.2	90.4	5.6 (11.1)	6.6	79.5
Tailors, dressmakers, sewers, upholsterers, and related workers	.5 (.8)	-1.6 (-1.5)	65.6	3.4	-3.0	82.6	.3 (.6)	-2.7	80.7

RECENT CHANGES IN THE FEMINIZATION OF 17 IMPORTANT OCCUPATIONS

Table 15.1. (contd.)

Occupation	Switzerland			United States		
	1970s	1980s	Latest year value (%)	1970s	1980s	Latest year value (%)
Typical "male" occupations						
Architects, engineers, and related technicians	.0		98.5	-4.9	-2.7	88.1
Legislative officials and government administrators	-.2		94.0	-11.6	-13.1	54.5
Managers	-1.1		94.2	-10.4	-16.1	53.9
Sales supervisors and buyers	4.8		67.9	-11.0	-6.5	65.7
Protective services workers	-2.8		92.4	-5.0	-3.8	84.8
Production supervisors and general foremen				-1.1	-1.4	96.8
Blacksmiths, toolmakers, sharpeners and related workers	-1.4		98.1	-.5	1.1	96.6
Bricklayers, carpenters and other construction workers	-.1		99.9	-.2	.7	99.0
Typical "female" occupations						
Nurses	-.4		89.8	-1.4	-.9	95.0
Teachers	1.6		49.9	1.5	3.2	68.9
Stenographers and typists	1.3[d]		62.1	1.5	.1	98.4
Bookkeepers, cashiers and related workers	11.3		48.2	4.7	-1.1	85.5
Salespersons, shop assistants and related workers	-2.6		83.5	5.1	.2	66.9
Cooks, waiters, bartenders and related workers	-2.1		61.0	-3.6	-9.2	58.3
Maids and related housekeeping service workers	-1.1		93.6	-10.2	4.1	89.7
Hairdressers, barbers, beauticians and related workers	11.4		77.6	7.7	5.5	81.4
Tailors, dressmakers, sewers, upholsterers, and related workers	-2.7		77.8	3.6	5.0	62.9

Occupation	Bahrain 1970s	Bahrain 1980s	Bahrain Latest year value (%)	Egypt 1970s	Egypt 1980s	Egypt Latest year value (%)	Jordan 1970s	Jordan 1980s	Jordan Latest year value (%)
Typical "male" occupations									
Architects, engineers and related technicians	-1.9	-1.5	96.1		-.4	94.4	-.1 (-.1)		98.8
Legislative officials and government administrators	5.5	11.1	93.0		5.6	88.5	-4.0 (-2.2)		95.6
Managers	-1.1	-2.0	95.1		-7.6	88.6	-3.7 (-2.1)		95.5
Sales supervisors and buyers					-2.4	92.1			
Protective services workers	-.9	.7	99.6		-.0	99.7	-.6 (-.3)		98.9
Production supervisors and general foremen					-.6	97.4			
Blacksmiths, toolmakers, sharpeners and related workers	.0	-.2	99.8		-.3	99.3	-.2 (-.1)		99.7
Bricklayers, carpenters and other construction workers	-.1	.1	99.9		-.1	99.7	.1 (.0)		100.0
Typical "female" occupations									
Nurses			64.1						
Teachers	10.4	-6.2	45.4		5.9	39.9	15.4 (8.6)		50.1
Stenographers and typists	35.3	3.0	74.5		49.5	65.5	31.3 (17.4)		76.0
Bookkeepers, cashiers and related workers	17.2[e]	2.8[e]	25.0		9.4	35.7	7.5 (4.1)		9.9
Salespersons, shop assistants and related workers	1.6	5.1	7.5		1.3	8.1	2.0 (1.1)		3.4
Cooks, waiters, bartenders and related workers	2.4[f]	4.4[f]	7.4		.7	3.6	2.7 (1.5)		3.4
Maids and related housekeeping service workers	21.0[g]	26.6[g]	69.5		-7.4	78.6	14.2 (7.9)		81.1
Hairdressers, barbers, beauticians and related workers	18.4	6.3	28.4		1.2	3.6	15.7 (8.7)		19.0
Tailors, dressmakers, sewers, upholsterers, and related workers	.9	14.2	19.5		-3.6	14.6	-32.7 (-18.2)		26.2

Table 15.1. (contd.)

Occupation	Kuwait			Tunisia			China		
	1970s	1980s	Latest year value (%)	1970s	1980s	Latest year value (%)	1970s	1980s	Latest year value (%)
Typical "male" occupations									
Architects, engineers and related technicians		-1.4	97.9		-8.1 (-5.8)	86.8		-4.5 (-5.6)	77.8
Legislative officials and government administrators		-2.0	95.9		-2.8 (-2.0)	89.8			89.8
Managers		-2.3	96.3		-5.7 (-4.0)	91.0		.2 (.2)	89.8
Sales supervisors and buyers		-1.9	96.8					-11.4 (-14.2)	83.5
Protective services workers		-.2	99.8		-.4 (-.3)	98.0		-.7 (-.9)	93.1
Production supervisors and general foremen		.2	100.0		-9.2 (-6.6)	89.6			
Blacksmiths, toolmakers, sharpeners and related workers		.0	100.0		-.2 (-.2)	98.4		.6 (.7)	68.4
Bricklayers, carpenters and other construction workers		.0	100.0		.1 (.1)	99.3		.6 (.8)	94.5
Typical "female" occupations									
Nurses		-2.0	97.9			43.7		.9 (1.2)	95.7
Teachers		5.6	56.6		5.8 (4.1)	30.4		5.4 (6.7)	44.4
Stenographers and typists		16.0	58.0		11.3 (8.1)	54.5		1.3 (1.6)	87.6
Bookkeepers, cashiers and related workers		9.6	13.1		4.1 (2.9)	20.6		7.9 (9.9)	78.3
Salespersons, shop assistants and related workers		1.1	3.7		-2.4 (-1.7)	3.3		4.6 (5.7)	56.2
Cooks, waiters, bartenders and related workers		.2	7.9		.6 (.4)	4.7		3.7 (4.7)	51.3
Maids and related housekeeping service workers		6.3	77.5		-20.5 (-14.6)	68.1			
Hairdressers, barbers, beauticians and related workers		-.6	22.4		8.5 (6.1)	30.0		22.8 (28.5)	48.8
Tailors, dressmakers, sewers, upholsterers, and related workers		-.6	4.7		-2.4[h] (-1.7)	83.0		-3.4 (-4.3)	82.9

Occupation	Fiji			Hong Kong			Japan		
	1970s	1980s	Latest year value (%)	1970s	1980s	Latest year value (%)	1970s	1980s	Latest year value (%)
Typical "male" occupations									
Architects, engineers and related technicians		−.8	96.3	−4.6	1.17	95.1	−.4	−1.42	97.6
Legislative officials and government administrators		1.7	92.3		−2.85	68.1	−.3	−.42	98.3
Managers		−2.0	90.6	−6.4	−9.23	77.1	1.0	−1.99	90.8
Sales supervisors and buyers		−4.4	81.6		−28.05	56.9			
Protective services workers		−1.0	97.1	−5.8	3.72	93.4	−.7	−.28	97.2
Production supervisors and general foremen		−2.4	94.0		7.54[l]	85.6			
Blacksmiths, toolmakers, sharpeners and related workers		−.8	91.8	−1.2	6.91	87.9	1.1	−.25	95.3
Bricklayers, carpenters and other construction workers		−.2	99.4	3.5[n]	2.25	97.1	1.0	1.18	95.4
Typical "female" occupations									
Nurses		3.3	53.1		−4.10	89.4	−.1	−1.09	96.5
Teachers		−1.9	93.7		−.35	61.4	4.9	.61	43.4
Stenographers and typists		11.7	43.4	5.8	21.42	94.0	−.5	−3.10	93.3
Bookkeepers, cashiers and related workers		4.9	34.5	23.0	17.78	70.3	5.1	6.24	75.6
Salespersons, shop assistants and related workers		12.3	44.1		10.40	43.8	2.9	4.11	64.6
Cooks, waiters, bartenders and related workers							−1.7	−1.53	63.1
Maids and related housekeeping service workers		−2.1	95.8		10.21	91.4	−1.0	.30	97.6
Hairdressers, barbers, beauticians and related workers		21.6	40.9	.8	15.42	35.5	−.3	−1.31	69.1
Tailors, dressmakers, sewers, upholsterers, and related workers		31.1	71.2	9.1	−7.57	65.5	1.8	−1.47	80.4

Table 15.1. (contd.)

Occupation	Costa Rica			Mauritius			Senegal		
	1970s	1980s	Latest year value (%)	1970s	1980s	Latest year value (%)	1970s	1980s	Latest year value (%)
Typical "male" occupations									
Architects, engineers and related technicians	-1.4 (-1.0)	-1.4 (-3.4)	96.2	-1.0 (-.8)	-3.5 (-4.9)	94.2		-5.4 (-4.5)	92.8
Legislative officials and government administrators	-20.0 (-14.3)	.6 (1.4)	74.0	-1.4 (-1.2)	7.2 (10.2)	89.2		-7.2 (-5.9)	90.4
Managers	-9.7 (-6.9)	-4.8 (-11.9)	73.9	-12.8 (-11.7)	-3.2 (-4.6)	81.9		13.6 (11.0)	93.9
Sales supervisors and buyers				-3.9 (-3.6)	-10.4 (-14.8)	77.7			
Protective services workers	-2.4 (-1.7)	1.9 (4.6)	99.4	.4 (.4)	-1.0 (-1.5)	97.5		-3.8 (-3.2)	95.4
Production supervisors and general foremen				-15.9 (-14.4)	-1.5 (-2.1)	80.8			
Blacksmiths, toolmakers, sharpeners and related workers	.0 (.0)	-.4 (-.9)	99.6	-10.2 (-9.3)	7.4 (10.6)	95.2		-4.1 (-3.4)	95.1
Bricklayers, carpenters and other construction workers	-2.4 (-1.7)	.3 (.7)	97.5	-.2 (-.2)	.1 (.2)	99.7		-2.2 (-1.8)	97.1
Typical "female" occupations									
Nurses						59.0			46.1
Teachers	3.7 (2.6)	1.9 (4.7)	73.4	6.0 (5.4)	3.3 (4.7)	50.4		8.0 (6.6)	24.0
Stenographers and typists	12.3 (8.8)	-4.2 (-10.4)	89.5	5.5 (5.0)	-7.1 (-10.1)	84.9		6.2 (5.2)	77.7
Bookkeepers, cashiers and related workers	1.9 (1.3)	15.5 (38.7)	45.7	12.5 (11.4)	8.9 (12.7)	43.3			
Salespersons, shop assistants and related workers	.6 (.4)	5.7 (14.2)	39.4	4.9 (4.4)	8.3 (11.9)	27.2		-5.3 (-4.4)	29.0
Cooks, waiters, bartenders and related workers				-14.4 (-13.1)	-6.8 (-9.7)	23.4			
Maids and related housekeeping service workers	-1.2 (-.9)	-.3 (-.9)	87.8	3.0 (2.8)	6.2 (8.9)	97.0			
Hairdressers, barbers, beauticians and related workers	19.2 (13.7)	12.5 (31.3)	81.0	15.0 (13.6)	10.4 (14.8)	38.3			
Tailors, dressmakers, sewers, upholsterers, and related workers	20.6 (14.7)	-1.2 (-2.9)	84.0	28.3 (25.7)	-3.0 (-4.2)	62.0			

Notes to Table 15.1.

[a] In brackets, observed percentage point change is adjusted so as to represent percentage point change for an equivalent ten-year period by taking into account that the period being observed is not always ten years. [b] See notes at bottom of tables in Chapter 11 for an indication of when occupational classification for latest year may have problem of comparability with classification in other countries. [c] For Austria, data for stenographers and typists refer to employees, administrative only (i.e. office clerks and secretaries). [d] For Switzerland, data for stenographers and typists refer to sales clerks and office clerks. [e] For Bahrain, data for bookkeepers, cashiers and related workers include cashiers only for 1991; 1971 and 1981 data also include bookkeepers and related workers. [f] For Bahrain, 1991 data for cooks, waiters and bartenders include cooks, waiters and bartenders; 1971 and 1981 data do not include cooks. [g] For Bahrain, 1991 data for maids and related housekeeping service workers refer to housemaids only; 1971 and 1981 data refer to cooks and maids. Therefore, for trend analysis, cooks and maids occupations are aggregated into one occupational group. [h] For Tunisia, 1989 data for tailors and dressmakers refer to workers in textiles. We assume this includes spinners and weavers and related workers. Data for 1976 have separate occupational categories of spinners and tailors. Note that spinners are three times more numerous than tailors in 1976 data. For trend analysis, spinners and tailors are combined into one occupational category for 1976. [i] For Cyprus, 1989 data for legislative officials and government administrators refer only to senior government legislators and administrators; 1981 data refer to government administrators and legislators (with no mention of senior level). [j] For Australia, 1991 data for managers refer to managers; 1971 and 1981 data also include employers and workers on own account. Therefore, 1971 and 1981 data are not comparable with 1991 data. [k] For Cyprus, data for trend analysis refer to buyers only. [l] For Hong Kong, data for sales supervisors for 1981 and 1991 include commercial travellers and technical salesmen. Comparable data for 1971 are not available. [m] For Australia, data for blacksmiths, toolmakers and machine tool operators include plumbers for 1970 and 1980 but not for 1990. [n] For Hong Kong, 1971 data include painters; therefore, for time series analysis, data refer to the combined occupational group of bricklayers, carpenters and painters. [r] For Italy, the unusually large decrease (and low average value) observed is due to values for an occupation entitled "administrative employees with managerial function" where percentage female decreased by 13.7 percentage points between 1971–81. This occupation was roughly five times larger than all of the other seven managerial occupations (various types of even higher level occupations consisting of managing directors and directors) put together which as a group had a decrease in percentage female of −4.8 percentage points between 1971–81.

Source: Study data.

Table 15.2. Summary of trends for the 1970s and 1980s in percentage male for eight typical "male" occupations and percentage female for nine typical "female" occupations, by region

Occupations	OECD							
	1970s				1980s			
	INC	DEC	Neutral[b]	Average change[a,c]	INC	DEC	Neutral[b]	Average change[a,c]
Typical "male" occupations								
Architects, engineers and related tech.	0	1	9	-2.1	1	3	8	-2.6
Legislative officials and government administrators	1	6	4	-4.9	0	8	2	-7.9
Managers	1	3	6	-2.6	1	7	4	-5.8
Sales supervisors and buyers	0	5	1	-7.0	2	3	2	-1.7
Protective services workers	0	2	9	-2.9	0	1	11	-1.1
Production supervisors and general foremen	0	0	4	0.7	0	1	5	-2.9
Blacksmiths, toolmakers, etc.	0	1	9	-1.1	1	0	10	0.2
Bricklayers, carpenters, etc.	0	0	10	-0.2	1	0	10	0.5
Total	**2**	**18**	**52**		**6**	**23**	**52**	
Typical "female" occupations								
Nurses	0	1	7	-1.1	0	0	8	-0.4
Teachers	3	0	7	3.2	1	0	11	2.3
Stenographers, typists, etc.	1	1	7	0.1	2	0	10	1.8
Bookkeepers, cashiers and related workers	6	0	4	9.0	7	1	3	6.3
Salespersons, shop assistants	2	1	7	-0.2	0	1	11	-1.5
Cooks, waiters, bartenders	2	1	7	0.3	1	5	6	-2.9
Maids and related housekeeping	0	2	7	-2.3	1	1	10	-1.6
Hairdressers, barbers	9	0	2	9.1	6	0	5	5.4
Tailors, dressmakers, etc.	3	1	6	2.6	0	0	10	-0.6
Total	**26**	**7**	**54**		**17**	**8**	**74**	
Percentage of non-agricultural labour force which is female (for latter year in time period)			**38.3**				**42.2**	

Notes: [a] Observed national percentage point changes are adjusted so as to represent percentage point change for an equivalent ten-year period by taking into account that the period being observed is not always ten years. [b] A clear increase (INC) or decrease (DEC) is considered to have occurred when percentage male for a "male" occupation or percentage female for a "female" occupation changed by at least 5 percentage points over an equivalent ten-year period for 1970–1980 or 1980–1990. [c] Regional averages are unweighted averages of country values. Regional average is not reported when data are available for only one country in region for time period. Countries included in this table have data for 1970s and/or 1980s.
Source: Table 15.1.

Occupations	Middle East and North Africa							
	1970s				1980s			
	INC	DEC	Neutral[b]	Average change[a,c]	INC	DEC	Neutral[b]	Average change[a,c]
Typical "male" occupations								
Architects, engineers and related tech.	0	0	2	−1.0	0	1	3	−2.3
Legislative officials and government administrators	1	0	1	1.6	2	0	2	3.2
Managers	0	0	2	−1.6	0	1	3	−4.0
Sales supervisors and buyers	0	0	0	−[c]	0	0	2	−2.1
Protective services workers	0	0	2	−0.6	0	0	4	0.0
Production supervisors and general foremen	0	0	0	−[c]	0	1	2	−2.3
Blacksmiths, toolmakers, etc.	0	0	2	−0.1	0	0	4	−0.2
Bricklayers, carpenters, etc.	0	0	2	−0.1	0	0	4	0.0
Total	**1**	**0**	**11**		**2**	**3**	**24**	
Typical "female" occupations								
Nurses	0	0	0	−[c]	0	0	1	−[c]
Teachers	2	0	0	9.5	2	1	1	2.4
Stenographers, typists, etc.	2	0	0	26.4	3	0	1	19.1
Bookkeepers, cashiers and related workers	1	0	1	10.7	2	0	2	6.2
Salespersons, shop assistants	0	0	2	1.3	1	0	3	1.5
Cooks, waiters, bartenders	0	0	2	1.9	0	0	4	1.4
Maids and related housekeeping	2	0	0	14.4	2	2	0	2.7
Hairdressers, barbers	2	0	0	13.6	2	0	2	3.2
Tailors, dressmakers, etc.	0	1	1	−8.6	1	0	3	2.1
Total	**9**	**1**	**6**		**13**	**3**	**17**	
Percentage of non-agricultural labour force which is female (for latter year in time period)			**11.2**				**17.5**	

Notes: [a] Observed national percentage point changes are adjusted so as to represent percentage point change for an equivalent ten-year period by taking into account that the period being observed is not always ten years. [b] A clear increase (INC) or decrease (DEC) is considered to have occurred when percentage male for a "male" occupation or percentage female for a "female" occupation changed by at least 5 percentage points over an equivalent ten-year period for 1970–1980 or 1980–1990. [c] Regional averages are unweighted averages of country values. Regional average is not reported when data are available for only one country in region for time period. Countries included in this table have data for 1970s and/or 1980s.
Source: Table 15.1.

Table 15.2. (contd.)

Occupations	Asia/Pacific							
	1970s				1980s			
	INC	DEC	Neutral[b]	Average change[a,c]	INC	DEC	Neutral[b]	Average change[a,c]
Typical "male" occupations								
Architects, engineers and related tech.	0	0	2	−2.5	0	1	3	−1.7
Legislative officials and government administrators	0	0	1	—[c]	0	0	3	−0.5
Managers	0	1	1	−2.7	0	1	3	−3.3
Sales supervisors and buyers	0	0	0	—[c]	0	2	1	−15.5
Protective services workers	0	1	1	−3.2	0	0	4	0.4
Production supervisors and general foremen	0	0	0	—[c]	1	0	1	2.6
Blacksmiths, toolmakers, etc.	0	0	2	−0.1	1	0	3	1.6
Bricklayers, carpenters, etc.	0	0	2	2.2	0	0	2	1.0
Total	**0**	**2**	**9**		**2**	**4**	**20**	
Typical "female" occupations								
Nurses	0	0	1	—[c]	0	0	3	−1.3
Teachers	0	0	1	—[c]	1	0	3	2.6
Stenographers, typists, etc.	1	0	1	2.6	1	0	3	4.5
Bookkeepers, cashiers and related workers	2	0	0	14.1	4	0	0	11.4
Salespersons, shop assistants	0	0	1	—[c]	2	0	2	6.3
Cooks, waiters, bartenders	0	0	1	—[c]	1	0	2	5.1
Maids and related housekeeping	0	0	0	—[c]	1	0	2	2.8
Hairdressers, barbers	0	0	2	0.3	3	0	1	16.0
Tailors, dressmakers, etc.	1	0	1	5.4	1	1	2	4.4
Total	**4**	**0**	**9**		**14**	**1**	**18**	
Percentage of non-agricultural labour force which is female (for latter year in time period)	36.2				35.6			

Notes: [a] Observed national percentage point changes are adjusted so as to represent percentage point change for an equivalent ten-year period by taking into account that the period being observed is not always ten years. [b] A clear increase (INC) or decrease (DEC) is considered to have occurred when percentage male for a "male" occupation or percentage female for a "female" occupation changed by at least 5 percentage points over an equivalent ten-year period for 1970–1980 or 1980–1990. [c] Regional averages are unweighted averages of country values. Regional average is not reported when data are available for only one country in region for time period.
Countries included in this table have data for 1970s and/or 1980s.
Source: Table 15.1.

Occupations	Other Developing							
	1970s				1980s			
	INC	DEC	Neutral[b]	Average change[a,c]	INC	DEC	Neutral[b]	Average change[a,c]
Typical "male" occupations								
Architects, engineers and related tech.	0	0	2	-0.9	0	0	3	-4.3
Legislative officials and government administrators	0	1	1	-7.8	1	1	1	1.9
Managers	0	2	0	-9.3	0	2	1	-1.8
Sales supervisors and buyers	0	0	1	[c]	0	1	0	-14.8
Protective services workers	0	0	2	-0.7	0	0	3	-0.0
Production supervisors and general foremen	0	1	0	[c]	0	1	1	[c]
Blacksmiths, toolmakers, etc.	0	1	0	[c]	0	0	2	2.1
Bricklayers, carpenters, etc.	0	0	2	-0.9	1	0	3	-0.3
Total	**0**	**5**	**8**		**1**	**5**	**14**	
Typical "female" occupations								
Nurses	0	0	0	[c]	0	0	0	[c]
Teachers	1	0	1	4.0	1	0	2	5.3
Stenographers, typists, etc.	2	0	0	6.9	1	2	0	-5.1
Bookkeepers, cashiers and related workers	1	0	1	6.4	2	0	0	25.7
Salespersons, shop assistants	0	0	2	2.4	2	0	1	7.2
Cooks, waiters, bartenders	0	1	0	[c]	0	1	0	-9.7
Maids and related housekeeping	0	0	2	0.9	1	0	1	4.0
Hairdressers, barbers	2	0	0	13.7	2	0	0	23.0
Tailors, dressmakers, etc.	2	0	0	20.2	0	0	2	-3.6
Total	**8**	**1**	**6**		**9**	**3**	**6**	
Percentage of non-agricultural labour force which is female (for latter year in time period)				30.9				30.3

Notes: [a] Observed national percentage point changes are adjusted so as to represent percentage point change for an equivalent ten-year period by taking into account that the period being observed is not always ten years. [b] A clear increase (INC) or decrease (DEC) is considered to have occurred when percentage male for a "male" occupation or percentage female for a "female" occupation changed by at least 5 percentage points over an equivalent ten-year period for 1970–1980 or 1980–1990. [c] Regional averages are unweighted averages of country values. Regional average is not reported when data are available for only one country in region for time period. Countries included in this table have data for 1970s and/or 1980s.
Source: Table 15.1.

are the only examples where the percentage female rose in a consistent and substantial way over the past two decades. In Norway, per cent male fell from 93.9 in 1970, to 86.2 in 1980 and to 79.9 per cent in 1990; in the United States the percentage female fell from 93.6 per cent in 1970, to 88.6 in 1980 and to 84.8 in 1990. It would be worthwhile investigating whether these two countries have had similar policies or programmes with respect to the hiring of women into protective service occupations.

For production supervisors and general foremen, there appears to be greater entry of women into this occupation in recent years in non-OECD countries as compared to OECD countries. The percentage female rose by more than 5 percentage points in 2 out of the 7 non-OECD country examples shown in tables 15.1 and 15.2 (Tunisia and Mauritius); there were no examples for OECD countries. While this might seem a positive sign for women in less developed countries, the small observed change needs to be interpreted in the context of the increased employment of women in labour-intensive factory-based occupations in some (often export-oriented) developing countries. Yet, **the vast gap, whereby women predominate in low paying production jobs while men dominate supervisory production jobs, is something which should be changing faster than it is.**

"Male" occupations with increasing feminization

There is in general an **observable increase** in percentage female for the other four typical "male" occupations analysed in this book. This trend is particularly clear for three of these occupations—**legislative officials and government administrators; managers; and sales supervisors and buyers**—as the percentage female increased by an average of 3 and 6 per cent per decade for these occupations on average, and there was a clear increase (i.e. at least a 5 percentage point increase per equivalent ten-year period) in almost one-half of the country-time period examples shown in tables 15.1 and 15.2. This increase in the feminization of these three "male" occupations caused these three occupations to become less male-dominated over the past two decades. Based on the earliest available national study data, these occupations were male-dominated in 75 out of 83 country examples as compared to 63 out of 83 country examples based on the latest available national data (table 15.3).

There has also been **a (smaller) decrease in the percentage male for architects, engineers and related workers** (at around 2 per cent per decade on average). This change is much more obvious in the 1980s as compared to the 1970s, as indicated by the seven clear national decreases in the percentage male in the 1980s and only 1 clear decrease in the 1970s (table 15.3).

While results are generally similar for OECD and non-OECD countries for these four "male" occupations (table 15.1), there are some interesting regional differences worth noting. There were *big increases in feminization of the sales supervisor occupation in three developing economies* (China, Hong

Kong and Mauritius). Another noticeable regional difference is that there was *a general increase in the feminization of legislators and government administrators in OECD countries* but not non-OECD countries. Whereas the percentage female clearly increased in 14 of 21 country-time periods in OECD countries (6 of 11 in the 1970s, and 8 of 10 in the 1980s), there were only 2 clear increases out of 14 country-time periods for non-OECD study countries. When we look at the five OECD study countries with data for the entire 1970-1990 period, we find that when percentage female rose by at least five percentage points in the 1970s, it also rose by more than five percentage points in the 1980s as well. In addition, changes in these five countries are quite substantial—with percentage female increasing by about 35 per cent in Norway, 25 per cent in the United States, 15 per cent in Finland and Spain, and 10 per cent in West Germany. This is a good example of how change often carries forward through time.

15.2   Changes in the feminization of nine typical "female" occupations

There is considerable variation across countries, regions and occupations in how percentage female has changed in the past two decades for our nine typical "female" occupations. This variability parallels the cross-national variability for "female" occupations observed in Chapter 11 for a recent year—and is in contrast to results observed above for "male" occupations where there is considerable similarity over time as well as across countries for a recent year. To facilitate discussion, our nine typical "female" occupations are grouped based on changes in percentage female.

"Female" occupations with increasing feminization

Two occupations (bookkeepers, cashiers and related workers; hairdressers, barbers, beauticians and related workers) have clearly become more feminized in the past two decades—and this has occurred throughout the world (figure 15.2). As a result, these occupations have become female-concentrated in many more countries over the past two decades (going from 11 out of 24 study countries based on earlier data to 16 out of 24 study countries based on latest available data for bookkeepers/cashiers; and from 17 out of 24 study countries to 21 out of 24 study countries for hairdressers/barbers). Indeed, percentage female increased by an average of about 9 percentage points per decade for the 1970s as well as the 1980s for each of these occupations—and this increase in percentage female was observed in all study regions. Furthermore, percentage female increased by at least 5 per cent per equivalent ten-year period in 25 out of 37 country-time period examples for

Figure 15.2. Average change in the percentage female for nine typical "female" occupations for the 1970s and 1980s, by region

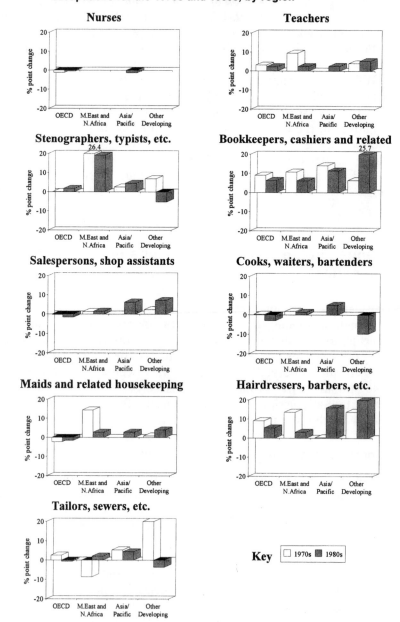

Notes: Percentage point changes are reported for an equivalent ten-year period.
Regional average is unweighted average of national values. Regional value is not reported only when one national value in the region is available for a time period.
Source: Table 15.2.

bookkeeper/cashier and in 26 out of 38 country-time period examples for hairdresser/barber.

Even most of the examples where the change in percentage female was less than 5 per cent for the 1970s or 1980s can be explained by either (i) a very large increase in percentage female in the adjacent decade (5 examples for bookkeeper/cashier, including the only clear decrease; 1 example for hairdresser/barber) and so represents a situation where percentage female increased substantially over the past two decades; or (ii) percentage female was already so high that further large increases were difficult (4 examples for bookkeeper/cashier and 6 examples for hairdresser/barber where percentage female exceeded 80 per cent in 1970 or 1980). In short, there were very few study country examples where percentage female was less than 80 per cent for bookkeepers/cashiers or for hairdressers/barbers and did not *clearly* increase during the 1970-1990 period.[2]

It is interesting to speculate on why there has been such a large worldwide increase recently in the feminization of these two occupations. Reasons cannot be country-specific, or region-specific or culture-specific. There has to be some common worldwide phenomena involved, which have encouraged women to seek work in these occupations and/or encouraged employers to prefer hiring women workers.

For bookkeepers/cashiers, one possible explanation is *computerization of activities* in financial services. For example, automated and computerized bank teller systems have become common place. This has reduced decision-making and independent responsibility which, in turn, has resulted in a de-skilling of the work. Accompanying this deskilling has been a *reorganization of work schedules* and an increase in part-time employment. These changes have, it seems, encouraged employers to hire women for these occupations, and increased the willingness of many women to accept work (often part-time) in these occupations.

For hairdressers/barbers, there have not been any major technological changes of which the author is aware. One possible explanation for the clear worldwide increase in the feminization of the hairdresser occupation is *women's increased entry into the labour force*. Because of this, women may have less time available for doing hairdressing at home, as well as less contact with informal, home-based hairdressing activities. In addition, working women may have greater need for hairdressing on a regular basis. These factors may have increased the "need" for women hairdressers: both to meet the growing demand of women workers for formal hairdresser establishments, as well as the demand from male workers who may no longer have a spouse available at home to do their hair. Another possibility is that there has been a general change in work organization with a move towards part-time, flexible employment.

Teaching has also experienced an increase in feminization around the world in the past two decades. While only one country-time period displayed a clear decrease, there were 11 clear increases (table 15.2). On average, percentage female among teachers increased by approximately 4 percentage points in the 1970s and by a further 3 percentage points in the 1980s.

There were, however, *regional differences for teachers* (figure 15.2). In particular, *increased feminization of the teaching profession was greater in non-OECD countries as compared to OECD countries* (an average increase in percentage female of 6.4 per cent as compared to 3.2 per cent for the 1970s, and 3.4 per cent as compared to 2.3 per cent for the 1980s). Indeed, the extent to which teaching is a female-concentrated occupation in OECD countries decreased over the past two decades (from 9 out of 13 study countries based on earlier data to 5 out of 13 study countries based on the most recent data), because the increase in percentage female among teachers in a number of OECD countries was smaller than for the non-agricultural labour force as a whole.

"Female" occupations with little change in feminization with female dominance of occupation continuing

Several of our nine typical "female" occupations experienced **little or no overall change in feminization.** For three of these occupations—**nurse; maid/related housekeeper; and secretary/typist**—this result can be explained by the fact that these occupations were already highly feminized earlier (as over 80 per cent of workers in these occupations were female earlier). This means that there was very little room for a further increase in percentage female. At the same time, a decrease in percentage female was unlikely because of the increased entry of women into the non-agricultural labour force as a whole.

This lack of change is particularly noticeable in OECD countries where percentage female is especially high in these three occupations. Actually, percentage female *decreased* slightly in two of these occupations (nurse; maid/related housekeeper) in OECD countries in the past two decades (decreasing by roughly 1 to 2 per cent per decade on average). This is perhaps a first sign that these occupations will become more gender-integrated in the future.

Among non-OECD countries, there are some interesting differences. For maids/related housekeepers, Middle Eastern countries had very large increases in percentage female, whereas North African countries had large decreases. Percentage female increased from 71 per cent (1975) to 78 per cent (1985) in Kuwait; from 54 per cent (1961) to 68 per cent (1979) in Jordan; and from 22 per cent (1971) to 43 per cent (1981) and 69.5 per cent (1991) in Bahrain. In contrast, percentage female decreased substantially from 89 per cent (1975) to 68 per cent (1989) in Tunisia and from 86 per cent (1976) to 79 per cent (1986) in Egypt. Reasons for these different patterns would be worth investigating. For the three Middle Eastern study countries at least, it seems reasonable to surmise that the observed increase in feminization was due to the importation of migrant labour with a sex composition more in keeping with that found in the remainder of the world.

For typist/secretary, the increase in percentage female observed for the world as a whole over the past two decades (an average increase of 4 to 5 per cent per decade) is due mainly to quite large changes in a relatively few countries, especially Middle Eastern/North African countries.

Percentage female increased by more than five percentage points in 5 out of the 6 available country-time periods in the ME region (with the exception, Bahrain 1981–1991, a country where percentage female had increased by 35 per cent in the previous decade). And observed increases were very large indeed. Percentage female went from 36 per cent (1971) to 74 per cent (1991) in Bahrain; from 16 per cent (1976) to 65 per cent (1986) in Egypt; from 6 per cent (1961) to 28 per cent (1979) in Jordan; from 42 per cent (1975) to 54 per cent (1989) in Tunisia. Typists and secretarial positions in offices are obviously among the few acceptable occupations for women in the Middle East and North Africa and it appears to have become one of the main destinations for women entering the non-agricultural labour force in these countries over the past two decades.

It is interesting that so few men have entered these three "female" occupations in recent years. For two of these occupations at least (nurse and typist), one might have expected that many more men would have sought out jobs here. Along with the increased use of computers and upskilling of the typist occupation, one would expect more men to seek out work in this occupation. And along with the general deterioration in job market prospects for men, one might have expected more men to take up nursing as a profession. That more men have not indicates that the sex-stereotyping of these occupations, especially in OECD countries, is very strong indeed; it would be worth further investigation to help establish whether this is due to discrimination faced by male applicants or to an unwillingness of men to apply for jobs in these "female" occupations.

"Female" occupations with little change in feminization but with considerable regional variation

There was relatively little change in the feminization of salespersons/shop assistants, as indicated by the lack of a clear change in 12 of 15 study country-time period examples in the 1970s and 17 of 23 study country-time period examples in the 1980s (with average decade changes of only 0.6 and 1.5 per cent respectively). This result can not be attributed to a very high percentage female, since percentage female for salesperson/shop assistant (42 per cent for the world, 68 per cent for OECD, 48 per cent for OD, 42 per cent for Asia/Pacific and 5 per cent for ME) leaves room for further increases. In addition, technological change (such as the introduction of digitized cash registers and optical scanners) has helped to deskill these occupations; and, work organization changes have increased demand for flexible, part-time workers. Both of these changes should have helped increase the feminization of this occupation. Why this has not occurred deserves further investigation.

The fact that there was little or **no change in percentage female of salespersons/shop assistants for OECD countries whereas there was a sizeable increase in the feminization of the labour force as a whole,** caused there to be a marked decrease in the extent to which salespersons/shop assistants is a female-concentrated occupation in OECD countries. Whereas this was a female-concentrated occupation in all 13 OECD study countries based on earlier study data, this was so in only 9 OECD study countries based on the latest study data.

Percentage female, however, increased in the 1980s among non-Middle East/North African developing study countries (figure 15.2). There was a clear increase in 4 of the 5 available country-time periods (and the exception was Senegal, where data quality is suspect), with the average increase approximately 10 per cent per equivalent ten years. We do not know of an obvious explanation for the different pattern for non-Middle East/North African developing countries as compared to OECD countries.

Cooks, waiters and waitresses (along with nurses as discussed above) is the only one of our nine typical "female" occupations where, on average, percentage female decreased in the world as a whole over the last two decades. While this decrease was small on average (approximately one per cent for both the 1970s and 1980s), it is nonetheless a striking result in light of the rapid increase in feminization of the non-agricultural labour force as a whole (approximately 3 to 4 per cent in the 1970s and in the 1980s). Among OECD study countries, this decreasing feminization caused the cooks, waiters and waitresses occupational group to be less of a female-concentrated occupation, going from 10 out of 14 OECD study countries based on earlier study data to 7 out of 14 OECD study countries based on the latest study data. Why there has been a relative decrease in the feminization of this occupation is worth further investigation. One might have expected increasing feminization in this occupation, since part-time employment is common. Perhaps experiences differed for the sub-occupations comprising this occupation (i.e. cooks and bartenders may have had different trends as compared to waiters and waitresses).

Among non-OECD countries, there was relatively little change in percentage female for cooks and waiters/waitresses among study countries—outside of the two small island states of Fiji (where percentage female increased from 32 to 44 per cent between 1976 and 1986) and Mauritius (where percentage female decreased from 45 to 23 per cent between 1972 and 1990). Indeed, percentage female changed by less than 5.0 percentage points in all nine of the other non-OECD country-time periods (with average change only 1.0 per cent for the 1970s and 1.4 per cent for the 1980s). The reasons for the substantial increase in Fiji and the substantial decrease in Mauritius would be worth understanding, since many of the workers in this occupation in these two countries are employed in tourism, which is growing in importance in the world.

"Female" occupations with relatively little overall change in feminization but with a distinct increase for small export-oriented countries

Over all, there was relatively little change in the world in feminization for **tailors, dressmakers, sewers, etc.** over the past two decades. It **remained very much a female-concentrated occupation,** in 20 of 23 study countries or areas based on the earliest available study data and in 19 of 23 based on the latest available study data.

There are, however, large increases for several small study economies which pursued an export-oriented development path that included textiles. Thus, there were large increases in feminization of the tailors, dressmakers, sewers, etc. occupational group for Hong Kong (from 64 to 73 per cent between 1971 and 1981), Costa Rica (from 65 to 85 per cent between 1973 and 1987), Mauritius (from 37 to 65 per cent between 1972 and 1983), and Fiji (from 41 to 61 per cent between 1976 and 1986).

Figure 15.3. Percentage female for tailors, sewers, etc. occupational group for small garment-exporting countries and areas, 1970–90

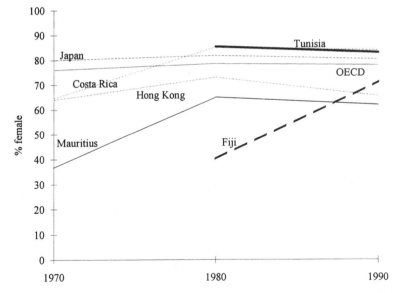

Note: Included in this figure are non-OECD economies with time series data and sizeable textile exports. OECD average and Japan are included for comparison.
National values are connected by straight lines for expositional purposes.
Source: Tables 15.1 and 15.2.

Table 15.3. Whether eight typical "male" occupations are male–dominated and nine typical "female" occupations are female–concentrated for earliest and latest available data years, by region

Occupation	Region[a]									
	OECD (N = 14)		Middle East and North Africa (N = 5)		Asia/Pacific (N = 4)		Other Developing (N = 2)		Total (N = 25)	
	x/y earliest data	x/y latest data	x/y earliest data	x/y latest data	x/y earliest data	x/y latest data	x/y earliest data	x/y latest data	x/y earliest data	x/y latest data
"Male" occupations										
Architects, engineers and related tech.	13/13	12/13	5/5	5/5	4/4	3/4	2/2	2/2	24/24	22/24
Legislative officials and government admin.	9/12	7/12	4/5	5/5	2/2	2/2	2/2	1/2	17/21	15/21
Managers	12/14	10/14	5/5	5/5	4/4	3/4	2/2	1/2	23/25	19/25
Sales supervisors and buyers	6/8	3/8	2/2	2/2	2/2	2/2	1/1	0/1	11/13	7/13
Protective services workers	14/14	13/14	5/5	5/5	4/4	4/4	2/2	2/2	25/25	24/25
Production supervisors and general foremen	6/6	6/6	3/3	3/3	1/2	2/2	1/1	1/1	11/12	12/12
Blacksmiths, toolmakers, etc.	13/13	13/13	5/5	5/5	3/4	4/4	2/2	2/2	23/24	23/24
Bricklayers, carpenters, etc.	13/13	13/13	5/5	5/5	4/4	4/4	2/2	2/2	24/24	24/24
Total	**86/93**	**77/93**	**34/35**	**35/35**	**24/26**	**24/26**	**14/14**	**11/14**	**158/168**	**147/168**
"Female" occupations										
Nurses	10/10	10/10	1/1	1/1	2/2	2/2	n/a	n/a	13/13	13/13
Teachers	9/13	5/13	4/5	5/5	1/3	1/3	2/2	2/2	16/23	13/23
Stenographers, typists, etc.	12/12	12/12	5/5	5/5	4/4	4/4	2/2	2/2	23/23	23/23
Bookkeepers, cashiers and related workers	8/13	10/13	1/5	2/5	2/4	4/4	0/2	0/2	11/24	16/24
Salespersons, shop assistants	13/13	9/13	0/5	0/5	1/3	1/3	1/2	0/2	15/23	10/23
Cooks, waiters, bartenders	10/14	7/14	0/5	0/5	1/3	1/3	1/1	0/1	12/23	8/23
Maids and related housekeeping	12/12	12/12	5/5	5/5	2/2	2/2	2/2	2/2	21/21	21/21
Hairdressers, barbers	14/14	14/14	1/5	4/5	1/4	2/4	1/1	1/1	17/24	21/24
Tailors, dressmakers, etc.	11/12	11/12	3/5	2/5	4/4	4/4	2/2	2/2	20/23	19/23
Total	**99/113**	**90/113**	**20/41**	**24/41**	**18/29**	**21/29**	**11/14**	**9/14**	**148/197**	**144/197**

Notes: For x/y, x indicates number of countries where "female" occupations are female-concentrated in a relative sense, see Chapter 5 (i.e. when per cent female is at least 1.5 times average per cent female for the non-agricultural labour force as a whole); or "male" occupations are male-dominated (i.e. at least 80 per cent of the workers are men). y indicates the number of countries with data for two or more years.
[a] Only countries with comparable occupations over time included in the comparisons.
N indicates the number of countries which have time series data.
See notes at bottom of tables in Chapter 11 and table 15.1 for information on possible problems with comparability of occupations across countries or time.
Source: Table 15.1.

At the same time, the demand for female *tailors, dressmakers, sewers, etc. seems to have an upper limit, at 60 to 90 per cent female* (figure 15.3), perhaps because some sub-occupations, such as upholsterers and pattern makers/cutters, tend to include sizeable numbers of male workers. Such an interpretation is consistent with the levels of percentage female found in other non-OECD countries which have large textile exports, such as Malaysia (80 per cent in 1980), Japan (80 per cent in 1990, with no change from the 80 per cent for 1970), Republic of Korea (62 per cent in 1983), China (83 per cent in 1990, down slightly from 86 per cent in 1982) and Tunisia (83 per cent in 1983, down slightly from 85 per cent in 1975). This interpretation is also consistent with the 79 per cent feminization rate found in OECD countries. One possibility is that the predominance of women workers in garment production in non-OECD countries may be in large part an industrialized country pattern which multinationals bring to other countries.

Notes

[1] The conclusion in this section that there has been little or no change in the masculinization of these four "male" occupations is based on fact that the male percentage has changed only slightly in study countries over the past two decades in these occupations. If instead, we looked at whether male percentage increased or decreased (without considering the size of the change), it is found that there are many more study countries where male percentage decreased than increased.

	1970s (number of countries)		1980s (number of countries)	
	Increase in % male	Decrease in % male	Increase in % male	Decrease in % male
Protective services workers	1	16	6	17
Production supervisors	2	4	3	9
Blacksmiths, toolmakers	8	12	10	13
Bricklayers, carpenters and other construction workers	4	12	15	8

My feeling is that the results shown in table 15.3 are more appropriate than the numbers in this footnote for understanding the situation, because a small change in a study country may (i) be due to measurement problems and (ii) need to be interpreted in part in relation to the general increase around the world in female labour force participation rates.

[2] The only three exceptions for bookkeepers/cashiers are in two Central European OECD countries (Austria 1980-90; West Germany 1976-80 and 1980-89); yet even here, percentage female rose in both the 1970s and 1980s and percentage female is now over 70 per cent. The only exceptions for hairdressers/barbers are Japan (for both 1970-80 and 1980-90) where percentage female is now 69 per cent and two Middle East countries (Egypt and Kuwait) where percentage female is very low.

PART V

MAIN FINDINGS

SUMMARY AND CONCLUSIONS

16

16.1 Importance of topic

This book documents the high levels of occupational segregation by sex in the world today (i.e. the tendency for men and women to work in different occupations). It is shown to be extensive in every region, at all economic development levels, in all political systems, and in diverse religious, social and cultural environments. In short, occupational segregation by sex is an important worldwide phenomenon.

Occupational segregation by sex is *not only detrimental for women, it is also a major source of labour market rigidity and economic inefficiency.* Excluding the majority of workers from the majority of occupations (as is shown to be the current situation), is wasteful of human resources, contributes to labour market rigidity, and reduces an economy's ability to adjust to change—labour market aspects which are taking on added importance in today's global economy.

In addition, the sex segregation of occupations is *not always bad for women and good for men;* in recent years, job growth has generally favoured typical "female" occupations (such as service occupations) rather than typical "male" occupations (such as production occupations).

16.2 Background on earlier studies and objectives of this book

Much of this book is based on detailed occupational data for 41 countries or areas. This cross-national focus has advantages over most previous studies of occupational segregation by sex, which have generally been national studies. Cross-national studies provide a global perspective and information on whether national levels and/or recent changes in occupational segregation by sex are universal, regional or national in nature. In the process, lessons can be drawn from experiences in other parts of the world, such as why occupational segregation by sex is changing in only some parts of the world, and the types of policies that can be used to reduce it. At the same time, of course, all cross-national studies suffer from the usual problem of comparability of national data. One must be especially cautious about drawing conclusions for particular occupations and occupational groups for specific countries, because of comparability problems.

The present book has several features which differ from previous cross-national studies of occupational segregation by sex. First and foremost, almost all the analysis and discussion in this book are based on relatively detailed occupational data, with an average of approximately 175 non-agricultural occupations classified per study country. This level of detail is unusual for a cross-national study of occupational segregation by sex that covers *a wide range of developing and industrialized countries.* Another feature is that *time series data* are analysed for 32 of the 41 study countries/areas. In contrast, virtually all previous cross-national studies which have included a substantial number of developing countries have relied on data for only about six non-agricultural occupations; in addition, previous cross-national studies which have used more detailed occupational data have included a much smaller selection of industrialized countries and time periods than in the present book. This book also contains some *methodological innovations,* that are discussed below, particularly development of a technique for increasing the comparability of national data which have greatly differing numbers of occupations classified. These adjustments are extremely important for cross-national analyses such as found here, because the observed level of occupational segregation by sex (see Chapter 6) is sensitive to the number of occupations classified. Another feature of this book is that *a number of different statistics are used* to examine the multi-dimensional nature of occupational segregation by sex.

16.3   Some major methodological findings

This book has paid considerable attention to methodological issues. This was necessary because of the great diversity around the world in labour markets and national occupational data. For example, there are wide variations across study countries in the female share of the non-agricultural labour force (which ranges from roughly 10 to 65 per cent across our study countries and areas); the reported employment share of agriculture (which ranges from less than 1 per cent to over 70 per cent); and, the number of occupations classified in the national data (which ranges from roughly 50 to 500 occupations). A number of methodological innovations were made in order to take this diversity into consideration.

Need for several inequality measures

It is important to use a number of different inequality statistics to provide a satisfactory *understanding of the multi-dimensional nature of occupational segregation by sex* (see table 4.1). For example, the percentage female and male in occupations (which are used in Chapters 11 and 15) indicate the extent to which there is concentration of women and men in an occupation. Representation ratios (which are used in Chapter 8) provide a simple, easy to understand statistic on the relative concentration, i.e. representativeness, of women in an occupational group as compared to women's share for the non-agricultural labour force as a whole. Inequality indices (which are used in Chapters 9 and 13) provide a summary statistic for the overall tendency for men and women to be segregated into different occupations. Percentages of the male and female workers in gender-dominated and gender-integrated occupations based on relative and absolute concepts (which are used in Chapters 10 and 14) provide *easily understood measures* of the extent to which the non-agricultural labour force is divided into gender-stereotyped "female" and "male" occupations. In Chapter 9, a new measure of gender inequality in the labour market is developed by combining two separate phenomena into one index number: women being left out of the non-agricultural labour force altogether, and occupational segregation by sex for those women who are in the non-agricultural labour force.

One interesting insight provided by the use of a variety of inequality statistics is the observation that there is more variation across countries in the feminization of typical "female" occupations than in the masculinization of typical "male" occupations (Chapter 11). This means that while men are often found working in "female" occupations, it is more unusual to find women in "male" occupations. This is also consistent with a factor analysis reported in Chapter 12, which indicates that *occupational segregation statistics form two distinct sets of factors,* with one factor representing the female side of the labour market and the other factor representing the male side of the labour market, measured together with the overall level of occupational segregation by sex.

Need for disaggregated occupational data

The level of detail in national occupational data greatly affects the level of occupational segregation by sex observed in a country. The more disaggregated occupational data are, the more sex segregation will be observed. Until now, no one has estimated the mathematical relationship between the observed level of occupational segregation by sex and the number of occupations on which this statistic is calculated.

Analysis in Chapter 6 indicates that *one-digit occupational data (usually representing six non-agricultural occupations plus agriculture) are not very good for analysing occupational segregation by sex.* Yet out of necessity, most previous cross-national studies of occupational segregation by sex have relied exclusively on one-digit occupational data, especially previous cross-national studies which have included a substantial number of developing countries (Chapter 3).

One-digit *occupational data are found to hide a large proportion of the existing sex segregation of occupations*. For example as shown in Chapter 6, ID (index of dissimilarity, the most commonly used inequality statistic) increases on average by about .25 (from around .38 to .63) when national occupational data are disaggregated from typical one-digit non-agricultural data to typical three-digit non-agricultural data; similarly, the percentage of the female non-agricultural labour force working in a female-dominated occupation increases by about 31 per cent on average when national occupational data are disaggregated from typical one-digit to three-digit non-agricultural data (with none or very few female-dominated occupations identified based on one-digit non-agricultural data). And, of course, it is obviously not possible to investigate the feminization of specific occupations (such as teacher, secretary and construction worker) using one-digit occupational data.

Worse than hiding considerable segregation, one-digit occupational data often provide a qualitatively different picture of occupational segregation by sex as compared to two- and three-digit occupational data—both for analysing occupational segregation by sex across countries as well as for analysing changes over time within a country (Chapter 6). For example, based on one-digit occupational data, Mauritius and Tunisia have relatively low ID values and are ranked second and third out of 26 study countries and areas while Norway is ranked sixteenth; based on two-digit data, in contrast, Norway is ranked eighth, Mauritius fourteenth and Tunisia twenty-second.

On the other hand, analysis in Chapter 6 indicates that *two-digit occupational data are often sufficiently detailed (and so three-digit data are not always necessary)* for analysing inequality indices such as ID, percentage of the male non-agricultural labour force in a male-dominated occupation and feminization of large occupational groups such as teacher, secretary/receptionist and transport worker. On the other hand, *two-digit data are found to be insufficiently detailed for analysing the extent to which the women are in a female-dominated occupation, or the feminization of smaller occupations* such as for pre-primary, primary, secondary and university teachers; in part, this is due to a bias in occupational classifications which tend to be more finely disaggregated for typical occupational groups where male workers tend to be concentrated as compared to those where women workers tend to be concentrated.

We estimated in Chapter 6 the *mathematical relationship between the number of occupations classified and the ID* which is observed. We found that over 80 per cent of the increase in a country's ID due to increased disaggregation of occupational data could be explained by knowing the number of occupations classified. Using this strong and consistent mathematical relationship, adjusted inequality statistics were calculated and used in the empirical analysis of differences in the levels and trends in occupational segregation by sex presented in Parts III and IV. Although these adjustments are only approximate, as there are, of course, national variations in this relationship, these adjustments none the less greatly increased the comparability of national estimates of occupational segregation by sex.

16.4 Some major findings for occupational segregation by sex in the world today

First of all, it is important to point out that **occupational segregation by sex is very extensive in each and every country.** According to study data presented in Chapter 9, ID (the most commonly used inequality statistic) is approximately .58 on average based on a typical two-digit classification (with 75 non-agricultural occupations) and approximately .66 based on a typical three-digit classification (with 265 non-agricultural occupations). More striking (as shown in Chapter 10) is the fact that approximately one-half of workers in the world are in an occupation where one sex dominates to such an extent that these occupations could be considered as "male" or "female" occupations (defined as occupations where at least 80 per cent of workers are male or female).

Second, **male-dominated occupations are much more common than female-dominated occupations;** according to study data, male-dominated non-agricultural occupations are over seven times as numerous as female-dominated ones (Chapter 10). Also according to study data based on 75 non-agricultural occupations, approximately 60 per cent of male non-agricultural workers are in a "male" occupation; in contrast, only about 25 per cent of female non-agricultural workers are in a "female" occupation (percentages which increase by about 3 and 12 per cent respectively based on more detailed three-digit data with about 265 non-agricultural occupations).

Third, the fact that many more male than female workers face little competition from the other sex (Chapters 10 and 11) takes on added importance because **"female" occupations tend to be less valuable** with lower pay, lower status and fewer advancement possibilities as compared to "male" occupations (Chapters 2 and 3). For example, roughly 88 per cent of managers and legislative officials/government administrators in the world are men. Women comprise approximately 42 per cent of salespersons and shop assistants in the world, yet only about 18 per cent of sales supervisors and buyers; and whereas the vast majority of pre-primary and primary school teachers are women, women are a distinct minority of university level teachers.

Fourth, **levels of occupational segregation by sex differ greatly across study regions.** The Asia/Pacific region has the lowest average level and the Middle East/North Africa region the highest. The level of sex segregation is also relatively high in the Other Developing region, while the OECD and Transition Economy regions have rather average levels of occupational segregation by sex for the world.

Fifth, surprisingly, the level of **occupational segregation by sex is quite similar in OECD and European Transition Economy study countries.** We had expected to find lower sex segregation in Transition Economy countries prior to the fall of communism, since several of the usual economic explanations for occupational segregation and pay inequalities by sex (as discussed in Chapter 2) did not seemingly apply under communism. These countries had a strong ideological commitment to equality of sexes, and managers were not overly concerned with either minimizing costs or maximizing profits. While differences in occupational classifications in communist and capitalist countries affects comparisons, the likelihood is that the observed similarity in levels of occupational segregation by sex in European capitalist and communist countries represents a real phenomenon. Previous analysts undoubtedly underestimated the long-lasting nature of the effect cultural and social values have on gender-stereotyping; they also, it seems, underestimated the important changes occurring in many capitalist countries and the lack of change in communist countries over recent decades (as described in Chapters 13–15) which caused differences in the sex segregation of occupations between capitalist and communist countries almost to disappear by the 1990s.

Sixth, another regional result which may surprise many readers is the relatively low level of occupational segregation by sex in Asia/Pacific (although this result has also been found in earlier studies, see Chapter 3). Given that female-male pay ratios are relatively low in Asia (Chapter 2), it seems reasonable to conclude that gender inequality in the labour market has a somewhat different character in **Asia** as compared to other parts of the world. First, there is evidence that **vertical segregation** within occupations, sometimes referred to as echelon segregation (whereby women and men in the same occupation hold different jobs in terms of grade, pay, authority and career possibilities) is relatively more important in Asia and the Pacific than in other regions. Secondly, women in Asia and the Pacific have a much better chance of working in a production occupation than in OECD countries, especially in Asian (as well as developing) countries that have pursued an export-oriented industrial path, since in these countries, women comprise a relatively high proportion of those employed in export production. But as these jobs are often low paying, entry into production occupations does not necessarily translate into an improvement in the female-male pay ratio. Third, many observers may be unconsciously focusing on the lower rate of female labour force participation in Asian countries as compared to OECD countries, for when we look at an inequality statistic which combines ID and female labour force participation into one index number (our IDHALF in Chapter 9), we find that inequality levels in Asia are no longer lower than in the OECD.

Seventh, just as there are large and significant differences in occupational segregation by sex across regions, there are also large and significant differences across OECD subregions. **The North American subregion has the lowest level** (see Chapters 9 and 10). It might surprise many readers (but not those familiar with the research literature, see Chapter 3) that **the Scandinavian subregion has the highest level of occupational segregation by sex among OECD subregions.** The reason for the relatively high level of occupational segregation by sex in Scandinavia is the unusually high proportion of non-agricultural workers in female-dominated occupations—almost half are in a female-dominated occupation as compared to about 33 per cent in North America and only about 20 per cent in the rest of the OECD region. Thus, *Scandinavia has a very large set of both "female" occupations and "male" occupations.* In light of the relatively equal rates of pay for men and women in Scandinavia (as shown in Chapter 2), it is obvious that a high level of occupational segregation by sex is not necessarily bad for women if, as in Scandinavia, separate but reasonably equal labour markets in terms of pay are created for men and women. On the other hand, as discussed in Chapters 9 and 10, it is uncertain whether this Scandinavian model is transferable to other countries or even sustainable into the future in Scandinavia in its present form, since it is based to a large extent on small wage differentials in the labour market in general and a large public sector that provides extensive support facilities for working women such as day care, in addition to public sector jobs for many women.

Eighth, regression analysis in Chapter 9 indicates that **occupational segregation by sex** (as proxied for by ID75) **is not related to socio-economic development** (proxied for by level of national income per capita, adult female education level and size of the agricultural sector). Nor is ID75 strongly related to two theoretically important labour market variables (female share of the non-agricultural labour force and proportion of the labour force working part-time) when the region a country comes from is taken into consideration.

Ninth, these regression results in Chapter 9 indicate that the region a country comes from is the most important determinant of differences across countries in occupational segregation by sex. This result is consistent with the fact that the level of occupational segregation by sex tends to be quite similar for study countries within regions and subregions. Indeed, approximately half of the differences in ID75 across study countries can be "explained" by simply knowing if a country is from the Asia/Pacific, Middle East/North Africa, OECD, Transition Economy or Other Developing region—and this result is more or less unaffected by taking into account the socio-economic and labour market conditions in study countries. These regression results strongly imply that **social, cultural and historical factors are of paramount importance in determining the extent to which occupations are segmented based on the sex of the worker.**

Tenth, as noted above in section 16.3 on methodological findings, factor analysis in Chapter 12 identified two separate groups of inequality variables, i.e. factors (one which represents the female side of the labour market, and the other which represents the male side and the overall level of occupational segregation by sex). Especially interesting is that **countries in each study region, as well as in some OECD subregions, have their own unique combination of factor scores.** Middle Eastern and North African countries have high scores on factor 1 and low scores on factor 2. Asian and Pacific countries, on the other hand, tend to have relatively low scores on factor 1 and average-to-low scores on factor 2. Other Developing countries/areas have high or average-to-high scores on both factors. OECD and Transition Economy countries tend to have average scores for both factors.

Eleventh, **there is considerable similarity across study countries in the degree to which typical "male" occupations are feminized** (Chapter 11). The percentage male is uniformly high in all study countries and areas for all eight of the typical "male" occupations we investigated in detail. For five of these eight "male" occupations (architects, engineers and related technical workers; protective services workers; production supervisors and general foremen; blacksmiths, toolmakers, etc.; bricklayers, carpenters and other construction workers), approximately 95 per cent of workers are men, and men comprise at least 80 per cent of workers in 154 out of 156 available occupation-country examples. There is clearly a need to break down barriers and enable women to enter traditional "male" occupations.

Twelfth, in contrast to the results for our eight specific "male" occupations, there is **considerable variation in feminization for the nine specific "female" occupations we investigated in detail** (Chapter 11). Three of these occupations (nurses; secretaries and typists; maids and related housekeeping workers) are highly feminized all across the world; they are approximately 85 per cent female on average, and there is a relative concentration of women workers in 79 out of the available 82 country-occupation examples. Despite this high percentage female, male nurses are fairly common (making up from one-third to one-half or more of nurses) in 6 out of 21 study countries with data; male houseboys are fairly common in 4 out of 30 study countries with data; and male secretaries are fairly common in 4 out of 31 study countries with data. Interestingly, all but one of these exceptions are outside of the OECD region. *These results show that even in the most feminized occupations around the world, there are countries where male workers are common and that men can and are willing to do "female" work.* Two other occupations (hairdressers, barbers and related workers; and tailors and sewers, etc.) follow the same pattern as the previous three "female" occupations, but in a more muted form. Again, these occupations are much more feminized in OECD countries as compared to non-OECD countries.

The remaining three supposedly "female" occupations investigated (teachers; bookkeepers/cashiers; cooks, waiters and bartenders) are female-concentrated in about one-half of the available country examples, with women comprising approximately 50 per cent of these workers; part of the reason for the mixed picture here in terms of feminization is the heterogeneous nature of these occupations (for example, women are much more likely to be pre-primary and primary school teachers as compared to secondary and university teachers; women are often much more likely to be waitresses than cooks). It is also worth noting that there are relatively few women in these last three occupations in Middle Eastern and North African countries, because this work requires public interaction of men and women and this is frowned upon in these countries. Again, *it seems clear that men in many parts of the world are able and willing to take up what we started out assuming are women's occupations.*

Thirteenth, **women have very limited labour market choices throughout the world,** as women tend to work in a small set of occupations. In addition, the most important occupations for women represent relatively poor jobs in terms of pay, status, decision-making authority and career opportunity. This situation is illustrated by analysis in Chapter 11 where we identified the five largest female-dominated occupations in terms of employment. In study country after study country, the same occupations were identified. Three occupational groups (nurses; secretaries/typists; maids/housekeepers) were responsible for approximately one-half of all entries and only seven occupational groups (also including bookkeepers/cashiers; building caretakers/cleaners; caregivers; tailors/sewers) were responsible for approximately three-quarters of the entries for all 41 study countries and areas. There is obviously *a need to broaden women's limited choice of occupations by having women enter in greater numbers into non-traditional occupations for women.*

Fourteenth, the **main occupations for women** workers throughout the world, such as those noted in the previous paragraph, **have characteristics which are highly consistent with typical female stereotypes in society at large** (see table 2.1). Indeed, the five largest female and female-dominated occupations in each study country are consistent with typical female stereotypes, such as a caring nature; honesty; manual dexterity, especially with fingers; experience and skill at typical household activities; and willingness to be subservient and take orders. There is *clearly a need to break down the very strong gender stereotypes* which exist around the world regarding the supposed capabilities, preferences and abilities of men and women. Only in this way will individual women begin to have the opportunity of a wide choice of occupations.

16.5   Some major findings for recent changes in occupational segregation by sex in the world

First, there is little doubt that **occupational segregation by sex has fallen in the past two decades in many study countries.** For the world as a whole (Chapter 13), the index of dissimilarity (i.e. ID) fell on average by approximately

−.025 in both the 1970s as well as the 1980s, from an ID75 of approximately .63 in 1970 to approximately .58 in 1990 (and there were similar decreases for the marginal matching index). There was also a large fall in the percentage of the total non-agricultural labour force in a gender-dominated occupation, as TDOM75 fell on average by almost 11 percentage points between 1970 and 1990 for study countries and areas, from approximately 66 per cent to approximately 55 per cent (Chapter 14).

Second, it is also clear that the observed decrease in occupational segregation by sex in the world in the past two decades is **mainly due to the increased integration of men and women within occupations rather than a shift in the occupational structure of employment.** This was established in Chapter 13 when we (i) divided observed changes in ID into the parts due to changes in the gender-integration of occupations and changes in employment structure and (ii) used other inequality statistics recommended for investigating changes in occupational segregation by sex. This finding is important, because most policy-makers and laypersons consider the greater integration of male and female workers within occupations as indicative of an improvement in occupational segregation by sex.

Third, although occupational segregation by sex decreased for the world as a whole over the past two decades, **decreases are observed in some but not other parts of the world.** While there were large falls in occupational segregation by sex in several of the small developing countries for which we had time series data as well as most OECD study countries, *this did not occur in large East Asian countries, most Middle Eastern and North African countries as well as several OECD and Transition Economy countries.* Asia, in particular, stands out as resistant to decreases in occupational segregation by sex as it contains the only two study economies where occupational segregation by sex seems to have clearly increased—China from 1982 to 1990 and Hong Kong from 1971 to 1991—and, in addition, there was no change in Japan in the 1980s or 1990s.

There are also major differences in recent experiences across OECD and Transition Economy subregions and countries. On the one hand, occupational segregation by sex (as measured by the integration of women and men within occupations) fell sharply over the past two decades in North America (the United States and Canada), Scandinavia (Finland, Norway and Sweden), Other English-speaking countries (Australia, New Zealand and the United Kingdom) and Western Europe (France, Luxembourg, and to a lesser extent the Netherlands). On the other hand, occupational segregation by sex remained basically unchanged in most of Central Europe (Austria and Switzerland and to a lesser extent West Germany, as well as Hungary and Poland) and Southern Europe (Italy, Spain and Cyprus, as well as former Yugoslavia).

Fourth, despite the dramatic improvement for many OECD countries, there is no room for complacency in this region. The fact is that occupational segregation by sex had previously been so high outside Southern Europe that levels in 1970 were similar to those found today in many developing countries from Africa, the South Pacific, the Middle East, North Africa and the Caribbean. Consequently, all OECD countries have considerable scope for (further) improvement.

Fifth, the **decrease in sex inequality in the labour market over the past two decades is especially large when measured by a new inequality index we developed (IDHALF)** which combines into one index number the female share of the non-agricultural labour force and the occupational segregation by sex for those in the non-agricultural labour force, which assumes that women comprise one-half of the non-agricultural labour force. This index decreased in all regions of the world in the past two decades except for Asia/Pacific, and in all OECD subregions except that this tendency was weak in our OECD Central European subregion.

Sixth, because occupational segregation by sex tended to fall in study countries and study regions/OECD subregions with relatively high levels and to remain unchanged or increase in study countries and study regions/OECD subregions with relatively low levels, **there has been a marked convergence around the world over the past two decades in levels of occupational segregation by sex.** Regression analysis in Chapter 13 indicates that this tendency of convergence is statistically significant, especially in the 1980s where a difference in ID75 of .08 (the difference between average ID75 values today in the Asia/Pacific and OECD regions) is associated with a change in ID75 of $-.024$ over a ten-year period, approximately the same magnitude as the average change in the 1980s for the world as a whole. This convergence implies that the present clustering of study countries with an ID75 value between .55 and .60, as observed in Chapter 9, is a recent phenomenon.

Seventh, regression analysis in Chapter 13 indicates that changes in the female share of the non-agricultural labour force and changes in occupational segregation by sex are negatively related (significantly related in the 1970s but not the 1980s). An increase in the female share of the non-agricultural labour force of three to four percentage points (similar to the actual average change for the 1970s and the 1980s) is associated with a change in ID of approximately $-.03$ for the 1970s (and $-.01$ for the 1980s). This relationship is twice as strong for countries with PFEM values above 35 per cent as compared to countries with below 35 per cent. Thus, **it does seem that women's entry into the non-agricultural labour force has tended to reduce occupational segregation by sex, as one would expect.** It is noteworthy, however, that the time series regression results reported in Chapter 13 differ from the cross-section results for a recent year reported in Chapter 9 where ID75 and PFEM were not significantly related when the region was taken into consideration (but significantly, and non-linearly related when the region was not specified, negatively related for PFEM values up to approximately 35 per cent and positively related for higher PFEM values).

Eighth, results from Chapter 14 indicate that **many men in the past two decades have lost their privileged position in the labour market of having their own "male" occupations** where they face little or no competition from women workers. On average, the percentage of male non-agricultural workers in a male-dominated occupation fell by about 10 percentage points over the past two decades (and by about 20 per cent as far as male workers are concerned)—from an MDOM75 of approximately 57 per cent to 47 per cent in this time period. This decrease in MDOM75 was as large as approximately 18 percentage points on average over the past two decades for the 11 OECD study countries outside of Southern and Central Europe.

Ninth, while in no study country were men able to clearly increase their protected position in the labour market, *men were able to maintain their position in a number of study countries*. This occurred in several large Asian economies (such as China, Hong Kong and Japan), several OECD and Transition Economy countries in Southern and Central Europe (such as Austria, West Germany, Switzerland, Spain, Hungary, Poland and former Yugoslavia) as well as in certain Middle Eastern/North African countries (such as Jordan and Tunisia).

Tenth, changes in the number and size of female-dominated occupations over the past two decades displayed considerable variability across study countries, regions and OECD subregions. In the 1980s, however, there was a general tendency (with considerable variation across study countries) for the percentage of the female non-agricultural labour force working in a female-dominated occupation to fall outside of the Asia/Pacific and Transition Economy regions. This result is interesting in that one would have expected FDOM75 to have increased along with increases in female labour force activity. It seems that the expansion of established female-dominated occupations was insufficient to absorb all of the new female labour force participants, and thus many women entered less traditional occupations.

Eleventh, when we looked in Chapter 15 at changes over the past two decades in percentage male for the eight specific "male" occupations investigated in Chapter 11, it was found that despite the increasing entry of women into the non-agricultural labour force, four of these "male" occupations (protective services workers; production supervisors and foremen; blacksmiths, toolmakers, etc.; bricklayers, carpenters and other construction workers) remained very much male enclaves. The male percentage changed by less than five percentage points per decade in 116 out of the 128 available country-time period examples (and by less than one percentage point in approximately one-half of these examples). Clearly *there is a need to increase gender sensitization and break down gender stereotypes for these occupations*. For this to be successful all three of the social partners need to get involved, as these occupations are often found in unionized sectors of the labour market.

Twelfth, sizeable numbers of women entered the other four typical "male" occupations we investigated (architects, engineers and related technical workers; legislative officials and government administrators; managers; sales supervisors and buyers), and this improvement is generally found in all study regions. One interesting exception is that major increases in the feminization of sales supervisors and buyers is restricted to non-OECD study economies (such as China, Hong Kong and Mauritius). A second interesting difference is that increases in the feminization of legislative officials and government administrators occur almost exclusively in OECD countries (in 14 out of 21 country-time period for OECD countries as compared to 2 out of 14 country-time periods for non-OECD study countries and areas). Particularly striking is that whenever there was a clear increase in feminization in an OECD study country in the 1970s, there was always a further clear increase in the 1980s. *This is a good example of how gender integration often carries forward through time.*

Thirteenth, when we looked at changes in the feminization of our typical specific "female" occupations in Chapter 15, it was found that there is **considerable variation in experiences both across these "female" occupations as well as across study countries and regions.** This variability parallels the variability observed in Chapters 10 and 11 based on a cross-section analysis of a recent year.

For two "female" occupations—bookkeepers, cashiers and related workers; and hairdressers, barbers and related workers—there has been a large increase in feminization around the world. According to study data, the female share increased by approximately 18 per cent per study country on average over the past two decades in these occupations, and this growth is found in all study regions. Although this is speculation, technological and work organization changes provide possible explanations for this worldwide phenomenon. There has been deskilling of the cashier occupation. In addition, both occupations have moved towards part-time and flexible work schedules, and women generally provided this type of flexible workforce. For a third supposedly "female" occupation (teachers), the female share also rose around the world, but the number of female teachers grew more or less in tandem with the number of female non-agricultural workers in general and consequently, the percentage female remained more or less unchanged on average.

The remaining six "female" occupations investigated did not have obvious worldwide trends in the female share. There were, however, some noteworthy differences between regions. There was a slight decrease in percentage female for two highly feminized occupations (nurses; maids and related household workers) in OECD countries (a decrease of 1 to 2 per cent per decade on average) as well as a slight decrease for nurses in other study countries. *This could be a first sign of male entry into these occupations.* Indeed, it is worth speculating in general about when sizeable numbers of men will decide to enter "female" occupations, especially better paying "female" occupations such as nurses. In industrialized countries with high unemployment rates, men may decide that a job in a "female" occupation is better than no job—women have faced a similar quandary for many years: whether a less desirable job is better than no job at all. Second, in the Middle East/North Africa, there were very large increases in female share (approximately 40 percentage points on average) for typists/secretaries. In this region, there are very few non-agricultural occupations that are socially acceptable for women, and study data indicate that secretarial work has been the destination of many of the new female non-agricultural labour force participants in this region in the past two decades. Third, for the tailors, dressmakers, sewers, etc. occupational group, there were very large increases in the percentage female for small study countries with large textile exports (e.g. the percentage female went from 37 to 65 per cent in Mauritius, from 41 to 61 per cent in Fiji and from 65 to 85 per cent in Costa Rica). It seems that multinational firms seeking low cost production sites not only bring the required capital and technology to developing countries, but also the western pattern where women do this work.

16.6   Concluding remarks

As shown above, the separation of men and women into different occupations is common throughout all regions of the world, and is a major source of labour market rigidity and inefficiency. This has had an especially negative impact on women, since "female" occupations generally have low pay, low status and fewer career opportunities.

In spite of the usual difficulties with data quality and cross-national comparability, study results indicate that not all is gloomy for women. Occupational segregation by sex was observed to have fallen considerably in a number of study countries in the past two decades. Although we did not do a detailed investigation of national policies or how they relate to observed changes in occupational segregation by sex, the analysis contained in this book provides a number of policy insights.

On the **data collection and analysis side,** it is clear that (i) disaggregated occupational data are required to measure and understand the sex segregation of occupations, and especially the situation faced by women workers; (ii) time series data are required to measure and understand progress, or the lack of it, toward greater gender equality in the labour market; and (iii) a comprehensive analysis of the various dimensions of occupational segregation by sex greatly increases understanding of its multifaceted nature and the best policy options.

On the policy side, study results indicate that the **sex segregation of occupations has affected men as well as women,** because recent job growth has been concentrated in service occupations where women often predominate, and job losses have been concentrated in production occupations where men predominate. In my opinion, this implies that equal opportunity policies and programmes to reduce occupational segregation by sex *should assist men who want to enter into traditional "female" occupations (especially less well paying "female" occupations) as well as assist women who want to enter into traditional "male" occupations.* This would also have the advantage of broadening support for policies and programmes to reduce the sex segregation of occupations. This would, in addition, help break down the gender stereotypes of women as subordinates and men as decision-makers; for example, the employment of sizeable numbers of men in typical "female" occupations such as maids, nurses and secretaries would in my opinion help to speed up the acceptability of women as managers, supervisors and doctors. In the longer run, it is hoped that these changes would increase the acceptability for men of taking on greater household and family responsibilities.

Achieving this goal of a wider occupational choice for women is not easy, as attested to by the high levels of occupational segregation by sex found throughout the world today. **There are many complementary ways to achieve this goal which reflect the multiple sources of occupational segregation by sex;** indeed because of this, comprehensive approaches are always the most effective. *Facilitating policies,* such as providing child-care and other services to working women (which is emphasized in Scandinavia and where occupational segregation by sex has fallen in the past two decades) are important, because all around the world, women, not men, are generally constrained by family and household responsibilities. *Affirmative action and equal opportunity programmes* as well as anti-discrimination laws can be important (as emphasized in North America, Other English-speaking countries and the European Union where occupational segregation by sex has fallen in the past two decades) to help break down barriers based on sex stereotypes. Economic development and the *opening up of Third World economies* to international trade and investment can be important (such as occurred in Mauritius and Fiji). And, of course, *increased education and training for women in non-traditional subjects* is required since, as observed in this book, there is a wide range of professional and other occupations (such as engineers, science and crafts) where relatively few women work anywhere in the world.

But in my opinion, **the most important changes required, if occupational segregation by sex is to be greatly reduced, are ideational in nature** (some of which are associated with the increased popularity of feminist ideas and the women's liberation movement). Simply put, it is necessary to *change gender-stereotypes and typical prejudices* inside and outside the labour market regarding the supposed abilities, preferences and the appropriate work and societal roles for men and women, as these beliefs and prejudices help to justify implicit and explicit discrimination against women. In addition to the *demonstration effect* of women entering and succeeding in non-traditional occupations, as discussed in a previous paragraph (possibly through affirmative action and equal opportunity programmes), this implies the importance of policies and programmes which attempt to *increase gender-sensitization and eliminate gender stereotypes*—such as through the media, in the workplace, in trade unions, in employers' organizations and in schools, in order to increase awareness that individual men and women have similar capabilities for all types of work. Study results are very clear on this. Not only is there a very close correspondence everywhere in the world between the characteristics of "female" occupations and typical female stereotypes; but in addition, statistical analysis in this book indicates that national levels of occupational segregation by sex are quite similar within regions and subregions of the world (where cultural and historical experiences, and therefore values, are similar), yet more or less unrelated to socio-economic or labour market conditions.

In conclusion, the segmentation of occupations based on the sex of workers is an important labour market phenomenon which deserves increased attention from policy-makers and laypersons interested in equality, efficiency and social justice—issues which, as it happens, lie at the heart of the ILO. It is hoped that this book helps in stimulating increased attention to this subject.

BIBLIOGRAPHY

Amsden, A. (ed.): *The economics of women and work* (Harmondsworth: Penguin Books, 1980).

Anker, R.: "Measuring women's participation in the African labour force", in A. Adepoju and C. Oppong (eds.): *Gender, work and population in sub-Saharan Africa* (London: James Currey; and Portsmouth, New Hampshire: Heinemann, 1994).

–: "Labour market policies, vulnerable groups and poverty", in H. Figueiredo and Z. Shaheed (eds.) *New approaches to poverty analysis and policy—II* (Geneva: International Institute for Labour Studies, 1995).

–; Anker, M.: "Measuring female labour force with emphasis on Egypt" in N. Khoury and V. Moghadam (eds.) *Women in the Arab World* (London: Zed Books, 1995).

–; Hein, C.: "Why Third World urban employers usually prefer men", in *International Labour Review* (Geneva: ILO), 1985, Vol. 124, No. 1, pp. 73–90.

–; –: *Sex inequalities in urban employment in the Third World* (London: Macmillan, 1986).

–; –: "Sex inequalities in Third World employment: Statistical evidence", in R. Anker and C. Hein (eds): *Sex inequalities in urban employment in the Third World* (London: Macmillan, 1986).

–; Khan, M.E.; Gupta, R.B.: "Biases in measuring the labour force: Results of a methods test survey in Uttar Pradesh, India", in *International Labour Review* (Geneva: ILO), 1987, pp. 151–167.

Baden, S.: *The impact of recession on women's employment in OECD countries*, Paper prepared for the Interdepartmental Project on Equality for Women in Employment (Geneva: ILO, 1993).

Bakker, I.: "Women's employment in comparative perspective", in J. Jenson, E. Hagen and C. Reddy (eds.) *Feminization of the labour force: Paradoxes and promises* (New York: Oxford University Press, 1988).

Barbezat, D.: "Occupational segmentation by sex in the world", in *Equality of women in employment*, Interdepartmental Working Paper No. 13 (Geneva: ILO, 1993).

Becker, G.S.: *The economics of discrimination* (Chicago, 2nd edition: University of Chicago Press, 1971).

Beller, A.: "Occupational segregation by sex: Determinants and changes", in *Journal of Human Resources* (Madison), 1982, Vol. 17, No. 3.

–: "Trends in occupational segregation by sex and race, 1960–1981", in B.F. Reskin (ed.): *Sex segregation in the workplace: Trends, explanation and remedies* (Washington, DC), 1984, pp. 11–26.

Bergmann, B.: "Occupational segregation, wages and profits when employers discriminate by wage or sex", in *Eastern Economic Journal* (Storrs, Connecticut), 1974, Vol. 1, Nos. 2–3.

Bianchi, S.M.; Rytina, N.: "The decline in occupational sex segregation during the 1970s: Census and CPS comparisons", in *Demography* (Washington, DC), 1986, Vol. 23, No. 1, pp. 79–86.

–; –: "Sex segregation within occupations and labour markets: A critical evaluation", in *American Economic Review* (Nashville), 1986, Vol. 26, No. 2, pp. 43–47.

Blackburn, R.M.; Jarman, J.; Siltanen, J.: "The analysis of occupational gender segregation over time and place: Consideration of measurement and some new evidence", in *Work, Employment and Society* (London), 1993, Vol. 7, No. 3.

Blau, F.: *Occupational segregation by gender: A look at the 1980s*, Paper presented at the American Economic Association Meeting (New York), Dec. 1988.

–; M. Ferber: *The economics of women, men and work*, (Englewood Cliffs, New Jersey: Prentice-Hall, 1992).

–; –: "Career plans and expectations of young women and men: The earnings gap and labour force participation" in *Journal of Human Resources* (Madison), 1991, Vol. 26, No. 4, pp. 581–607.

–; Hendricks W.: "Occupational segregation by sex: Trends and prospects", in *The Journal of Human Resources* (Madison), 1979, Vol. XIV, No. 2, pp. 197–210.

–; Jusenius, C.: "Economists approach to sex segregation by sex: An appraisal", in M. Blaxall and B. Reagan (eds.): *Women and the workplace* (Chicago: University of Chicago Press, 1976).

–; Khan, L.: "The gender earnings gap: Learning from international comparisons", in *American Economic Review* (Nashville), 1992, Vol. 82, No. 2.

–; –: *The gender earnings gap: Some international evidence* (Cambridge, Massachusetts: National Bureau of Economic Research, Working Paper No. 4224, Dec. 1992).

Bodrova, V. and Anker, R.: *Working women in Socialist countries: The fertility connection.* (Geneva: ILO, 1985).

Boserup, E.: *Women's role in economic development* (London: George Allen and Unwin Ltd., 1970).

Boulding, E.: *Handbook of international data on women* (Beverly Hills, California: Sage, 1976).

Bradley, H.: *Men's work, women's work* (Oxford: Basil Blackwell, 1989).

Brown, W. et al.: "Occupational pay structures under different wage fixing arrangements: A comparison of intra-occupational pay dispersion in Australia, Great Britain and the United States", in *British Journal of Industrial Relations* (Oxford), 1980, vol. 18, No. 2, pp. 217–230.

Buvinic, M.: "The feminization of poverty? Research and policy needs" in J. Figueiredo and Z. Shaheed (eds.) *New approaches to poverty analysis and policy—II* (Geneva: IILS, 1995).

Canadian Union of Public Employees: *Toronto Pay Equity Plan Facts* (Toronto), 1992, mimeo.

Charles, M.: "Cross-national variation in occupational sex segregation", in *American Sociological Review* (New York), 1992, Vol. 57, pp. 483–502.

Chapman, B.; Ross Harding J.: "Sex differences in earnings: An analysis of Malaysian wage data", in *Journal of Development Studies* (London), 1986, Vol. 21, No. 3, pp. 362–376.

Chiplin, B.; Sloane P.: *Sex discrimination in the labour market* (London: Macmillan, 1976).

Cohen, B.; House, W.: "Women's urban labour market status in developing countries: How well do they fare in Khartoum, Sudan?", in *Journal of Development Studies* (London), 1993, Vol. 29, No. 3, pp. 461–483.

Cohen, B.; Bechar, S.; Raijman, R.: "Occupational sex segregation in Israel, 1972–1983", in *Israel Social Science Research* (Beersheva), 1987, Vol. 5, Nos. 1 & 2, pp. 97–106.

Cohn, S.: *The process of occupational sex typing* (Philadelphia: Temple University Press, 1985).

–; –: "Sex-role socialization and occupational segregation: An exploratory investigation", in *Journal of Post Keynesian Economics* (New York), 1987, Vol. IX, No. 3, pp. 330–346.

Dex, S.: *The sexual division of work* (New York: St. Martin's Press, 1985).

Dixon-Mueller, R.; Anker, R.: *Assessing women's contribution to development* (Geneva: ILO, 1988).

Doeringer, P.; Piore, M.: *Internal labor markets and manpower analysis* (Lexington, Massachusetts: D.C. Heath and Co., 1971).

Duncan, D.; Duncan, B.: "A methodological analysis of segregation indexes", in *American Sociological Review* (New York), 1955, No. 20, pp. 210–217.

Economist, The: "Womb to tomb" (London), 5 Nov. 1994.

Edgeworth, F.Y.: "Equal pay to men and women for equal work", in *Economic Journal*, (Oxford), 1922, Vol. 32, No. 4.

EEC: *Bulletin on Women and Employment in the EU* (Brussels), 1993, No. 3; 1994, No. 5; 1995, No.7.

–: *Equal pay for work of equal value* (Brussels, 1993).

England, P.: "The failure of human capital theory to explain occupational sex segregation", in *Journal of Human Resources* (Madison), 1982, Vol. 17, No. 2, pp. 358–370.

–, et al.: "Explaining occupational sex segregation and wages: Findings from a model with fixed effects", *in American Sociological Review* (New York), 1988, Vol. 53, No. 4, pp. 544–558.

EUROSTAT: *Women in the European Community* (Luxembourg: Statistical Office of the European Communities, 1992).

Fergamy, N.: *An attempt to improve upon age-specific activity rates for women in Arab countries, 1950–1990* (Cairo), 1995, mimeo.

Fields, J.; Wolff, E.: "The decline of sex segregation and the wage gap, 1970–1980", in *Journal of Human Resources* (Madison), 1991, Vol. 26, No. 4, pp. 608–622.

Fox, B.; Fox, J.: "Occupational gender segregation of the Canadian labour force, 1931–1981", in *Canadian Review of Sociology and Anthropology* (Montreal, Quebec), 1987, Vol. 24, No. 3, pp. 374–397.

Gannicott, K.: "Women, wages and discrimination: Some evidence from Taiwan", in *Economic Development and Cultural Change* (Chicago), 1986, Vol. 34, No. 4, pp. 721–730.

Gindling, T.: "Women's wages and economic crisis in Costa Rica", in *Economic Development and Cultural Change* (Chicago), 1993, pp. 277–297.

Goldschmidt-Clermont, L.: *Unpaid work in the household: A review of economic evaluation methods* (Geneva: ILO, 1982), Women, Work and Development series, No. 1.

–: *Economic evaluations of unpaid household work: Africa, Asia, Latin America and Oceania*, (Geneva: ILO, 1987), Women, Work and Development series, No. 14.

Gonzalez, P.: *Indicators of the relative performance of women in the labour market* (Geneva: ILO, 1991), mimeo.

–; Watts, M.: *Measuring gender wage differentials and job segregation* (Geneva: ILO, Dec. 1996).

Gregory, J.: "Equal pay for work of equal value: The strengths and weaknesses of legislation", in *Work, Employment and Society* (London), 1992, Vol. 6, No. 3, pp. 461–473.

Gregory, R.G.; Duncan, R.: "Segmented labour market theories and the Australian experience of Equal Pay for Women", in *Journal of Post Keynesian Economics* (New York), 1981, Vol. 3, No. 3.

Groshen, E.: "The structure of the female/male wage differential: Is it who you are, what you do, or where you work?", in *Journal of Human Resources* (Madison), 1991, Vol. 26, No. 83, pp. 457–472.

Gruber, J.: "The incidence of mandated maternity benefits", in *American Economic Review* (Nashville), 1994, Vol. 84, No. 3, pp. 622–641.

Gunderson, M.: "Male-female wage differentials and policy responses", in *Journal of Economic Literature* (Pittsburgh), 1989, Vol. 27, No. 1.

–: *Comparable worth and gender discrimination: An international perspective* (Geneva: ILO, 1994).

Gwartney-Gibbs, P.: "Sex segregation in the paid work force: The New Zealand case", in *Australian and New Zealand Journal of Sociology* (Bundoora, Victoria), 1988, Vol. 24, No. 2, pp. 264–278.

Haavio-Mannila, E.; Kauppinen, K.: "Changes in the status of women in Russia and Estonia", in T. Piirainen (ed.): *Changes and continuity in Eastern Europe* (Aldershot, Hampshire: Dartmouth, 1994).

Hakim, C.: "Job segregation: Trends in the 1970", in *Employment Gazette* (London), 1981, pp. 521–529.

–: "The myth of rising female employment", in *Work, Employment and Society* (London), 1993, Vol. 7, No. 1, pp. 97–120.

–: "Explaining trends in occupational segregation: The measurement, causes and consequences of the sexual division of labour", in *European Sociological Review* (Oxford), 1992, Vol. 8, No. 2, pp. 127–152.

–: "Segregated and integrated occupations: A new approach to analysing social change", in *European Sociological Review* (Oxford), 1993, Vol. 9, No. 3.

Horton, S.: *Women and industrialization in Asia: Overview of 7 country studies,* Institute for Policy Analysis (University of Toronto, 1993), mimeo.

House, W.: "Occupational segregation and discriminatory pay: The position of women in the Cyprus labour market", in *International Labour Review* (Geneva), 1983, Vol. 122, No. 1.

–: "The status and pay of women in the Cyprus labour market", in R. Anker and C. Hein (eds): *Sex inequalities in urban employment in the Third World* (London: Macmillan, 1986).

Hunter, J.: *Japanese women working* (New York: Routledge, 1993).

Hutchens, R.: "Segregation curves, Lorenz curves, and inequality in the distribution of people across occupations", in *Mathematical Social Sciences* (Amsterdam), 1991, No. 21, pp. 31–51.

ILO: *International Standard Classification of Occupations-68* (Geneva, 1968).

–: *Employment, incomes and inequality: A strategy for increasing productive employment in Kenya* (Geneva, 1972).

–: *International Standard Classification of Occupations-88* (Geneva, 1990).

–: *Active labour market policies in a wider context,* paper prepared for ILO Governing Body Committee on Employment and Social Policy (Geneva, 1993a), Nov.

–: *Statistical measurement of gender wage differentials,* Equality of Women in Employment, Interdepartmental working paper No. 3 (Geneva, 1993b).

–: *Workers with family responsibilities,* Report III, Part 4B, International Labour Conference, 80th Session (Geneva, 1993c).

–: *Changing role of women in the economy: Employment and social issues,* Governing Body Committee on Employment and Social Policy, 261st Session (Geneva, 1994a), Nov.

–: *Elements of a child care strategy for the Republic of Korea* (Geneva, 1994b), mimeo.

–: *ILO action on discrimination in employment and occupation,* Governing Body Committee on Legal Issues and International Labour Standards, 261st session, (Geneva, 1994c), Nov.

–: *Part-time work,* International Labour Conference, 81st Session, 1994, Report IV (2B), (Geneva, 1994d).

–: *Recent developments in the clothing industry* (Geneva, 1994e).

–: *The remuneration of nursing personnel, an international perspective* (Geneva, 1994f).

–: *Women and work: Selected ILO policy documents* (Geneva, 1994g).

–: "Gender issues in conditions of work and welfare facilities", "Gender issues in labour legislation, labour-management relations and remuneration", "Gender issues in labour market policies", "Gender issues in poverty alleviation and employment of people with disabilities" in *Gender issues in the world of work* (Geneva, 1995a).

–: *Women workers: An annotated bibliography, 1983–94* (Geneva, 1995b).

–: *Equality in employment and occupation*, International Labour Conference, 83rd Session (Geneva, 1996).

–: *Yearbook of Labour Statistics*, Geneva, various years.

–: *Labour force estimates and projections, 1950–2010* (Geneva, forthcoming).

–; Asia-Pacific Skill Development Programme: *Making it: Women in new occupations* (Islamabad, 1988).

–; Commonwealth Association of Polytechnics in Africa: *Women in technical trades* (Geneva: ILO and CAPA, 1990).

–; INSTRAW: *Women in economic activity: A global statistical survey (1950–2000)*, (Santo Domingo, 1985).

Izraeli, D.: "Sex structure of occupations", in *Sociology of Work and Occupations* (Newbury Park, California), 1979, pp. 406–429.

Jacobs, J.: "Long-term trends in occupational segregation by sex", in *American Journal of Sociology* (Chicago), 1989, Vol. 95, No. 1, pp. 160–173.

–: "Introduction to the special issue on sex segregation and gender stratification", in *Work and Occupations* (Newbury Park, California), 1992, Vol. 19, No. 4.

–; Lim, S.: "Trends in occupational and industrial sex segregation in 56 countries: 1960–80", in *Work and Occupations* (Newbury Park, California), 1992, pp. 450–486.

Jahn, J.A.; Schmid, C.F.; Schrag, C.: "The measurement of ecological segregation", in *American Sociological Review* (New York), 1947, Vol. 12, pp. 293–303.

Jain, M.: "The changing women", in *India Today* (New Delhi), 15 July 1992, pp. 52–61.

Jenson, J.; Hagen, E.; Reddy, C.: *Feminization of the labour force: Paradoxes and promises* (New York: Oxford University Press, 1988).

Jose, A.V.: *Employment and wages of women workers in Asian countries: An assessment* (New Delhi: ILO, 1987), Asian Employment Programme Working Paper.

Joseph, G.: *Women at work: The British experience* (Oxford: Philip Allan, 1983).

Jusenius, C.: "Occupational change, 1969–71", in *Dual careers: Longitudinal study of labour market experience of women*, (Columbus, Ohio: Centre for Human Resource Research), 1975, Vol. 3.

–: "The influence of work experience, skill requirement, and occupational segregation on women's earnings", in *Journal of Economics and Business* (Philadelphia), 1977, Vol. 29, No. 2, pp. 107–115.

Karmel, T.; MacLachlan, M.: "Occupational sex segregation—increasing or decreasing?", in *Economic Record* (Sydney, Australia), 1988, No. 64, pp. 187–195.

Khan, M.; Ghosh, D.; Anker, R.: "Inequalities between men and women in nutrition and family welfare services: An in-depth enquiry in an Indian village", in P. Caldwell and G. Santow (eds.): *Selected readings in the cultural, social and behavioural determinants of health* (Canberra: Highland Press, 1989).

Kaupinen-Toropainen, K.; Kandolin, I.; Haavio-Mannila, E.: "Sex segregation of work in Finland and the quality of women's work", in *Journal of Organizational Behavior Manaegement* (New York), 1988, Vol. 9, pp. 15–27.

Kidd, M.; Shannon, M.: "Does the level of occupational segregation affect estimates of the gender wage gap?", in *Industrial and Labour Relations Review* (Ithaca, New York), 1996, Vol. 49, No. 2.

King, M.: "Occupational segregation by race and sex, 1940–1988", in *Monthly Labour Review* (Washington, DC), 1992, Vol. 115, No. 4, pp. 30–37.

Lam, A.: *Women and Japanese management: Discrimination and reform* (London: Routledge, 1992).

Leigh-Doyle, S.: "Increasing women's participation in technical fields: A pilot project in Africa", in *International Labour Review* (Geneva: ILO), 1991, Vol. 130, No. 4.

Lewis, D.: "The sources of changes in the occupational segregation of Australian women", in *Economic Record* (Sydney, Australia), 1985, Vol. 61, pp. 719–736.

–; Shorten, B.: "Occupational segregation, labour force participation and the relative earnings of men and women", in *Applied Economics* (London), 1991, Vol. 23, No. 1b, pp. 167–177.

Lim, L.: *More and better jobs for women: An action guide* (Geneva: ILO, 1996).

Lloyd, C.; Niemi, B.: *The economics of sex differentials* (New York: Columbia University Press, 1979).

Manpower: "Women on slow track to the top in Japan", in *Manpower Digest* (Milwaukee, Wisconsin), Sep., 1994.

Martens, H.; Mitter S.: *Women in trade unions: Organizing the unorganized* (Geneva: ILO, 1994).

Martin, J.; Roberts, C.: *Women and employment: A lifetime perspective* (London: Her Majesty's Stationery Office, 1984).

Mason Oppenheim, K.: *Gender and demographic change* (Liège, IUSSP, 1995).

Melkas, H.; Anker, R.: *Occupational segregation in the Nordic countries* (ILO: Geneva, forthcoming).

Meulders, D.: *Women and the five Essen priorities* (Brussels: Economie du Travail et de l'Emploi, Université Libre de Bruxelles, Feb. 1996), mimeo.

Mihye, R.: "A study on male-female wage differentials", in *Women's Studies Forum* (Seoul: Korean Women's Development Institute), 1991, Vol. 7, pp. 5–38.

Miller, A.: *The industrial distribution of women's employment: An international comparison* (Philadelphia: University of Pennsylvania, Population Studies Center, 1972).

Moghadam, V.: *Economic reform and women's employment in Egypt: Constraints and opportunities* (Helsinki: UNU/WIDER, May 1995).

–: "Economic restructuring and women in the labour force", in *WIDER Angle* (Helsinki: WIDER), 1995, No. 2, pp.15–16.

Moir, H.: "Segregation in the New Zealand labour market", in *Pacific Viewpoint* (Wellington), 1977.

Neumann, S.: "Occupational sex segregation in the Kibbutz: Principles and practice", in *Kyklos* (Basel), 1991, Vol. 44, No. 2, pp. 203–219.

Nordic Council of Ministers: *Women and men in the Nordic countries. Facts on equal opportunities yesterday, today and tomorrow* (Stockholm: Nordic Council of Ministers, 1994).

Oaxaca, R.: "Female-male wage differentials in urban labour markets", in *International Economic Review* (Philadelphia), Vol. 14, 1973.

OECD: *Women and employment: Policies for equal opportunity* (Paris: OECD, 1980).

–: *The integration of women into the economy* (Paris: OECD, 1985).

–: "Women's activity, employment and earnings: A review of recent developments", in *OECD Employment Outlook* (Paris), Sep. 1988.

Ogawa, N.: *Sex differentials in labour force participation and earnings in Japan* (Tokyo: Nihon University Population Research Institute, Reprint no. 25, 1987).

–; Clark, R.: "Earnings patterns of Japanese women: 1976–1988", in *Economic Development and Cultural Change* (Chicago), Vol. 43, No. 2.

Omori, M.: "Gender and the labor market", in *The Journal of Japanese Studies* (Seattle), 1993, Vol. 19, No. 1, pp. 79–102.

Papola, T.S.: "Women workers in the formal sector of Lucknow, India" in R. Anker and C. Hein (eds.): *Sex inequalities in urban employment in the Third World* (London: Macmillan, 1986).

Paukert, L.: *Women's employment in East-Central European countries during the period of transition to a market economy system* (Geneva: ILO, 1994), mimeo.

Petersen, T.; Morgan, L.: "Separate and unequal: Occupation-establishment sex segregation and the gender wage gap", in *American Journal of Sociology* (Chicago), 1995, Vol. 101, No. 2, pp. 329–365.

Presser, H.; Kishor, S.: "Economic development and occupational sex segregation in Puerto Rico: 1950–80", in *Population and Development Review* (New York), 1991, Vol. 17, No. 1.

–; Yi, H.: *Women's gender-type occupational mobility during economic development: The case of Mexico,* paper presented at the Annual Meeting of the Population Association of America, (San Francisco), California, April 6–8, 1995.

Psacharopoulos, G.; Tzannatos, Z.: *Women's employment and pay in Latin America: Overview and methodology* (Washington, DC: The World Bank, 1992).

Reilly, B.: "Occupational segregation and selectivity bias in occupational wage equations: An empirical analysis using Irish data", in *Applied Economics* (London), 1991, No. 23, pp. 1–7.

Reskin, B.; Hartmann, H.: *Women's work, men's work: Sex segregation on the job* (Washington, DC: National Academy Press, 1986).

–; Padavic, I.: *Women and men at work* (Thousand Oaks, California: Pine Forge Press, 1994).

–; Roos, P.: *Job queues, gender cues: Explaining women's inroads into male occupations* (Philadelphia: Temple University Press, 1990).

–; –: "Jobs, authority and earnings among managers: The continuing significance of sex", in *Work and Occupations* (California), 1992, Vol. 19, No. 4.

Reubens, B.; Harrison, J.: "Occupational dissimilarity by age and sex", in B. Reubens (ed.) *Youth at work: An international survey* (Towa, New Jersey: Rowman and Allanhead), 1983, pp. 39–85.

Rimmer, S.: "Occupational segregation, earnings differentials and status among Australian workers", in *Economic Record* (Sydney, Australia), 1991, pp. 205–216.

Roos, P.: *Gender and work: A comparative analysis of industrial societies* (Stoneybrook, New York: SUNY Press, 1985).

Rosenfeld, R. and Kalleberg, A.: "Gender inequality in the labour market: A cross-national perspective", in *Acta Sociologica* (Oslo), 1991, Vol. 34, No. 1, pp. 207–225.

Rubery, J.; Fagan, C.: "Occupational segregation of women and men in the European Community", in *Social Europe* (Luxembourg), 1993, Supplement no. 3.

–; –: *Wage determination and sex segregation in employment in the European Community: Summary*, Report for the Equal Opportunities Unit, DGV (Brussels: Commission of the European Communities, 1993), Aug.

Rubery, J.; Smith, M.: *Factors influencing the integration of women into the economy*, paper presented at ILO/European Commission Seminar on Women and Work in Europe (Turin), 18–19 April, 1996.

Rytina, N.: "Occupational segregation and earnings differences by sex", in *Monthly Labor Review* (Washington, DC), 1981, pp. 49–53.

–: "Occupational reclassification and changes in distribution by gender", in *Monthly Labour Review* (Washington, DC), 1984.

Schultz, P.: "Women's changing participation in the labour force: A world perspective", in *Economic Development and Cultural Change* (Chicago), 1990, Vol. 38, No. 3.

Scott, A.: "Economic development and urban women's work: The case of Lima, Peru", in R. Anker and C. Hein (eds): *Sex inequalities in urban employment in the Third World* (London: Macmillan, 1986).

Silber, J.: "On the measurement of employment segregation", in *Economics Letters* (Lausanne), 1989, No. 30, pp. 237–243.

Siltanen, J.: "Social change and the measurement of occupational segregation by sex: An assessment of the sex ratio index", in *Work, Employment and Society* (London), 1990, Vol. 4, No. 1, pp. 1–29.

–; Jarman, J.; Blackburn, R.: *Gender inequality in the labour market: Occupational concentration and segregation—A manual on methodology* (Geneva: ILO, 1995).

Standing, G.: *Global feminization through flexible labour* (Geneva: ILO, 1989), Labour Market Analysis and Employment Planning Working Paper No. 31.

–: *Cumulative disadvantage? Women industrial workers in Malaysia and the Philippines* (Geneva: ILO, 1992), Labour Market Analysis and Employment Planning Working Paper No. 60.

Steinberg, R.: "Gendered instructions: cultural lag and gender bias in the Hay system of job evaluation", in *Work and Occupations* (Newbury Park, California), 1992, Vol. 19, No. 4.

Strober, M.; Arnold, C.: "The dynamics of occupational segregation among bank tellers", in C. Brown and J. Pechman (eds.): *Gender in the workplace* (Washington, DC: The Brookings Institution, 1987).

Sziraczki, G.; Windell, J.: "Impact of employment restructuring on disadvantaged groups in Hungary and Bulgaria", in *International Labour Review* (Geneva: ILO), 1992, Vol. 131, No. 4–5, pp. 471–496.

Tae-Hong K.: "An analysis of female employment ratio in Korea's manufacturing industry", in *Women's Studies Forum* (Seoul: Korean Women's Development Institute), 1992, Vol. 8.

Terrell, K.: "Female-male earnings differentials and occupational structure", in *International Labour Review* (Geneva: ILO), 1992, Vol. 131, No. 4–5.

Thomas, C.; Taylor, R.: *Enforcement of equality provisions for women workers, equality of women in employment,* Equality for Women in Employment Working Paper No. 20 (Geneva: ILO, 1994).

Tomoda, S.: *Women workers in manufacturing, 1971–91,* Sectoral Activities Programme Working Paper (Geneva: ILO, 1995).

Treiman, D.; Hartmann, H. (eds.) : *Women, work, and wages: Equal pay for jobs of equal value,* (Washington, DC: National Academy Press, 1981).

–; Roos, P.: "Sex and earnings in industrial society: A nine nation comparison", in *American Journal of Sociology* (Chicago), 1983.

Tzannatos, Z.: "Employment segregation: Can we measure it and what does the measure mean?", in *British Journal of Industrial Relations* (London), 1990, Vol. 28, No. 1, pp. 105–111.

United Nations: *The role of women in the ECE Region,* Economic Commission for Europe (New York: UNECE, 1980).

–: *The economic role of women in the ECE Region: Developments 1975/85* (New York, 1985a).

–: *Women's employment and fertility* (New York: UN, 1985b).

–: *The World's Women 1970–1990: Trends and Statistics* (New York: UN, 1991).

–: *Women and Economic Decision-Making, Expert Group Meeting* (New York, 7–11 Nov. 1994).

–: *Report of the Fourth World Conference on Women* (Beijing, 4–15 Sep.) (New York: UN, 1995).

–: *The World's Women 1995: Trends and Statistics* (New York: UN, 1995b).

–: *Population and women* (New York: UN, 1996).

United Nations Children's Fund: *Women and gender in countries in transition: A UNICEF perspective* (New York, 1994).

United Nations Development Programme: *Human Development Report* (New York: Oxford University Press, 1993; 1995).

United Nations Industrial Development Organization: *Participation of women in manufacturing: Patterns, determinants and future trends: Regional analysis*, ESCAP Region (UNIDO, 1994).

United Nations Fund for Population Activities: *Guidelines for UNFPA Support for Gender, Population and Development Activities* (New York: UNFPA, 1995).

US Commission on Civil Rights: *Social indicators of equality for minorities and women* (Washington, DC: Government Printing Office, 1978).

US Merit Systems Protection Board: *A question of equity: Women and the glass ceiling* (Washington, DC, 1992).

Van der Eecken, T.: *Gender equality in employment in Mozambique* (Lusaka, 1994), mimeo.

Van Mourik, A.; Poot, J.; Siegers, J.: "Trends in occupational segregation of women and men in New Zealand: Some new evidence", in *New Zealand Economic Papers* (Wellington), 1989, Vol. 23, pp. 29–50.

Walby, S.; Bagguley, P.: "Sex segregation in local labour markets", in *Work, Employment and Society* (London), 1990, Vol. 4, No. 1, pp. 59–81.

Watts, M: "Measuring Job Segregation by marginal matching: A critical examination", in P. Gonzalez and M. Watts (eds.) *Measuring gender wage differentials and job segregation,* Equality for Women in Employment Working Paper (Geneva: ILO, 1995), No. 24.

–: "Explaining trends in occupational segregation: Some comments", in *European Sociological Review* (Oxford), 1993.

–: "How should occupational sex segregation be measured?", in *Work, Employment and Society* (London), 1992, Vol. 6, No. 3, pp. 475–487.

–; Rich, J.: "Equal employment opportunity in Australia: The role of part-time employment in occupational sex segregation", in *Australian Bulletin of Labour* (Adelaide), 1991, Vol. 17, No. 2, pp. 160–179.

–; –: "Labour market segmentation and the persistence of occupational sex segregation in Australia", in *Australian Economic Papers* (Adelaide), 1992.

–; –: "Occupational sex segregation in Britain, 1979–1989: The persistence of sexual stereotyping", in *Cambridge Journal of Economics* (London), 1993, Vol. 17.

Whitworth, S.: "Gender, international relations and the case of the ILO", in *Review of International Studies* (Cambridge, United Kingdom), 1994, pp. 389–405.

Williams, G.: "The changing U.S. labour force and occupational differentiation by sex", in *Demography* (Washington, DC), 1979, Vol. 16, No. 1, pp. 73–87.

Williams, J.: "Another commentary on so-called segregation indices", in *American Sociological Review* (New York), 1948, Vol. 13, pp. 298–303.

Wong, A.: "Planned development, social stratification, and the sexual division of labor in Singapore", in E. Leacock et al. (eds.): *Women's work: Development and the division of labor by gender* (South Hadley, Massachusetts: Bergin and Garvey Publishers, 1986), pp. 207–223.

World Bank: *Enhancing women's participation in economic development* (Washington, DC, 1994), mimeo.

Yi, H.; Presser H.: *Women's gender-type occupational mobility during economic development: The case of Puerto Rico*, Paper presented at the annual meeting of the Population Association of America (San Francisco), 6–8 April, 1995.

INDEX

Figures and tables are indicated by *italic page numbers*, major text sections by **bold numbers**.

A

absenteeism   17

absolute concept, gender dominance *72–73*, 85–86

accountants   289

adjusted data   61, *62–63*, 63–65

adjusted index of dissimilarity *see* ID75

administrative and managerial occupations
    female employment   49, 164–165, 250, 289
    gender dominance   268–269
    see also legislative officials and government administrators; managers

affirmative action   417

Africa
    female-dominated occupations   283
    sales occupations   166
    teachers   268
    see also Middle East and North Africa; sub-Saharan Africa

aggregation   46, 155, 251–252

agriculture
    Asia and Pacific   147
    exclusion from analysis   58–59
    Middle East and North Africa   145
    OECD countries   139
    Other Developing countries and areas   150
    sub-Saharan Africa   48
    Transition Economies   144

Angola
    data   125
    economy   150
    inequality statistics   303
    maids and related housekeeping   272
    professional and technical occupations   163

    sales occupations   118, 271, 290
    stenographers and typists   269

Anker, M.   58

Anker, R.   8, 18
    and Anker   58
    and Bodrova   144, 181
    and Dixon-Mueller   196
    and Hein   4, 17, 23, 34, *39*, 47–48, 49, 81, 85, 250
    and Khan and Ghosh   184
    and Khan and Gupta   58, 196

architects, engineers and related technicians   264, *265*
    feminization   *374*, 390

armed forces   57–58

Asia and Pacific   **147**, *148*, **150**
    administrative and managerial occupations   164–165, 269
    clerical occupations   165, 270
    female-dominated occupations   223, 283–284, 367
    gender-dominated occupations   212, 230, 233
    ID75   175, 177, 184–185, 319, 321, 331
    IDHALF   197, 339, 341, 342
    male-dominated occupations   215, 360
    occupational segregation by sex   34, 48, 50, 408
    occupational structure   156–157, *156*
    production occupations   166–167, 275
    see also East Asia; Fiji; India; Pakistan

Australia
    data comparability   64
    dump categories   60
    female–male pay differentials   30
    ID75   116

Austria   46

Austria *contd.*
  ID75 326
  IDHALF 339
  male-dominated occupations 355, 359, 360
  occupational classification schemes 60–61

B

Bahrain 145
  data comparability 64
  ID75 322–323
  male nurses 264
  occupational classification schemes 61
  service occupations 290, 394
  stenographers and typists 269, 395
  teachers 289
Bakker, I. *39*, 48, 49
Balu, F. *39–40*
Barbezat, D. 34, 35, 81, 99, 103
bartenders *see* cooks, waiters and bartenders
Becker, G.S. 18
Beijing Conference on Women 1995 5–6, 196
Bergmann, B. 21
Blackburn, R.M. 69, 75
blacksmiths and toolmakers *265*, 274–275
  feminization *374*
Blau, F. 34, 48, 49, 76, 77, 89, 329
Bodrova, V. 144, 181
bookkeepers and cashiers *267*, 270
  classification problems 61
  feminization 391, *392*, 393
Boserup, E. *40*, 46
Boulding, E. *40*, 48, 49
bricklayers and carpenters *265*, 274–275
  feminization *374*
Brown, W. 33
Bulgaria
  gender-dominated occupations 233
  ID75 116, 183
  male-dominated occupations 215, 217, 219
Buvinic, M. 8, 16

C

Canada
  administrative and managerial occupations 165, 268, 269
  female employment 289

gender-dominated occupations 233
  ID75 116
  inequality statistics 306
  male-dominated occupations 217, 219
  occupational classification schemes 61
CAPA 268
Caribbean
  salespersons and shop assistants 271
  see also Latin America and Caribbean
cashiers *see* bookkeepers and cashiers
censuses 56–57
Charles, M. *40–41*, 46, 48
China 125, 147, 150
  clerical occupations 165
  female-dominated occupations 118, 367
  gender-dominated occupations 126, 233
  ID75 116, 184, 186, 321
  IDHALF 197
  male-dominated occupations 217, 219, 355, 360
  occupational classification schemes 61
  production occupations 157, 166, 167, 274, 400
  sales occupations 271, 390–391
  service occupations 273, 274
clerical occupations
  female employment 165, 250, 289
  gender dominance 269–270
  regional variation 49, 157, 284–285
  see also bookkeepers and cashiers; stenographers and typists
coding 53, 56–57, **59–60**, 251
Commonwealth Association of Polytechnics in Africa 268
communism 408
comparable worth regulations 81, 84
computerization 393
convergence 413
cooks, waiters and bartenders *267*, 273–274
  feminization *392*, 396–397
Copenhagen World Summit on Social Development 6
correlation matrix, inequality statistics 298–299, *298*
Costa Rica 150
  data 125
  service occupations 290
  tailors, dressmakers, sewers and upholsterers 397

education contd.
  Transition Economies   144
Egypt
  administrative and managerial
    occupations   165
  agriculture   145
  clerical occupations   269, 395
  data   125
  dump categories   60
  employment definition and
    measurement   58
  female employment   80, 145, 289
  gender-dominated occupations   230
  ID75 values   186
  maids and related housekeeping   272,
    394
  teachers   266
employers, prejudice   18–19
employment, definition and
  measurement   53, **58–59**
engineers *see* architects, engineers and
  related technicians
enterprise size, and female–male pay
  differentials   34–35
equal opportunity policies   8, 417
establishment surveys   56
Europe, female–male pay differentials   34
European Union, cross-national studies   47
export-oriented countries   397, *397*
extended labour force   196

F
facilitating policies   417
factor analysis
  inequality statistics   299–301, *299, 300*
  OECD countries   304–306, *304*
  regional variations   409–410
Fagan, C.   *43–44*, 47, 48, 49, 75, 98, *117*
female-concentrated occupations   *73*, 87,
  87, 88
  hairdressers and barbers   272–273
  teachers   266
female-dominated occupations   68,
  252–253, *267*, 276, *277–282, 284*, 285, 414
  clerical occupations   269
  definitions   **80–81**, *82–84*, **84**
  and disaggregation   118
  feminization   391, *392*, 393–397,
    398–399, 405, 410–411, 415–416

gender stereotypes   276, 283
indices   *72*
  and marginal matching index   78
  masculinization   *376–389*
  pay and status   20–21, 285, 407
  percentage female   222–223, *224–225*,
    226–227, *226, 227*, 253, *254–257, 262*,
    264
  professional and technical
    occupations   264
  recent changes   *356–357*, 365, *366*, 367,
    367, 368, 369
  regional variations   283–285, 395–397
  service occupations   272–273
female-headed households   16
female labour force participation   16
  Asia and Pacific   147, 150, *150, 151*
  definition and measurement   58
  and hairdresser occupations   393
  industrialized countries   48
  and marginal matching index   79–80
  Middle East and North Africa   145, *150,
    151*
  and occupational segregation by sex   48
  OECD countries   139, 141, *141, 142*
  Other Developing countries and
    areas   150–151, *150, 151*
  Transition Economies   144–145
  see also female share of non-agricultural
    employment
female–male pay differentials   7–8, 14, 30,
  31, 32–35
  female-dominated occupations   285
  Toronto   *33*
  Washington State public service   *32*
  and working conditions   19
female share of non-agricultural employment
  70, 413
  difference between ID and MM   79, *79*
  and gender-integrated occupations   81,
    87–88, *87, 88*
  and ID75   189, *190–191, 192*, 193–195,
    193, 194, 195, 345–346, *345, 346*
  and index of dissimilarity   89–92, *91, 92*
female-underrepresented occupations   *74,
  87, 87, 88*
female workers *see* women
feminist theories   22–23
  cultural restrictions   29–30
  flexible occupations   29

training *see* education
Transition Economies   138, **142**, *143*, **144–145**, 408
  exclusion from study   253
  female-dominated occupations   223, 227, 367
  gender-dominated occupations   212
  ID75   175, 181–183, 186
  IDHALF   197
  inequality statistics   303
  male-dominated occupations   215
  managers   269
  unemployment rates   57
  see also Bulgaria; former Yugoslavia; Hungary; Poland
Treiman, D.   32–33, *44*, 48
Tunisia
  data   125
  data comparability over time   64
  female-dominated occupations   223
  female employment   145, 289
  ID75   116, 322–323
  inequality statistics   302
  maids and related housekeeping   272, 394
  male nurses   264
  production occupations   167, 390, 400
  stenographers and typists   269, 395
Turkey   30, 139, 164
typists *see* stenographers and typists
Tzannatos, Z.   *42*, 48, 50, 89

U
UN *see* United Nations
unadjusted data   61, *62–63*, 63–65
unclassifiable occupational groups   59–60
UNDP *see* United Nations Development Programme
unemployment rates   57
United Kingdom
  aggregation levels   126
  Department of Employment   69
  exclusion from study   253
  ID75   116
  number of occupations classified   125
United Nations
  Economic Commission for Europe   *44*, 49, 181
  The World's Women 1970–1990   16

unpaid household activities   196
United Nations Development Programme   16, 196
United States
  administrative and managerial occupations   165, 268, 269
  aggregation levels   126
  bookkeepers and cashiers   270
  in cross-national studies   46
  female-dominated occupations   367
  female employment   289
  GDP   139
  gender-dominated occupations   233
  ID75   116, 186
  IDHALF   197
  inequality statistics   306
  male-dominated occupations   217, 219
  national studies   38
  production occupations   274, 275
  professional and technical occupations   164, 264, 266, 268
  service occupations   274, 375, 390
unmapped data   61, *62–63*, 63–65
unpaid housepersons and care givers   196
USSR, former   138

V
vertical segregation   35, 184–185

W
wage differentials *see* pay differentials
waiters and waitresses *see* cooks, waiters and bartenders
Washington (State)   30, 32, *32*
Watts, M.   69, 78
WE (women and employment) index   69
West Germany   61, 116, 336
Windell, J.   28
women   9–10
  in clerical occupations   269–270
  effect of occupational segregation by sex   6–9, 403
  in female-dominated occupations   222–223, *224–225*, 226–227, *226, 227, 235–237, 238–240, 356–357*
  in gender-dominated occupations   *247–249*
  labour market choices   411, 417
  in male-dominated occupations   415